THE HABIT MECHANIC

Fine-Tune Your Brain and Supercharge How You Live, Work, and Lead

DR. JON FINN

tougherminds.co.uk

The Habit Mechanic
Fine-Tune Your Brain and Supercharge How You Live, Work, and Lead

ISBN 978-1-5445-2895-3 *Hardcover*
978-1-5445-2896-0 *Paperback*
978-1-5445-2897-7 *Ebook*

Ten Percent of This Book's Profits Help Disadvantaged Young People Succeed and Thrive in Their Lives

Thank you for buying this book and helping other people improve and transform their lives. Time and again, we've seen the positive and life-changing impact of training young people to become Habit Mechanics. That's why 10 percent of this book's profits are used to train volunteers to help disadvantaged young people become Habit Mechanics. This will help them thrive and succeed in their education and in their future working lives.

Thank you!

To learn more, visit tougherminds.co.uk/habitmechanic and click on "Helping Others."

Advance Praise

"I have read countless bestselling personal development and leadership books, but none are as powerful as* The Habit Mechanic.** *In my opinion it is the missing piece of the 'how to be your best' puzzle. It will help you optimize your personal performance and leadership.* ***I have not seen anything as insightful or instructive as this from any other expert in this space. *The book is packed with straightforward but powerful science-backed tools that help myself, my family, and my businesses to thrive.* ***I will use this book and the tool kit it provides for the rest of my life."***

—MIKE JONES, serial technology entrepreneur

"If there is one book you buy this year make it The Habit Mechanic. *This is not just a self-help book;* ***it is a manual for life****. It is brimming with practical examples, real life case studies, and steps to help you put the learning into action.* ***Grounded in science****, this is a powerful, enlightening, and interesting read that* ***will help you alter habits and make positive changes not only in your life but in those around you****."*

—JO HERRINGTON, leading learning and development expert in the City of London, Thrive Group Founder

"I've always struggled with the 'self-help' literature due to the lack of being able to find a way of transferring the 'help' into action. **The Habit Mechanic *really is different.*** *The combination of* ***simple, actionable, and effective*** *plans with a* ***truly compelling and readable*** *narrative makes it a* ***really powerful enabler for any leader or individual who wants to do (and live!) better****."*

—JONATHAN HEWLETT, former President Diesel Europe, Venture Founder

"The Habit Mechanic *offers a* ***new, exciting, and practical way to harness the power of cutting-edge science*** *so everyone can be their best. I believe* ***becoming a Habit Mechanic is essential if you want to fulfill your potential in the new hybrid workplace****. This book is* ***not only helping me, but it's also going to help my people and teams*** *develop the habits they need to succeed in the new world of work."*

—**MICHAEL ELSON, Managing Director at UNIT Film and TV**

"A self-confessed self-help book addict, ***I've finally found the one that has made all the difference.*** The Habit Mechanic *is different. It's* ***packed full of science-based but simple and practical tools*** *that make my life so much easier."*

—**HARRISON EVANS, Collaboration Manager, University of Leeds**

"The Habit Mechanic *is different because it* ***actually shows you how to make positive changes in your life****. It is based on good science, but* ***super easy to put into practice****. One habit I have now built is creating a daily 'Tiny Empowering Action' Plan (one of the Habit Mechanic Tools I've learned). It* ***only takes me two minutes per day, but it saves me hours and makes me feel great****.* The Habit Mechanic *is* ***both empowering and life-changing****!"*

—**DR. JO-ANN ROLLE, Dean, School of Business, Medgar Evers College, The City University of New York**

"Unlike other books I've read, this one actually shows you what to do to be your best and fulfill your potential. ***It is like a Swiss Army knife for personal and leadership success.*** *The depth of content is amazing.* ***I wish I'd been able to read it 30 years ago!****"*

—**PHIL CLARKE, former Wigan and Great Britain Rugby League Captain, winner of 12 major titles, and Co-founder of The Sports Office**

"I read a lot of books in this space that promise a lot, but this is different because it actually delivers! *It is based on great science; it's super easy to understand and extremely practical.* ***It really is exceptional and provides powerful tools and accessible language that my team and I can use to help us continually improve.*** *This is not a book to read once; it is a* ***performance and leadership companion for life****!"*

—NIGEL ADKINS, leading English soccer manager, winner of three league titles and four league promotions, and manager of two Premier League teams

"I have found The Habit Mechanic *a great book for* ***providing me with tools that I can apply to both my personal and professional lives.*** *I now feel equipped with the knowledge and skills to develop better habits to* ***enable me to be the best version of myself every day****! The benefits from working on your habits can be transformational. Give it a go!"*

—ALISON WHITE, Business Development & Relationship Manager, KPMG, UK

"The Habit Mechanic *is* ***packed full of powerful, practical skills that I've been able to use immediately to help myself, players, and coaches*** *think differently and improve our performance."*

—KEVIN SHARP, leading English cricket coach who helped develop some of the best batsmen in the world

"I've always wondered why, no matter what I tried, I couldn't make the positive changes I wanted in my life. ***But*** **The Habit Mechanic** ***has given me the answers and the tools to finally be my best.*** *I am* ***not stabbing in the dark anymore*** *and* ***I feel so empowered! I know I will use this book for the rest of my life****, and that it will help millions of other people."*

—MICHELLE SHORTHOUSE, Administrator

"I've worked in high-performance sport for over 20 years. I know world-class performers and teams employ expert coaches to help them be their best. But that's not an option for most people. ***The Habit Mechanic is like having a personal performance coach.*** *It's shown me* ***how to make important and achievable changes that help me to be my best at work and at home****. If you're looking for that extra edge to help you achieve your goals, then I certainly recommend this book."*

—MARTIN BLAND, League Partnership Manager, Stats Perform

"I don't think there's been a single day since I started learning to be a 'Chief Habit Mechanic' that I haven't told someone how great it is or taught someone in my team a new skill it's taught me. *This book doesn't just give you the undisputable science-backed facts but* ***actually teaches you really simple yet highly effective ways of achieving the changes*** *it talks about. I finish every day on a list of positives rather than focusing on the negatives and* ***am so much more productive than I've been in years****."*

—JOHN MCMAHON, CEO, MCM Digital Marketing Agency

"Learning how to become a 'Chief Habit Mechanic' has shown me ***how to use cutting-edge science to help my clients make positive change in their lives. It is also helping me stand out from the crowd and grow and drive my business****. It has* ***taught me how to maximize and get more out of my working day****. This has reduced my stress levels and* ***freed up more quality family time****. My Habit Mechanic journey so far has been both fascinating and rewarding. I am only at the beginning of this journey, and* ***I'm really excited about how these insights are going to help me in the future****!"*

—PHIL HOLMES, PH Sports Nutrition Founder, performance coach, and former professional rugby player

"I am on a constant journey to improve my performance as a teacher and a leader. After spending time with Jon and reading The Habit Mechanic, ***I have been able to take a step back and understand my performance and how I can give myself the best opportunity to be at my best more often. The impact it's had on my ability to manage heavy workloads both physically and mentally has been life-changing. EVERYONE who wants to feel and do better should read*** **The Habit Mechanic.***"*

—ROBERT BELL, Headteacher at the Consilium Evolve Academy

I created the "Habit Mechanic" approach, the language,
the tools, the app, and this book to make it easier for people to
build better habits so they can be their best and
make a positive impact on the world.

Habit Mechanics proactively put their best foot
forward to be their best. They take control of their own future.
They take responsibility for their health, happiness, and success.
This means they are also in a much better position
to help others be their best.

Habit Mechanics are changing the world,
one habit at a time!

This book is dedicated to all those people who are,
or who aspire to be, Habit Mechanics.

CONTENTS

Step 4: CHIEF HABIT MECHANIC SKILLS

BRINGING IT ALL TOGETHER

FOREWORD

—Professor Jim McKenna, world-leading behavior change researcher, Carnegie Faculty, Leeds Beckett University, UK

I am delighted to introduce Dr. Jon Finn's *The Habit Mechanic*. Friends and colleagues who have seen sample sections described them as "unique," "practical," "powerful," and "an excellent approach." I agree that these same terms also apply to the full book. What I also see is an innovative, scientifically based framework that captures some of the most compelling and effective practices for dealing with everyday challenges faced by literally millions of people and teams, in life and work. These techniques work, time after time and across settings. By implication, then, becoming a Habit Mechanic literally changes people's lives.

Crucially, *The Habit Mechanic* emphasizes that behavior is the underlying imperative of all performance, resilience, and wellbeing. In clear steps, it shows how to establish positive behavioral routines so they become habits. Without that foundation, any aspiration to feel well, perform well, or achieve great things will be built on shifting sand. *The Habit Mechanic* also attacks two profound and widespread human biases: (1) overconfidence that we are already doing the right things and (2) our human tendency to downplay the anticipated effectiveness of these processes.

Given the timing, with changing expectations regarding post-COVID ways of working, the key messages could hardly be more relevant. Never before has the uncertainty of the VUCA (volatile, uncertain, complex, and ambiguous) world, amplified by hybrid notions of work, depended on people who can effectively self-manage. Indeed, *The Habit Mechanic* goes well beyond a one-eyed fixation on self-regulation and motivation. In an accessible, practical style, it shows how to integrate active influences on behavior to ensure individuals spend more time on meaningful tasks.

Just as influential will be those organizations who use *The Habit Mechanic* to reinforce the ways of working that encourage self-management. Importantly, *The Habit Mechanic* challenges every organization to adjust its ways of working toward what has become known as the "Deliberately Developmental Organization." This allows employees—at different levels—to work together to improve their management of every daily action and routine. In my experience, this approach is far better than relying on conventional feedback, which tends to reinforce hierarchies where higher-ups provide lower-downs with unhelpful, and unwanted, criticism. In the post-COVID world, every self-determined individual, team, or organization will accent ways of working that ensure personal progress in meaningful work and optimal support as the work is done.

The Habit Mechanic provides a treasure trove of engaging examples of real-world people, individuals, teams, or organizations using these same techniques and approaches. These examples will support any mindset or company philosophy to deal with an often-unacknowledged reality—that top performers need to keep working hard to improve, especially when they want to stay at the top. In turn, *The Habit Mechanic* encourages far-sighted employers to offer this support "on-the-job."

While the careful integration of effective practices is impressive, I am also drawn to the style of the book. The short sections meet the realities of real-world working where people are time-poor. Further, many sections of *The Habit Mechanic* can be easily used to support "just-in-time" staff development training.

Drawing on years of successful implementation with individuals and international organizations, this work offers an exciting new approach to helping people thrive and succeed. *The Habit Mechanic* adds a much-needed new dimension to the Generalist-Specialist axis: effective implementation. *The Habit Mechanic* occupies the space at the heart of the Generalist-Specialist-Deliverer triangle. As such, it puts the essential skills underpinning better performance—regardless of context—into your hands.

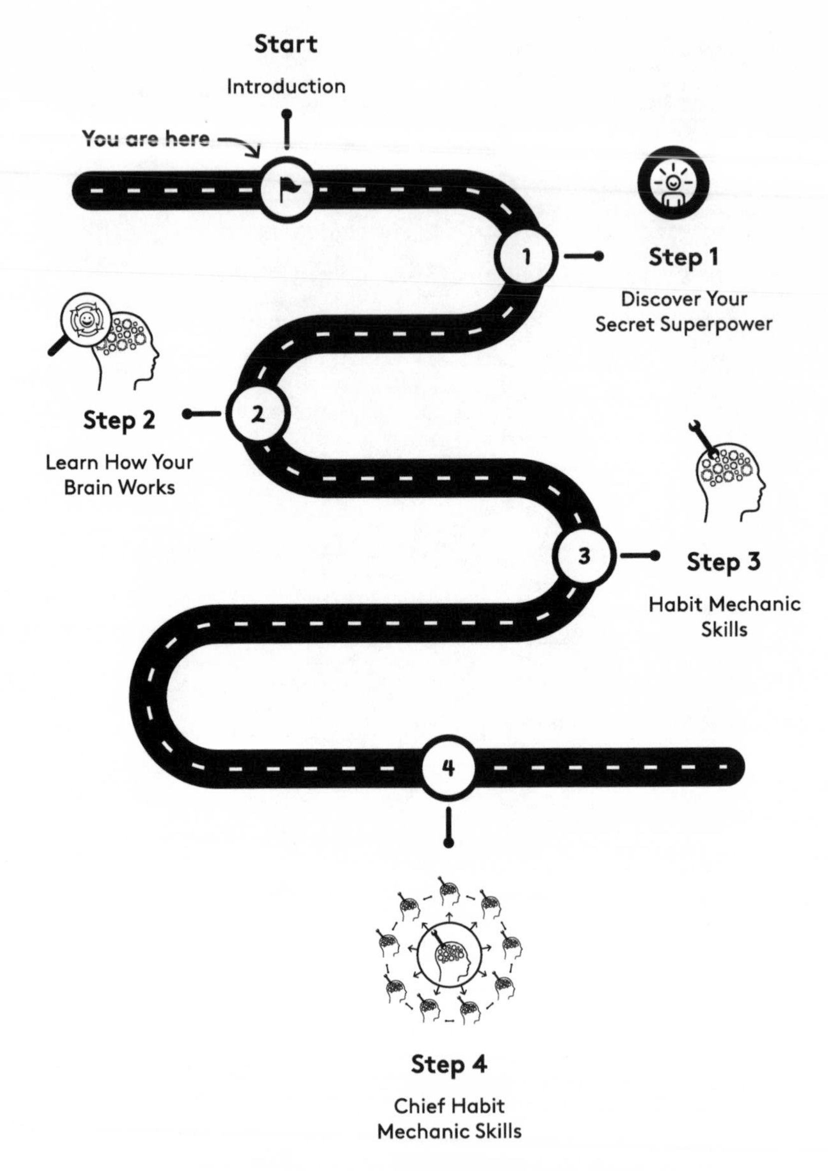

Figure S0.1: An overview of your journey through this book.

INTRODUCTION

How to Get the Most Out of This Book

This book is not intended to be read once and left on the shelf to collect dust. It is a book for life, and the ideas in it have already helped over 10,000 people thrive and succeed in our challenging modern world.

It is packed full of simple and practical, science-based, tried-and-tested, award-winning "Habit Mechanic Tools." They have been designed to make your life easier. But you will only get the most out of these tools if you use them regularly, which is really easy to do.

TO GET THE MOST OUT OF THIS BOOK, I RECOMMEND:

First, read it cover to cover (although you can skip Step 4 [Chief Habit Mechanic skills] if helping other people be their best is not a high priority for you right now). Fully engage in the simple and practical exercises in each section. If it is helpful to you, make notes and annotate the areas you find most interesting.

Second, keep it close by so you can pick it up regularly and revisit the sections that are most helpful for you. The more you use the Habit

Mechanic Tools, the more powerful they will become in helping you fulfill your potential.

Nothing in this book, or the Habit Mechanic approach, is prescriptive. The key is to try things out and see what works best for you.

WHAT IF I DON'T HAVE A LOT OF TIME RIGHT NOW?

Flick through the book and see which chapters and sections look most interesting to you. Some tools in the book will take you as little as five minutes to learn how to use, but the benefits can last a lifetime.

If you have any questions about any area of this book, I am here to help. Just send me an email at:

thehabitmechanic@tougherminds.co.uk

Or contact me via our website:
tougherminds.co.uk

I am confident that the ideas you are about to learn will be as powerful for you as they have been for my colleagues, myself, and all the Habit Mechanics and Chief Habit Mechanics we have trained so far.

—Dr. Jon Finn

1

QUICK START

A Two-Minute Daily Exercise to Make Your Life Easier

Welcome! My name is Dr. Jon Finn. At the time of writing, I have been working in the fields of resilience, performance, and leadership psychology for over 20 years. I have completed three degrees in these areas, including a PhD.

Through my work I know that many people try to be their best, but they fail. However, this is not their fault. It is the advice they are given that is faulty, and sometimes dangerous (e.g., as exposed in the BBC's 2021 documentary *Bad Influencer: The Great Insta Con*). Later, I will explain more about the flaws in how we have traditionally been taught to be our best.

MY MISSION?

To make it easier for people from every background to consistently feel better, do better, and (if they want to) lead better. If you want to unlock your amazing potential, I wrote this book to help you.

On top of my academic qualifications, I have also spent over 25,000 hours developing and delivering training and coaching programs. I have learned that the key to ACTUALLY consistently feeling, performing, and (if you want to) leading better is to fine-tune your brain. But the ONLY reliable way to do this in our challenging world is by becoming what I call a "Habit Mechanic." This is a NEW approach that I have created to help people be their best.

My team and I have also designed a range of simple, practical, science-based, and award-winning tools to help individuals and teams become Habit Mechanics, and leaders become Chief Habit Mechanics. These are tried and tested, and have already helped over 10,000 people be their best more often. These tools are proven to change people's lives.

CREATE YOUR FIRST "DAILY TEA PLAN"

The first Habit Mechanic Tool I will show you how to use is called the "Daily TEA (Tiny Empowering Action) Plan." It is based on cutting-edge science but is simple to use. It only takes two minutes to complete and will help you do a little bit better every day.

Step One—Rate Yourself

First, ask yourself this question:

How well did you do your best to be your best and achieve your goals yesterday (or so far today, if yesterday feels like too long ago to remember ☺)?

You could say you did great, or you failed. But I'd like you to be a bit more accurate because this will be more helpful for you. So please rate yourself from 1 (you failed) to 10 (perfect). You are probably somewhere in between.

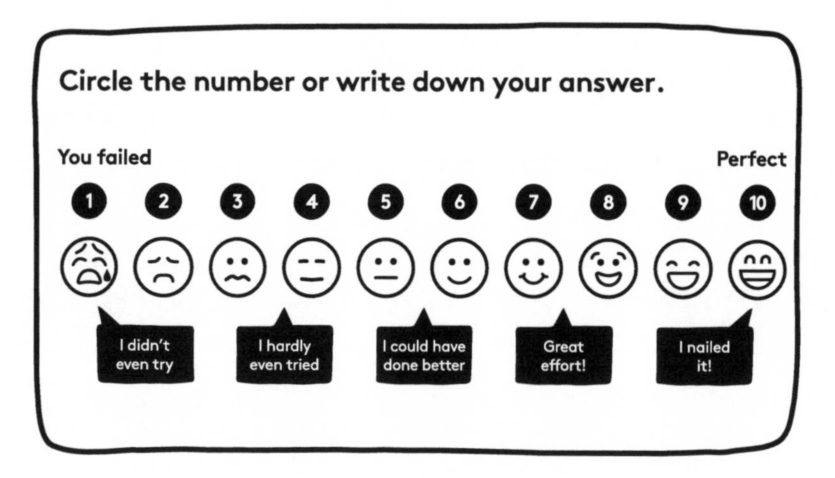

Figure 1.1: Don't worry if you are not 100% sure about your score; just go with your best guess or gut feeling.

This is what I call an intelligent "Self-Watching" exercise.

When I think about how well I did my best to be my best, I consider things like how well I managed my sleep, diet, exercise, stress, and productivity, and how helpful I was to others. You might judge yourself against a different set of criteria.

Step Two—Create a Tiny Empowering Action

After you have given yourself a score, I want you to write down a Tiny Empowering Action (TEA) that will make your life easier over the next 24 hours. Here are some examples I use as my TEAs:

- Only check the news once today.
- Go for a five-minute walk at lunchtime.
- Eat a piece of fruit for breakfast.
- Write down a positive reflection at the end of the day.

Write down your **T**iny **E**mpowering **A**ction (just one thing):

Step Three—Explain Why

Finally, I want you to consider why doing this will help you be your best.

Here are some examples I use:

- Only check the news once today because it will be less distracting, I will get more done, and I will feel better about myself.
- Go for a five-minute walk at lunchtime because it will make it easier to have a productive afternoon.
- Eat a piece of fruit for breakfast because it is a healthy way to start the day and will trigger other healthy behaviors.
- Write down a positive reflection at the end of the day because it will help me finish the day well, switch off, and sleep better.

Write down why doing this (your TEA) will help you be your best.

Here is a complete example for the three steps:

1. Best doing score—7/10.
2. TEA—Only check the news once today.
3. Why?—It will be easier to focus and be productive.

CONGRATULATIONS! You just completed your first Daily TEA Plan! ☺

This is a quick and practical way to take more control over your day and boost your resilience, wellbeing, and performance.

It is not a quick tip or trick—they don't work! (I will explain why later.)

It might look simple, but it is based on complex and cutting-edge insights from neuroscience, behavioral science, and psychology. It has been deliberately designed to give you the maximum positive impact on your day for the minimum amount of time taken to complete it. This is just one of the many simple, practical, and science-based Habit Mechanic Tools I will show you how to use throughout this book.

Don't worry if you didn't find it very easy to do, because you will improve with practice.

Completing a Daily TEA Plan on a regular basis will literally change your brain via a process called neuroplasticity. These changes will strengthen your ability to think constructively about yourself and to successfully plan to be your best. I will talk about these brain-changing processes in much more detail throughout the book.

MAKING DAILY TEA PLANS EASIER

To make it easier to complete regular Daily TEA Plans, I have created a PDF template. I use this, and if you want to use it go to tougherminds.co.uk/habitmechanic and click on "Resources" to download your copy.

I will also remind you to complete exercises like the Daily TEA Plan in The Habit Mechanic podcast (listen to it here: tougherminds.co.uk/podcast).

Finally, our Habit Mechanic app is also designed to make completing regular Daily TEA Plans easier. To learn more, go to tougherminds.co.uk/habitmechanic and click on "Habit Mechanic app."

Daily TEA Plan FAQs

If you want more help completing your first Daily TEA Plan, check out the following FAQs.

Question 1. Should I focus on the same TEA every day, for example, "Go for a five-minute walk at lunchtime"?

Answer 1. When you first begin using the TEA Plan process, your number one aim is to achieve a tiny bit of success. So it makes sense to keep focusing on the same TEA until you feel it is a habit. For example, going for a walk at lunchtime becomes part of your normal routine, just like eating lunch.

You can then focus on a new TEA, for example, "Write down a positive reflection at the end of the day." Taking this **one tiny habit at a time** approach will make it easier for you to make positive changes in your life.

Question 2. How long does it take to build a new habit?

Answer 2. The answer is not simple, and it is definitely not 21 days! Habits are complex. For example, what you think is one habit might be several interconnected habits. Some habits you want to develop might be easier to build than others. This is because elements of a new habit you want to build might already be embedded in habits you have already developed. Another new habit you want to build might have to be started from scratch.

The simplest rule to apply is that you get good at what you practice. For example, if you practice writing down a positive reflection at the end of the day for the next 30 days, you will start to develop the habit. But if for the subsequent 30 days you check your social media instead of writing down your end-of-day positive reflection, you will develop better social-media-checking habits and unravel the work you've done on developing your end-of-day-reflection habit.

Mental conditioning is just like physical conditioning. If you stop training, you lose the gains you have made through practice. As they say, "Use it or lose it!"

I will talk lots more about the habit building process throughout the book, but I hope this is useful insight for the time being.

Question 3. Can I create more than one TEA each day, for example, "Go for a five-minute walk at lunchtime AND write down a positive reflection at the end of the day"?

Answer 3. Yes, go for it. But if you find that you are struggling to do both, just focus on one until it is a habit.

Question 4. What should I do if I'm very good at overthinking and talking myself out of doing what I know I should do?

Answer 4. Just go ahead and do what you think you should do. You will only truly learn what works best for you by trying things out. I call this doing "personal research."

Question 5. Do I need to be 10/10 every day?

Answer 5. No. I think if you are scoring 7s and 8s you are doing very well!

Don't overthink the Daily TEA Plan. Just put it into practice and adapt it so that the process works well for you.

Remember, the Daily TEA Plan is only one small tool in a set of tools you will discover in this book. The tools are designed to be used together. For example, when you combine the Daily TEA Plan with the "Future Ambitious Meaningful (FAM) Story" tool (which I will introduce in Chapter 16), both become more powerful.

Nothing in this book is prescriptive. All the tools can be used in a flexible way. You will only learn what works best for you through trial and error.

2

MY STORY AND WHY BECOMING A HABIT MECHANIC IS ESSENTIAL FOR HAPPINESS AND SUCCESS IN OUR CHALLENGING WORLD

"I've just come back from the supermarket.
The cupboard's so full of chocolate biscuits that I
can't close the door... I'll start the detox on Monday.
The trouble is, there are 52 Mondays in a year.
I say that every week!"

—PETER KAY, comedian

Knowing what you want to do is one thing. Doing it is another. By becoming a Habit Mechanic, you will learn how to put your best foot forward and do your best to be your best using an award-winning, science-based approach that has already changed thousands of people's lives. Habit Mechanics are not looking to be perfect. We just want to do a little bit better every day. These tiny daily wins quickly add up to help us achieve big results.

USING FAILURE AS A CATALYST

We all fail, which is a good thing (even though it doesn't feel like it at the time) because it is the only way we can learn how to get better. I have failed many times and continue to do so. But I do my best to use these failures to spur me on. Without failure, I would not have become a Habit Mechanic.

Let me tell you a little bit more about my journey.

I was a 19-year-old university student and playing in one of the most important rugby matches of my life. It was a cold, wet, windy day in the north of England. I looked up at the sky and the ball was plummeting and swirling toward me. I stood on my own goal line; two opposition players were closing me down quickly and I had to catch the ball. My heart was pounding, my mind was racing, but all I had to do was not mess this up. The pressure was on!

It was the warm-up game before we played Australia in a student international. Australia was one of the best student teams in the world.

I had made the same catch hundreds of times before, but this time my mind was playing tricks on me. I was telling myself: "Don't drop it, don't drop it... you are going to drop it."

What happened next? Did I catch the ball, make a break, and score a try? No.

I dropped the ball and the opposition scored. My confidence drained and I was hoping a hole in the ground would appear so I could hide in it. I got substituted and, unsurprisingly, I was not selected for the Australia match.

I was kicking myself. I had messed up. Not because I didn't have the physical skills, but because I had not yet developed the mental skills. And to make it worse, sport psychology was a central part of my undergraduate degree. Clearly, I needed to pay closer attention to my studies!

But this was the setback I needed to spur me on.

Fast forward a few months, and it was becoming clear that a ruptured quad muscle in my right leg had put an end to playing competitive rugby. I could not train without sustaining injuries. So I decided I was going to become an expert in performance psychology. I was going to help other people fulfill their potential.

I will explain more about my journey and research later in the book (Chapter 8). But this work eventually led to me founding the award-winning Tougher Minds consultancy and creating the Habit Mechanic and Chief Habit Mechanic training programs.

CREATING TOUGHER MINDS

What does "Tougher Minds" mean? As I will show in this book, most of what you are doing, most of the time, is mindless. You are running on autopilot. Significantly, a lot of these mindless thoughts are typically **not** very helpful for your health, happiness, and performance.

So, to help ourselves manage the parts of our brain that are responsible for some of this unhelpful mindless behavior, we need to be "tougher" on them (in the nicest possible way ☺). We can think of this as strengthening and conditioning them, so they can help us be at our best in today's challenging world. Hence, we say "Tougher Minds."

Figure 2.1: At Tougher Minds, we help people be their best, and also equip them with the skills to help others fulfill their potential. We do this by teaching people to be Habit Mechanics and Chief Habit Mechanics.

Tougher Minds (my colleagues and myself) has trained and coached over 10,000 people. We work with global businesses, high-growth start-ups, individuals, elite athletes, coaches and teams, leading educational institutes, and families. We advise government and think tanks, and have been featured in major UK publications including *The Times*, *Sunday Times*, *Sunday Telegraph*, and *People Management*.

WHAT IS THE MAIN LESSON I HAVE DRAWN FROM ALL MY EXPERIENCE?

Fine-tuning your brain is the key to consistently feeling, performing, and (if you want to) leading better. But the ONLY reliable way to do this in our challenging world is to become a Habit Mechanic.

Why Do We Need a New Approach to Help Us Be Our Best?

The well-intended traditional approaches you might have tried to help you be your best (e.g., self-help, training, and coaching) are

- typically NOT rooted in cutting-edge science about how your brain and habits ACTUALLY work; and
- in my experience, NEVER grounded in comprehensive behavioral science that can ACTUALLY empower you to fulfill your potential.

Therefore, these well-intended traditional approaches are suboptimal at helping you be your best because they are not designed to help you change your brain.

Similarly, quick tips and tricks are not designed to help you change your brain or consistently be your best. And on a very serious note, some of the advice given in these tips and tricks is misleading and potentially dangerous. (To learn why, start by watching the BBC documentaries *Bad Influencer: The Great Insta Con* and *I Can Cure You: Online Mental Health Cures.*)

Hence why I said earlier that if you have not been able to make successful changes before, it is not your fault. It is the advice and training you have been given that is faulty.

Why Are Traditional Approaches and Quick Tips Suboptimal in Helping You Be Your Best?

Traditional support to help us fulfill our potential typically comes in the form of knowledge and skills. But we don't run on knowledge and skills. We run on habits. Therefore, traditional approaches can do more harm than good. For example, we try, we fail, and then we beat ourselves up and develop a negative mindset about ourselves.

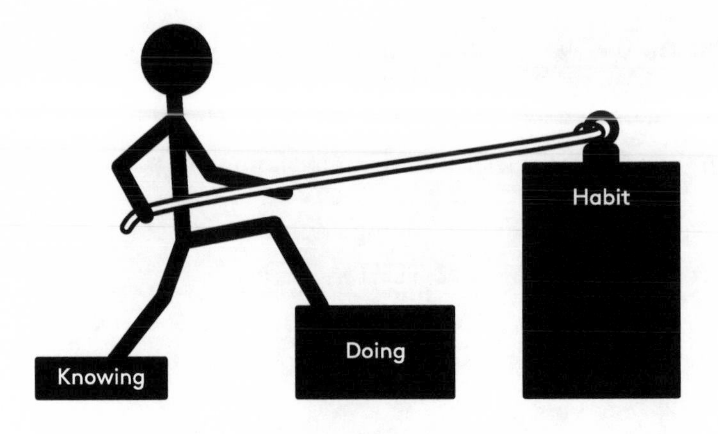

Figure 2.2: To truly be your best more often, you need to learn how to build better habits.

Let me show you what I mean. The vast majority of people now **know** what they need to do to live a healthy lifestyle. And the vast majority of people also have the skills and resources necessary to lead a healthy lifestyle (e.g., eating five portions of fruit and veg per day). Yet, even if people agree these are good things to do, they do not necessarily do them. In the UK, poor diet alone is reported to contribute to 64,000 deaths per year and cost the economy £74 billion ($100 billion)—simply because many people do not follow advice they agree with.

In a similar vein, most people know that beating themselves up less often and getting more good quality sleep would be helpful. But they don't do those things.

We don't do what we KNOW we should do. Instead, we do what we are in the HABIT of doing.

THE VOLATILE, UNCERTAIN, COMPLEX, AND AMBIGUOUS (VUCA) WORLD

The modern world can be extremely challenging because every day others are trying to infect and infest your brain with negative habits (I will explain more in Chapter 6). If you want to let these negative habits control you forever, stop reading this book now ☺. But if you want to learn simple and practical ways to stop and get rid of these negative habits, carry on reading.

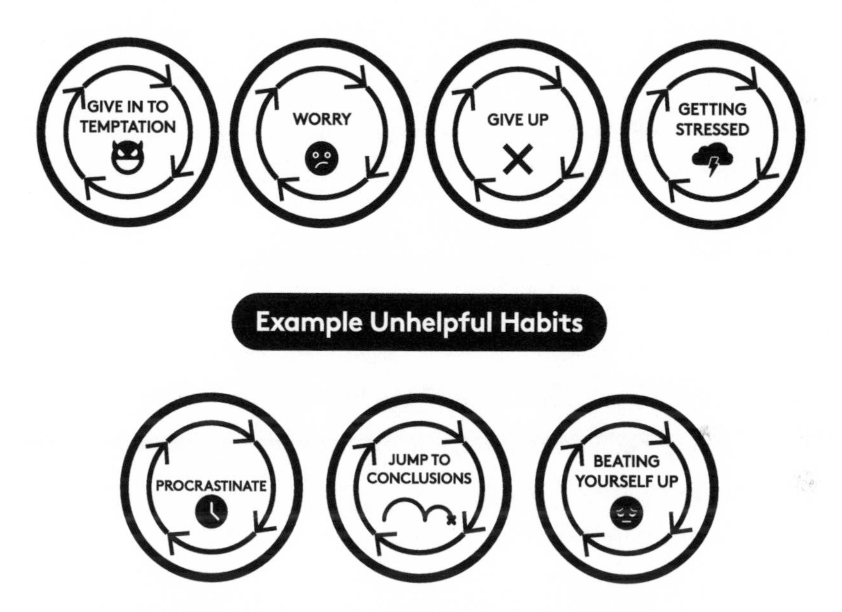

Figure 2.3: You can spend so much of your time on these negative habits that it can be like having a second job that you don't get paid for, and that makes everything you want to achieve in your life more difficult.

WHAT IS A HABIT MECHANIC?

Habit Mechanics know how to use powerful insights from neuroscience, psychology, and behavioral science to actually feel better and do better.

What does this mean in plain English? By becoming a Habit Mechanic, you will learn how to use a range of simple and practical tools that will change your brain (neuroscience and psychology) and help you design your environment (behavioral science) to make it easier to be your best.

Figure 2.4: Neuroscience and psychology + behavioral science = Habit Mechanic.

First, Habit Mechanics learn how to do "Me Power Conditioning." This means deliberately working toward being your best by:

1. Analyzing your current habits—including those connected to worrying, being too self-critical, procrastinating, and sabotaging your own success.
2. Building more new helpful habits.

What Is a Chief Habit Mechanic?

Some Habit Mechanics want to help others fulfill their potential. So, they learn how to be "Team Power Leaders" so they can develop more helpful leadership habits. Building better Me Power Conditioning and Team Power Leadership habits are the foundations of becoming a Chief Habit Mechanic.

Figure 2.5: Me Power Conditioning + Team Power Leadership = Chief Habit Mechanic.

How Can I Become a Habit Mechanic?

1. Commit to reading this book.
2. Commit to implementing the ideas you learn and testing them out in your day-to-day life.
3. Create "Habit Building Plans" to help you do this (I will show you how).
4. Use this book as a guide for your future happiness and success, dipping in and out of it as new challenges and opportunities arise in your life.

How Can I Become a Chief Habit Mechanic?

First become a Habit Mechanic. Then commit to using the tools in Step 4 of this book (I will explain more about Step 4 shortly).

Learn What Works Best for You

Nothing I say in this book is prescriptive. You are unique and will only understand what works for you by trying things out (i.e., put some of the ideas in this book into practice to learn what works best for you). I call this "doing personal research."

Learning how to become a Habit Mechanic and a Chief Habit Mechanic is a bit like a jigsaw puzzle. But you now have all the pieces (they're inside this book), and I will show you how to put them together.

Habit Mechanic Mindset

To be our best in this challenging world, we must adopt a proactive "Habit Mechanic Mindset." This means thinking of your life as a journey where you will travel through peaks and troughs. When you notice yourself going into a trough, you deliberately build new habits to help yourself get out of it faster than you otherwise would. When you feel like you are on a peak, you might want to build new habits that allow you to push yourself even higher and stay there for longer.

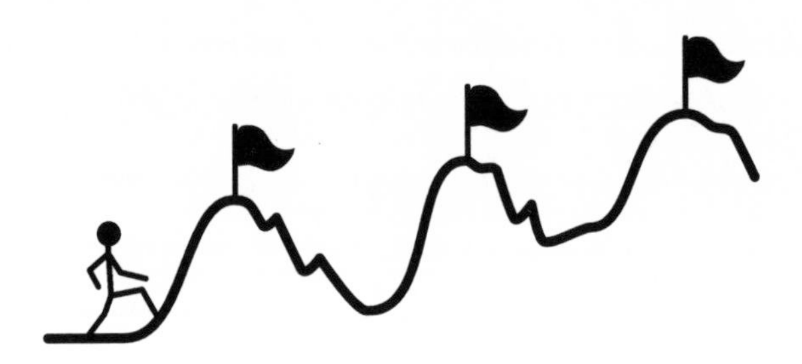

Figure 2.6: Learning to become a Habit Mechanic will make it much easier to successfully navigate your life.

WHO DOES TOUGHER MINDS TRAIN TO BE HABIT MECHANICS AND CHIEF HABIT MECHANICS?

Individuals: Anyone who wants to do better, feel better, and fulfill their potential.

Businesses: From big businesses to start-ups, the one thing our clients have in common is their desire to beat the competition. So they naturally want to help their people and teams be at their best, especially in the new hybrid workplace.

Elite sports people: Managers, coaches, and athletes who want to use cutting-edge science to give themselves a competitive advantage.

Education: Schools, colleges, universities, and families that want to give their young people the very best chance of fulfilling their potential in life.

WHAT RESULTS DO HABIT MECHANICS AND CHIEF HABIT MECHANICS GET?

Building new helpful habits improves every area of life for people of all ages. The benefits include...

Time Savings

"I've always been a well-organized and productive person, but learning how my brain works, and putting these skills (Habit Mechanic Tools) into practice saves me at least one hour every day. It's amazing!"

—ZDENEK BURDA, Chief Technology Officer, BOSCO

Stress Management

"The program has taught me simple and practical skills (Habit Mechanic Tools) that make it so much easier to manage stress. I now sleep better, I'm more productive, and I get more quality time to spend with my young family. I wish I'd learned these skills years ago!"

—ABI LIDDLE, Chief Operations Officer, Modo 25

Accelerated Academic Performance

With a 12-week training program, on average our students improve their exam results by half-a-grade more per subject than those who are not trained to be Habit Mechanics. This is seismic, and something we have consistently replicated in both the state and independent sectors, at schools with greatly differing levels of typical pupil examination attainment, and with children and young people from across a huge range of socioeconomic backgrounds.

Cutting-Edge Leadership, Team, and Culture Development

Chief Habit Mechanics can demystify the "dark arts" of creating a winning culture, because they understand that habits are the foundations of individual and collective success or failure. As the managing director of the UK arm of a Fortune 500 company said to me after a leadership residential I ran for his team: *"You have just given them the highway code for leadership and team success."*

BECOMING A HABIT MECHANIC MAKES LIFE EASIER

When you actually understand what you are designed to do, and how to fine-tune your brain, life gets a lot easier.

Here are other benefits people report experiencing when they learn how to become Habit Mechanics:

"I do more clever work, not just busy work."

"I deal with stress better and am less distracted by negative thoughts."

"I eat healthier food that helps my brain to function properly. I feel better, and it is easier to think clearly and cleverly."

"I have improved my sleep and feel better in the mornings."

"I feel less stressed because I have simple skills to refocus my thinking."

"I get distracted less easily, and get more work done as a result."

"I say fewer unhelpful things to myself, which saves me time because I spend less time dwelling on the negatives."

"I am more confident, which helps me to be my best at home and work."

"I have learned to perform better when the pressure is on."

"I interact with my partner and children in a more helpful way and feel like I have become a better parent."

"I have become a better role model for my direct reports."

"I understand how to lead my team more effectively."

"I am better able to collaborate with colleagues, and as a result we are performing better as a team."

"Our team is more effective and getting better results."

"This training has changed my life!"

SHOULDN'T SOMEONE HAVE ALREADY TAUGHT ME HOW TO DO THIS?

You might be asking: "If becoming a Habit Mechanic is so great, why has no one ever taught me how to do this before?" This is a great question.

Uniquely, Habit Mechanics capitalize on new insights from cutting-edge neuroscience, behavioral science, and psychology. This science is complex, making it hard to understand and apply in everyday life. But my unique career has allowed me to unlock the most important secrets in this science. I have been able to connect different insights from different experts. By combining their work with my own (and my team's) research, consultancy, and life experiences, I have created a NEW and uniquely powerful approach that anyone can use to thrive and succeed.

WHAT WILL I GET FROM THIS BOOK?

I want to help you understand just how much potential you have and how to tap into it. The value you will get from this book is at least the equivalent of doing a degree. But unlike other degree courses, where the main focus is learning academic theory, I will teach you simple and practical science-based, habit building tools. You can use these for the rest of your life, and they will make it much easier for you to be resilient, perform to your potential, and (if you want to) become an outstanding leader.

You do not need any other qualifications to learn how to use the tools in this book. The only requirement is a desire to be your best.

I have broken the book down into four simple steps.

Step 1— Discover Your Secret Superpower

First, I will introduce you to your Secret Superpower and explain why NOT knowing how to use it means the challenging modern world can turn it into your greatest weakness. I will also share with you the secret science behind a story of iconic sporting success. This will help you truly understand what it means to be a Habit Mechanic. You will also begin to understand yourself by developing your "Habit Mechanic intelligence."

Figure 2.7: Your potential is amazing; you just need to know how to unlock it.

Step 2—Learn about the Secret Brain Science That Will Unlock Your Potential

Next, I will focus on Me Power Conditioning. You will learn about the Lighthouse Brain model and how your brain works. You will also learn how to use emotional regulation to develop your resilience.

Figure 2.8: Actually understanding how your brain works makes being your best so much easier.

Step 3—Habit Mechanic Skills

Next, I will show you how to use your "Habit Mechanic's Tool Kit." Here you will learn simple and practical skills to boost your motivation, analyze your habits, and use behavioral science to build new habits that will have the following benefits:

- Make you feel better
- Improve your work-life balance
- Supercharge your performance
- Save you time because you will be more efficient and effective
- Reduce your stress levels
- Stop you from beating yourself up
- Improve your sleep, diet, exercise, brain health, and performance
- Build your confidence
- Help you perform under pressure
- Boost focus and productivity (whether working from home or in the office)

- Sharpen your creativity and problem-solving abilities

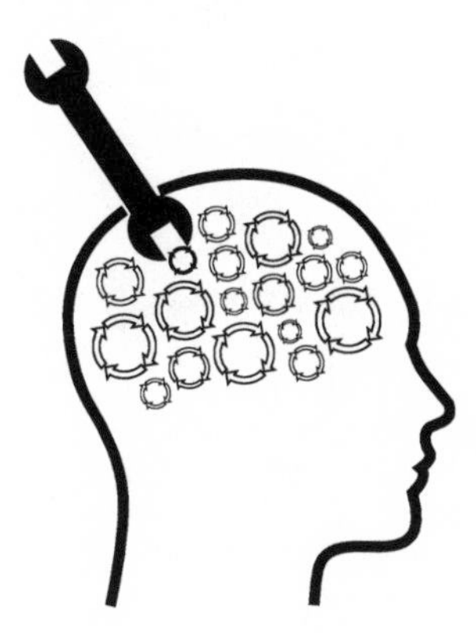

Figure 2.9: Actually understanding how your habits work makes building new ones so much easier.

Step 4—Chief Habit Mechanic Skills*

**This section is optional and will benefit anybody who wants to help others do better, from team members to business leaders and managers, through to coaches (sports and personal), teachers, and parents.*

Finally, I will focus on helping you become a Team Power Leader and show you how to use your "Chief Habit Mechanic's Tool Kit." You will learn how to use Leadership Science and create high-performing teams using our "Team Power Building" tools. You will also learn how to analyze and build new Team Power Leadership habits across four core areas:

- Role Model
- Action Communicator
- Cultural Architect
- SWAP Coach

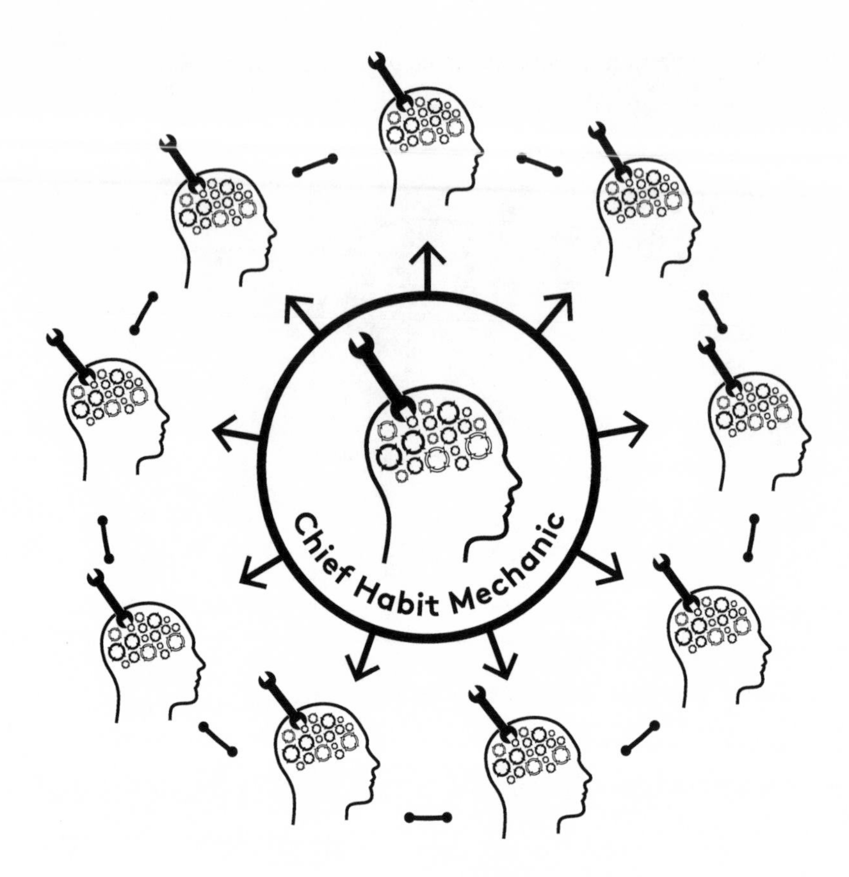

Figure 2.10: Once you are a Habit Mechanic, you can help others become Habit Mechanics.

As we work through the book, I will also share stories from some of the world's top performers, including:

- Groundbreaking scientist Marie Curie, on how she persisted to become the first woman to be awarded a Nobel Prize, and the only person to be awarded a Nobel Prize in two different sciences (physics and chemistry)
- Tennis star Novak Djokovic on monitoring and improving daily habitsAuthor J.K. Rowling, Microsoft founder Bill Gates, golfers

Rory McIlroy and Georgia Hall, and inventor Elon Musk on the power of intelligent goal setting

- NASA's pioneering aeronautical engineer Mary Jackson on being a role model
- All Black rugby legend Richie McCaw on improving productivity and minimizing distractions
- Tennis great Serena Williams on sharpening your focus and concentration for important tasks
- England rugby star Jonny Wilkinson on how to perform under pressure
- World champion athlete Jessica Ennis-Hill on reducing stress and building confidence
- World-cup-winning rugby coach Sir Clive Woodward on creating a high-performing culture
- Soccer manager Sir Alex Ferguson on developing people
- Bridgewater Associates (arguably the world's most successful hedge fund) founder Ray Dalio on creating a "purposefully developmental organization"
- Sir James Dyson on helping teams fail so they can succeed
- Self-made billionaire (and founder of undergarment brand Spanx) Sara Blakely on team communication

3

HABIT MECHANIC LANGUAGE AND TOOLS

As you read through Steps 1–3, you will be introduced to specific language and a range of helpful tools I have created (with the help of my team). I have listed them here so that you can refer back at any point. I will also recap them throughout the book, and I've created A–Z indexes at the end of the book. You don't have to learn all the language and tools by heart. That is why I have written this book, so you will have them forever and can revisit the language and tools that are most helpful for you as and when you need to.

BUT, do tell others about this language, because the more people in your network (family, friends, colleagues) who understand it, the more powerful it will become in helping you be your best.

Note: I will introduce the "Chief Habit Mechanic Tools" in Step 4 (Chapters 27–35).

CORE LANGUAGE

Me Power Conditioning—This means deliberately working toward being your best. (Chapters 2 and 9)

Focused or deliberate practice—Where you focus hard, make mistakes, and use feedback about your mistakes to get better. (Chapters 5 and 26)

10 Intelligence Factors—Once we have the opportunity to learn something, I have concluded that 10 factors (some genetic and some environmental, but all changeable) can supercharge or block our learning. (Chapters 5 and 26)

Habit Mechanic intelligence—Your ability to acquire and apply Habit Mechanic knowledge and skills to develop new helpful habits. (Chapter 5)

Super Habits—Habits that trigger other positive behaviors/habits. (Chapter 8)

Destructive Habits—Habits that trigger lots of other unhelpful behaviors/habits. (Chapter 8)

Lighthouse Brain—A simple model to help you understand the gist of how your brain works so you can begin to improve your thinking. (Chapter 10)

HUE (Horribly Unhelpful Emotions)—An imaginary character who lives in your brain who can make you worry and make it difficult for you to be your best. (Chapter 10)

Willomenia Power or Will Power—An imaginary character who lives in your brain who can help you manage HUE. (Chapter 10)

APE (Alive Perceived Energy) Brain—An easy acronym to help you understand your survival brain/limbic regions of the brain. (Chapter 11)

HAC (Helpful Attention Control) Brain—An easy acronym to help you understand your prefrontal cortex. (Chapter 11)

Self-Watching—Reflecting and thinking about yourself in a focused and systematic way. (Chapter 12)

Me Power Wish List—A list of all the small new helpful habits you would like to build. (Chapter 12)

Hedonism (pleasure)—This focuses on seeking short-term gratification and immediate rewards. (Chapter 14)

Eudemonia (Habit Mechanic development)—This focuses on delaying short-term gratification and sometimes enduring pain, boredom, and stress in order to develop yourself, grow, and achieve big meaningful goals. (Chapter 14)

TRAIT (Trigger, Routine, APE Incentive, Training) Habit Loop—A unique habit model created to help people understand how their habits actually work. (Chapter 17)

Nine Action Factors framework—Created to make it easy for you to use the latest insights from behavioral science to build sustainable new habits. (Chapter 18)

DES—Simple shorthand for diet, exercise, and sleep. (Chapter 19)

Activation levels—A concept created to make it easier to understand and manage your energy levels, alertness, and anxiety. (Chapter 21)

Focus Words and Focus Pictures—Skills you can use to help manage your thoughts. (Chapter 21)

The House of Confidence—A concept created to make confidence easier to understand and build. (Chapter 23)

The Igloo of Confidence—A concept created to make it easier to understand and develop the two core components of confidence (belief [self-esteem] and evidence [self-efficacy]). (Chapter 23)

Brain States—A concept created to help a person think about their brain as being like a battery that has three specific operating states: recharge, medium charge, and high charge. (Chapter 25)

Ice Cubes and Ice Sculptures—Terms created to help a person separate their daily tasks into two distinct categories: easy work (ice cubes) and mentally challenging work (ice sculptures). (Chapter 25)

SELF-REFLECTION TOOLS

APE Brain Test—A quick Self-Watching exercise to help you reflect on your helpful and unhelpful habits. (Chapter 12)

In-Depth Habits Reflection—An in-depth exercise to help you begin identifying your most unhelpful habits. (Chapter 17)

Helpful Habits Reflection—An exercise to help you reflect on which new habits it would be most helpful to build. (Chapter 17)

How HUE Hinders Change—An exercise to help you reflect on all the ways HUE might make it more difficult for you to build new habits. (Chapter 20)

Performance HAC Plan—An exercise to help you reflect on how well your practice helps you perform under pressure. (Chapter 24)

The Learning Strengths Plan—An exercise to help you reflect on your current learning habits and build better ones. (Chapter 26)

PLANNING TOOLS

Daily TEA (Tiny Empowering Action) Plan—A two-minute daily exercise to make your life easier. (Chapter 1)

Daily 3:1 Reflection—A daily positive reflection tool. (Chapters 5 and 23)

FAM (Future Ambitious Meaningful) Story—A tool to help you create, connect, and periodically review and update your long-, medium-, and short-term goals. (Chapter 16)

SWAP (Self-Watch, Aim, Plan)—A simple tool to help you begin building any new habit. (Chapter 19)

Seven-Day "Diet, Exercise, and Sleep" SWAP tool—A tool to help you build better DES habits daily. (Chapter 19)

The Habit Building Plan—A tool to help you activate all Nine Action Factors when you are developing a new habit. (Chapter 20)

Me Power Weekly Wall Chart—A tool to help you set meaningful goals for the week, and achieve them. (Chapter 18)

Optimal Activation Review—A tool to help you track, compare, and improve your Activation levels throughout the day. (Chapter 21)

WABA (Written APE Brain Argument)—A structured approach to managing unhelpful thoughts. (Chapter 22)

FAB (Fortunate, Adapt, Benefits) Thinking—A structured approach to reframing unhelpful thoughts. (Chapter 22)

RABA (Running APE Brain Argument)—A structured approach to managing unhelpful thoughts. (Chapter 22)

RAW (Reduce Activation and Write)—A summary of how to manage your stress. (Chapter 22)

Expressive Writing—A long-form stress management and confidence-building tool. (Chapter 22)

The Confidence Profile—A simple tool to help you reflect on and build confidence in different areas of your life. (Chapter 23)

KOSY (Knowledge, Others, Skills, You) Confidence—A simple confidence-building framework. (Chapter 23)

TE–TAP (Task, Environment, Timings, Activation, and Physical) Learning—A simple framework to pressure-proof your ability to perform. (Chapter 24)

Will Power Story—A tool to help you be more focused and productive every day and improve work-life balance. (Chapter 25)

Will Power Boosters and Strengths—Tactics you can use to supercharge your Will Power Stories. (Chapter 25)

E3 Learning—A framework to highlight that the most impactful types of practice include three core factors: Effort, Efficiency, and Effectiveness. (Chapter 26)

Focused Practice framework—Designed to help you improve the quality of your current learning. It helps you break down the learning process into four distinct parts, making it easier to do high-charge ice sculpture building work. (Chapter 26)

Now, let's dive into Step 1.

I will begin by sharing the scientific secrets behind one of the most famous and inspirational sporting stories of all time.

Step 1

DISCOVER YOUR SECRET SUPERPOWER

An Introduction to Being Happy and Successful in a Challenging World

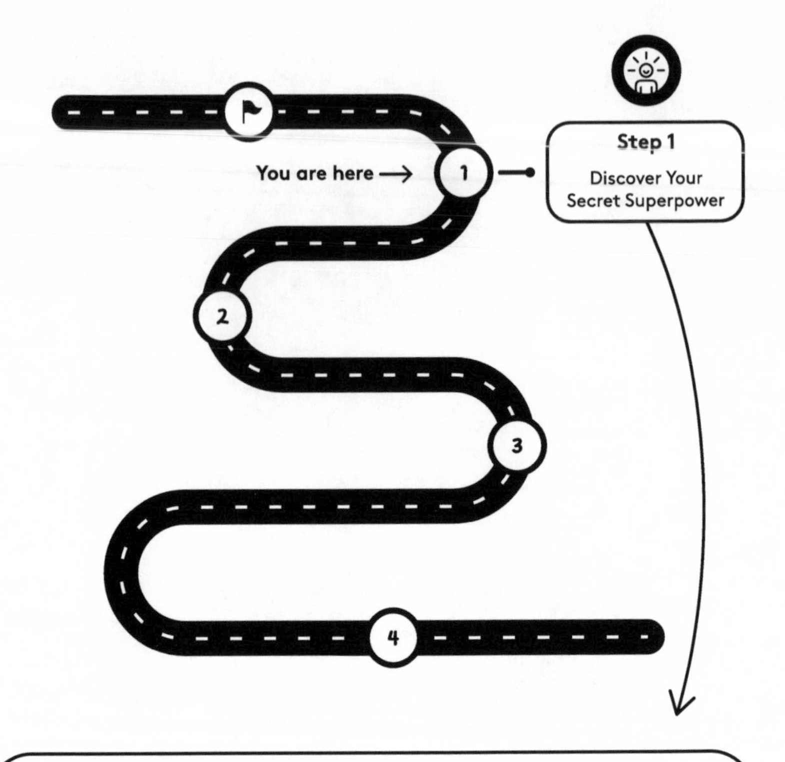

Chapter 4: The Secret Science behind a Story of Iconic Sporting Success

Chapter 5: Your Own Secret Superpower

Chapter 6: We're All Fighting a Learning War

Chapter 7: How to Win the Learning War and Break through Barriers in Your Own Life

Chapter 8: My Lightbulb Moment! Why I Made It My Mission to Help Others Become Habit Mechanics

Figure S1.1: An overview of your journey through Step 1.

4

THE SECRET SCIENCE BEHIND A STORY OF ICONIC SPORTING SUCCESS

They said it couldn't be done. They said it was not possible, but on May 6, 1954, Roger Bannister became the first person to run a sub-four-minute mile. Some of the world's best runners and coaches had been attempting to break this record since the 1880s, and it was beginning to look impossible.

In the 1950s, Bannister was not the only elite athlete trying to break that four-minute barrier. The record was also being pursued by American Wes Santee and Australian John Landy.

So why did Bannister succeed, where many others had failed?

BANNISTER'S SECRET ADVANTAGE

Running was only Bannister's hobby; his profession was medicine. At Oxford University, he was training to be a medical doctor. He was also a research scholar studying the respiratory system. As his research participants were running on treadmills in the university laboratory, Bannister was investigating the effects of oxygen levels on their performance. This was cutting-edge research.

As stated in Neal Bascomb's *The Perfect Mile*, "... few had examined the body's capacity to withstand punishment to the extent that Bannister did."

Bannister stated that he knew enough about medicine and physiology to know it was physically possible to run a sub-four-minute-mile. He was not interested in the art of running fast. He was interested in the science.

It's clear that Roger Bannister was an early pioneer in what we now call sports science. He wanted to understand the inner workings of his body and how it responded to training, much like a Formula 1 racing car mechanic understands the inner workings of an engine.

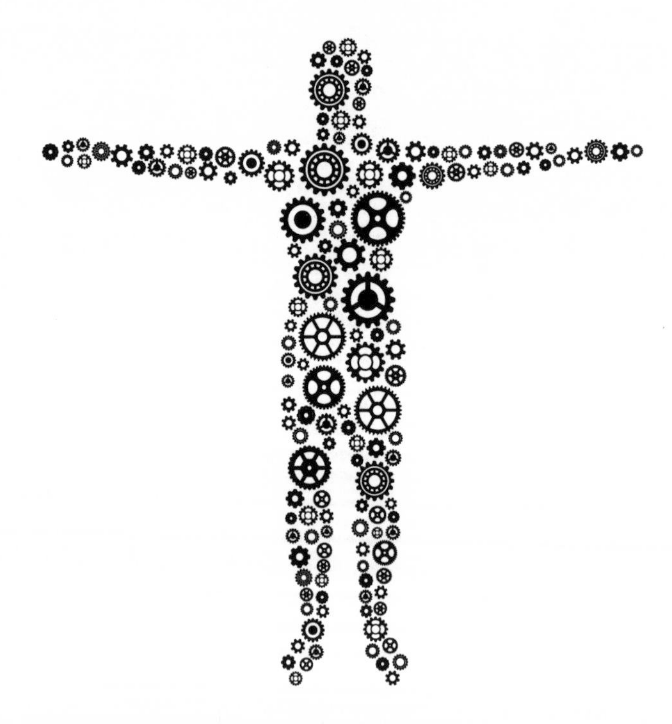

Figure 4.1: If you understand the inner workings of your mind and body, you will be better able to make positive changes in your life.

In contrast, his competitors had a less sophisticated understanding of how their training impacted their bodies.

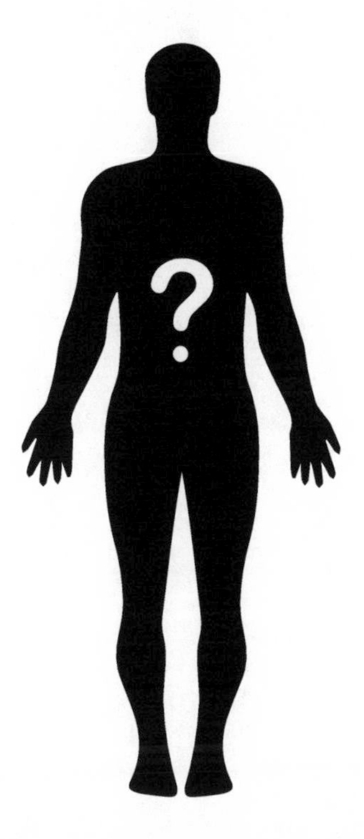

Figure 4.2: If you do not truly understand how your brain and body work, it will be more difficult to maximize your potential.

Bannister's opponents were taking what scientists call a "black-box" approach. In science, a black-box approach means examining or testing a complex system or process (e.g., how your brain works) without actually understanding what is going on inside it.

Figure 4.3: "Black-box" testing.

For example, you are told off by your boss (input). This makes you feel stressed and angry (output). But you don't actually know what being told off did to your brain and body. You just know that it made you feel angry.

In the case of Bannister's opponents, they were focusing on the type of training they were doing (the input) and the running times they were achieving (the output). They were not scientifically measuring the effect their training was having on the inner workings of their bodies. They were treating it like a black box.

So What?

Well, in simple terms, these detailed scientific insights allowed Bannister to gain a competitive advantage. He made his training more efficient and effective than his competitors' and was able to shave precious seconds off his running time.

BANNISTER WAS A HABIT MECHANIC

By studying the inner workings of his body, Bannister uniquely understood that he had to get better at conserving oxygen as he ran. To do this, he needed to build some new habits. He created a specific running style to optimize oxygen consumption and drilled it until it became his habitual technique.

He also adjusted his training habits. He designed new training to put exactly the same physical demands on his body as those created when attempting the four-minute mile.

Bannister's scientific approach to performance allowed him to fulfill his potential and inspire countless others to do the same.

Roger Bannister was what I would call a Habit Mechanic, and you can be one, too.

The process is simple:

1. First, understand how your brain and habits work.
2. Then build the new habits you need to fulfill your potential.

I am going to guide you through this process and make it easy for you to put cutting-edge insights from neuroscience, behavioral science, and psychology into practice.

Just like Sir Roger Bannister, building new habits will allow you to fulfill your potential.

If you want to become a Habit Mechanic, you first need to learn about your Secret Superpower.

5

YOUR OWN SECRET SUPERPOWER

"Environments [nurture] can be deterministic as we once believed only genes could be and...the genome [nature] can be as malleable as we once believed only environments could be."

—DR. DANIELA KAUFER and DR. DARLENE FRANCIS from University of California, Berkley, summarizing the findings from cutting-edge nature-nurture research

If you are not 100 percent sure what this quote means, don't worry (I am not sure I would if I didn't have a PhD in performance psychology ☺). I will fully unpack it during this chapter. The reason I have included the quote is to show that although the ideas in this book might sound very simple, they are often based on extremely complex scientific insights, which are not always easy to understand. I see one of my roles as helping everyone access this powerful science so that we can benefit and make our lives easier.

LEARNING TO BE YOUR BEST

For me, the most important things about Roger Bannister's story are the lessons it teaches us about learning. These lessons are more important than ever before because, whether you realize it or not, we are all in a Learning War (more about this in Chapter 6).

First, let me explain why learning is at the heart of Bannister's story.

To achieve a sub-four-minute time, Wes Santee, John Landy, and Roger Bannister had to *learn* how to run faster.

How do we learn? We can train, practice, rehearse, study, revise, experience, and observe.

The unique scientific insights Bannister had collected supercharged his learning and gave him a competitive advantage. He was able to make his training more efficient and effective than his competitors'. Or, in other words, he was able to "learn" how to shave precious seconds off his running time more quickly than his competitors.

HUMANS ARE DESIGNED TO LEARN

Now, let's think about learning in our own lives. The modern science is clear. When we are born, we *cannot* do very much. It is only by experiencing, doing, and practicing things that we develop basic life skills, including walking, talking, and problem-solving. This also includes things as basic as learning to smile, something that research has shown babies do in the first hours and days of life, aided by their mirror neurons.

Here is one specific insight about how our early learning is invisible to us. It is from the book *Peak* by the late preeminent Professor Anders Ericsson, author of nearly 300 publications about developing expertise, and whom I was fortunate to study with.

...Nine-month-old infants who paid more attention to a parent as that parent was reading a book and pointing to the pictures in the book grew up to have a much better vocabulary at five years of age than infants who paid less attention.

You are learning all the time. It is what humans are designed to do. You are learning now as you read this book. Think about what you have learned today from the news, gossip, the TV shows you watched, social media, the internet, your daily life.

It is perplexing to me when people say that others "cannot learn." For example, many people have said something like, "Jane just can't learn math. She will never be any good at it."

A statement like this simply is not true. Everything Jane can do, from walking and talking through to knowing how to use her smartphone, she has learned. She definitely can learn, but she just might not have learned as much about math as others expect.

YOUR BRAIN IS LIKE PLASTICINE

Contemporary science shows that, with *deliberate or focused practice,*[1] we can improve any skill.

When we practice anything, our brains change. It is these changes that allow us to improve our skills and abilities. The brain-changing process is called *neuroplasticity.* There are about 100 billion neurons in your brain, and they are malleable like plasticine. This means that our abilities are not fixed. You can improve anything with the right type and quantity of practice.

WARNING! I know this research has been misunderstood in the past, so let me be very clear about what it means. It does not mean that anyone

[1] Where you focus hard, make mistakes, and use feedback about your mistakes to get better.

can become the best in the world at anything. It simply means that with focused practice we can improve anything.

For example, Sara Blakely, self-made billionaire and founder of undergarment brand Spanx, could not have become so excellent at sales if she had not practiced selling. However, practicing sales skills will not necessarily turn you into a billionaire. But if you do the right type of practice, it will make you better at sales.

A QUICK OVERVIEW OF HOW WE LEARN

Let's go a little deeper. Learning can be broken down into some simple steps. First, you pay *attention* to some new information. For example, you meet a new family (with seven members) and you ask them their names. The names go into your short-term memory, which can ONLY hold around five to seven pieces of information at any one time. In this example, each name (of which there are seven) would count as one piece of information.

If you don't repeat these names within about 30 seconds, your short-term memory will dump them. They will disappear without a trace.

However, if you repeat the names before they disappear—for example, by saying them to yourself, writing them down, or saying them to someone else—this information will start to be turned into a memory. In other words, your brain will begin to form neurological connections that represent the new information you have learned. The more you repeat the information, the thicker the connections become. Think of thin cobwebs transforming into solid cables, or "cobwebs to cables."

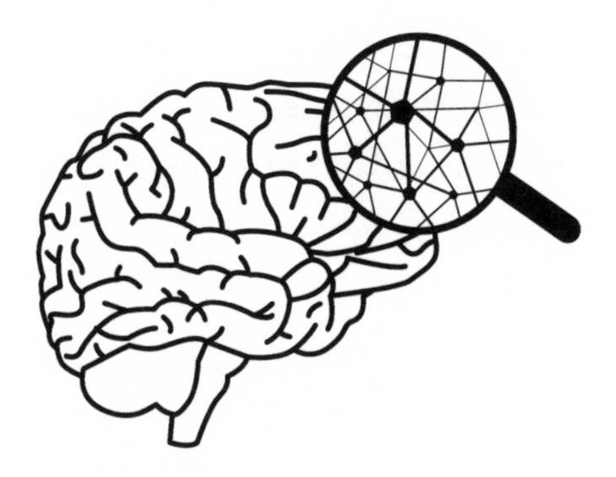

Figure 5.1: Practice changes your brain by strengthening neurological pathways.

But if you stop using the information, the cables will reduce to cobwebs —and eventually disappear. That means you will no longer be able to remember this information. For example, when you were at primary or elementary school, you knew everyone's name in your class. But because you do not see these people anymore, and have stopped paying attention to their names, the neurons in your brain associated with their names have died. But this will not have happened to the neurons of the names of the people you still stay in touch with.

This cobwebs-to-cables process works exactly the same for anything you have learned. Your ability to do anything is only possible because you have specific neurons for each thing in your brain.

For example, babies are constantly acquiring knowledge by watching people and experiencing things. We do not just learn in the classroom or by reading. We are learning all the time.

KNOWLEDGE-TO-SKILL-TO-HABIT

To learn how to run faster, Roger Bannister first acquired **knowledge** about the role of oxygen. He then used this knowledge to develop new running and training **skills** (think of putting skills into practice as "doing"). Finally, he repeated those skills until they became **habits**. All learning that changes our behavior (what we think and do) follows this same knowledge-to-skill-to-habit path.

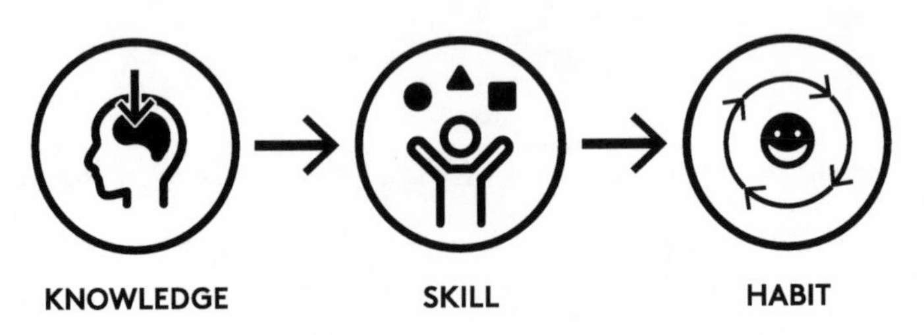

Figure 5.2: All learning that changes our behavior can be broken down into these three simple steps.

Learning how to improve anything starts with acquiring **knowledge**. When you learned the alphabet, you received the knowledge from a book, teacher, or parent. Then you had to practice your alphabet **skills**.

With practice, skills become **habits**, making them easy to use with almost no conscious effort. So the more you practiced your alphabet, the easier and more habitual it became. Eventually, you could say the alphabet without really thinking about it. This process can take a long time, but the more we practice a skill, the more neurons we grow for that skill.

BUILDING YOUR LEARNING ONE BLOCK AT A TIME

Imagine that practice, and moving from knowledge-to-skill-to-habit, involves freezing neurons in the brain until they become **solid ice cubes**.

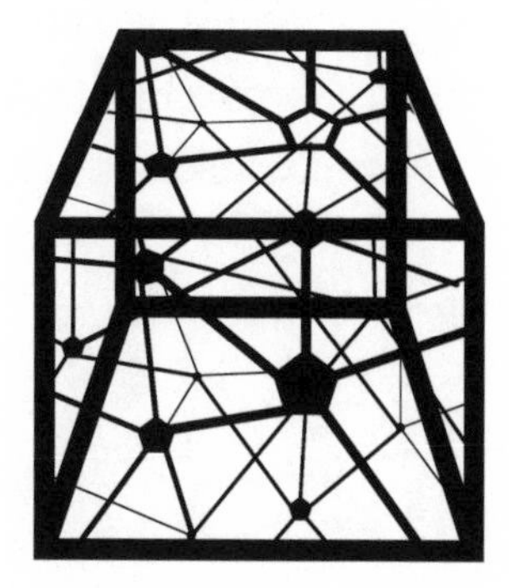

Figure 5.3: A neuron ice cube.

Once an ice cube is frozen, the habit is built. But if we stop using the habit, the ice cube melts, because neurons that are not being used become weaker.

Figure 5.4: Your neuron ice cubes can be strengthened through practice but weakened through lack of practice.

We can imagine that we then organize our ice cubes into an igloo that represents how good we are at any particular activity. For example, here is an igloo for a professional salesperson.

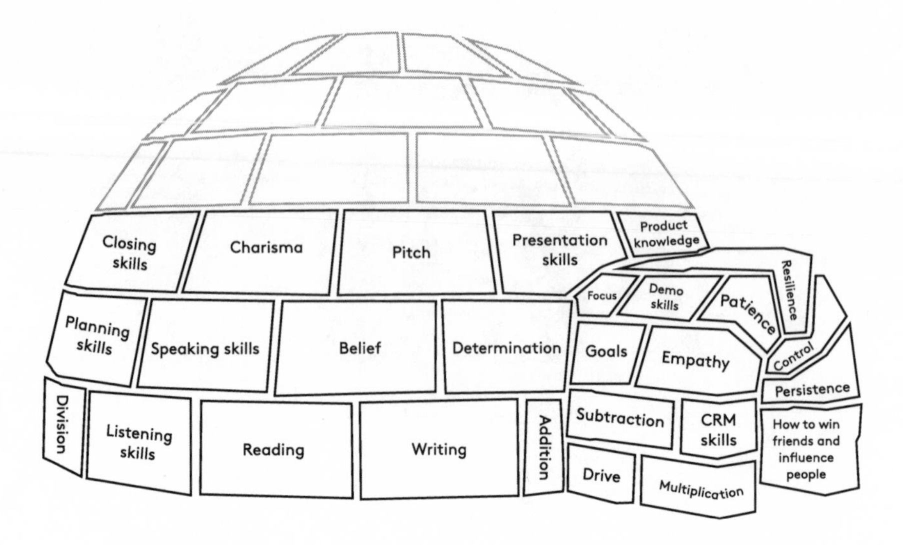

Figure 5.5: Notice how some of the ice cubes are very basic things you might take for granted, but things that you could not do when you were born (e.g., speaking), and things that not every adult is able to do (e.g., reading and writing). Also notice that there is still room for improvement/ice cubes to freeze.

The more complete our igloo, the better we are at the activity. But there will always be new ice cubes we need to freeze and add onto our igloo to develop our abilities and advance to the next level.

We can also imagine that we have a group of igloos (like an igloo housing estate [Figure 5.6]). Each represents the different areas in our work and life that are important to us for happiness and success.

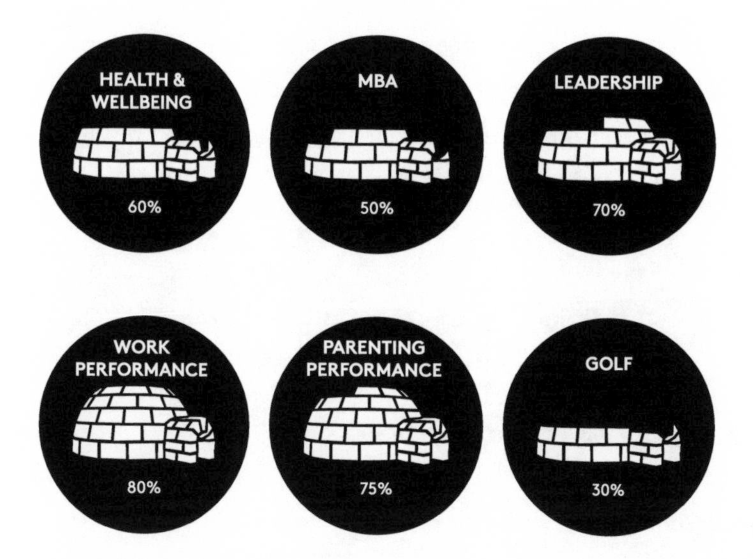

Figure 5.6: Different igloos will be at different stages of development, but they can each be built up and improved with the right type, quality, and quantity of practice.

Focused practice can help improve everything that's important for us to live a healthy and happy life, where we fulfill our potential.

CAN YOU DELIBERATELY PRACTICE HAPPINESS?

The same knowledge-to-skill-to-habit process applies to any area of our lives we want to improve (be that physical or mental).

For example, **we can learn to be happier**. The first thing we might need is some new knowledge about what it means to be happy. I will address this question in a lot more detail later in the book (Chapter 14), but here is a quick overview of my understanding.

To feel we are truly happy, we first need our brain to be working well. This is more likely to happen if we have good sleep, diet, and exercise habits, and positive personal relationships.

Next, we need to experience both pleasure (think short-term gratification) and personal achievement and growth. Achieving the latter can require delaying short-term gratification in pursuit of bigger, more meaningful goals. This sometimes means experiencing pain, boredom, and stress.

Balancing Short-Term Gratification and Personal Growth

Striking a good balance between pleasure and personal growth can be difficult because of the way the brain is naturally wired. For survival reasons, we are designed to prioritize pleasure and dwell on problems and challenges. This can make achieving personal growth difficult. For example, I know that finishing this book (writing it) will result in feelings of personal achievement, making me happier in the long-term. But the writing process is very stressful, and there are many other fun things I would rather be doing right now that will give me short-term happiness.

For example, I might find myself thinking (as I am writing this book)...

This is too difficult. I shouldn't be in my office writing on a Sunday afternoon; I should be at home with my feet up, relaxing and enjoying a nice Sunday lunch with my family. That's it, I am going home!

But this type of thinking will make it more difficult for me to finish the book and impede my personal growth and therefore my happiness.

The good news is that we can all learn to get better at controlling our thoughts and use them to help us achieve our goals. For example, I could think...

Giving up is the easy option. Finishing this book will help lots of other people feel and do better every day. And on a selfish note, I know that completing and publishing it will make me feel happy for a long time. I am lucky to be able to write it, and I should be proud of myself for persisting. This is only one Sunday, and my family understands.

Another example might be seeing a piece of cake in a coffee shop that looks really delicious. I might find myself thinking, "That looks delicious; it will taste amazing and make me feel good."

However, I am on a diet and eating the cake will not help me achieve my weight-loss goal. So instead I could say to myself, "Eating the cake might make me feel good for a few minutes, but I will feel bad for much longer if I don't achieve my weight-loss goal this week. Resisting the cake will help me feel a sense of personal achievement and help me feel proud of myself."

Thinking in a more helpful way is a skill we can all learn to improve. By doing this, it will be easier to resist the temptation to give in, beat ourselves up, and only focus on the negatives. If you keep practicing the skill (thinking in a helpful way), it will become a habit.

Ultimately, thinking more helpfully makes it easier to strike a better balance between experiencing pleasure and personal growth.

Daily 3:1 Reflection

A Habit Mechanic Tool you could use to think more helpfully is our "Daily 3:1 Reflection." You can use this at the end of each day to help you think in a more helpful way about your day. Why not have a go:

Write down three (or more) positive or helpful reflections about today, and one area you can improve tomorrow. Then, if it helps, discuss/share your reflections with others.

Here is an example:

- + I was able to have breakfast with my family this morning.
- + I love the company I work for. I feel so lucky to work here.
- + I was able to help my children with their homework.

You can also set a goal to work toward in the next 24 hours:

- – Do 10 more minutes walking tomorrow than I achieved today.

If we keep practicing this process of writing down thoughts that are helpful to us, we move it from knowing (knowledge about the Daily 3:1 Reflection), to doing (the Daily 3:1 Reflection), to habit (habitually thinking in a more helpful way).

There are many Habit Mechanic Tools we can learn to help us be happier, and this book is packed full of them. Our Daily 3:1 Reflection is just one.

To make it easier to complete regular Daily 3:1 Reflections, I have created a PDF template. I use this, and if you want to use it, go to tougherminds.co.uk/habitmechanic and click on "Resources" to download your copy.

WHAT ABOUT MY GENES?

A person's genes make it more likely that they are able to get good at certain things, but scientific research shows that genetics are malleable. People do have "raw genetic material," which is their genotype. However, the physical expression (e.g., height, ability to catch, how you handle stress) of this is strongly influenced by environmental interactions (practice) resulting in their phenotype. This understanding is called epigenetics.

Science now shows that our environments can have just as great an influence on our development as our genes. How good you are at anything (e.g., stress management, sleep, productivity, leadership, reading) is not a case of nature (genes) versus nurture (practice), but nature PLUS nurture.

BUT AREN'T SOME PEOPLE JUST NATURALLY MORE INTELLIGENT THAN OTHERS?

I understand why it can appear this way. For example, imagine three girls at your school were called Sarah, Lisa, and Jane.

Sarah always got the top grades. Lisa always got average academic grades. Jane always came bottom of the class. It would be easy to conclude that Sarah must be more intelligent than Lisa and Jane. And that Lisa must be more intelligent than Jane. But it is not as straightforward as this.

To understand why, let's first consider what intelligence means, using the *Oxford Dictionary* definition:

"The ability to acquire and apply knowledge and skills."

In other words, it is a person's ability to learn, and then to use what they have learned. So, learning and intelligence are interconnected.

We know that everyone can learn because it is a fundamental part of being human. So, do different people have different capacities for learning (e.g., some people find it easier to do academic learning than others)? Kind of.

The reason it can sometimes appear that some people are more intelligent than others (i.e., because one person can learn something faster or more easily) is that certain factors can supercharge or block learning. Some of these factors are genetic (nature) and some are environmental (nurture).

Let's think more about Sarah (top grades), Lisa (average grades), and Jane (worst grades).

Sarah

Sarah's genetics and life circumstances meant she was able to get good at reading and writing much more quickly than Lisa and Jane. Sarah's father was a highly skilled teacher and encouraged Sarah to practice her reading and writing skills from a very young age. Sarah then had to teach her younger sister how to read and write. She also had a natural attentional style[2] that was perfect for reading, writing, and academic work.

Lisa

Lisa's genetics and life circumstances meant she developed her people skills (e.g., abilities to listen, empathize, and make others laugh) much more quickly than Sarah and Jane. Each of Lisa's parents had two jobs. This meant that Lisa had to look after her younger siblings after school from a young age, almost acting like their third parent. She also had a large extended family, and every weekend the family got together and hung out. Lisa spent a lot of time playing with her cousins and listening to her aunts and uncles and grandparents. She noticed how they listened and cared for each other, but also teased each other, making people laugh. Her natural attentional style made it easy for her to listen closely to others and to show empathy.

Jane

Jane's genetics and life circumstances meant that she was able to get good at playing tennis much more quickly than Sarah and Lisa. Jane's mother was a highly skilled tennis coach. Jane grew up next door to a tennis court where she was coached by her mother from a very young age. She had a younger brother, and they played tennis together most nights of the week after school and every weekend. She was tall and powerful for her age, and also had a natural attentional style that was perfect for playing tennis.

I have created these examples to highlight how genetic (nature) and

[2] Different types of learning require different attentional styles. Some learning requires a narrow focus of concentration (e.g., academic learning), others a broad focus of concentration (e.g., playing soccer). Yet everybody seems to have a different natural attentional style. The good news is you can learn how to focus your attention more narrowly or widely.

environmental (nurture) factors interact to make it easier for some people to learn some things. Sarah, Lisa, and Jane are all intelligent; they have just spent their time practicing different things and so developing their intelligence in different areas.

Note: I am not saying that people who get top grades cannot also be good at playing tennis and have good people skills ☺; these are just examples.

To develop their intelligence, they all had to move through the learning process I explained earlier: going from **knowledge** to **skill** to **habit.** But because each individual had different genetics and life circumstances, progressing through this learning process was easier in some areas of their lives than others.

Could Jane have ever outperformed Sarah or Lisa academically? That is not a very helpful question in my experience. Could Jane have outperformed *herself* had she been introduced to and taught Habit Mechanic knowledge and skills? That is a better question, and one to which we know the answer is yes. With this kind of support, all three girls could have become better and more confident in any and all aspects of their lives, whatever their starting point in each.

Let's dig a little deeper.

10 Intelligence Factors

Once we have the opportunity to learn something, I have concluded that 10 factors (some genetic and some environmental, but all changeable) can supercharge or block our learning. I call them the "10 Intelligence Factors."[3]

[3] Professor David Perkins' work has been instrumental in helping me think about intelligence and learning in this way. He was Professor of Education at Harvard Graduate School, where he worked closely with Professor Howard Gardner (creator of the theory of multiple intelligences) on Project Zero.

The 10 Intelligence Factors are (underneath each I've shown how this book will help you get that factor working for you):

1. **Your motivation to learn (including your belief that you can learn)**
   I will show you how to boost your motivation and personal drive in Chapter 16, and throughout this book, I will help you understand that you can learn to get better at anything you put your mind to.
2. **Your diet, exercise, and sleep habits**
   I will show you how to develop better ones in Chapter 19.
3. **Your emotional state while learning**
   By learning to become a Habit Mechanic, you will get much better at managing your emotions.
4. **Your Activation levels while learning**
   I will explain this concept and how to use it to help you in Chapter 21.
5. **Your attentional style**
   By learning to become a Habit Mechanic, you will get much better at managing and focusing your attention.
6. **Your working memory and memory recollection capacities**
   By fully engaging in this book and learning to become a Habit Mechanic, you will sharpen and enhance your memory capacities.
7. **The brain friendliness and quality of the learning material (or how you encode information)**
   I have used insights about how brains work, and how people learn, to make this book and our training brain friendly.
8. **The skill of your teacher(s)**
   The ideas in this book have already helped over 10,000 people feel and do better, so you are in safe hands.
9. **The volume and quality of your prior learning (i.e., what you have already learned)**

This book is structured to build up your Habit Mechanic knowledge, skills, and habits one tiny step at a time.

10. **The volume and quality of your current learning (i.e., are you doing lots of focused practice?)**
    Throughout the book, and explicitly in Chapter 26, I will show you how to do focused/deliberate practice so that you can optimize every minute you spend practicing.

I will explain the 10 Intelligence Factors in much more detail in Chapter 26. But the important point I want to make here is that we can all learn how to unblock any factor we feel is blocking our learning. In fact, we can learn how to turn the blocker into a learning supercharger.

Habit Mechanic Intelligence

The best way to do that is by improving your "Habit Mechanic intelligence" (i.e., your ability to acquire and apply Habit Mechanic knowledge and skills to develop new helpful habits). By reading this book and learning to be a Habit Mechanic, you are doing exactly that!

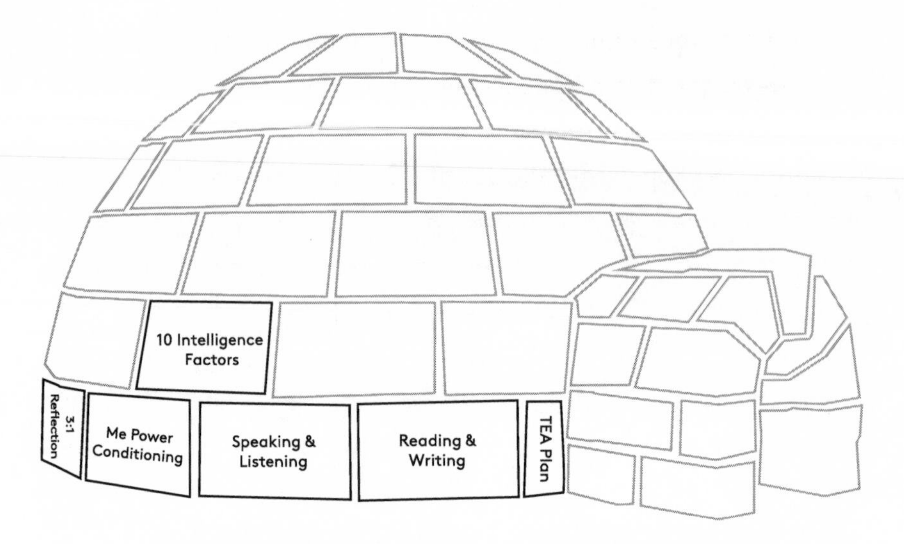

Figure 5.7: Your "Habit Mechanic intelligence igloo." To help you see your Habit Mechanic intelligence developing, I will use the igloo structure (introduced earlier in this chapter). As you work through the book your Habit Mechanic intelligence igloo will become increasingly developed. I have deliberately put speaking, listening, reading, and writing into the igloo, because these are all essential for developing your Habit Mechanic intelligence.

LEARNING FROM AN OLYMPIC CHAMPION

British athlete Jessica Ennis-Hill finished her career as multiple world champion and Olympic gold medalist in heptathlon. In a BBC interview with fellow former world champion athlete Michael Johnson, she revealed that as a junior, she had never even heard of the event (the heptathlon), much less aspired to be a dominant force in the discipline.

So, at one point in her life, she had no knowledge of an event that she became the best in the world at. She was not born to do it. She worked amazingly hard to achieve this exalted status.

The learning science I have shared in this chapter does not say that everyone can become a world champion athlete. It simply says that whatever your current abilities (in any area of your life), you can improve them with practice.

This is the process Ennis-Hill used to become a world champion. Over a long period of time she incrementally (one tiny step at a time) improved her heptathlete abilities (or intelligence), until she had some of the best heptathlete abilities in the world. It was probably the case that most, if not all, of the 10 Intelligence Factors were working in her favor. This would have made it easier for her to develop heptathlete abilities (moving from heptathlete **knowledge** to heptathlete **skills** to heptathlete **habits**).

The learning process is always the same, and you can use it to improve your abilities (or intelligences) in any area of your life.

LEARNING IS YOUR SECRET SUPERPOWER!

Until the 1990s, it was commonly accepted that once you stopped growing (in height) your ability to develop new skills and abilities was extremely limited. It was also commonly accepted that your genetics determined your potential. But modern science has transformed our understanding of the power of learning. Frustratingly, the old views about human potential still dominate.

It is easy to underestimate the power of your ability to learn. This is because you have always been able to learn and are doing it all the time. You have also probably been given some inaccurate and disempowering information about your learning abilities.

But the evidence is clear: whatever you want to get better at, you can. This includes improving your wellbeing, resilience, performance, and leadership.

Learning is your Secret Superpower. But next I want to give you an important warning about why it can easily be misdirected, making your life more difficult!

6

WE'RE ALL FIGHTING A LEARNING WAR

There is a problem! The challenges of the modern world can turn your greatest strength into your greatest weakness. More than ever before, it is easier to *accidentally learn* how to get good at some really unhelpful things, which make being happy and at our best very difficult.

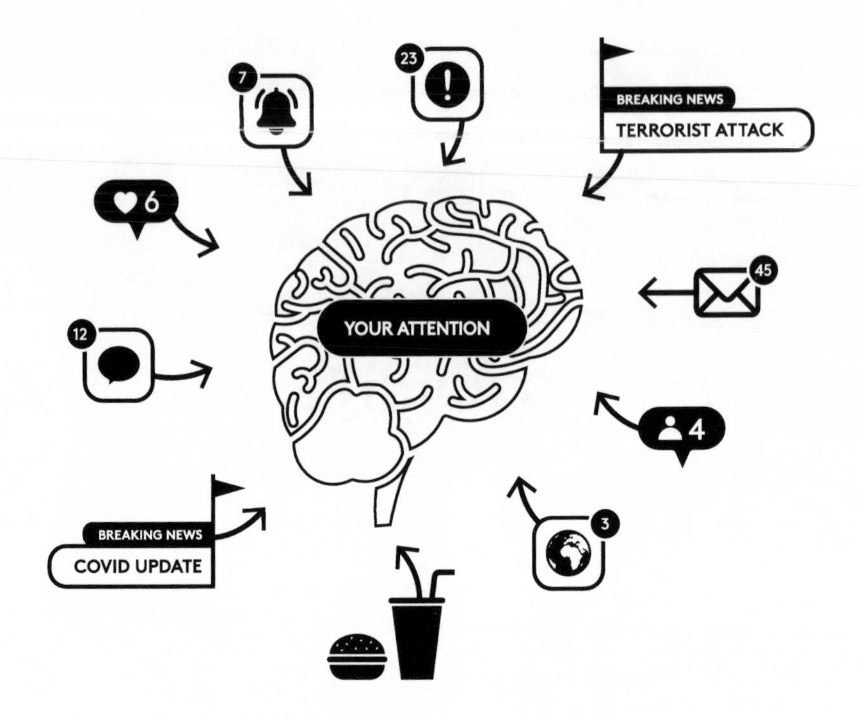

Figure 6.1: Some have said that the most valuable real estate on the planet is the human eyeball because it is the gateway to your most precious resource—your attention.

LEARNING HOW TO BE A WORSE VERSION OF YOURSELF

We live in the VUCA (volatile, uncertain, complex, and ambiguous) world—a term originated from the US military. There is only one constant in this world: change.

Here are some examples of recent, profound changes to our lives and work:

- New approaches (agile, hybrid, flexible) have changed the way we work.

- Smartphones, social media, and videoconferencing have changed the way we communicate and socialize.
- Online stores have changed the way we shop.
- Contactless payments, online banking, and easy access to credit have changed our personal finances.
- And—by allowing us to see edited versions of other people's lives—social media has promoted narcissism and increased our anxiety, stress, and lack of confidence.

There is widespread recognition that the root cause of these changes is the rapid advance of technology and the disruption it brings to our lives and work.

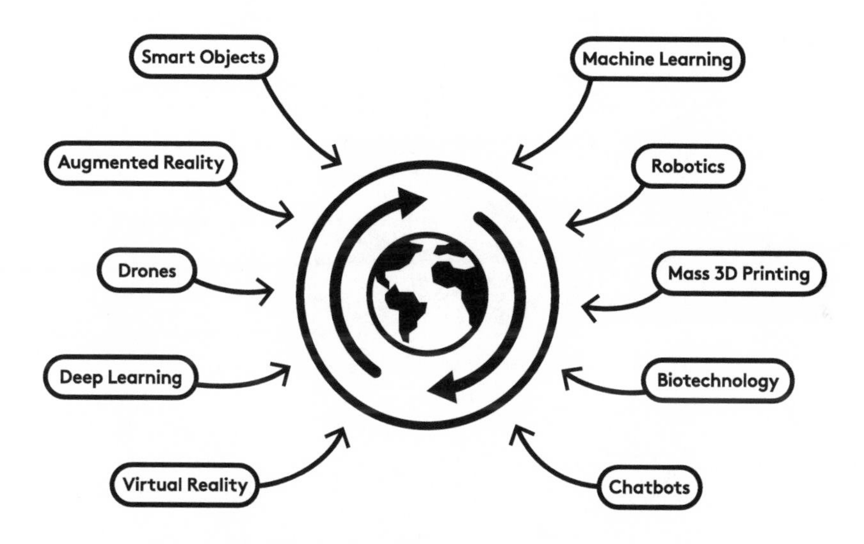

Figure 6.2: The COVID-19 pandemic has accelerated the role technology plays in our daily work and lives.

These constant changes create stress and challenges. In turn, this makes it easier to get good at things like

- beating ourselves up;
- getting stressed;
- getting distracted;
- feeling anxious;
- sleeping less;
- exercising less;
- consuming more junk food;
- getting into debt; and
- becoming more selfish.

Remember: when you practice something, your brain changes. You learn how to get better at the thing you are practicing—even if the thing you practice is unhelpful or harmful.

Do you want to learn how to do all this unhelpful stuff? Of course not. But the VUCA world and those who run it are making it really easy.

The reality is that we are in a Learning War with some of the most powerful people in the world.

THE ATTENTION ECONOMY

Businesses understand that to make money they need to capture our attention, hence the "attention economy."

You will no doubt understand that smartphones, social media, the internet, and other technologically driven interruptions are constantly hijacking our attention, which is leading to outcomes like the average adult attention span dropping to about eight seconds (it was about 12 seconds in 2000). A recent Ofcom report (from 2021) also showed that adults in the UK are spending nearly six hours a day watching TV and online video content. This is an increase of 47 minutes on the previous year.

These issues are highlighted in the book *Stand Out of Our Light: Freedom and Resistance in the Attention Economy.* It was written by former Google advertising strategist Dr. James Williams, who completed his PhD at Oxford University's Internet Institute.

Its central theme is an appeal to society and the tech industry to help ensure our smartphones and other electronic devices do not distract us so much that we fail to live meaningful, fulfilled lives. Williams highlights how our attention becomes a scarce resource, as information becomes plentiful and abundant. He says that in the attention economy, we need to recognize the damaging impact of this on our work and lives. For example, the internet is funded largely by advertising, so tech companies need people to be glued to their apps and sites or they don't make money. This means they are incentivized to consume as much of people's time and conscious attention as possible.

The reality is that your attention is constantly being hijacked. Here are some examples:

***Social media*:** Why do these companies want you to use their services? To make you happy? Or so they can sell your attention and the data they collect about you to advertisers?

***Streaming services*:** The more use you get out of a streaming service, the more likely you will keep subscribing. A recent *Vanity Fair* article cited the CEO of one of these companies saying that his company's real competitor is sleep. "You get a show or a movie you're really dying to watch, and you end up staying up late at night, so we actually compete with sleep," the CEO said. "And we're winning!"

***Online retailers*:** Do they want you to be happy? Or do they want you to spend as much money with them as possible?

***Supermarkets*:** Do they want you to be healthy? Or do you think they deliberately place unhealthy and high-profit foods in the places you are most likely to be tempted to buy them?

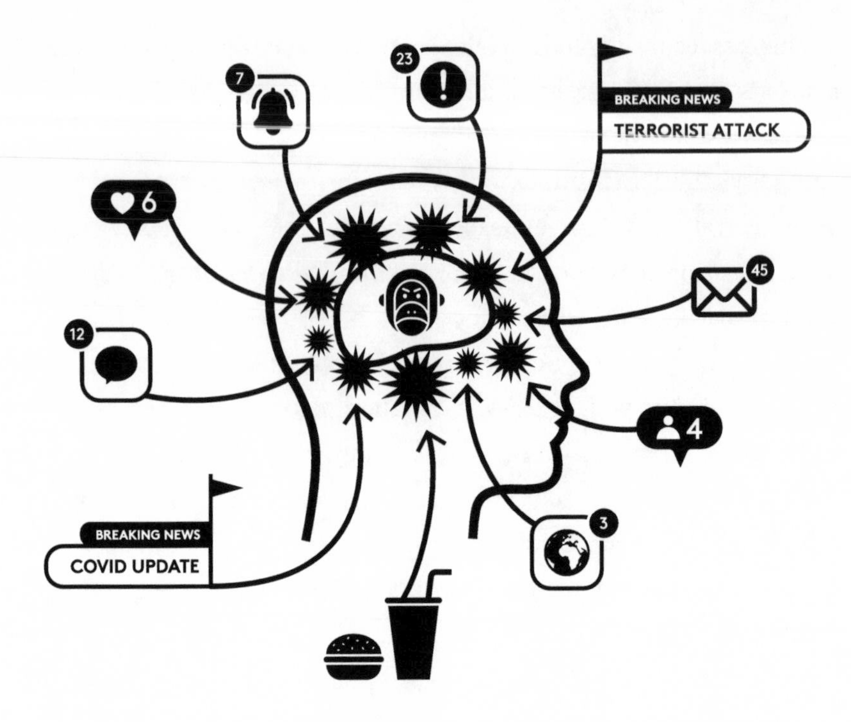

Figure 6.3: It is easy to feel bombarded and overwhelmed, and spend more time than is helpful doing things that are not good for your health, happiness, or performance.

We are surrounded by distractions and diversions that are tricking us into practicing things that are not very helpful for our health, happiness, or performance.

THE BIGGEST PROBLEM?

We are not consciously practicing these things. We are doing them on autopilot.

It turns out that our brains are designed to learn some things more easily than others. Unfortunately, many of the things that make our lives more difficult are really easy to learn, while many of the things that help us be happy and successful are more difficult to learn.

In the Learning War, you are being hoodwinked into learning bad habits that make it harder than ever to do the important things that help you be at your best.

So how can you respond? What can you do to win this war?

7

HOW TO WIN THE LEARNING WAR AND BREAK THROUGH BARRIERS IN YOUR OWN LIFE

The bad news is that learning how to get good at eating donuts and beating ourselves up is far easier than developing good health and happiness habits. The good news is we can use secrets from the new science of learning to improve our resilience and be our best more often.

I know that many people have tried to stop doing unhelpful things but ultimately failed. Others have been able to achieve some success but always fallen short of their true potential. If this is you, it's not your fault. You have been let down. The advice you were given was not good enough. For too long, your brain has been treated like a black box!

However, it does not have to be this way. You can learn how to use cutting-edge science to run your own version of the sub-four-minute mile. In other words, you can achieve your long-term goals, overcome obstacles that seem insurmountable, and succeed and thrive in your work and life. I know these things sometimes feel impossible, but I am going to show you how to achieve them by taking more control of your journey through life.

To do this, I am going to teach you how to become a Habit Mechanic. It's easy to learn how, and by understanding your internal mechanics (how your brain and habits work, and how to supercharge your learning so you can change them), you will be able to unlock your true potential.

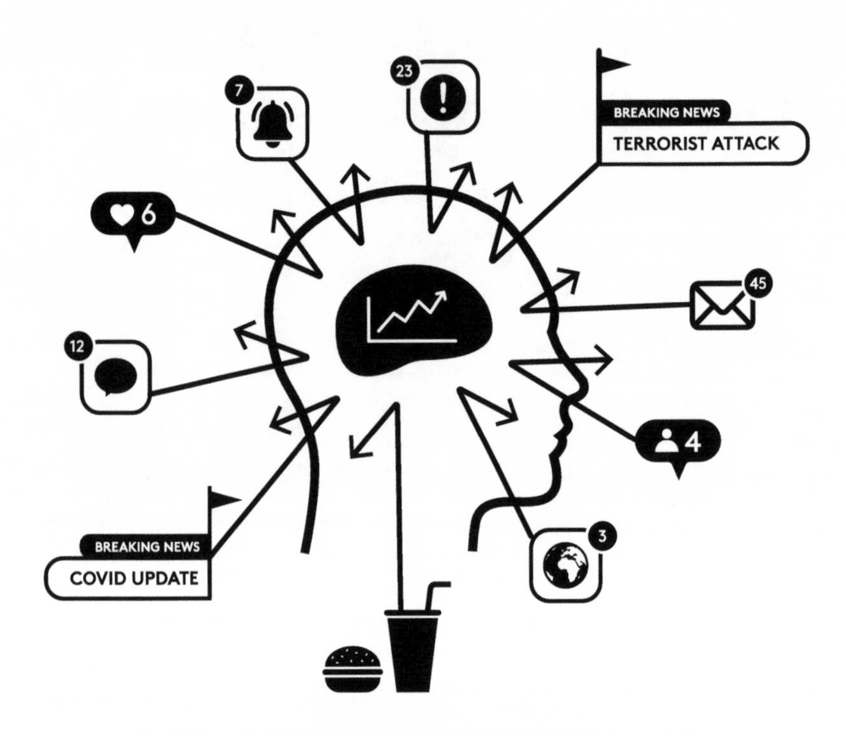

Figure 7.1: You don't have to be a victim of the attention economy; you can learn how to fight back.

8

MY LIGHTBULB MOMENT! WHY I MADE IT MY MISSION TO HELP OTHERS BECOME HABIT MECHANICS

You might be asking yourself, who is Dr. Jon Finn and why should I trust what he says? To answer these questions, I have provided a few insights about my career to show you how I have come to know what I know. These research, consultancy, and life experiences helped me to create the Habit Mechanic concept and training programs.

Tip: If you are not interested in my personal experiences, just skip ahead to Part 7 ☺.

PART 1—USING FAILURE AS A CATALYST

After the rugby setback I explained in Chapter 2, and my decision to focus on helping other people fulfill their potential, I intensified my commitment to my university studies.

I not only studied sport psychology but also physiology, motor control (how humans learn skills), and nutrition. I became fascinated by mental skills training and completed a dissertation that explored how golfers use mental imagery to improve their performance. It was graded First Class. That meant I could study the master's program of my choosing.

I had overcome the first obstacle in my future career.

PART 2—THE BLACK-BOX APPROACH!

As I studied my Master's in Sport Psychology, I was fortunate to learn from some of the world's leading human-performance scientists. Some were undertaking research for NASA. Others were pioneering the use of neuroscience in sports performance. And others were helping British athletes win gold medals and break world records by optimizing their training in state-of-the-art facilities.

What made this period particularly exciting was that a new technology called "functional magnetic resonance imaging" (fMRI) was becoming widely available. This meant that, for the first time ever, researchers were able to look inside the human brain in real time.

Until this point, psychologists had been forced to use "black-box" theories (see Chapter 4) to understand human behavior. This meant psychology theories (about what goes on inside the human brain and why people do what they do) were created without actually looking at what goes on inside the human brain. Believe it or not, black-box theories still dominate today. This is a huge problem, which is why I have highlighted it in this book.

During my master's, the ideas and research I was exposed to were very different from the traditional black-box approach of looking at why humans do what they do. This has given me a huge advantage in my career, and I will be eternally grateful to those amazing scientists who taught and nurtured me.

I was extremely focused during my master's degree, because I knew I wanted to work in the field of performance psychology. I sharpened my applied psychology skills by working with athletes, carrying out research (that was published), and digging deeper into the neuroscience of mental skills training. I was building solid, science-based foundations for my chosen career.

PART 3—THE SCIENCE OF SUCCESS

After completing my master's, I was thrust straight into the world of elite sport. I began working as a consultant for a performance analysis company whose clients included some of the world's highest-profile soccer and rugby teams.

This company used lower-league teams to give their junior employees training experience. I was posted to the English professional soccer team Scunthorpe United. I built good relationships at the club and ended up becoming part of the backroom staff, using my psychology and analysis skills to support the first-team players and coaches.

At the start of the 2006–07 season, we were more favored for relegation than success because we had such a small budget. We were the underdogs. But against all odds, we won the league and gained promotion.

The statistics told a fascinating story. We spent around 50 percent less on player wages than our rivals. It only cost us approximately £25,000 ($34,000) to acquire a single league point. The team that finished second spent £66,000 ($89,000) per point and the team that finished third spent £41,000 ($55,000) per point. For us to be able to secure league points so cheaply was amazing.

Other interesting performance stories also emerged. Scunthorpe was very successful at recruiting and nurturing talent. We bought young players cheaply from bigger teams and often sold them on for huge profits. One young player was sold back to the team we purchased him from at a 95 percent profit. This was not an easy thing to achieve, because successful talent development is extremely complex.

The promotion also created a leadership transition within the team, which sparked my interest in the science of leadership development.

These experiences inspired me and made me want to deepen my understanding of how successful, effective, and powerful teams are created—the sort of teams in which every member consistently performs to their potential. So I began a PhD to help me understand more.

I researched emotional regulation and how this created the mental resilience needed to fulfill your potential, as well as the foundations of outstanding leadership. More importantly, I began working with Professor Jim McKenna, one of the world's foremost behavioral science and behavior change experts.

My PhD allowed me to research and work with some of the most talented athletes in the UK and the coaches who were experts at nurturing them. My aim was to demystify what helped young athletes fulfill their potential, and what stopped them. However, unlike previous research in this area, I used a neuroscience and behavioral science lens. I wanted to cut through the noise and understand what was going on inside their brains.

This research set me on the path to seeking out the secret science that we can all use to make our lives easier.

PART 4—BRAINS RUN ON HABITS

"Can you help our golf coaches teach their golfers how to control their thoughts under pressure?"

This was the challenge my colleagues and I were presented with by the Professional Golfers' Association (PGA) of Great Britain and Ireland as it set up a golf psychology module for its trainee professionals.

I was confident we could help the PGA's coaches, but we needed a different approach.

By this point in my career, I was gaining a lot of experience and starting to work with (and, more importantly, learn from) many world-class coaches and athletes. I worked in professional sports including soccer, rugby, cricket, golf, tennis, and track and field.

Alongside my applied work, university lecturing, and imagery research, I continued to work on my PhD. It was becoming clear to me that the traditional approaches used in coaching and performance psychology were not as effective as they might be. This was because they were based on black-box theories, and not on how brains actually worked.

I used the PGA opportunity to train golf coaches to try something new. I wanted to put into practice what I was learning from neuroscience and behavioral science. I created a tool called the Pre-Shot Training System. It was designed to make it easier for coaches to help their golfers develop better thinking habits and improve their performance under pressure. This method included physical tools—big colored square boxes that could be placed on the floor and used to plan out mental pre-shot routines. This allowed golfers to make their invisible thoughts real. Instead of simply knowing what they should be thinking under pressure, Pre-Shot made it easier for them to practice these thoughts in real time. It allowed them to move from knowing (knowledge), to doing (skill), to habit.

Pre-Shot was not only embedded into the PGA's training, it was also adopted by a range of other sports. Some universities also embedded it into their applied sport psychology and coaching curriculums. It was also adapted to help train people how to perform under pressure and optimize their focus and learning in many other different activities. Many coaches, including those working with world champion and world-class athletes, told me this was the best mental training system they had ever used. It was an essential building block in developing what came next in my career.

PART 5—WHY DON'T WE TEACH EVERYONE SPORT PSYCHOLOGY TECHNIQUES?

"Sport psychology has not only benefited my sporting success, but also my professional and personal life. So why don't we teach these skills to young people?"

I'm paraphrasing words I believe Olympic silver medalist Sir Colin Moynihan said to influence the creation of the Haberdashers' Performance Psychology Fellowship—a new position in education to which I was appointed.

The Haberdashers' Company is one of the Great Twelve Livery Companies of the City of London. It has a long tradition of supporting schools and young people through its education foundation. As part of this work, it funds fellowships to give schools in its network access to specialist support.

The London 2012 Olympic Games were fast approaching, and the next Haberdashers' fellowships were being discussed. Moynihan was the chairman of the British Olympic Association, a former Minister for Sport in the UK government, an Olympic medalist, and a former Haberdashers' school pupil. It is my understanding that he proposed or influenced the idea of deliberately teaching young people sport psychology skills.

The Haberdashers' Performance Psychology Fellowship was created, and I was given the job. I was tasked with embedding performance psychology into school life at the Haberdashers' Monmouth Schools (a family of schools)—one of the top private school groups in the UK.

I was armed with all the neurons I had developed from my teaching, consultancy work, PhD, and broader research, as well as my Pre-Shot kits and a blank piece of paper. It was a fascinating project that received national newspaper attention. I was very fortunate to work with some excellent people (including Dave Vickers and Kate Callaghan), without whom the project would have failed because it was such a groundbreaking piece of work. I will be eternally grateful for their support and for the opportunity to work on such a fantastic project.

For me, the most exciting part of this work was to create a practical, accessible language that conveyed complex science that, when accessible, made people's lives easier. I wanted both young and old (parents, teachers, coaches) to use it and benefit so they could do better. This language (now called Habit Mechanic [see Chapter 3] and Chief Habit Mechanic [see Chapter 27] language) helps people understand how the brain works and how to build better habits, motivate themselves, manage stress, build confidence, focus, optimize learning, perform under pressure, and become better leaders.

This language, and associated techniques, would form the foundations of Tougher Minds, and the essence of what it means to be a Habit Mechanic and Chief Habit Mechanic.

The impact of this work immediately led to other exciting projects, including working with Colfe's (one of London's oldest independent schools, with a longstanding association with the Leathersellers' Company) and many global businesses based in the City of London that were attracted by our cutting-edge and science-based approach to improving performance and leadership. During this period, I began working with our fantastic Head of Education, Andrew Foster (at Colfe's), and I also met our excellent Head of Business, Catherine Grant, who was working as a senior leader in the City of London.

PART 6—WHY DON'T WE TEACH EVERYONE HOW THEIR BRAIN WORKS, AND HOW TO USE BEHAVIORAL SCIENCE TO FULFILL THEIR POTENTIAL?

This was the question I started to ask myself when I saw the profound impact of training based on cutting-edge science, when compared to old-school training methods. It was like the difference in physical performance achieved when using insights from sport science versus traditional but outdated training methods. The latter is more likely to leave you with a hamstring strain than a personal best.

At this point in my career, I found it astonishing that the vast majority of training, self-help, and coaching that people used to try to fulfill their potential was still based on outdated black-box theories. As I write this today, not much has changed. This means that when we seek advice about how to be our best, that advice is typically NOT rooted in science about how our brains work (neuroscience) or the factors that influence our ability to make sustainable changes (behavioral science).

Insights about brain evolution, brain structure, neuroplasticity, and maturation are typically not given serious consideration in the vast majority of approaches on offer. And, in the very few instances where some of these insights are considered, I am not aware of any that are also based on cutting-edge behavioral science.

Beware of people who tell you that "new science" does not have much to tell us about being our best. This is simply not true. Sure, some of the insights confirm what we thought we already knew. But many others allow humans to think about themselves in a completely different way. Here are some of the key concepts this new science has taught us:

Neuroplasticity: Our brains are changing all the time via a process called neuroplasticity. Until quite recently, scientists thought that when you stopped physically growing, your brain stopped changing—meaning your skills and abilities were fixed after that point. This is the view most people still believe is true.

Your brain is a threat detection machine: The overarching organizational principle that motivates human behavior seems to be to minimize threat and maximize reward. Yet the human desire to minimize threats is much stronger than the desire to find rewards. The scale of brain circuitry dedicated to detecting negative emotions means that one negative can require up to 11 positives to neutralize it. The well-worn, established management technique of "give them a positive, then give them a negative, then give them another positive" highlights just how much we have misunderstood our emotions in the past.

What do other people think of me?: Closely connected same neural circuitry processes both social thoughts (not wanting to look bad in front of others) and basic survival thoughts (the need to find food and water). Yes, this means that Maslow's hierarchy of needs got it very wrong, because positive connections with others are part of our most basic needs. Yet many people still use Maslow's hierarchy at the heart of their approach.

We run on habits: Most of our thoughts and actions (behaviors) are mindless, or habits. In fact, modern science shows that at least 98 percent of our behavior is unconscious or semi-unconscious. We run on habits; yet the vast majority of training, self-help, and coaching treats us like our brains are logical, meaning that we will do what we "know" is the right thing. WRONG! We do what we are in the habit of doing.

The list goes on, and I will explain other new powerful findings later in the book.

Does This Mean That Old Training Approaches, Which Do Not Factor in This New Science, Are Ineffective?

YES! Or, at least, they are not nearly as effective as they would be if they factored in the new science. Old training approaches are well intended, but ultimately offer ineffective advice about what we need to do to bring about successful and sustainable change in the challenging VUCA world. For example, an old-school approach might be telling you what you need to do (give you knowledge) to reduce stress. But knowing how to manage stress is very different from building better stress management habits.

PART 7—HELPING PEOPLE BECOME HABIT MECHANICS

Taking all of the above into account, I want to help people actually do better in work and life. That's why I created training to help people become Habit Mechanics and Chief Habit Mechanics.

The Habit Mechanic Manifesto

I am a Habit Mechanic.

I DON'T USE OUTDATED SELF-HELP AND COACHING METHODS that are becoming less and less effective in the challenging modern world.

I use proven insights from cutting-edge neuroscience, behavioral science, and psychology to develop my own resilience and performance habits.

Then I use the same techniques to help those around me thrive and succeed.

I change people's lives by empowering them to be their best.

My fellow **Habit Mechanics** help me to be my best.

I am only **ONE HABIT AWAY**!

What Does "Only One Habit Away" Mean?

It means the next habit you build could be the one that unlocks your potential.

Super Habits

Through my work helping others, and myself, I have identified some "Super Habits." Once you develop these, they can literally transform your life. For example, one of my Super Habits is completing the Daily TEA Plan. Doing this one simple thing, that only takes me two minutes each day, triggers many other positive behaviors that make my life so much easier.

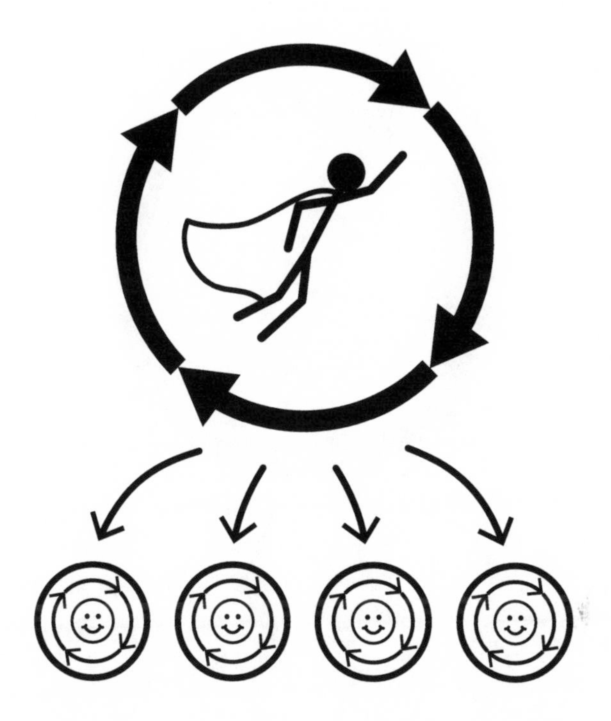

Figure 8.1: It is amazing how one small Super Habit can unlock many other helpful habits.

Here are some other examples of Super Habits I have developed. Writing a positive end-of-day reflection (I will show you some techniques for doing this in Chapter 22) has transformed my ability to manage stress and improved my sleep. Exercise (walking or running) first thing in the morning has transformed my productivity levels throughout the day. Completing a monthly intelligent goal-setting exercise (I will show you how to do this in Chapter 16) has supercharged my motivation.

Destructive Habits

As well as Super Habits, I have also found that some habits are disproportionately damaging for people's health, happiness, and performance. I call these "Destructive Habits" because they unlock lots of unhelpful behaviors.

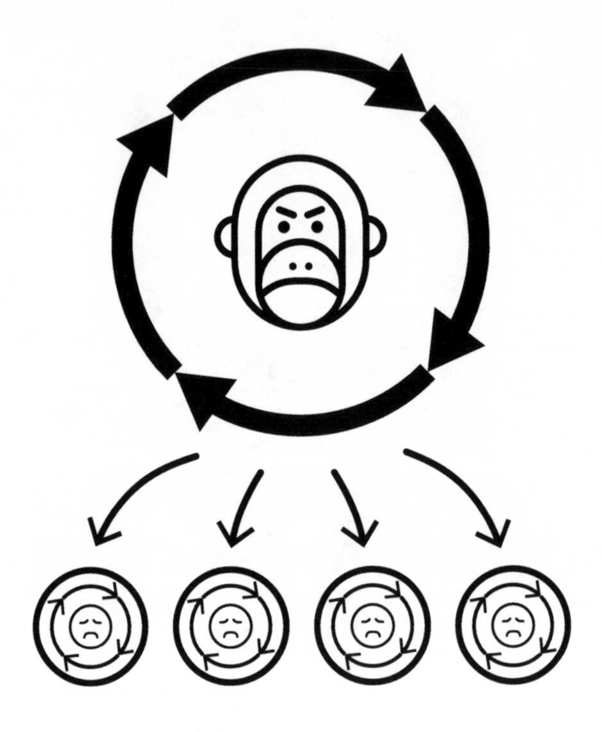

Figure 8.2: One small Destructive Habit can quickly activate lots of other unhelpful habits.

For example, eating late is a Destructive Habit for some people. Because it is late, they are really hungry so they eat too much. Then they can't sleep properly, and poor sleep makes them unfocused and unproductive the following day. This increases their stress levels. On top of all this, they also gain weight. All this unhelpful behavior is unlocked by developing a habit of eating too late.

Here are some other examples of habits people report being destructive:

- Regularly having a glass of wine in the evening (which leads to two, or the entire bottle) to unwind, but this leads to poor quality sleep, which also means feeling sluggish and unproductive at work the following day.
- Having emails/inbox open and a smartphone close by when trying to do focused work, leading to constant distractions, more mistakes, wasted time, increased stress, lower levels of productivity, and poorer quality sleep.
- Not leaving their desk at lunchtime (even for as little as five minutes) because they are too busy, leading to a tired and unfocused mind in the afternoon, which means reduced productivity levels, more mistakes in their work, having to work longer hours, increased levels of stress, unhelpful eating habits, and poorer sleep quality.

Finding your Super and Destructive Habits

The good news is that this book contains the tools to help you discover both your Super Habits and your Destructive Habits. But you will only find them by putting the ideas you read about into practice. This will help you learn more about what is actually holding you back, and what ACTUALLY helps you feel and perform better.

Still Want to Be a Habit Mechanic?

If YES, keep reading and I will show you how ☺!

HABIT MECHANIC LANGUAGE AND TOOLS YOU HAVE LEARNED SO FAR...

Core Language

Me Power Conditioning—This means deliberately working toward being your best. (Chapters 2 and 9) ☑

Focused or deliberate practice—Where you focus hard, make mistakes, and use feedback about your mistakes to get better. (Chapter 5) ☑

10 Intelligence Factors—Once we have the opportunity to learn something, I have concluded that 10 factors (some genetic and some environmental, but all changeable) can supercharge or block our learning. (Chapter 5) ☑

Habit Mechanic intelligence—Your ability to acquire and apply Habit Mechanic knowledge and skills to develop new helpful habits. (Chapter 5) ☑

Super Habits—Habits that trigger other positive behaviors/habits. (Chapter 8) ☑

Destructive Habits—Habits that trigger lots of other unhelpful behaviors/habits. (Chapter 8) ☑

Planning Tools

Daily TEA (Tiny Empowering Action) Plan—A two-minute daily exercise to make your life easier. (Chapter 1) ☑

Daily 3:1 Reflection—A daily positive reflection tool. (Chapter 5) ☑

Step 2

LEARN ABOUT THE SECRET BRAIN SCIENCE THAT WILL UNLOCK YOUR POTENTIAL

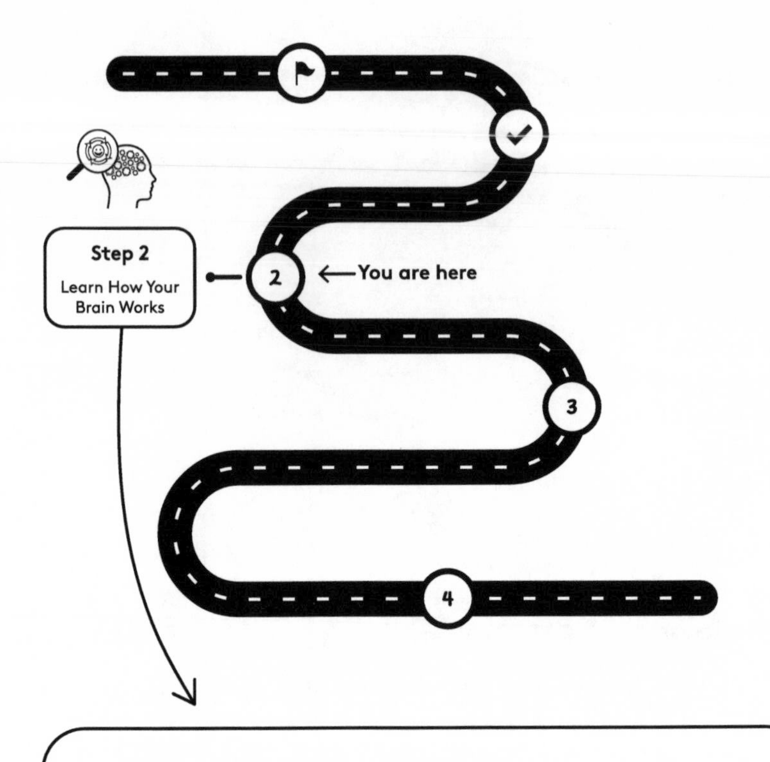

Chapter 9: How Your Brain Works

Chapter 10: The Lighthouse Brain

Chapter 11: What Actually Happens inside My Brain?

Chapter 12: How to Start Me Power Conditioning

Chapter 13: Using Will Power to Self-Watch, HAC and Develop Resilience

Chapter 14: The "Secret" Science of Fulfilling Your Potential: Emotional Regulation

Figure S2.1: An overview of your journey through Step 2.

9

HOW YOUR BRAIN WORKS

HOW CAN I ACTUALLY START DOING BETTER? TRY ME POWER CONDITIONING

Each of us can choose to take responsibility for our wellbeing and performance, and purposefully work toward being at our best.

If we think in terms of a scale, at one end we could *refuse* to try to be at our best. This means that you are passive and let the VUCA world control you and what you learn to become good at. This can result in people getting really good at lots of unhelpful things. I call this end of the scale "VUCA World Conditioning." If you want to lose the Learning War, *refusing* to try to be at your best will guarantee it!

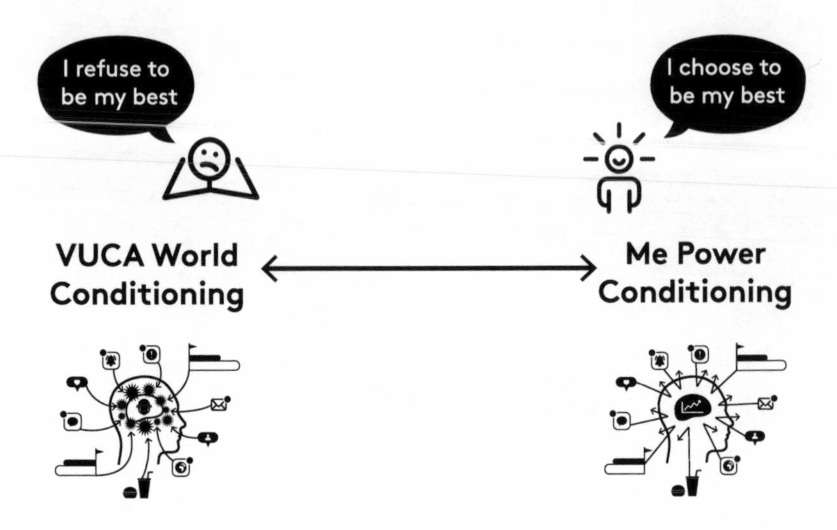

Figure 9.1: The Best Doing continuum.

At the opposite end of the scale, we could purposefully *choose* to work toward being at our best. It turns out that choosing to be at your best gives you a much better chance not only of fulfilling your potential but also of being happy.

I call deliberately choosing to do this "Me Power Conditioning." Learning how to do this is at the heart of becoming a Habit Mechanic.

To help you do more Me Power Conditioning, I want to help you understand more about how you think. We pay attention to things by thinking about them, and this leads to learning. In other words, attention drives learning.

THINKING ABOUT YOUR THINKING

First, let's take a few moments to consider how we think.

Thinking Exercise

Please take a moment now to complete this simple task, which will help you understand more about how you think.

Imagine you are wearing a pair of headphones (place your hands on your ears if that is helpful). Describe them to yourself. Are they large or small (e.g., earbuds or large noise-cancelling headphones)? What color are they? What song is playing?

Now, notice how you are talking to yourself inside your own head. If you don't think you are talking to yourself, notice how you are saying to yourself: "I'm not talking to myself; I'm not crazy."

The aim of this exercise is to highlight that we are always thinking. Recognizing that fact is an important part of the Me Power Conditioning process. Our brain is always on: it's designed to keep paying attention.

However, our attention span is naturally short—and it's becoming shorter because of how we use it in the modern world. We can think of our brains as "frog brains" that jump from one thing to another.

Figure 9.2: The attention economy is shortening our attention span and making it more difficult to focus.

Our brains are designed to pay attention to things that bring us short-term gratification (pleasure). This can stop us achieving long-term objectives that would bring truly great satisfaction and fulfillment (personal growth).

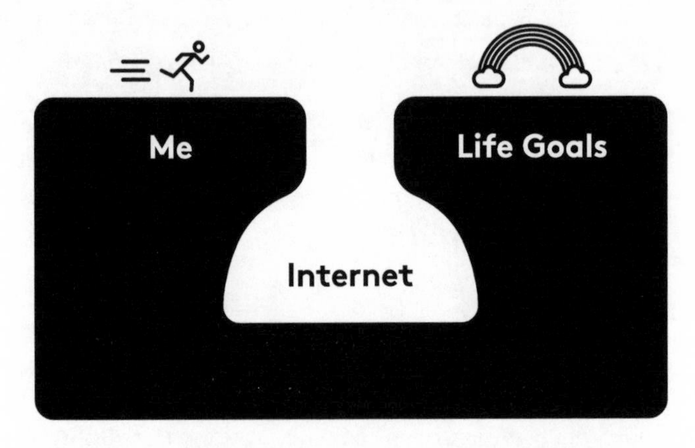

Figure 9.3: Even with the best intentions to get things done, it is easier than ever to get sidetracked.

Remember, the more we think and do unhelpful things, the better we become at them.

These unhelpful behaviors (thoughts and actions) also make us less efficient and effective. For example, it feels easier than ever to spend 10 minutes doing a task that we could do in five minutes because we become easily distracted by our smartphones or emails. It also feels easier than ever to waste time beating ourselves up.

Figure 9.4: It is easy to waste a lot of time each day doing and thinking unhelpful things.

By the end of the day, we find we've lost 30 minutes. And by the end of the week, we are three hours down. We will never get this time back. We will probably have to stay at work later, spend less time with our loved ones, and beat ourselves up even more as a result. We find ourselves trapped in a negative cycle. But it doesn't have to be this way. We can all strike a better balance between work and home life by learning how to do more Me Power Conditioning, so we build more helpful habits.

HOW DO YOU USE YOUR DAY?

All of us have just 24 hours in any single day. We can be doing (and thinking) either things that are helping us achieve our health, happiness, and performance goals, or things that are unhelpful and stopping us from achieving them. Think of it like a barcode (see Figure 9.5): The white lines represent helpful thoughts and actions (e.g., sleeping properly, doing focused work, speaking to yourself in a positive way, practicing your stress management skills). The black lines represent when you are doing and thinking things that are unhelpful for your health, happiness, and performance (e.g., beating yourself up, eating the wrong foods, procrastinating, staying up too late). To be at our best more often, we need to get better at recognizing our unhelpful behaviors and removing one unhelpful black line at a time.

Figure 9.5: I will show you how to identify your black lines and eradicate them one at a time.

"HELPFUL VERSUS UNHELPFUL"—NOT "POSITIVE VERSUS NEGATIVE"

It is important to say that **helpful thinking** is NOT necessarily the same as **positive thinking**, and **unhelpful thinking** is NOT necessarily the same as **negative thinking**. For example, receiving negative feedback about something you are trying to improve can be really helpful (e.g., if delivered in the right way, it will help you improve). Eating a donut every morning for breakfast (which if you like them will be a VERY positive experience) can be really unhelpful (e.g., it might make it more difficult to achieve your weight loss or healthy eating goals).

But why is it so easy to think and do unhelpful things? To understand this, we need to consider how our brains work.

I am going to show you how your brain works using three different but interconnected models. They range from simple to complex.

1. Simple—Lighthouse Brain
2. Intermediate—APE Brain vs. HAC Brain
3. Complex—Emotional Regulation

I created the insights I am about to share to make it as easy as possible to understand how we can all begin to spend more time doing and thinking more helpful things, by building more helpful habits.

10

THE LIGHTHOUSE BRAIN

We might know what we want to do or achieve, but accomplishing it is a different story. To help you understand why, I want to tell you a story about how your brain works. The concepts in this will be the basis for everything else that follows in this book. They will provide a solid foundation so you can understand exactly how you, or you and your team, can fulfill your potential. I've created this story to make complex psychology, neuroscience, and behavioral science easy to understand. I will provide more details about the science later.

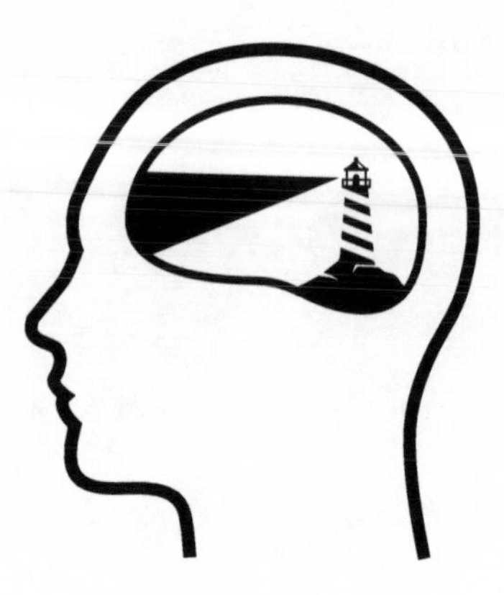

Figure 10.1: The Lighthouse Brain.

First, imagine you have a lighthouse in your brain. Two characters live there. The first is HUE. This stands for Horribly Unhelpful Emotions. The second is Willomenia Power, or Will Power for short. Most importantly, Will Power is HUE's guide and mentor.

HUE

HUE works in the lighthouse's control room. Its first instinct is to search for threats. Imagine HUE using a beam of light emitted from the lighthouse to mindlessly scan your thoughts, your feelings, and the environment around you. It scans for past mistakes or regrets. It projects worst-case scenarios about what might happen in the future. And it searches for any immediate problems.

HUE's second instinct is to find easy, new, and exciting things that make it feel good. HUE loves doing things and having experiences that give it short-term gratification.

Figure 10.2: Meet your Horribly Unhelpful Emotions (HUE).

WILL POWER

There is a training room in the lighthouse. Will Power likes to learn about how to help you fulfill your potential and spends most of its time in there, studying and learning. When HUE notices a problem, or a short-term gratification opportunity, it sometimes calls Will Power for help. When everything in your brain is working properly, Will Power guides HUE to solve the problem or manage unhelpful impulses.

This makes it easier for HUE to deal with similar problems if they occur again.

Figure 10.3: Meet Willomenia Power, or Will Power, HUE's guide and mentor.

The Will Power Mentoring process looks something like this:

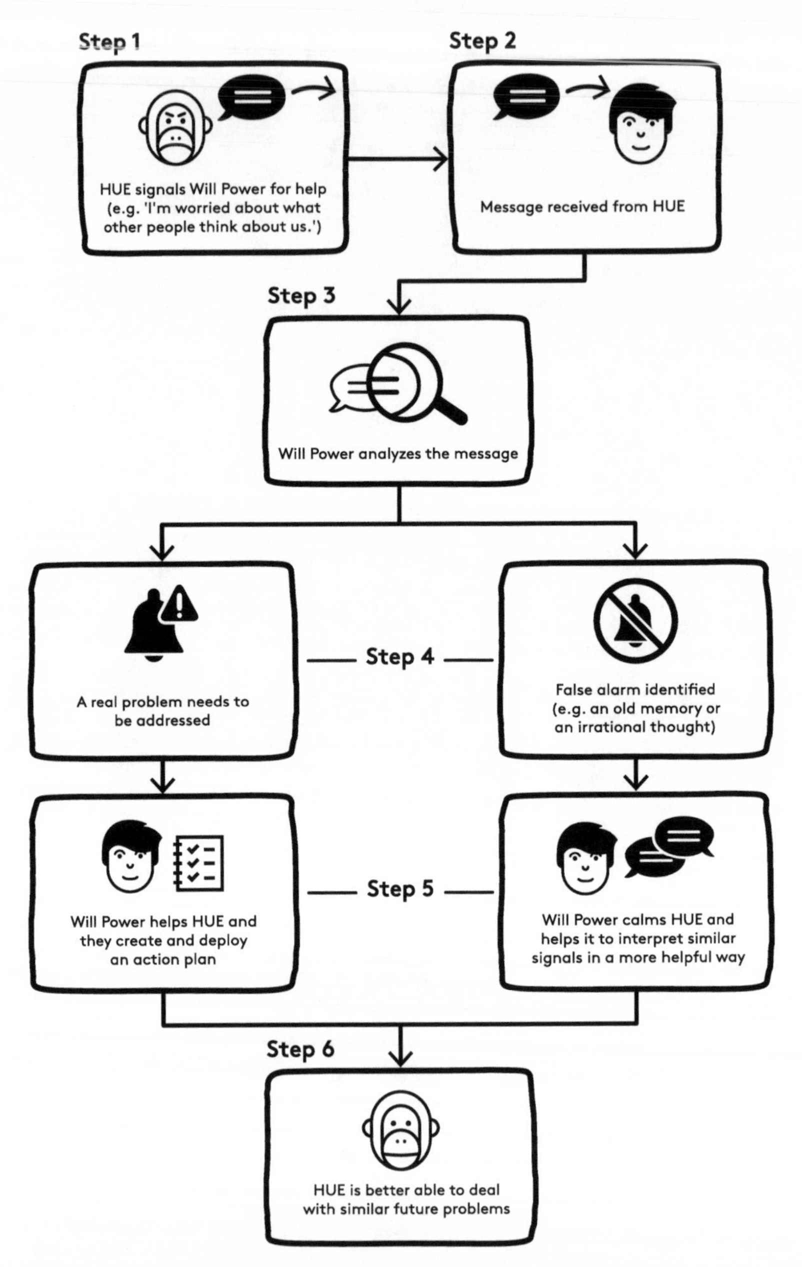

Figure 10.4: A simple overview of how Will Power and HUE can work together successfully.

When Will Power can do its job properly, your HUE will be calmer, and it should be easier for you to:

- build good diet, exercise, and sleep habits;
- successfully manage stress;
- spend less time thinking unhelpful thoughts;
- build and maintain robust levels of confidence;
- be focused, productive, creative, and good at solving problems;
- perform well under pressure;
- be a better leader; and
- be a better team member.

"Calmer HUE, better you."

But, as I have already shown, the modern world presents many new challenges that can overwhelm us.

- We can find it hard to switch off, which can negatively affect sleep, rest, and recovery.
- Social media leads us to compare our lives to others', and we can beat ourselves up too much.
- We are tempted to eat bad food, buy things we don't need, and spend money we don't have.
- We become distracted, so a 10-minute job takes 20 minutes. Over a week, this accumulates into several wasted hours.

These types of challenges result in an unhelpful imbalance between HUE and Will Power. HUE can become overactivated, and Will Power can quickly get overwhelmed and exhausted. This makes it very difficult to be healthy, happy, and at your best.

If you want to win the Learning War, be your best, and help others do the same, your first job is to get HUE and Will Power working together efficiently and effectively, creating more balance between these two powerful assets.

To help you do this, let's dig deeper into the inner workings of your brain.

Test?

If it is helpful, write down what HUE stands for to test your memory!

11

WHAT ACTUALLY HAPPENS INSIDE MY BRAIN?

Obviously, there isn't really a lighthouse in your brain! I created this story to make some very complex processes easy to understand. Let me explain in more detail what is going on.

HUE

HUE operates the limbic regions of the brain. I call these areas the APE (**A**live, **P**erceived, and **E**nergy) Brain. This was partly inspired by neuroscientist Paul MacLean's seminal "triune brain" metaphor, and also the fact that Homo sapiens (humans) are Great Apes. The APE Brain makes us prioritize survival.

Note: I sometimes use the terms "APE Brain" and "HUE" interchangeably.

WILL POWER

Will Power operates the prefrontal cortex, or the HAC (**H**elpful **A**ttention **C**ontrol) Brain (pronounced *hack* brain). We can use the HAC Brain to manage the APE Brain and build better habits.

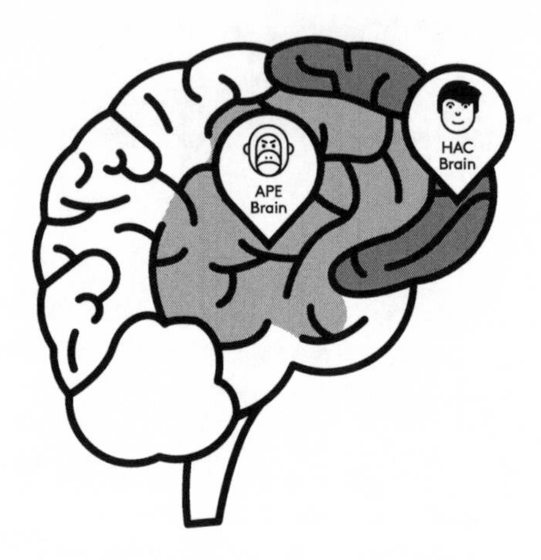

Figure 11.1: A cartoon drawing of the human brain to show the broad regions where the APE and HAC Brains are located in my model.

YOUR APE BRAIN PRIORITIZES SAVING ENERGY, MAKING CHANGE DIFFICULT

To understand more about the APE Brain, please read aloud the following passage.

> To make sense of words it deosn't mttaer in what order the ltteers in a wrod are, the olny ipmoratnt tihng is taht the frist and lsat ltteer are in the rghit pclae.

Even though the letters are mixed up, you can still understand the meaning. This is because most of our thoughts and actions (behaviors) are mindless. We mainly guess and predict. In fact, science shows that at least 98 percent of our behavior is unconscious or semi-unconscious, meaning it is habit.

You have the equivalent of over one trillion microscopic biological moving parts in your brain that mindlessly drive most of what you do and think.

So you did not need to read the passage consciously, taking the time to process each individual letter in each word. Your brain reads each word as a picture, meaning that even if some of the letters are not in the correct place, the picture still makes sense.

Because habits make thinking and doing things more energy efficient, we have evolved to run on them. This means we do not think about most of the things we do.

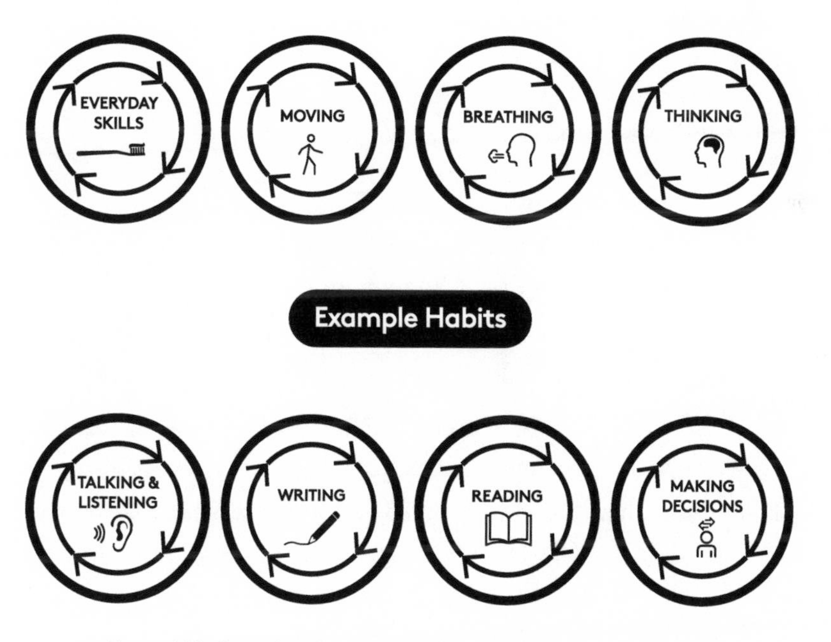

Figure 11.2: Examples of everyday things you do that are mainly habit.

Our habits dominate what we do and how we think. Our experience of the world is what we are in the habit of paying attention to. For example, if we only pay attention to our failures in life and the setbacks we've experienced, that becomes our reality. Equally, if we only pay attention to how fantastic we think we are, and how nothing is ever our fault, that becomes our reality.

Our family, friends, colleagues, teams, and organizations all run on habits. The most dominant habits are those they practice most, because of the process I explained earlier known as neuroplasticity.

Some of our habits are helpful for us being at our best, and some are unhelpful.

We Are Not Designed to Be Healthy, Happy, and at Our Best

Homo sapiens have been around for about 300,000 years. Our primal instincts, driven by our APE Brain, mean we are not designed to be happy and at our best in the context of our 21st century lives.

Alive

Instead, we are designed to survive. To stay **Alive**, we prioritize all the things that are essential for doing that. Although for most people things like food, shelter, and warmth are a given in the modern world, notice how quickly the supermarket shelves emptied during the COVID-19 pandemic.

We are also instinctively concerned about our physical safety. Notice your reaction to a loud bang or a stranger getting too close to you, or your heightened sensitivity to shadows in the dark after watching a horror movie.

Perceived

Closely connected to staying alive is our concern about how we are **P**erceived by other people who are important in our lives—think social status, peer pressure, and how social media is used. Communication, cooperation, and alliances with other humans support our survival. Humans are not the biggest or strongest animal on the planet, but they are the best at working intelligently in teams. Teamwork has been the foundation of human survival and success (i.e., historically, if you got kicked out of the team or the tribe, your survival chances were significantly reduced, as were your chances of passing on your genes). Our success in life can be closely connected to how we are viewed by people who are important in our lives. So, we often worry too much about what others think.

Energy

Finally, as food—our main source of energy—has not always been readily available (i.e., we used to be hunters and gatherers, and not supermarket shoppers), we make every effort to conserve **E**nergy. This is why we sometimes prefer to sit and watch TV instead of exercising, and we avoid work that is mentally challenging. Thinking hard burns a lot of energy! For example, it will take less mental energy to perform a well-practiced task than it will to learn a new skill or perform a difficult task.

We can even see this in our food preferences. Your brain knows that it is more energy efficient to eat a donut than an apple. It takes just as much energy to eat both, but there are more calories in the donut.

Survival Habits

The collective APE result is what I call "survival habits." Here are some examples:

- Worrying too much
- Being unfairly self-critical or beating yourself up
- Giving in to temptation
- Easily getting distracted
- Procrastinating
- Giving up easily
- Jumping to conclusions
- Easily becoming stressed

These habits operate like any other: the more you practice, the better you get. For example, if you want to get better at worrying, all you have to do is practice worrying a lot and you will become a world champion worrier. This is because the more you practice it, the more you grow and strengthen the neurons in your brain that are connected to worrying.

In the Learning War, these types of habits are becoming increasingly problematic because of the challenges we face in the VUCA world. These unhelpful habits mean we can beat ourselves up too much or procrastinate on things that we really do need to get done.

In fact, these habits are often the biggest waste of personal resources in any 24-hour period.

And if they are the biggest waste of resources for an individual, they are also the biggest waste of resources for a team, business, or family unit.

Think back to the black and white barcode (Chapter 9, Figure 9.5). The white lines represent helpful habits and the black lines represent unhelpful habits (the barriers to your happiness and success).

Habits underpin everything we do:

- How we think and feel
- What we eat
- How much we exercise
- How well we sleep
- How we manage stress
- Our confidence levels
- How productive we are
- Our creativity and problem-solving abilities
- Our performance under pressure
- Our performance as a leader
- Our performance as a team member
- Our performance as a parent

If we want to be at our best more often, individually and collectively, we need to learn how to build more new helpful habits.

The first step to building new habits is called "intelligent Self-Watching." The Daily TEA Plan (Chapter 1) and the Daily 3:1 Reflection (Chapter 5) both require you to do intelligent Self-Watching. Let's do some more now.

Test?

If it is helpful, write down what APE and HAC stand for to test your memory!

12

HOW TO START ME POWER CONDITIONING

To start identifying some of your unhelpful habits, I want you to do some intelligent Self-Watching. This simply means thinking about yourself in a focused and systematic way, so that you can precisely identify your unhelpful behavior. This can be difficult to do because you are designed to run on habits.

Figure 12.1: Self-Watching is like switching on a CCTV camera that monitors your thoughts and actions.

To help you do this, I have created a short "APE Brain Test."

There are no right or wrong answers. This is just about what you think about yourself right now. The more you practice Self-Watching exercises like the APE Brain Test, the better you will become at understanding yourself. I complete this type of test about once a month to help me stay on top of my APE Brain. The more I practice intelligent Self-Watching, the better I get.

You could complete the test either from your own point of view, or on behalf of a person you want to help. Score each statement from 1 to 10, where 1 equals never and 10 equals always.

Note: It doesn't matter what your scores are. The important thing is that you are thinking about yourself and identifying your strengths and areas for improvement. Don't overthink your scores; just go with your gut instinct. The more you practice intelligent Self-Watching, the better you will get at it.

1. I reflect on my diet, exercise, and sleep, and plan to make daily improvements in these areas. *Score:* ______
2. At the end of the day, I always reflect and highlight what went well, and what I can improve tomorrow. *Score:* ______
3. At the end of every week, I reflect on what went well, and plan how I can improve next week. *Score:* ______
4. From time to time, I think about my future. I set long-, medium-, and short-term goals to focus my efforts and achieve major objectives. *Score:* ______
5. I regularly update my yearly and monthly calendar to add important work and life activities. *Score:* ______
6. I recognize when I'm stressed and successfully plan to reduce my stress. *Score:* ______
7. I monitor my confidence levels and successfully build up confidence in areas where it is low. *Score:* ______

8. I recognize when my emotions are unhelpful and can successfully keep them under control. *Score:* _____
9. I successfully plan to improve my productivity levels. *Score:* _____
10. I successfully plan to spend less time dwelling on unhelpful thoughts. *Score:* _____
11. I successfully plan to improve my performance as a leader. *Score:* _____

What next?

1. Circle the area you think it will be most helpful to make a small adjustment to today to help you be your best.
2. Write down one small thing you will do differently to improve this area.

   (Tip: Writing "Be less stressed" is too vague to be helpful. Instead, be more specific—e.g., "Write a 3:1 Daily Reflection at the end of the working day.")

   ____

   ____

   ____

3. Explain why (e.g., "It will make it easier to de-stress, switch off, sleep well, and be at my best tomorrow").

   ____

   ____

   ____

Don't worry if you are not sure how to improve the area you have selected, because I am going to cover all of the core APE Brain Test themes throughout the remainder of the book.

Although this book has been written to be read sequentially, you can jump ahead to get some improvement ideas—if you promise to come back to this point in the book and continue reading ☺. I have listed where you can learn more about each core APE Brain Test area below:

- I want to improve my sleep and/or diet and/or exercise. (Chapter 19)
- I want to improve my long-, medium-, and short-term goal setting. (Chapter 16)
- I want to get better at managing stress and thinking more helpfully. (Chapter 22)
- I want to improve my confidence. (Chapter 23)
- I want to get better at performing under pressure. (Chapter 24)
- I want to improve my focus and productivity. (Chapter 25)
- I want to improve my leadership. (Step 4—Chief Habit Mechanic skills)

If you do jump ahead, remember that the key to Habit Mechanic success is learning how to build sustainable new habits. Knowing what you need to do is very different from doing it. For the remainder of this section of the book (Step 2) and the beginning of the next (Step 3), I am going to really get under the hood (or bonnet) of what it takes to develop more new sustainable helpful habits.

But first, I want to finish this chapter by introducing a concept called the "Me Power Wish List."

By taking the APE Brain Test, you will have identified the most significant challenge(s) or problem(s) your APE Brain poses in your life right now. (If you complete it again next month, the scores might be different because your life circumstances and habits might be a little bit different.)

You may now want to begin creating your Me Power Wish List. This is a list of all the small new helpful habits you would like to build and changes you would like to make based on your APE Brain Test results.

YOUR ME POWER WISH LIST

Create your list where it is most helpful for you, for example, a notebook, Word file, phone note.

Please remember it's only realistically possible to **make one tiny change/ build one tiny new habit at a time**. This is a wish list for a reason: nobody has the resources to make all the changes they want at once.

I have a list of daily, weekly, and monthly habits I developed over many years that started on my Me Power Wish List and are now cables in my brain. Remember: knowing (knowledge), to doing (skill), to habit.

EXAMPLE ME POWER WISH LIST

Daily

- 6.30 a.m. run (if this sounds too difficult, you could go for a five-minute walk instead)
- Core—40 push-ups and 40 sit-ups (if this sounds too difficult, you could start with one push-up)
- Stretch
- Post my Daily TEA Plan in my Habit Mechanic app
- Will Power Boosters (e.g., one fewer check of my phone, apps off my phone, phone off, no TV news during the week, no emails at night) (learn more in Chapter 25)
- Drink two liters of water per day
- Aim for approximately eight miles of running/walking per day
- End-of-day positive reflection/Expressive Writing (learn more in Chapter 22)
- Complete my "Me Power Weekly Wall Chart" goals for the day (learn more in Chapter 18)

Weekly

- Structured weekly reflection (learn more in Chapter 36)
- Plan week ahead using Brain States method (learn more in Chapter 25)
- Create my Me Power Weekly Wall Chart (learn more in Chapter 18)

Monthly

- Habit review (learn more in Chapter 17)
- "Future Ambitious Meaningful Story" review (learn more in Chapter 16)
- "Team Power Leadership" review (learn more in Step 4)

Next, let's think about what happened in your brain as you were completing the APE Brain Test.

13

USING WILL POWER TO SELF-WATCH, HAC, AND DEVELOP RESILIENCE

In my model, the prefrontal cortex is the HAC (Helpful Attention Control) Brain. We can use it to manage the APE (Alive Perceived Energy) Brain. We imagine the HAC Brain is operated by Will Power.

Will Power is our first line of defense against the APE Brain because it allows us to resist temptations (e.g., eating too much junk food) and distractions (e.g., checking our social media).

WHAT IS RESILIENCE?

Using your Will Power to HAC (pronounced "hack") your brain is a two-step process:

Step 1. Regular Self-Watching to help you recognize when you are doing and thinking things that are unhelpful and that make it more difficult for you to be at your best (e.g., recognizing that you are beating yourself up too much).

Step 2. Refocusing your attention* onto things that are more helpful and make it easier for you to be at your best (e.g., focusing on thoughts that make you feel more positive about yourself).

**I find the most powerful way to refocus my attention is to write down my thoughts, that is, create a written reflection or plan (I will say more about this in Chapter 22).*

The outcome of this two-step process is **resilience**. So being resilient is an outcome you can achieve in this way. And this is exactly what you did when you completed the APE Brain Test in the last chapter. You highlighted your unhelpful behavior (i.e., by answering the test questions), and then you focused your attention onto doing something that was more helpful for you (e.g., completing a Daily 3:1 Reflection at the end of each day to help you de-stress).

Like anything else, resilience is something we can all learn to improve. We just need to practice it properly.

Resilience makes it easier to

- build better habits;
- be healthier;
- be happier;
- persist;
- manage stress effectively;
- increase your confidence;
- focus your attention;
- be more efficient and effective;
- be a better problem solver;
- be more creative;
- perform better under pressure; and
- be an outstanding leader.

When you HAC your brain to activate your resilience, you are actually managing your emotions. The centrality of emotions during this process is evident when we look at the different terms different scientists use to describe what I call HACing (pronounced "hacking").

- Social scientists call this emotional self-control.
- Neuroscientists call this emotional regulation.

Whichever term you use to describe the process, the outcome is the same: it helps people manage their emotions so they can be more resilient.

RESILIENCE IS LIKE YOUR SWISS ARMY KNIFE FOR LIFE SUCCESS

Many preeminent scientists have studied this process since the 1960s and large sets of compelling research data have been collected about its importance.

Professor Roy Baumeister is one of the world's most respected and prolific social psychologists. His work has been cited by other academics over 200,000 times, he has over 650 publications, and he has written 40 books.

He lists the outcomes you are far more likely to experience if you are good at managing your emotions:

- Succeeding in education
- Experiencing better mental and physical health
- Feeling happier
- Achieving enhanced creativity
- Being more popular with others
- Enjoying stronger marriages and relationships
- Being more trusted
- Having fewer drinking problems and addictions

- Being less likely to commit crime
- Being less abusive
- Living longer
- Enjoying success in life

In short, if we can HAC our brain (manage our emotions) effectively, we become more resilient. This makes it easier to do important things really well. Remember, the first step of the HACing process is recognizing helpful and unhelpful behavior. We use Will Power to Self-Watch our thoughts and actions. Then, if we notice we are doing unhelpful things, we can also use our Will Power to deliberately begin switching our attention to more helpful things.

It is also important to say that Will Power is a limited resource, and this is why we need to use insights from behavioral science to build robust new habits. We will talk about habits, and how to develop more long-lasting helpful ones, in much greater detail a little bit later.

Right now, let's take a deep dive into our emotions and learn more about the role Will Power plays in emotional regulation.

14

THE "SECRET" SCIENCE OF FULFILLING YOUR POTENTIAL: EMOTIONAL REGULATION

WARNING! This short chapter is science heavy, but I will guide you through it and try to make it as easy as possible to understand. One of the big differences with Tougher Minds and the journey to becoming a Habit Mechanic is that cutting-edge science is the foundation of our work. If you understand the scientific underpinnings of the habit building techniques you learn in this book, they will be more powerful in helping you and those around you make lasting beneficial changes.

Here we go...

The scientific name I prefer to use to describe "HACing" (pronounced "hacking") is *emotional regulation.*

Effective emotional regulation underpins all aspects of wellbeing and high performance. Getting good at it is central to becoming a Habit Mechanic. Professor Barbara Fredrickson's work persuaded me that emotions are immediate biological signals that command us to act. This means emotions drive attention, and attention drives learning.

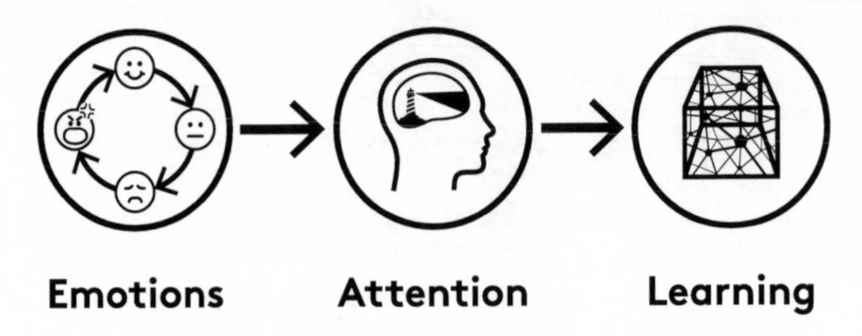

Figure 14.1: Emotions demand your attention and therefore drive what you learn/get good at (for better or for worse).

Emotional regulation is the engine that drives your abilities to learn. If you want to win the Learning War, the first thing you need to focus your learning superpower on is improving emotional regulation.

Both helpful and unhelpful emotional regulation brain regions (see Figure 14.2) can be strengthened with practice. So, we can all learn how to get worse at regulating our emotions. The good news is you have already begun improving your emotional regulation skills and habits by using Habit Mechanic Tools (e.g., Daily TEA Plan, Daily 3:1 Reflection, APE Brain Test, etc.).

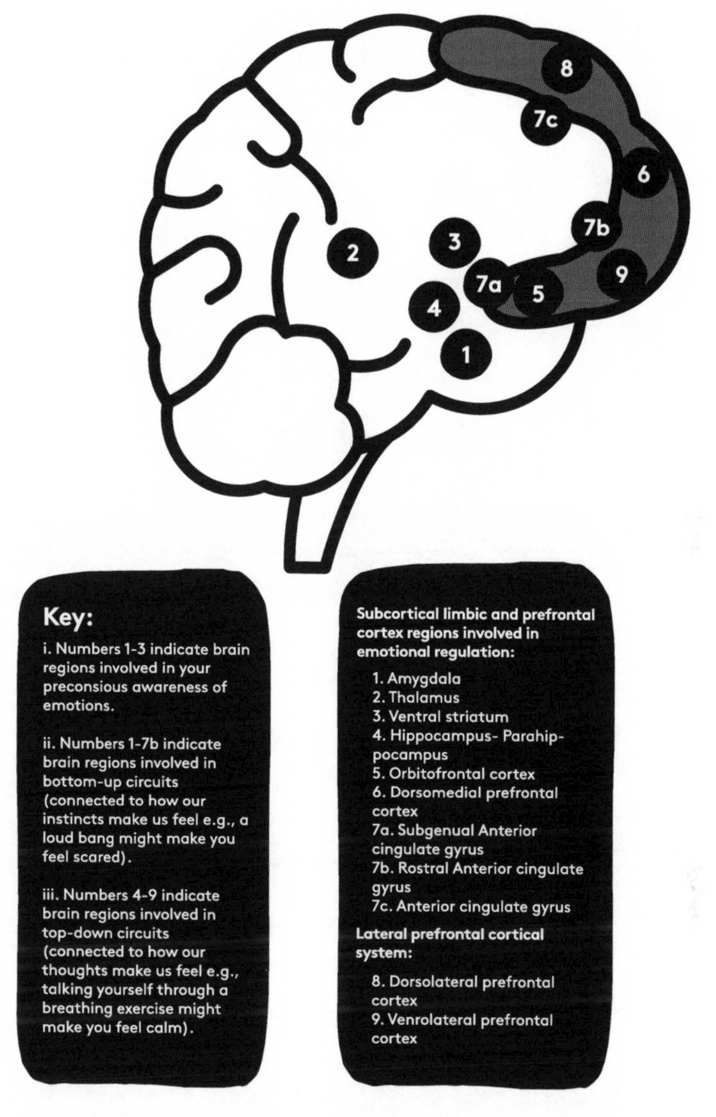

Figure 14.2: A cartoon of a neural map of emotional regulation systems (adapted from Phillips, Ladouceur, and Drevets 2008[4]). To learn how these brain circuits change with focused practice, check out Professor Richard Davidson's research and Dr. John Arden's work (I have studied with Dr. Arden).

[4] M. L. Phillips, C. D. Ladouceur, and W. C. Drevets, "A neural model of voluntary and automatic emotion regulation: implications for understanding the pathophysiology and neurodevelopment of bipolar disorder," *Molecular Psychiatry* 13, no. 9 (September 2008): 833–57.

FAST AND SLOW EMOTIONAL REGULATION

Insights about the specific neural circuitry involved in emotional regulation have revealed that emotional regulation operates on a continuum.

Conscious, effortful, and controlled regulation is at one end of this. This is called **explicit emotional regulation** (or slow).

On the other end of the continuum is unconscious, and possibly effortless, regulation. This is called **implicit emotional regulation** (or fast).

Both fast (or implicit) and slow (or explicit) systems work together to regulate emotions.

Most importantly, this means we can automate some elements of emotional regulation. Or, in other words, turn it into helpful habits.

Don't worry if this still feels intangible, because understanding the specifics of the science is not essential for learning how to get good at managing your emotions and becoming a Habit Mechanic.

We'll now consider emotional regulation in more practical terms.

PROACTIVELY MANAGE YOUR EMOTIONS

Emotions arise from a combination of your thoughts and feelings. The first step to managing your emotions is being more aware of them. We know HUE's (Horribly Unhelpful Emotions) first instinct is to use the lighthouse searchlight to seek out and dwell on threats and problems. But we are not always fully aware when and why this is happening, so negative emotional states can last for longer than necessary.

To deal with this more effectively, we can use Will Power to help us Self-Watch. For example, at the end of every day, we might take a few moments to think about our thoughts and feelings (emotions) and whether they are helping us be our best. If they are not, we can take action. Successfully regulating your emotions might take some time, but if you are proactive, you will do it faster and waste less time dwelling on unhelpful thoughts.

YOU CAN TAKE MORE RESPONSIBILITY FOR MANAGING YOUR EMOTIONS

Kristina Vogel is a former record-breaking German cyclist. She won two gold medals and a bronze at the Olympic Games, and 11 world titles. She was a genuine global sports star and champion.

Unfortunately, at age 27, she suffered serious spinal and chest injuries in a training accident at her home velodrome in Cottbus, Germany. The incident in June 2018 left her paralyzed; Kristina will never walk again. In the aftermath of the accident, she explained her feelings in an article on the BBC Sport website.

"I realized quickly I would not walk again," she said.

"Tears will not help. It is what it is. I am ready to take on this challenge and make the best of it."

In a news conference at the Berlin hospital where she was treated, Vogel described to the BBC the moments following the crash.

"I said 'breathe, breathe, breathe' and then I checked," she said. "Then I saw where I lay, how I was. When my shoes were off, I knew that this was it with the walking.

"Asking 'why me?' does not bring you any further. I want to get back into life, not depend on a lot of help. I must use this strength I had in competitions for my life."

In 2019, Kristina Vogel gave a follow-up interview to the BBC. This was done by British cycling great Sir Chris Hoy.

In a supporting article on the BBC Sport website, Hoy wrote about Vogel's take on her situation. He explained how the German told him: "This is the toughest challenge ever, but what do you do? Lie in bed and do nothing each day? Or take it on and achieve what you can?" Kristina also said: "I am still happy to be here, and my situation could have been worse than it is... it could be that I have no movement in my arms."

Sir Chris also outlined how Kristina "talked about having new goals and new things you can look forward to in life. She talked about how lucky she felt to have support from all around the world to help get an adapted car, a new wheelchair and a new house that is going to be a bungalow with wider door frames and better access."

This is what we might call a world champion example of somebody taking responsibility for what they can control and regulating their emotions. In other words, doing their best to be their best.

Vogel successfully reappraised the meaning of her life-changing accident. She began to think about how things could have been worse and looked for benefits. She asked how she could adapt her personal goals. And she identified what sporting opportunities she still had.

Just like Kristina, you can also learn to think about your life circumstances in a much more helpful way.

HOW TO START REGULATING YOUR EMOTIONS

There is another useful way of understanding your emotions. Psychologists use a tool known as the *Positive and Negative Affect Schedule (PANAS)* to help people monitor and measure their emotions and mood in a given situation. The PANAS emotions are shown in Figure 14.3.

I will use the PANAS emotions to explain an example emotional journey after a stressful experience, and show how we can take more control over our emotions than we imagine.

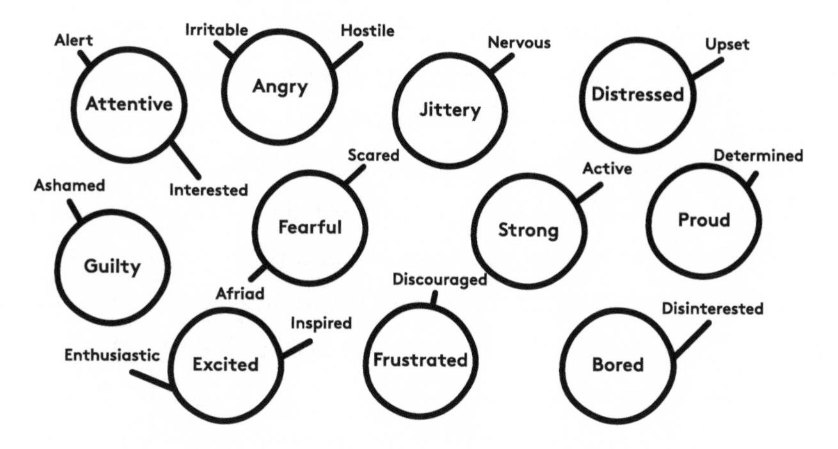

Figure 14.3. The PANAS emotions organized as main emotions and subcategory emotions—as detailed on the PANAS questionnaire.

AN EXAMPLE OF SUCCESSFUL EMOTIONAL REGULATION

Imagine going into a pay review meeting at work. You are very confident. You've been telling your friends and family you'll receive an increase. But in the meeting, you are told otherwise. There is a major disconnect between what you expected and what actually happened. HUE's natural response is to make you ***angry***.

Then you might start to feel ***guilty*** for letting people down (no new house for your family—you were planning to move to a better school district). Then you get ***fearful***. Will your family think you've let them down?

The above response is natural. If you think back to the Lighthouse Brain model, you will remember that HUE's first instinct is to dwell on threats and problems.

However, you can intervene.

Step 1. You can use your Will Power. First, you can use it to notice these unhelpful thoughts and feelings. This will shift your emotional focus from fear to being more ***attentive*** to the fact that you are dwelling on the negatives. By doing this, you are stepping back and using perspective, which makes refocusing and reframing your thoughts easier.

Step 2. Then you can use your Will Power to look for beneficial aspects in what has happened. For example, you now know what to do to get a pay raise next year. Or you can see that a different workplace is more suitable for you. You start to feel ***excited*** about the future. You realize you can make your family ***proud*** again after this setback. You start to feel much ***stronger***.

This may happen over days or weeks. The key is to proactively manage your thoughts and deliberately pay attention to more helpful ones (I will show you how in Chapters 22 and 23). Doing this will help you manage your emotions and thinking and take more control over your life. This is the essence of successful emotional regulation and central to becoming a Habit Mechanic.

When we encounter a stressful situation, we cannot avoid feeling stressed. But Habit Mechanics recognize that they do have some level of control over their emotional states, and they definitely have more control over them than anybody else. Me Power Conditioning (deliberately working toward being our best) empowers us to do our best to be our best. Habit Mechanics take responsibility for doing this.

Proactively shifting your attention from unhelpful to helpful thoughts will save you time. Instead of spending weeks dwelling, you could deal with negative emotions in a day... an hour... or even minutes. This makes it much easier to achieve your health, happiness, and performance goals.

If it is helpful, take a moment to make a few notes about, or think about, how good you are at noticing and managing your unhelpful emotions.

If you manage people, take a moment to make a few notes about, or think about, how good they are at noticing and managing their unhelpful emotions.

HOW WILL IMPROVING MY EMOTIONAL REGULATION MAKE ME HAPPIER?

What is happiness?

My understanding of what it means to be happy is drawn from two broad schools of thought.

One is called the **hedonic approach**. This focuses on achieving a state of happiness—via experiencing positive emotions—by pursuing pleasure (doing things that make you feel good in the short-term) and avoiding pain, boredom, and stress.

The other is called the **eudemonic approach**. This focuses on delaying short-term gratification in pursuit of bigger, more meaningful goals. This sometimes means experiencing negative but helpful emotions, for example, pain, boredom, and stress. This could mean, for example, resisting the desire to check your phone so you can focus on writing your book; defying HUE's desire to watch the next episode of your favorite TV show so you can get to bed on time; and making yourself do your daily, weekly, and monthly planning and reflection exercises even though it is not always that enjoyable and there are other things your HUE would prefer to do.

For simplicity, we will refer to the hedonic approach as **pleasure**, and to the eudemonic approach as **Habit Mechanic development**.

To achieve happiness, first we need our brain to be working well. Therefore, we need good sleep, diet, and exercise habits (we will cover this in Chapter 19), and to have positive personal relationships (think of the "P"/ Perceived in APE).

Then we need to strike a balance of both pleasure and Habit Mechanic development.

Why Is Striking This Balance Difficult?

HUE can have a profoundly negative impact on how engaged, fulfilled, and satisfied you feel with life. The problem is that the activities we engage in to pursue pleasure (the hedonic part of the happiness equation) can be very rewarding for HUE, meaning that we can become addicted to them, and they become unhelpful habits. By addiction I mean that we continue to engage in behaviors even though they are having negative consequences on our health, happiness, and being our best. For example, you know that checking your phone as regularly as you do is not good for you, but you can't stop yourself.

The trouble is that the states of pleasure we derive from these experiences disappear quickly, and our happiness returns to levels it was at prior to the experience, or worse still even lower.

So, wanting to feel good (pleasure) all the time is leading to lots of people feeling happy for short periods but deeply unsatisfied for most of the time.

Also, wanting to feel good (pleasure) all the time is not always compatible with great sleep, diet, and exercise habits, and great relationships with other people.

What Will Make You Happier?

To sustain feelings of happiness, we must also challenge ourselves to grow by becoming Habit Mechanics. This means that we will experience the highs and lows of pushing ourselves to our limits. We will expose our weaknesses but also discover our strengths. People who engage in this type of purposeful development experience flourishing and higher levels of wellbeing.

The challenge is that HUE is incentivized to do things that help you stay alive, focus on what important people think about you, and conserve energy. So pushing and challenging ourselves to grow can be difficult because not all of the work you will do to become a Habit Mechanic will give you immediate gratification. You will have to expose your weaknesses and fail from time to time. None of these ideas are appealing to HUE, so it resists.

Is Being Unhappy Addictive?

HUE can become addicted to pursuing pleasure (hedonic states). And it can compel you to avoid Habit Mechanic development activities (eudemonia). This is because challenging yourself to do better can expose your weaknesses. So HUE talks you out of engaging in challenging developmental processes, or talks you into giving up, and then beats you up for failing or not trying at all. So pursuing happiness is one thing, but achieving a good balance of pleasure and Habit Mechanic development is another.

I believe the best way to strike a pleasure/Habit Mechanic development balance is by developing our emotional regulation skills and habits (in other words, becoming a Habit Mechanic). This makes managing HUE and becoming truly happy much easier.

HOW CAN I IMPROVE MY EMOTIONAL REGULATION SKILLS?

For the remainder of the book, I am going to show you how to strengthen your abilities to regulate your emotions. I will do this by showing you how to analyze your habits and build more helpful ones for improved

- work-life balance;
- Habit Mechanic intelligence;

- motivation;
- stress management;
- sleep, diet, and exercise;
- confidence;
- performance under pressure;
- focus and productivity; and
- leadership.

Do You Want to Practice Regulating Your Emotions Right Now?

Use the Daily TEA Plan or the Daily 3:1 Reflection I introduced earlier.

To learn more simple and practical emotional regulation tools, keep reading. I call these Habit Mechanic Tools.

I think of Habit Mechanic Tools like bicycle stabilizers. They are designed to help you learn how to become a Habit Mechanic. The more skilled you become, and the more helpful habits you develop, the less reliant you will be on your Habit Mechanic Tools. But the tools will always be there to fall back on when you notice your habits slipping and during the more challenging periods of your life.

Congratulations! You have now completed Step 2!

Before you move on to Step 3, please take a moment to notice (in the Habit Mechanic language and tools list) everything you have learned so far. You are doing great!

HABIT MECHANIC LANGUAGE AND TOOLS COVERED IN STEP 2...

Core Language

Lighthouse Brain—A simple model to help you understand the gist of how your brain works so you can begin to improve your thinking. (Chapter 10) ☑

HUE (Horribly Unhelpful Emotions)—An imaginary character who lives in your brain who can make you worry and make it difficult for you to be your best. (Chapter 10) ☑

Willomenia Power or Will Power—An imaginary character who lives in your brain who can help you manage HUE. (Chapter 10) ☑

APE (Alive Perceived Energy) Brain—An easy acronym to help you understand your survival brain/limbic regions of the brain. (Chapter 11) ☑

HAC (Helpful Attention Control) Brain—An easy acronym to help you understand your prefrontal cortex. (Chapter 11) ☑

Self-Watching—Reflecting and thinking about yourself in a focused and systematic way. (Chapter 12) ☑

Me Power Wish List—A list of all the small new helpful habits you would like to build. (Chapter 12) ☑

Hedonism (pleasure)—This focuses on seeking short-term gratification and immediate rewards. (Chapter 14) ☑

Eudemonia (Habit Mechanic development)—This focuses on delaying short-term gratification, and sometimes enduring pain, boredom, and stress in order to develop yourself, grow, and achieve big meaningful goals. (Chapter 14) ☑

Self-Reflection Tools

APE Brain Test—A quick Self-Watching exercise to help you reflect on your helpful and unhelpful habits. (Chapter 12) ☑

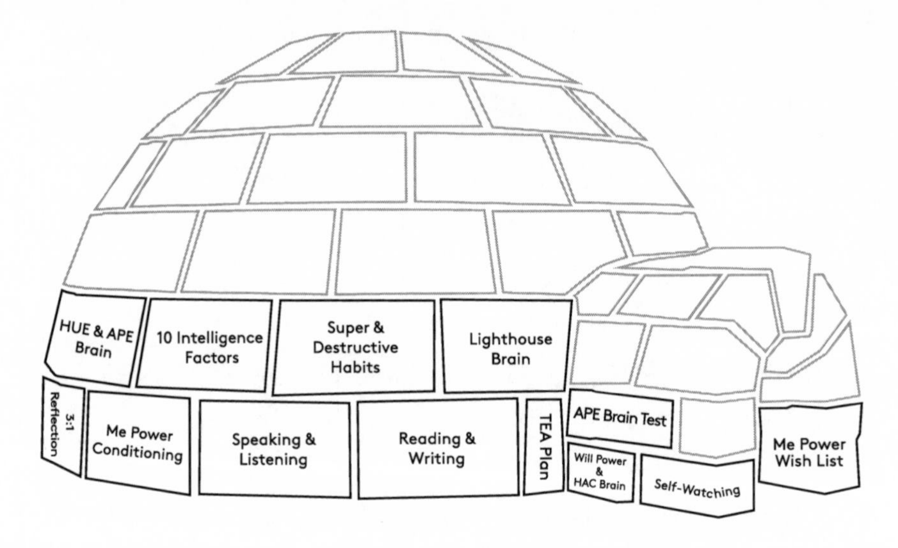

Figure 14.4: Your Habit Mechanic intelligence igloo is building up!

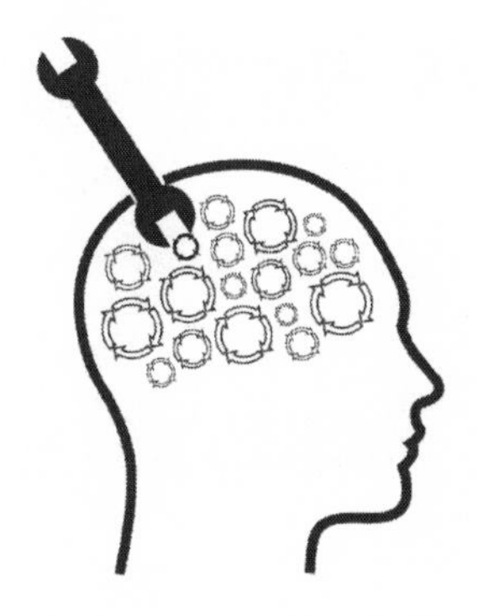

Step 3

HABIT MECHANIC SKILLS

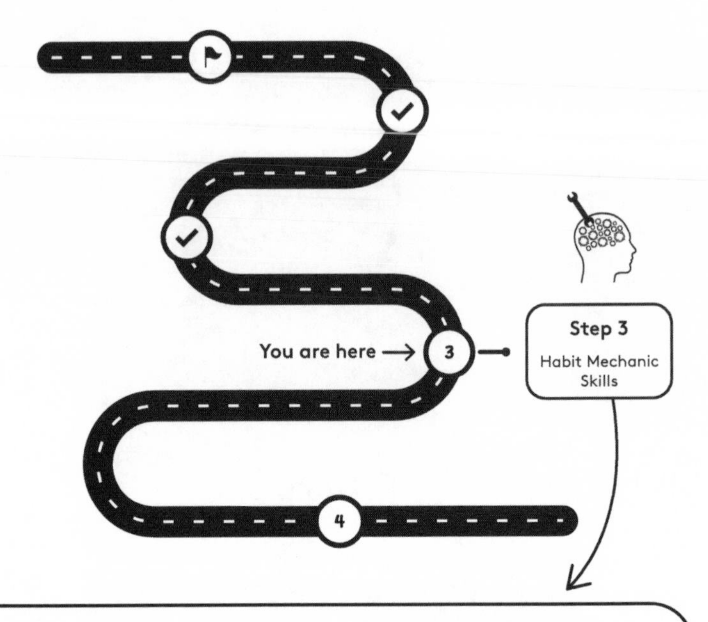

Chapter 15: Train Your WILL POWER to Help You Be Your Best More Often

Chapter 16: Boost Your MOTIVATION and Personal Drive with One Simple Tool

Chapter 17: Analyze and Improve Your HABITS to Achieve Your Long-Term Goals in Life and Work

Chapter 18: The Secret NINE FACTORS That Really Control Your Life

Chapter 19: Improve Your SLEEP, DIET, EXERCISE and Brain Health in Three Simple Steps

Chapter 20: Create Your Own HABIT BUILDING PLAN Using the Secrets of Behavioral Science

Chapter 21: Control Your ACTIVATION Levels to Feel Better and Make Everything You Do Easier

Chapter 22: Simple and Practical STRESS MANAGEMENT SKILLS to Stop Negative Thinking in Its Tracks

Chapter 23: Develop Rock-Solid CONFIDENCE with Our Science-Based Skills

Chapter 24: PERFORM UNDER PRESSURE Using Secrets from World-Class Performers

Chapter 25: Supercharge Your PRODUCTIVITY and FOCUS (In the Office or At Home) for Better Work-Life Balance

Chapter 26: Practice Smarter, Boost Your Intelligence, and Build Any Habit Faster by Using Our Learning Strengths Plan

Figure S3.1: An overview of your journey through Step 3.

15

TRAIN YOUR WILL POWER TO HELP YOU BE YOUR BEST MORE OFTEN

Instead of thinking about learning how to regulate your emotions, I want you to think of it like this: you're training your Will Power so it's stronger and better equipped to guide and mentor HUE.

The better trained your Will Power, the more effortlessly you will be able to be your best.

This is because it will be easier for you to build and sustain helpful habits. Remember, at least 98 percent of everything you do and think is a habit.

Remember, too, that there is a training room in the lighthouse. Will Power spends most of its time there, studying and learning so it can help you be your best.

YOUR HABIT MECHANIC'S TOOL KIT

What follows in this book is a series of simple and practical guides that show you how to use key Habit Mechanic Tools. These are designed to help you be your best. In Step 4, you will also learn how to use Chief Habit Mechanic Tools so you help others be their best.

These simple and practical tools will help you build daily, weekly, and monthly habits that make you feel and do better.

Think of using these guides and tools to stock the training room's shelves, so they are readily available when Will Power needs to draw on them to help HUE.

In Step 3, you are going to learn how to use Habit Mechanic Tools that will help you do the following things:

- Further develop your Habit Mechanic intelligence
- Improve your work-life balance
- Improve your ability to learn and change
- Supercharge your motivation
- Analyze your habits…
- …and build better habits for:
  - Sleep
  - Diet
  - Exercise
  - Energy management (I call this Activation)
  - Stress management
  - Confidence
  - Focus
  - Productivity
  - Problem-solving and creativity
  - Performing under pressure

At the heart of these tools are written plans. They will help you break the automatic nature of your current behavior and build better habits. If you have already begun using tools like the Daily TEA Plan or the 3:1 Reflection, you have already experienced the power of written plans.

WHY DOES WRITING OUT A PLAN WORK?

Short-term memory only lasts about 30 seconds, and HUE is very powerful. So you might set a goal "not to check your phone." But because you have not written it down, you literally forget and very quickly find yourself checking your phone again. Writing or typing out a plan commits you to your goal in a much more powerful way. In scientific terms, it switches on your neocortex. This makes you much more likely to stick to your goal and in turn strengthens your emotional regulation habits.

I write plans down in my workbook, diary, and Habit Mechanic Planner. I also type them out on my laptop or in the notes section of my phone. I have also tried using voice memos/audio recordings. I have not found this as effective as writing, but I know others who have.

Try out some different methods to see which type of written plans work best for you.

> *Now, let's think about how to fire up our motivation and personal drive.*

16

BOOST YOUR MOTIVATION AND PERSONAL DRIVE WITH ONE SIMPLE TOOL

In the build-up to golf's 2015 Masters, sportswear giant Nike released a TV commercial featuring professional golf greats Tiger Woods and Rory McIlroy. The ad focused on the development of McIlroy from an enthusiastic youngster to a successful professional golfer. It highlights how, as McIlroy grew up, Tiger Woods was a constant influence and inspiration.

A nine-year-old McIlroy even wrote to Woods to tell him a young golfer from Northern Ireland was "coming after him."

McIlroy's motivation to become a world champion golfer played a huge role in helping him become one of the best golfers on the planet.

The good news is that we can all learn how to use motivation to achieve our goals.

WHAT IS MOTIVATION?

If you want to become a Habit Mechanic so you can build new helpful habits, being motivated is crucial.

We define motivation as the "direction and intensity of effort."

This makes goal-setting essential for motivation. When we set a goal, we can direct and focus our efforts and energies on achieving it.

Imagine throwing a dart at a target. The target is your goal, and the dart represents your effort. How important the goal is will inform how much effort you put into throwing the dart.

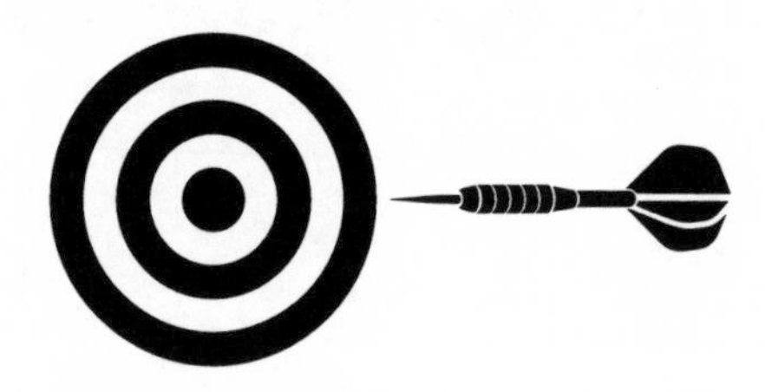

Figure 16.1: Creating goals makes it easier to focus your effort and energy in the right direction.

Completing the APE Brain Test may have highlighted a specific area you want to change (e.g., improved sleep, stress management, productivity, etc.). But once you have targeted a specific area, you may ask yourself:

Can I Really Improve in This Area?

The answer is yes, you can. Learning is your superpower. You can learn to improve any area of your life. I discussed the reasons for this in Chapter 5, and will go into even more detail in Chapter 26.

Then you may ask yourself:

Is Improving in This Area Worth the Effort?

To help you answer this question, I want to introduce a useful story about a successful individual.

WHAT CAN WE LEARN FROM J.K. ROWLING?

During an in-depth Oprah Winfrey interview, *Harry Potter* author J.K. Rowling explained how she had a long-term ambition to become a published author.

She explained how she struggled early on. But she persisted and eventually found the inspiration for the story of the young wizard. Yet this was not enough. She had to keep persisting, because *Harry Potter* was turned down by 12 publishers before she finally got a book deal. This is amazing when we consider that the *Harry Potter* series became the biggest-selling children's books of all time, and one of the highest-grossing movie franchises.

J.K. Rowling's story highlights a critical aspect of motivation: goals that are deeply meaningful are very powerful in helping us persist and achieve.

Research shows that (as detailed in Jim Collins and Jerry Porras's book, *Built to Last: Successful Habits of Visionary Companies*), when they began doing business, some of the world's most successful companies had what the researchers termed Big Hairy Audacious Goals (BHAGS)—clear, long-term, and ambitious goals. If we don't have a clear vision of what we want to achieve, it is difficult to persist and work to our potential each day.

There are many more examples of successful people using BHAGS for motivation. A common theme among all these individuals is that they have not let others dictate or control their destiny. Instead, they have been proactive and controlled the controllable factors in their lives.

- Henry Ford, the founder of Ford Motor Company, wanted to make cars affordable for everyone—not just rich people.
- As a child, Rory McIlroy set himself the future target of becoming a professional golfer and winning every major championship.

- Ten years before he did it, entrepreneur Elon Musk published a blueprint of how he would build electric sports cars, and the infrastructure to charge them with clean electricity.
- Tennis sisters Venus and Serena Williams didn't just stumble into becoming two of the greatest players of all time. They had a clear vision in place from a young age.

However, knowing the importance of a clear vision for the future is one thing. Achieving it is another. The problem is that HUE is only interested in the next 10 minutes of our time, and not what will happen at the end of the year, or in 10 years.

To make it easier to set and connect short-, medium-, and long-term goals, I have developed a special goal-setting system called the "FAM (Future Ambitious Meaningful) Story." It is designed to give you more control over your motivation.

THE POWER OF STORIES

American author and scholar Jonathan Gottschall calls humans "the storytelling animal." He believes we are conditioned to tell stories. From a neurobiological perspective, we understand that stories are so central to individuals and societies because they are easy for our brains to remember.

We have powerful autobiographical memory centers in our brains. Our brains really like structuring knowledge and memories as stories, with a beginning, a middle, and an end.

Will an average person be more likely to remember a list of facts, or an interesting story that incorporates those facts? Most find it much easier to remember the latter. This is why people studying for tests are encouraged to create memory palaces and mnemonics (stories about words).

Habit Mechanics create positive stories about their future lives because stories are powerful in helping us create change and achieve our goals.

FAM STORY BASICS

When we see someone successful, we often only notice what they are good at—and not the years of practice and effort that went into developing their excellence. We only see the ice on the surface, NOT the larger chunks below the waterline.

To get more control over your own story (your future), I will show you how to create your own FAM Story Iceberg.

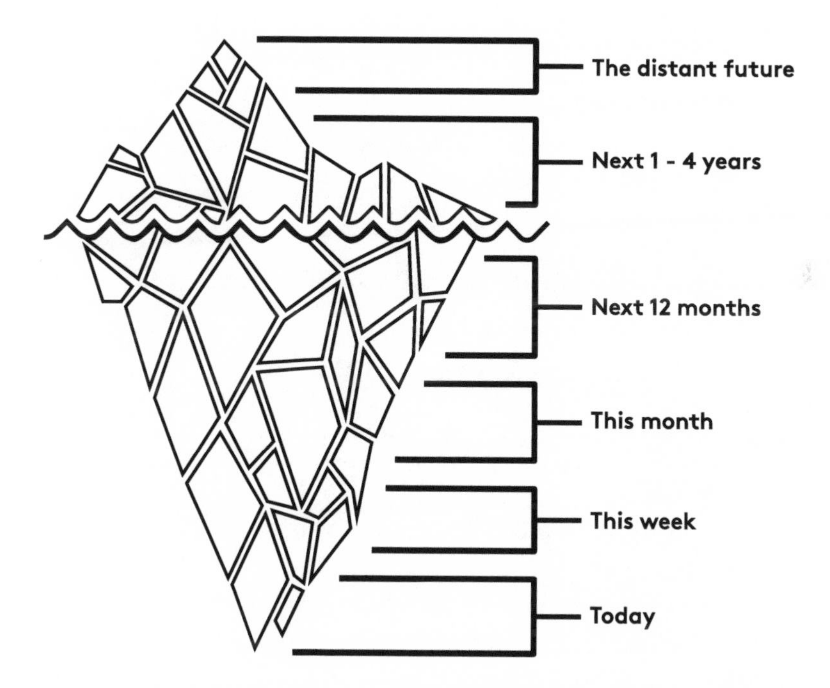

Figure 16.2: The FAM Story Iceberg helps you understand and better control the impact your daily habits have on your health, happiness, and performance in the future.

To build your own FAM Story Iceberg, you need to:

- Think about what you want to achieve, and where you would like to be, in the long-term future—say, **10 years**. This is the top of the iceberg (the distant future). If this sounds daunting, don't worry; I will help you generate some ideas.
- Then think about what you need to do in the next **one to four years** to achieve those big, long-term goals. This is just above the waterline.
- Then think about what you need to achieve in the next **12 months**. This is just below the waterline.
- Then think about what you need to achieve **this month**.
- Then think about what you need to achieve **this week**.
- Then think about what you need to do **today**. This is the bottom of the iceberg.

I will give you detailed guidance on how to create your own FAM Story Iceberg later. You can re-draft this as many times as you like.

THE BENEFITS OF FAM STORIES

1. Create a Wave of Motivation

FAM Stories create what I call a "wave of motivation." This helps direct our efforts and our energies. This also helps us focus by developing an understanding of exactly what we need to accomplish in the short-term to achieve our long-term objectives.

2. Track Your Progress

Setting structured goals allows us to track our progress. This makes it easier to strike the important balance between hedonism (pleasure) and eudemonia (Habit Mechanic development).

World-leading creativity expert and Harvard psychologist Professor Teresa Amabile coined the term *The Progress Principle* (also the title of her book). She highlighted how people feel better if their daily activity helps them make progress toward a meaningful goal. She showed how small wins, or pieces of progress, make it easier to keep persisting in the face of challenges. According to some researchers, the single biggest cause of work burnout is not overload but working for too long without experiencing personal progress.

When we do not feel like our efforts are being rewarded with progress, we can feel stifled and overwhelmed. In contrast, feeling that we are making progress in our lives can make us feel happier, more fulfilled, and more motivated.

3. Manage Stress

Setting and monitoring goals also makes it easier to reset and recalibrate when we falter. When set correctly, goals are excellent stress management tools. If goals are too challenging or too easy, you can adjust them accordingly—because they are not set in stone.

4. Prophesize Your Future

Goals create self-fulfilling prophecies. Walt Disney famously said: "If you can dream it, you can do it." Work by Columbia University Professor Robert Merton also showed that if you believe that you can achieve something, you have a better chance of success. Merton's self-fulfilling prophecy theory has had far-reaching implications for how we understand human behavior.

FAM STORY POWER

There is a useful case study from the world of golf that helps us understand the power of FAM Stories even more.

In 2018, Georgia Hall became only the third British winner of The Women's British Open since the event became a major. After the event, Hall revealed part of her FAM Story. She said: "It was my goal when I was nine to win the British Open. I am so happy."

Comments from Wayne Hall, Georgia's father and caddie, underlined this. He said: "We've been dreaming about this since she was seven years old, practicing and knocking in putts for the British Open. Now it's actually happened."

Georgia Hall fulfilled her own prophecy by winning The Open. Her father also explained how his daughter progressed through her FAM Story: "[She had] a 36-handicap at nine. At 10 years old she progressed to a 10-handicap, then set a course record when she was 11 that still stands now. Then she was selected for the England squads and just improved from there."

Wayne Hall also revealed that his daughter's goal had been to win The Open the previous season, in 2017. But her failure was not fatal to her career. Instead, she reset and tried again. He explained: "This is the biggest tournament for her, and for us, and we really, really went for it after last year, when we finished third."

This emphasizes that goals are not set in stone, and how having them allows us to pivot if things do not go to plan.

Georgia's experience shows us that our goals do not have to be completely rigid. Simply creating them appears to be far more beneficial than not.

Test?

If it is helpful, write down what FAM stands for to see how good your memory is!

DEVELOPING YOUR FAM STORY

To get you thinking about your future, write down answers to these questions.

1. Who inspires you? Be specific and name names.

Some ideas (in no particular order) to spark your thoughts:

- Parents
- Siblings
- Grandparents
- Family
- Colleagues
- People who have changed society
- Scientists
- Nobel Prize winners
- Entrepreneurs
- Mentors
- Writers
- Sporting champions
- Political leaders
- High achievers
- Musicians

2. Why do they inspire you?
(Be specific. Identify their shared and individual qualities.)

Some ideas (in no particular order) to spark your thoughts:

- Dedication
- Persistence
- Self-sacrifice
- Determination
- Desire
- Work ethic
- Success
- Tolerance
- Progress
- Excellence
- Innovation
- Humility
- Dependability
- Resilience
- Attitude
- Guts

3. Select at least three, and no more than eight, examples of what you do to feel at your best.

- Have fun
- Help others
- Develop myself
- Relax
- Do meaningful work
- Show humility

- Give my best
- Have a good work-life balance
- Achieve results
- Be dedicated
- Be determined
- Persist with difficult challenges
- Be resilient
- Show the right attitude
- Make personal progress
- Be diligent
- Be dependable
- Be tolerant
- Eat well
- Sleep well
- Show self-control

Write down other areas if they are not on the list.

4. Why is it important for you to do these things, and what outcomes do they help you achieve?

---

5. Write down or select at least three, and no more than eight, of your top strengths.

Some ideas (in no particular order) to spark your thoughts:

- Achievements
- Dedication
- Desire

- Persistence
- Self-sacrifice
- Positive attitude
- Calm
- Work ethic
- Reflective
- Success
- Humility
- Tolerance
- Diligence
- Dependability
- Excellence
- Attitude
- Innovative

Write down other areas if they are not on the list.

6. Write down the most important and difficult things you have achieved in your life so far, or in the past 12 months.

---

7. Briefly explain how you managed to be persistent to secure this achievement.

CREATING YOUR FAM STORY WITH THE "FAM FORM"

I have created a Habit Mechanic Tool I call the "FAM Form."

It helps you create your own FAM Story Iceberg and make the connection between the tip of the iceberg (your long-term future goals) and the bottom of the iceberg (the here and now and the small steps you will take to begin working toward your major goals).

Broadly, it makes you think about the future and present in the following terms:

- What do I want to achieve in the distant future?
- What do I need to do in the next one to four years to achieve my distant future goals?
- To achieve the above, what do I need to achieve in the next 12 months?
- To achieve the above, what do I need to achieve next month?
- To achieve the above, what do I need to achieve this week?
- To achieve the above, how do I begin today?

Sometimes we might feel reluctant to commit to achieving a major, long-term objective. But the beauty of the FAM Form is that it allows us to be flexible. We can decide to pivot and change our goals. They are not set in stone.

I encourage everyone who wants to be their best to periodically think about their own long-term goals. I step back to reflect and use the FAM Form to update my FAM Story every four to eight weeks. My FAM Story goals change because my life circumstances change. Sometimes the changes to my goals are tiny, and sometimes they are big. But what is most important is that I am engaging in a purposeful reflection and planning process. This helps me learn about myself and how to be at my best. This is what Habit Mechanics do.

LEARNING FROM BILL GATES

Microsoft founder and billionaire philanthropist Bill Gates provides us with another useful example of the value of creating long-term goals. In *Decoding Bill Gates,* the Netflix three-part docuseries about his life, Gates says that in his younger years, he and his best friend, Kent, constantly looked ahead to their futures to develop a vision of what they wanted to achieve.

"We were always scheming about what we'd be doing in the next five years," Gates said. "Kent had an interest in business and so he got me reading *Fortune* magazine."

Gates added that he and his friend discussed different career paths, what types of remuneration were available in each profession, and what type of impact on the world different people in various jobs could make. He also said that they both believed that they would achieve great things in the future.

COMPLETING THE FAM FORM

So, just like young Bill Gates and his friend, you can use the questions on the FAM Form to begin brainstorming ideas about your future. You can begin creating your own future, ambitious, and meaningful story.

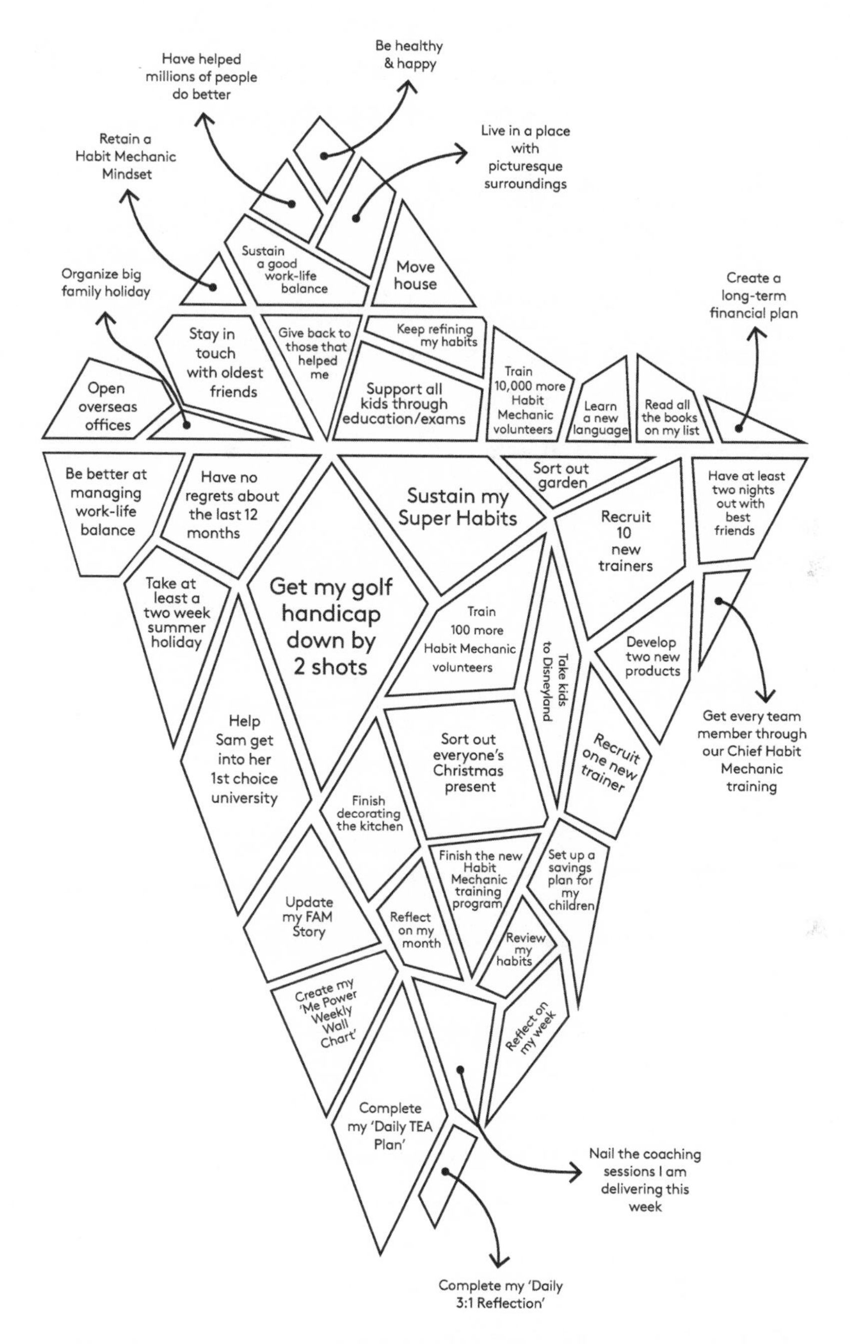

Figure 16.3: Example of a filled-in FAM Story Iceberg. But this is never complete because your life constantly changes, so you need to keep updating it (I do this every four to eight weeks).

FAM Form Questions to Help You Create Your Own FAM Story

Remember, the answers you give and the goals you set are not set in stone. They are flexible and can be changed at any time to make them more helpful for you.

1. What would you like to do and have in the distant/medium future (e.g., 10 years or more)?

Some words to get you thinking about your future goals:

- Location
- Family
- Possessions
- Friends and relationships
- Health
- Home
- Money
- Roles and responsibilities
- Job

Tip: If you are not sure, start by thinking about what you DO NOT want your future to look like.

Developing your long-term goals will take time. The aim of this exercise is not to create perfect goals but to get you thinking and started on your journey to having a clearer understanding about what you want your future self and life to look like. Remember, whatever you write down can be changed.

Should you set goals that might feel unrealistic?

I do because I have found that even if I do not achieve these goals, having a high level of expectation is helpful. It means I achieve a higher level of happiness and performance than I would have if I'd set myself less ambitious goals. This is something I have learned through practice.

Should you copy my approach?

No! You need to develop an approach that works best for you. You will only work out the best way to set the type of goals that work best for you by trying things out. Goals are powerful tools, but it can take a lot of trial and error to learn how to use them effectively.

Why × 5?

To make your long-term goals more meaningful and powerful, try to understand "Why?" you want to achieve them. An effective way to do this is to ask yourselves "Why?" five times.

For example, if you want to get a promotion at work, you might ask yourself "Why?" The answer might be, "Because you want to earn more money."

So you would then ask yourself, why do you want to earn more money? That answer might be, "Because you want to move to a bigger house."

Then, you would ask yourself, why do you want to live in a bigger house? This answer could be, "So my young children have a garden to play in."

The next question you might ask yourself is why is it important for you to have a garden your children can play in? The answer could be, "I understand the importance of outdoor play for healthy development and I want to provide a space at home where they can do this."

By the time you have asked yourself "Why?" at least five times, you will develop a clear understanding of the deeper reasons for your goals and ambitions. The more meaningful your reasons for wanting to achieve a goal, the more powerful they will be in helping you persist and succeed.

Now, let's get back to our FAM Form questions.

2. What do you need to achieve in the next one to four years to make distant/medium future goals attainable?

3. What do you need to achieve in the next 12 months to make your one-to-four-year goals attainable?

4. Write down at least three things, and no more than five, that you need to prioritize to help you feel good about yourself this month.

Think about these as your priorities for the month. It might also be helpful to write **why** you want to achieve these priorities.

5. Write down at least three things, and no more than five, that you need to prioritize this week to help you achieve your goals this month.

Think about these as your priorities for the week. It might also be helpful to write **why** you want to achieve these priorities.

When you start to consider the bottom of your FAM Story Iceberg, you need to use the insights you gained about yourself from the APE Brain Test (Chapter 12). This will help you begin understanding your current habits, and the ones that it might be helpful to change as you embark on your journey to becoming a Habit Mechanic. I will show you how to do an in-depth habit analysis in Chapter 17.

6. Write down at least three things, and no more than five, that you need to do today to help you achieve your goals this week.

Think about these as your priorities for today (e.g., eat an extra piece of fruit; go for a five-minute walk at lunchtime; turn my phone and emails off when I am doing work that requires my full concentration). Using other Habit Mechanic Tools like the Daily TEA Plan and 3:1 Daily Reflection will help you achieve these goals.

FIRING UP YOUR MOTIVATION

You now have the outline of a story about what you want your future to look like. To help you keep building and refining this story, I have created a list of quick questions and reminders below.

1. Make your goals more meaningful by asking yourself "Why?" five times.
2. On a scale of 1 to 10, how well are you doing your best to be your best and achieve your weekly goals?
3. Remind yourself it is possible to make changes because you are a combination of nature PLUS nurture.
4. Update your FAM Story (e.g., every four to eight weeks).
5. Can you connect your short-term goals and habits (i.e., today) to your future goals?
6. Write a "Fail Story" (i.e., what don't you want your future to look like?).
7. Reflect on your Fail Story and use it as a mirror to help you develop and refine your FAM Story.

HABIT MECHANIC PLANNING TOOL YOU HAVE LEARNED IN CHAPTER 16...

FAM (Future Ambitious Meaningful) Story—A tool to help you create, connect, and periodically review and update your long-, medium-, and short-term goals. ☑

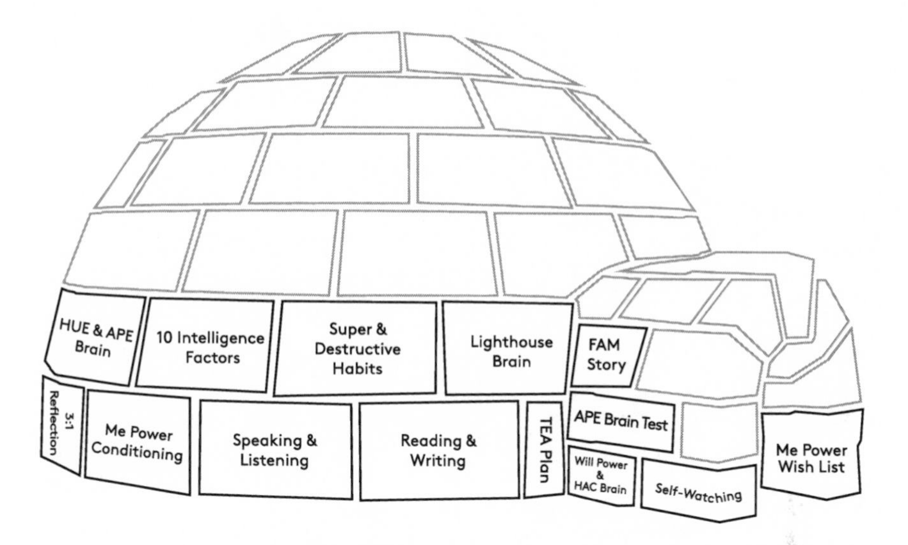

Figure 16.4: Your Habit Mechanic intelligence igloo is building up!

Next, I'll help you identify the most significant challenges your APE Brain poses by taking a closer look at how habits work and introducing our "TRAIT Habit Loop."

17

ANALYZE AND IMPROVE YOUR HABITS TO ACHIEVE YOUR LONG-TERM GOALS IN LIFE AND WORK

A TV commercial by sportswear brand Under Armour finished with the line: *"It's what you do in the dark that puts you in the light."*

It showed the world-record-breaking US swimmer Michael Phelps grinding and struggling through arduous winter training. Phelps was preparing for the 2016 Rio Olympics. It was his last appearance at the Games.

He won five gold medals and a silver, making him the most decorated Olympian of all time.

The commercial highlights the essential role your daily habits play in achieving your long-term goals.

Let's think about how habits and goals are connected.

HABITS DRIVE YOUR GOALS

Your ability to achieve your FAM (Future Ambitious Meaningful) Story will depend on your habits.

Think about the FAM Story Iceberg in a different way. Imagine you've turned the FAM Story Iceberg on its side. The tip of the iceberg, which represents your long-term future and goals, is now on the right-hand side.

The bottom of the iceberg is on the left, representing the present (today, right now) and the habits you need to develop to help you achieve your long-term goals.

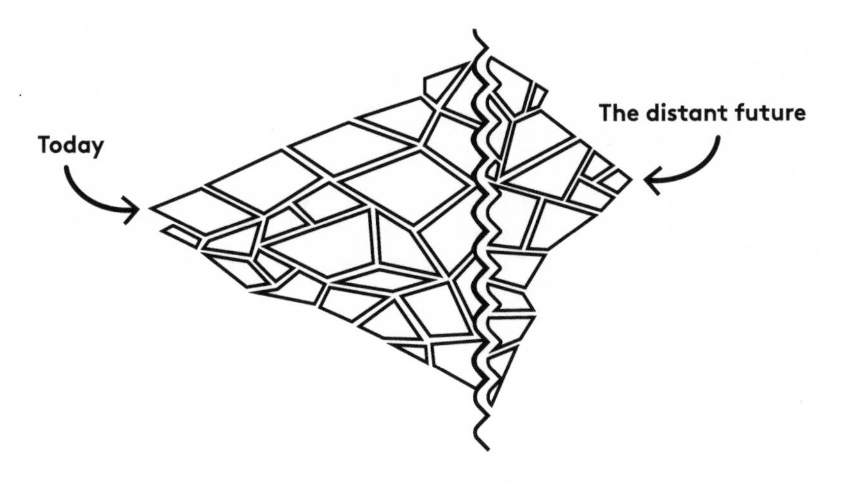

Figure 17.1: The FAM Story Iceberg tilted on its side to represent a timeline.

We all need to work on developing more helpful habits, often beginning by improving the basics like sleep, diet, and exercise.

But the challenges of the modern world mean helpful habits are not always easy to build and maintain. We need to constantly work on them.

YOUR THOUGHTS AND ACTIONS ARE MAINLY HABIT

To help you identify which habits will help you be at your best more often, let's think about how habits work in greater depth.

First, it is important to remember that habits are all-pervading in our lives.

You will hopefully recall the statistic, which is based on the work of Professor George Lakoff from University of California, Berkeley, that at least 98 percent of all human behavior—how you think and what you do—is habit.

This means that the vast majority of what we do and think, every day, is a habit. It's also important to recognize that unhelpful thinking can be a habit.

A useful quote to help us understand just how powerful habits are in our lives is from William James—the founding father of American psychology. In his book *The Principles of Psychology, Vol.1*, he said:

"My experience of the world is what I am in the habit of attending to [doing and thinking]."

The good news is that becoming a Habit Mechanic allows you to change your habits via the process of Me Power Conditioning (deliberately working toward being your best).

INTRODUCING THE TRAIT HABIT LOOP

To help you think in detail about how habits work, I've developed the TRAIT Habit Loop.

Figure 17.2: Other habit loops I have seen did not make perfect sense to me, so I created my own using insights from cutting-edge neuroscience and behavioral science.

Other habit models I've seen don't get to the heart of what really drives our behavior. TRAIT does, because it is based on cutting-edge science. Time and again, it has helped people develop powerful new sustainable habits.

Let me explain TRAIT in more detail.

T Is for Trigger

Triggers are the first part of the habit loop. They remind us what to do, for better or for worse.

All triggers are ultimately driven by our emotions, hence why emotional regulation is so important. But because emotions are implicit, we don't always think of them in these terms. It is easier to think of a trigger as a feeling, thought, smell, sound, or sight. Smartphones are among the most powerful triggering devices ever created. They provide endless visual, aural, and physical triggers, and are always close by.

Here is another example. Think about walking into a coffee shop. Triggers are all around you. There is high-energy, tempting, APE Brain-friendly food strategically placed when you order your drink. You might have gone to the coffee shop because you were feeling low on energy, so you will be tempted to make an impulsive purchase of a sugary treat.

R Is for Routine

Before I explain this, I want to introduce the AI (in TR**AI**T), because the Routine part of the loop will then make more sense.

AI Is for APE Incentive

The APE (Alive, Perceived, Energy) Brain is the driving force behind our behavior. So habits connected to survival, maintaining and enhancing social status, and saving energy are easy to build because these factors are most rewarding for the APE Brain. For example:

Stereotyping Is Connected to "Staying Alive"

We quickly judge—within just a tenth of a second—who is friend or foe. For example, we quickly (and possibly inaccurately) make judgments about someone we have only just met.

Thinking Habits Focusing on How You Are "Perceived by Important People"

We can mindlessly spend a lot of time thinking about what important people in our lives think about us. This can include worrying and beating ourselves up.

Thinking Habits Connected to "Conserving Energy"

We can default to high-calorie food choices when hungry or resist expending energy that does not result in a fast reward. When you feel hungry, you might eat an unhealthy sugary snack loaded with calories because it is more energy efficient than eating a piece of fruit. Or you might avoid exercise by driving to places that you could walk to. Or stop mentally challenging work to do something less mentally challenging that will consume less energy (e.g., stop writing a report to check your phone).

More on "R Is for Routine"

A trigger is always followed by a routine. The action you take, or how you think, is an automatic or semi-automatic response to the trigger. For example, your phone buzzes (trigger), you check it, see a message from your partner, and respond (routine). The routine is driven by an APE Incentive. You respond quickly to stay in your partner's good books. This might be a subconscious attempt to manage your partner's perception (the P in APE) of you (e.g., by replying quickly, you're showing them how important they are to you).

Sometimes the APE Brain can gain more than one reward from a habit. Imagine your phone buzzes on the desk while you're listening to a presentation. Your routine is to stop and check your phone. This probably takes a lot less energy (the E in APE) than concentrating on the presentation. And it might be a message from a friend that makes you feel good about yourself, rewarding the perception (the P in APE) part of the APE Brain, too (i.e., your friend must like you because they are taking the time to message you).

T Is for Training

The more you practice a habit, the more neurons in your brain become dedicated to it. More neurons make habit loops more powerful and easier to execute.

APE Brain-Friendly Habits

You can build new habits. But this ability is a double-edged sword. On one hand, it is beneficial because you can build more new helpful habits. On the other, it can be damaging because you can develop more unhelpful habits. The latter is easier than ever in the context of the VUCA world and the Learning War (described in Chapter 6).

APE Brain-friendly habits, which are typically unhelpful for modern life, are easier to build because the APE Brain is so central to the habit building process. These APE Brain-friendly habits can become addictive, meaning you continue to do them despite their negative consequences for your health, happiness, and performance. These can often be the seeds of the "Destructive Habits" that I mentioned earlier (Chapter 8, Part 7) because they unlock lots of other unhelpful habits/behaviors.

Here are some examples:

Example 1

Trigger: feeling hungry

Routine: eating an unhealthy snack that tastes good

APE Incentive: getting energy into your body—fast

Training: If this behavior is repeated often enough to become an unhelpful habit, you will gain weight, feel worse about yourself, and increase your risk of long-term health problems.

Example 2

Trigger: feeling frustrated at missing your favorite TV show because you need to go to bed

Routine: staying up late to watch the next episode

APE Incentive: It takes less energy and is more immediately rewarding to watch the next episode rather than go upstairs to bed.

Training: If this behavior is repeated often enough to become an unhelpful habit, you will not get enough sleep and will feel tired the next day, have reduced productivity, do less exercise, eat worse food, and increase your risk of long-term health problems.

Example 3

Trigger: feeling bored while doing a challenging piece of work

Routine: checking your phone

APE Incentive: It takes less energy, and is more immediately rewarding, to check your phone rather than complete your work.

Training: If this behavior is repeated often enough to become an unhelpful habit, you will have reduced productivity, need to work longer hours, become more easily distracted, and find it more difficult to do your best work.

Example 4

Trigger: feeling annoyed by something that happened at work

Routine: having a cigarette

APE Incentive: fast and energy-efficient way to relieve stress

Training: If this behavior is repeated often enough to become an unhelpful habit, you will increase your risk of long-term health problems, develop stained teeth and bad breath, and become addicted.

Example 5

Trigger: feeling stressed by your workload

Routine: drinking alcohol

APE Incentive: fast and energy-efficient way to relax

Training: If this becomes an unhelpful habit, you will have poorer sleep quality, potentially leading to poorer brain function and higher stress levels the following day. In turn, this might make it more difficult to be efficient and effective at work and lead you to eat unhealthy food, because it makes you feel better in the short-term. This will all lead to increased risks of long-term health problems.

Example 6

Trigger: feeling unhappy about yourself

Routine: buying some new clothes

APE Incentive: fast and energy-efficient way to change the way others perceive you—meaning you feel better

Training: If this behavior is repeated often enough to become an unhelpful habit, you might get deeper into debt and feel worse about yourself in the long-term.

Example 7

Trigger: You receive an email from your boss that gives you some negative feedback about your work, which your APE Brain takes personally.

Routine: beating yourself up

APE Incentive: The APE Brain is making you aware that your social status (how you are perceived by others) is under attack.

Training: If this behavior is repeated often enough to become an unhelpful habit, you will become really good at worrying about what other people think of you, become an expert in looking for personal slights or what I would call perception threats, and become an expert at beating yourself up. This might lead to long-term mental health problems.

Test?

If it is helpful, write down what TRAIT stands for to test your memory!

Reflection?

If it is helpful, why not write out one of your unhelpful habits using the TRAIT framework:

Trigger:

Routine:

APE Incentive:

Training:

HABIT MECHANIC HABIT ANALYSIS TOOLS

In-Depth Habits Reflection

Now that you understand more about how habits work, you can begin to analyze your own in more detail and do what I call an "In-Depth Habits Reflection" exercise. This builds on the APE Brain Test you completed earlier.

Remember, habits are the foundation of your FAM Story Iceberg. You will fail if your habits are not helpful to achieving your daily, weekly, and monthly goals. Creating more helpful habits will make it easier to make progress, succeed, and thrive.

To help you understand which new habits would be helpful to build this month, score yourself for each of the following statements from 1 to 10, where 1 equals "never" and 10 equals "always." Adding notes and specific examples next to statements that really resonate with you will be useful.

1. I give in to temptation and act impulsively. *Score:* _____
   Notes: ____
2. I do things I regret. *Score:* _____
   Notes: ____
3. I jump to conclusions. *Score:* _____
   Notes: ____
4. I have no discipline to keep going when things get difficult.
   Score: _____
   Notes: ____
5. I have no discipline to stay on a task and complete it. *Score:* _____
   Notes: ____
6. I stay in my comfort zone, and this stops me from being my best.
   Score: _____
   Notes: ____
7. I cannot resist temptations to quit. *Score:* _____
   Notes: ____
8. I do not continue to work when the reward is a long time in coming. *Score:* _____
   Notes: ____
9. I beat myself up when I have messed up. *Score:* _____
   Notes: ____
10. I am overconfident, and this has unhelpful consequences.
    Score: _____
    Notes: ____
11. I make excuses for my bad behavior. *Score:* ___
    Notes: ____

12. I do not push myself out of my comfort zone because I do not want to fail. *Score:* ____

    Notes: ____________________

13. I avoid taking personal responsibility for the quality of my own work. *Score:* ____

    Notes: ____________________

14. I let people down by NOT completing tasks on time to expected standards. *Score:* ____

    Notes: ____________________

15. I worry about things I cannot control. *Score:* ____

    Notes: ____________________

Now consider your scores. Identify the highest scores and the connected habits. Now, try to write down a typical way you use your most unhelpful habit, for example: "I beat myself up when I make a mistake." Don't worry if you are not sure what to write; I will help you think about your unhelpful habits in even more detail shortly.

____

____

____

____

____

Super Habits

Now that you have reflected on some of your unhelpful habits, I want to revisit the Super Habits concept I mentioned earlier (Chapter 8, Part 7).

Through Tougher Minds' work with over 10,000 people, I repeatedly see a set of core habits (Super Habits) that seem to be more powerful than other habits in helping people be healthier, happier, and at their best.

When people develop Super Habits, many other aspects of their lives become easier because these habits trigger other helpful habits/behaviors. They enable people to manage HUE (Horribly Unhelpful Emotions) and make the type of personal progress (Habit Mechanic development) essential for feeling happy and fulfilled.

Super Habits make it easier for people to achieve the following outcomes:

1. Improving diet, exercise, and sleep for better brain performance
2. Better stress management
3. Spending less time thinking unhelpful thoughts
4. Being focused to drive productivity, creativity, and problem-solving
5. Building and maintaining robust levels of confidence
6. Performing well under pressure
7. Better leadership for improved individual and team performance

All of which lead to better work-life balance.

Finding your Super Habits will help you unlock your potential.

I have developed and refined my Super Habits over many years. They naturally develop and change as you improve your Habit Mechanic intelligence and develop more helpful habits.

Here is an overview of my current Super Habits and the other helpful habits/behaviors each one triggers. They might sound simple, but they have emerged through years of Habit Mechanic training and trial and error. Remember, there is a huge difference between knowing these things are helpful and turning them into habits.

Daily

1. **Morning run:** activates my brain and means it is easier to think clearly, focus, and be productive; triggers healthy eating habits; contributes to my overall daily exercise, which makes sleeping easier at night; helps me manage my weight.

2. **Completing a Daily TEA Plan:** makes it easier for me to get the most out of my day; triggers a lot of the productivity habits I have developed; having a productive day makes me feel better about myself at the end of the day, and helps me better manage work-life balance.
3. **Five-minute lunchtime walk where I deliberately focus on my breathing:** helps me manage stress; be productive in the afternoon; finish work on time; better manage work-life balance; sleep better.
4. **End-of-day planning for the next day, combined with a written reflection on the current day:** helps me manage stress; see progress; build confidence; finish work on time; activates my evening routine/habits, helping me sleep better.

Weekly

1. **Weekly reflection and planning for week ahead:** improves my motivation, productivity, and confidence; helps activate my daily Super Habits.

Monthly/Bimonthly

1. **Review and update my FAM (Future Ambitious Meaningful) Story:** improves my motivation, productivity, and confidence; helps activate my daily and weekly Super Habits.
2. **Complete the Team Power Leadership self-assessments (which are in Step 4 of this book):** improves my leadership; helps the business, my team, and me fulfill our potential; helps activate my daily and weekly Super Habits.

Because of life's ebbs and flows, being at our best is an ongoing journey. This means that my Super Habits are not set in stone, because I am still learning how to be my best. Also, as my life changes, I might have to adjust some of my Super Habits so they better serve me in my new life circumstances (e.g., going into the office every day versus working remotely).

It is not essential for you to understand your Super Habits right now. You will discover them over time.

The first step to uncovering your Super Habits is developing more helpful habits, in tandem with developing your Habit Mechanic intelligence. That is what this book is designed to help you do.

So, next I want you to complete an exercise designed to help you begin identifying your helpful habits. Some you will have already developed, but others you will need to purposefully build.

Helpful Habits Reflection

The "Helpful Habits Reflection" is designed to help you build on what you learned from the In-Depth Habits Reflection. This helped you think about your unhelpful habits. So at this point, it might be useful to reflect on your In-Depth Habits Reflection notes and scores.

To complete the Helpful Habits Reflection, follow these instructions:

Below are 13 statements. Read them, and choose your current position for each one from this list of three options:

a. Not a priority.
b. I already do this well.
c. I need to do this better.

1. I reflect on my diet, exercise, and sleep, and plan to make daily improvements in these areas.
   ☐ a ☐ b ☐ c

2. At the end of the day, it would be helpful to reflect and highlight what went well and what I can improve tomorrow.

   ☐ a ☐ b ☐ c

3. At the end of every week, it would be helpful to think about what went well and to plan how I can improve next week.

   ☐ a ☐ b ☐ c

4. From time to time, it would be helpful to think about my future, and set long-, medium-, and short-term goals to focus my efforts and achieve my future ambitions.

   ☐ a ☐ b ☐ c

5. It would be helpful to regularly update my yearly and monthly calendar to add in important work and life activities.

   ☐ a ☐ b ☐ c

6. It would be helpful to recognize when I am stressed and successfully plan to reduce my stress.

   ☐ a ☐ b ☐ c

7. It would be helpful to monitor my confidence levels and successfully build up confidence in areas where it is low.

   ☐ a ☐ b ☐ c

8. It would be helpful to recognize when my emotions are unhelpful and successfully keep them under control.

   ☐ a ☐ b ☐ c

9. It would be helpful to successfully plan to improve my productivity levels.

   ☐ a ☐ b ☐ c

10. It would be helpful to successfully plan to improve my learning and performance in areas where I want to improve.

    ☐ a ☐ b ☐ c

11. It would be helpful to successfully plan to improve my performance under pressure.

☐ a ☐ b ☐ c

12. It would be helpful to plan out my day to improve my productivity.

    ☐ a ☐ b ☐ c

13. It would be helpful to learn how to become an even better leader.

    ☐ a ☐ b ☐ c

Now that you have reflected, give each area you have rated "c" (I need to do this better) a priority score (1 = lowest; 10 = highest).

If it is helpful, write down some reflections about what you have learned. Make a note of the helpful habits you already have that make your life easier. But also begin to consider which new helpful habits you could develop to replace your unhelpful ones.

Remember, you don't need to highlight your Super Habits yet. These will emerge over time as you develop your Habit Mechanic intelligence. The first step to uncovering your Super Habits is developing more helpful habits.

____

____

____

____

____

____

YOUR ME POWER WISH LIST

By reflecting on your habits, you will have identified the most significant challenge(s) or problem(s) your APE Brain poses. You may now wish to add any important habits you have identified to your Me Power Wish List (you started to create this in Chapter 12).

Remember, it's only realistic to make one tiny change at a time, or build one tiny new habit at a time. Nobody has the capacity to completely overhaul and change their behavior in one go. It is a gradual process.

HABIT MECHANIC LANGUAGE AND TOOLS YOU HAVE LEARNED IN CHAPTER 17...

Core Language

TRAIT (Trigger, Routine, APE Incentive, Training) Habit Loop—A unique habit model created to help people understand how their habits work. ☑

Self-Reflection Tools

In-Depth Habits Reflection—In-depth exercise to help you begin identifying your most unhelpful habits. ☑

Helpful Habits Reflection—An exercise to help you reflect on which new habits it would be most helpful to build. ☑

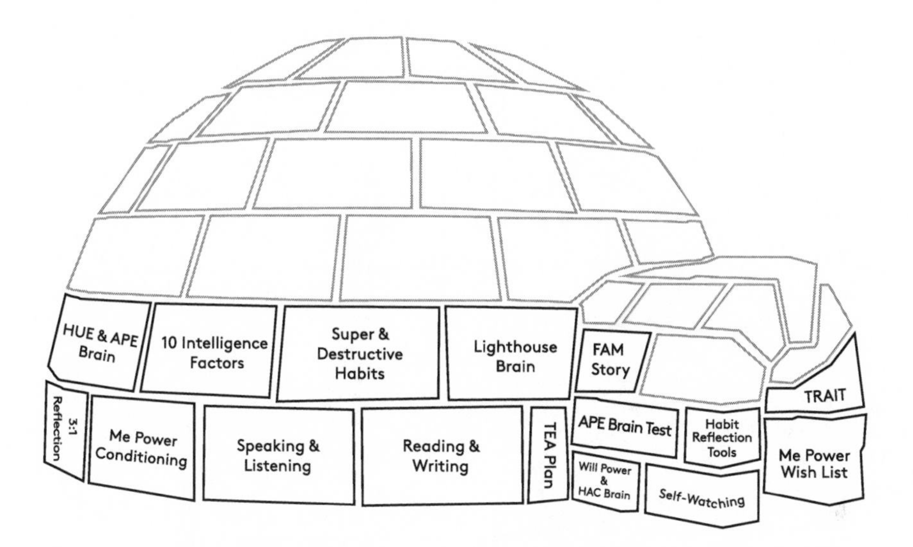

Figure 17.3: Your Habit Mechanic intelligence igloo is building up!

> *Next, we'll look at how our behavioral science-based Nine Action Factors framework can supercharge the habit building process.*

18

THE SECRET NINE FACTORS THAT REALLY CONTROL YOUR LIFE

If we did not already recognize that it is challenging for anyone to build new helpful habits, a story about former US president Barack Obama can help us understand more. It is also worth noting that Obama was not just the first African American president but the third youngest in over 100 years.

CBS News showed Mr. Obama taking questions from the press shortly after announcing new laws to regulate the American tobacco industry. A reporter asked him several questions about his own smoking habits. How many cigarettes does he smoke every day? Does he smoke in the presence of others?

Barack Obama is regarded by many as a consummate statesman, a highly capable leader, and a powerful role model. But even he admitted that stopping smoking was a "struggle." "Have I fallen off the wagon?" he said. "Occasionally, yes."

He added: "I'd say I am 95 percent cured, but there are times when I mess up. Like folks who go to Alcoholics Anonymous... smoking is something you continually struggle with."

In this chapter, we'll explore the science and the simple practice steps you can use to build the sustainable new habits that will make it easier to be your best.

VERBAL PERSUASION DOESN'T WORK!

Changing our habits (the foundations of all human behavior) is complex. We often fail because we do not understand the science of behavioral change.

When we try to build a new habit in any area of our life, the default (but faulty) behavior change technique we have been taught is what I term "verbal persuasion."

We notice an unhelpful habit and persuade ourselves we really DO need to stop. For example, we tell ourselves, "We are beating ourselves up too much... we must stop." We may even tell somebody else of our intention to stop this unhelpful behavior.

We use the same verbal persuasion technique if we want someone else to change a behavior. You might say: "I think it would be a good idea if you turned up for meetings on time, because this would be helpful for team performance." But even if people agree that your behavior change suggestion is a good idea, this is not enough to help people build the new habits that will deliver the change.

The behavioral science is clear: this traditional approach to changing our habits is overreliant on Will Power. Wanting to make a change is not enough to build a new habit. To make sustainable change, we must use insights from behavioral science to create a precise step-by-step approach.

WILL POWER IS THE CONDUIT FOR CHANGE– BUT IT IS LIMITED

All behavior change begins with using Will Power to resist the old habit. For example:

Trigger and APE Incentive: You notice the urge to check your phone, NOW, meaning you will have to break your focus on an important piece of work you need to complete ASAP. This is HUE (Horribly Unhelpful Emotions) looking for short-term gratification—driven by the *APE Incentive*. Having the phone in your eyeline is part of the *trigger* for your desire to check it.

Routine: You use Will Power to regulate your emotions and resist the temptation of entering the old routine of checking the phone. By doing this, you are starting to create a new routine, that is, when you feel the urge to check your phone, you show resolve and stay focused on the task on which you are working.

But if you only rely on your Will Power, it is likely HUE will eventually win and you will check your phone.

Although Will Power is the conduit for building new helpful habits, it is a limited resource. So we need to use Will Power PLUS behavioral science to secure new habits.

THE NINE ACTION FACTORS FRAMEWORK

To help people regulate their emotions and supercharge the habit building process, I used the latest insights from behavioral science to create the proprietary Tougher Minds "Nine Action Factors" framework. I use this framework, and the 200+ tactics I have created, to help my clients create personal and cultural change (i.e., a habit building program across a team or entire business). Here I will show you how to use a simple version to help you build new habits that last.

All of the nine factors are interconnected. Each is also connected to the TRAIT (Trigger, Routine, APE Incentive, Training) Habit Loop. Here is a simple overview of the nine factors (I will explain each in greater detail later):

1. Habit Mechanic Mindset Factor (*APE Incentive*)

Figure 18.1: If you don't believe you can improve, you never will. The right mindset is essential for changing your habits.

2. Brain State Optimization Factor (*Training*; *APE Incentive*)

Figure 18.2: To successfully build new habits, your brain needs to be neurobiologically ready for change.

3. Tiny Changes Factor (*APE Incentive*)

Figure 18.3: You can change but only one tiny step at a time.

4. Personal Motivation Factor (*APE Incentive*)

Figure 18.4: It is easier to change if there is a meaningful reason why.

5. Personal Knowledge and Skills Factor (*Routine*)

Figure 18.5: Building new habits often requires you to learn new things.

6. Community Knowledge and Skills Factor (*Routine*)

Figure 18.6: If the people around you already know how to do *the thing you want to learn (e.g., manage stress), it will be easier for you to learn it.*

7. Social Influence Factor (*APE Incentive*)

Figure 18.7: If the people around you are already doing *the thing you want to do, it will be easier for you to do it.*

8. Rewards and Penalties Factor (*APE Incentive*)

Figure 18.8: Rewards encourage behavior and penalties discourage it.

9. External Triggers Factor (*Trigger*)

Figure 18.9: It is easier to do things if you get triggered (reminded) to do them.

Figure 18.10: Activating all Nine Action Factors together makes building and sustaining new habits easier.

WHY DO WE NEED TO KNOW SO MUCH TO BUILD NEW HELPFUL HABITS?

Many of the thoughts and actions that are unhelpful for our health, happiness, and performance are what I call *simple behaviors*, like eating donuts, checking your phone too often, and beating yourself up. These behaviors are APE (Alive, Perceived, Energy) Brain–friendly and driven by human instincts connected to staying alive, achieving and maintaining social status, and conserving energy. These simple behaviors are increasingly agitated and exploited in the Learning War we are all fighting.

Unfortunately, many of the thoughts and actions that are most helpful for being our best in the modern world are what I call *complex behaviors*, like sleeping well, eating healthily, exercising sufficiently, not dwelling on negatives for too long, and becoming an outstanding leader. These behaviors are not APE Brain–friendly. They require us to learn new knowledge and skills and become expert habit builders or, in other words, Habit Mechanics and Chief Habit Mechanics.

The Nine Action Factors are constantly influencing your behavior (for better and for worse), but we are largely unaware of them. To help you take more control over your own thoughts and actions, I'll show you how to use the Nine Action Factors framework to your advantage.

USING THE NINE ACTION FACTORS

I use learning to drive as an example to understand more about how we can use the Nine Action Factors to help us build new helpful habits. Just like many of the things we would like to improve, driving is also a *complex behavior*, which is why it is a good example to use. Even if you haven't learned how to drive, this example will still make sense. Here are the nine factors and how they influence us when we learn to drive.

1. Habit Mechanic Mindset

Think of mindset as belief and what we believe. People with a *Habit Mechanic Mindset* believe they can improve anything with practice and take responsibility for being their best. People with an *APE Brain Mindset* believe they are only good at certain things, cannot change, and become victims of VUCA World Conditioning (Chapter 9, Figure 9.1). If we did not believe we could learn to drive and were not prepared to put the effort into learning, we would not have achieved this milestone. A Habit Mechanic Mindset is essential for learning to drive.

(To learn more about the origins of how I began to understand this factor, start with Professor Carol Dweck's work on mindset and Professor Walter Mischel's work on mastering your mindset by understanding your self-control, and see how these theories have developed over time.)

2. Brain State Optimization

In simple terms, this relates to how ready your brain is to learn. If you were sleep-deprived and took a driving lesson, you would unlikely be in the right Brain State to concentrate or gain anything helpful from the lesson. Equally, if you are stressed or in a bad mood, it will also be more difficult to learn. Remember: emotion drives attention; attention drives learning.

If we want to learn something new, we must be in the right Brain State.

(To learn more about the origins of how I began to understand this factor, start with Professor John Medina's "Brain Rules" work.)

3. Tiny Changes

This factor relates to the size or scale of the change we want to make (e.g., lose 15 pounds, get an extra hour of sleep per night, become the best leader in my business). In simple terms, we can make changes to behavior, but we can only make one tiny change at a time. If we want to learn to do something new, it is far more efficient to do it in stages and focus on making one tiny change at a time. For example, we learn to drive over extended periods and build a surprising amount of tiny new interconnected habits. We do not simply climb in the car and immediately gain a complete understanding of how to drive. Often, many first lessons just involve the student working out where all the controls are in the vehicle.

So, to best use the Tiny Factor, we should work toward an accumulation of tiny changes and improvements, instead of trying to make a single massive leap of progress. Here are some other examples:

- Want to lose one stone (or 14 pounds)? First focus on losing half a pound.
- Want to get an extra hour of sleep per night? Aim for one minute of extra sleep tonight, then build up to five minutes and so on.
- Want to be the best leader in your business? Start by building one tiny new habit that will improve your leadership.

In this book, I've deliberately used **"tiny" and "small" interchangeably**.

(To learn more about the origins of how I began to understand this factor, start with Professor BJ Fogg's work on tiny habits and see how these theories have developed over time.)

4. Personal Motivation

It's easier to make a change or build a new habit if you can connect it to a bigger meaningful goal in your life. This is one of the reasons why I asked you to create a FAM (Future Ambitious Meaningful) Story Iceberg (Chapter 16).

In the case of driving, you may have needed or wanted to learn how for work reasons, or to take your children to school, or to be the first qualified driver in your peer group, or some other reason. If we can connect the change we want to make to our bigger goals, dreams, and desires, this will provide motivation and make it easier to keep persisting with difficult changes.

(To learn more about the origins of how I began to understand this factor, start with Professor Edwin A. Locke's, and Professor Edward Deci and Professor Richard Ryan's, work on motivation and self-determination and see how these theories have developed over time.)

5. Personal Knowledge and Skills

We do not need to acquire new knowledge and skills to eat a donut, but it is often essential for complex behavior change—like learning to drive, improving our confidence, or enhancing our sleep or productivity, etc.

(To learn more about the origins of how I began to understand this factor, start with Professor Anders Ericsson's work on expertise and see how these theories have developed over time.)

6. Community Knowledge and Skills

What knowledge and skills do our families, peers, and communities have that might help us? Having a parent who knows how to drive can be helpful if you also want to learn (think of free driving lessons in supermarket car parks). A colleague knowing how to build better stress management habits is helpful if you also want to develop some.

The reason I try to make all our insights simple is so they can be easily shared among colleagues and families and across the Habit Mechanic community. The more people there are in your network who understand the Habit Mechanic Tools and language, the more powerful they become.

(To learn more about the origins of how I began to understand this factor, start with Professor Albert Bandura's work on social learning and see how this theory has developed over time.)

7. Social Influence

Our APE Brain is strongly influenced by the behavior of those people we look up to and respect. Remember, P stands for Perceived. So we implicitly worry about how we are perceived by these people because we want them to like us. In the case of learning to drive, if our parents think that speed limits can be ignored or there is no need for car insurance, they won't be good *role models* for us as learner drivers.

(To learn more about the origins of how I began to understand this factor, start with Dr. Stanley Milgram's and Professor Robert Cialdini's respective work on social influence and see how these theories have developed over time.)

8. Rewards and Penalties

Our APE Brain is strongly influenced by rewards and penalties. These can be social, intrinsic, or extrinsic. In the case of driving, people are rewarded for driving well and penalized for driving poorly. If you drive well, you will eventually pass your test and gain a full license (a reward). A long period of accident-free driving usually means a lower motor insurance premium (another reward). But breaking the speed limit can mean a fine, points, higher insurance, and, if you do it too many times, a lost license (in other words, penalties!). We can use rewards and penalties to help us build new helpful habits.

(To learn more about the origins of how I began to understand this factor, start with Professor B. F. Skinner's work on variable rewards and see how these theories have developed over time.)

9. External Triggers

External triggers in our modern world can be physical and digital. The smartphone is one of the most powerful external triggers ever designed. In a vehicle, we are surrounded by triggers. The speedometer shows us how fast we are traveling. A line in the middle of the road indicates which side we should drive on. A pedestrian crossing will remind us to stop. All of these are triggers, and they are often loaded with rewards and penalties. I will explain more about this later.

(To learn more about the origins of how I began to understand this factor, start with Professor Richard Thaler and Professor Cass Sunstein's "nudge" work and see how these theories have developed over time.)

SUMMARY OF THE NINE ACTION FACTORS

Think of each factor like a switch that you can turn on or off. If you "turn the switch on" for each factor, they will work for you, and building a new habit will become easier. But if the "switches are turned off," each factor will work against you, and building the habit will be more difficult. Learning how to turn each switch on is an essential Habit Mechanic skill, and something you will be much better at by the time you finish the book.

Test?

If it is helpful, write down the Nine Action Factors to see how good your memory is!

LEARNING HOW TO "SWITCH ON" THE NINE ACTION FACTORS

How Can I Learn to Develop a Habit Mechanic Mindset?

You are already developing one by reading this book. First, you are learning about science-based insights that show your abilities are not fixed and that you can change and improve. Second, you are learning how to build small new helpful habits so you can directly experience positive personal change. For example, if you have been using the Daily TEA Plan regularly, I would imagine you are already starting to see some success. This will build your confidence in your ability to make changes that help you feel and perform better.

How Can I Learn to Optimize My Brain State?

Start by using the insights shared in:

- Chapter 19 to improve your sleep, diet, and exercise habits
- Chapter 21 to improve your Activation
- Chapter 22 to improve your stress management
- Chapter 23 to calm your brain by building robust confidence
- Chapter 25 to supercharge your focus and productivity

These insights will help you become an expert at optimizing your Brain State, making it easier for you to build new habits and be your best.

Will You Remind Me to Focus On Making Tiny Changes?

Yes. This idea is built into the Habit Mechanic self-reflection and planning tools within this book, for example, Daily TEA (***Tiny*** Empowering Action) Plan.

How Can I Learn to Increase My Personal Motivation?

The Future Ambitious Meaningful (FAM) Story (Chapter 16) has been purposely designed to help you do this and has already helped thousands of other Habit Mechanics fire up their motivation.

An important motivation theory embedded into the Habit Mechanic self-reflection and planning tools is called self-determination. I will explain more about this and how to use it in "The Cultural Architect" (Chapter 32).

How Can I Learn the Knowledge and Skills to Help Me Develop the Habits I Want to Build?

If you want to develop habits to help you achieve the following outcomes, I am going to show you how throughout the remainder of the book.

- Improving diet, exercise, and sleep for better brain health and performance (Chapter 19)
- Better stress management (Chapter 22)
- Spending less time thinking unhelpful thoughts (Chapters 22 and 23)
- Being focused to drive productivity, creativity, and problem-solving (Chapter 25)
- Building and maintaining robust levels of confidence (Chapter 23)
- Performing well under pressure (Chapter 24)
- Better leadership for improved individual and team performance (Step 4—Chief Habit Mechanic skills)

To turn these insights into **Community Knowledge and Skills** (the sixth Action Factor), share what you have learned and encourage others to become Habit Mechanics.

How Can I Learn More about Using the Social Influence Factor?

In the "Chief Habit Mechanic skills" section (Step 4), you will learn more about:

- How people influence each other's behavior and habits
- How you can get better at influencing others by becoming a Team Power Leader
- How you can develop other Team Power Leaders who also positively influence other people's behavior in your team, group, or organization

How Can I Learn More about Using the Reward and Penalty Factor?

There are lots of "reward and penalty systems" deliberately built into the self-reflection and planning tools in this book. However, explaining the nuances of all of these is beyond the scope of this book. But I do want to spend a little bit of time explaining how you can deliberately create reward and penalty systems to help you build new habits.

"Carrot (reward) and stick (penalty)" is probably the most popular phrase used to explain this factor. But this phrase oversimplifies the complex inner workings of your brain. As I explained earlier, the APE Incentive component of the TRAIT Habit Loop drives your behavior. So when we are thinking about rewards and penalties, we must think in terms of what is rewarding for the APE Brain and what is not. I covered some of the basics of APE Incentives in the example APE Brain–friendly habits detailed in Chapter 17. Some of the key words used to describe APE Incentives were "using less energy," "immediate rewards," and "energy efficient," which is no surprise since your brain is designed to conserve energy. But now let's dig a little deeper to learn what else your APE Brain finds rewarding.

Familiar Reward and Penalty Systems

It is important to recognize the **reward and penalty systems** that influence our day-to-day lives. For example, why don't you speed when driving? There could be several answers to this question:

- I want to be a responsible citizen.
- I don't want to get a speeding fine or risk the cost of my car insurance increasing.
- Losing my license would be embarrassing.

Your answer could be a combination of the above, or a range of other answers. But broadly they will fall into three categories:

1. Intrinsic—how it makes me feel (e.g., being a responsible citizen makes me feel good).
2. Extrinsic—what I will get (e.g., cheaper car insurance saves me money).
3. Social—what people will think of me (e.g., losing my driving license might make people think less of me).

Some of your answers might fall into more than one category (e.g., being a responsible citizen makes you feel good [intrinsic] and might make others think you are a good person [social]).

Reward and penalty systems are built into our societies through laws that are designed to encourage people to behave in a way that is beneficial for society. Rules of conduct are used in a similar way at school, at work, and in other groups. For example, if you go to work, you get paid (reward).

Reward and penalty systems are also built into the products and services businesses are trying to sell you. It is said that all products and services can be put into three broad and overarching categories:

1. Health
2. Wealth
3. Relationships

If you purchase the product or service, it will increase one or more of these areas (reward), but if you don't make the purchase nothing will change (penalty).

Understanding this is helpful, because you can reflect on which laws, rules, and products or services (or reward and penalty systems) were, or are, most successful in influencing your behavior—and which are not. Further, you can begin to consider why some reward and penalty systems have more impact on your behavior than others. This will help you begin thinking about how you can better use rewards and penalties to help you build new habits.

The Secret Science of Achievement

We are hardwired to find improving and achieving both rewarding and motivational. For example, if you are on a diet and you are losing weight, it is easier to keep going because the feeling of achieving (or making progress) gives your brain a dopamine hit. However, if you step on the scale and you have gained weight, you are more likely to feel like giving up because you don't feel the efforts you are putting into changing yourself are paying off.

In simple terms, you get a brain reward (a prolonged hit of dopamine) when you feel like you are making progress, but a brain penalty (your dopamine levels and mood are lowered) when you are not.

Practical Actions

Set tiny goals—By setting tiny goals (remember the Tiny Factor) that are easy to achieve, you will more likely make progress, feel good, and keep going. For example, one minute of extra sleep tonight; five minutes of extra walking today; do one sit-up; write down one positive about your day at the end of each day. If you persist with tiny changes, they become the foundations of bigger results. For example, losing half-a-pound per week soon adds up to losing a significant amount of weight; starting with one minute of extra sleep per night can eventually result in gaining extra hours of sleep per week; five minutes of extra walking per day turns into extra miles every week; one sit-up per day quickly turns into 20 per day; one positive reflection each day turns into a more positive outlook on life.

Track your progress—Setting and reviewing your goals makes it easier to see the progress you are making. Also, if you notice you are not achieving the desired results, you can adjust your goals to make them easier to achieve and create some positive change momentum.

This book is packed full of Habit Mechanic Tools to help you monitor your progress. Here is another, which I call the "Me Power Weekly Wall Chart." I created it to help me plan for the week. I fill it in and stick it on my fridge at the beginning of each week.

Me Power Weekly Wall Chart

What are your goals for this week?	Why do you want to achieve these goals?	What will help you achieve your goals?

Mon	Tues	Wed	Thurs	Fri	Sat	Sun

Figure 18.11: Me Power Weekly Wall Chart

It has built-in reward and penalty systems. Here's how it works.

1. First, make a list of your goals for the week.
2. Next, answer the question, "Why do you want to achieve these goals?"
3. Then answer the question, "What will help you achieve these goals?"
4. Each day you achieve what you wanted to achieve, give yourself a tick (or a cross if you fail).
5. Aim to get as many consecutive ticks as possible, and create a "tick streak" (i.e., an unbroken run of days with a tick).
6. Set a new record for creating a tick streak (e.g., my previous personal best unbroken run was 3 days, now I want to break that record by achieving 4 days).
7. Finally, keep setting new records by breaking your longest tick streak.

To make it easier to complete, I have created a PDF template. I use this, and if you want to use it go to tougherminds.co.uk/habitmechanic and click on "Resources" to download your copy.

Gamification

By using something like the Me Power Weekly Wall Chart, you are beginning to gamify your reward and penalty systems. You can of course go much further (think "likes," points, badges, leaderboards, etc.). These techniques and others are what your favorite games, apps, restaurants, and brands increasingly use to hook you into coming back time and again.

Other techniques used are

- scarcity (sale, happy hour, buy-one-get-one-free offers, only limited places available);

- unpredictability (making a bet, scratch cards, playing the lottery, product drops); and
- loss (fear of missing out, breaking your longest streak, losing all your data if you unsubscribe, countdown timers to encourage you not to miss out on this fantastic offer).

All these tactics are being used against you every day in the Learning War.

The more knowledge you have of these reward and penalty systems, the better you will be able to use them to your advantage in building the habits that help you be your best. So I hope these introductory reward and penalty insights provide a good starting point for you.

How Can I Learn More about Using the External Triggers Factor?

The good news is you already have. For example, the Me Power Weekly Wall Chart is an external trigger (if you print it out and stick it in a prominent place). And like all powerful triggers, it doubles as a reward and penalty system.

Examples from Your Smartphone

What are the most powerful external triggers ever designed? I would argue that smartphones and watches are among them. This is because they are deliberately loaded with rewards and penalties, and are always very close by/strapped to you! A report by BBC News editor James Reevell detailed some of the science used by phone companies to get us hooked on their devices. He focused on several areas.

The "Dot Dot Dot" That Comes Up When You're Waiting For Someone to Reply to Your Text

This is designed to induce a small stress and dopamine response (dopamine is released in anticipation of a reward). It is connected to the "unpredictability" gamification idea I mentioned above. It is also called a "variable reward."

"Like" Buttons on Our Social Media Apps

This feeds directly into the APE Brain's subconscious concerns about how much other people like us.

Red Notification Dots

Most of us have been conditioned to relate red to mean danger, stop, and pay attention. So seeing the red dot can create a little stress response in your brain that compels you to take action (e.g., check the message NOW, because it could be an important one!).

Speed Camera Lottery

Another great example of an external trigger with a supercharged reward and penalty system is Kevin Richardson's speed camera lottery idea. Speed cameras already contain a powerful reward and penalty system, but Richardson took it a step further. He wanted to provide extra incentives for obeying the speed limit.

Here's how it works: Speeders get fined and money goes into a pot. If you are obeying the speed limit, your details will also be recorded and you will be entered into a lottery to have a chance of winning some of the money paid in fines by those who broke the speed limit.

Hot Triggers

When I was a teenager, I worked for one of the biggest fast-food companies on the planet. Back then, people had to physically come into the restaurant to buy their burger and fries. But that is not the case anymore. People can now use an app to order at home while sitting on their couch. So the fast-food companies' advertisements, whether on TV or the internet, have become what psychologists would call "hot triggers."

Remember, triggers are the first part of the habit loop. They remind you what to do. But some are more powerful than others.

When I was a teenager, a TV ad for a fast-food company might have reminded me that I liked their food. But it would not have compelled me to get up, go out of the house, and walk to their closest outlet (one mile away) to go and buy the food. It was too much effort.

But these new ads are hot triggers because they tell your APE Brain what to do right now (order some food via your smartphone), knowing that you can immediately place an order on your phone and the food will be with you within 30 minutes.

Also note that companies continually change their ads to keep them fresh—otherwise they become boring and less interesting to your APE Brain. Remember, it likes fun, exciting, new things.

Here are some other examples of hot triggers:

- Your phone buzzing in your pocket
- A piece of chocolate cake in your fridge (the place you look when you are hungry!)
- The seat belt alert noise to remind you to put it on

Why am I telling you this? Hot triggers have a powerful effect on what you do, and if you are aware of them, it is easier to make them work for you. For example, if your phone keeps distracting you when you are trying to complete a piece of work, turn it off and put it out of sight. If you want to create a Daily TEA Plan at the beginning of each day, print out the PDF and put it in a place where you will see it first thing (e.g., your desk).

If you have not already, go to tougherminds.co.uk/habitmechanic and click on "Resources" to download your copy of the Daily TEA Plan PDF.

Also, keep your hot triggers fresh. For example, I create bespoke monthly planners for some of my clients. But every month my designers create a new planner cover to make the planner more interesting for those using it.

ACTIVATING THE NINE ACTION FACTORS TOGETHER

You will be far more successful in building new habits if you plan to use all Nine Action Factors together. To help you do this, I have created the "Habit Building Plan," which I will show you how to use shortly.

> *But first we'll look at how you can begin to build better diet, exercise, and sleep habits to boost your brain health and performance.*

HABIT MECHANIC LANGUAGE YOU HAVE LEARNED IN CHAPTER 18...

Core Language

Nine Action Factors framework—Created to make it easy for you to use the latest insights from behavioral science to build sustainable new habits. ☑

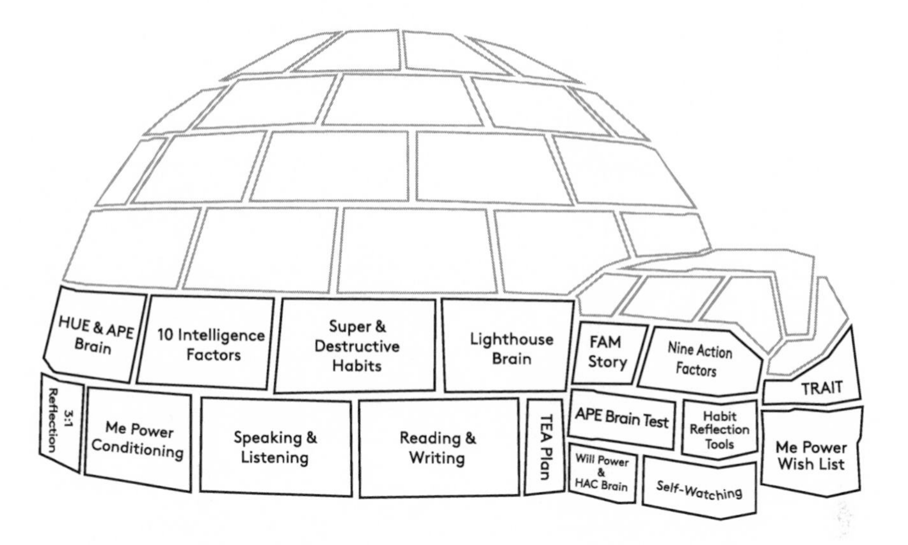

Figure 18.12: Your Habit Mechanic intelligence igloo is building up!

19

IMPROVE YOUR SLEEP, DIET, EXERCISE, AND BRAIN HEALTH IN THREE SIMPLE STEPS

Record-breaking and serial tennis Grand Slam winner Novak Djokovic gave a fascinating pre-Wimbledon interview in 2015. Djokovic explained to *Daily Telegraph* journalist Simon Briggs that he uses Self-Watching techniques.

That led Briggs to suggest Djokovic had the equivalent of a small CCTV camera on his shoulder, which allowed him to observe and break bad habits. The Serbian ace apparently liked the image and agrees he is constantly monitoring himself for negative energy and wasted potential. Essentially, he uses his "camera" to intelligently Self-Watch his behavior.

BUILDING MORE HELPFUL HABITS

Now that we have an understanding of the Nine Action Factors, we'll use this to help you build more helpful habits.

Step 1

The first step to building more helpful habits is to target the habit you want to improve.

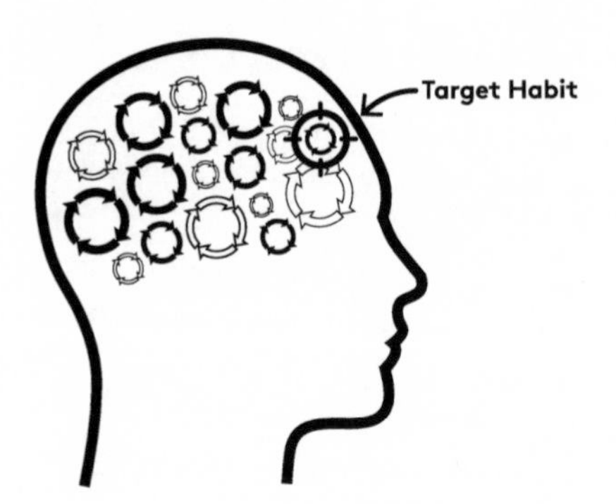

Figure 19.1: Although there might be lots of unhelpful habits you want to change, you will be more likely to experience "habit building success" if you start by targeting one.

Poor DIET, EXERCISE, and SLEEP habits are destructive for your short- and long-term health, happiness, and performance. If you have unhelpful habits in any of these three areas, your brain will not function properly—making it difficult to do anything to the best of your ability.

Most people can make improvements to at least one of these three areas. So this is often the first place people begin to build new habits.

Step 2

The second step to building a new helpful habit is to consider the knowledge and skills required to build the habit. Some habit building knowledge and skills will apply to building any habit. Others will be habit specific.

Figure 19.2: Steps 1 and 2 of the habit building process.

THE IMPORTANCE OF GOOD DIET, EXERCISE, AND SLEEP HABITS

Our Diet, Exercise, and Sleep (DES) habits are crucial for wellbeing and success. Diet, exercise, and sleep help maintain the hippocampus (or hippocampi—as there is one in each brain hemisphere), which is the main part of the human brain that produces new brain cells. These new cells are very important for helping us manage stress, perform well, and learn new things. Poor diet, exercise, and sleep can lead to the hippocampus becoming damaged. That makes managing stress and consistent high performance more difficult.

Good exercise and diet also help the brain release a protein called brain-derived neurotrophic factor (BDNF). This helps brain cells grow and flourish, so we can manage stress and learn more with less effort. Diet, exercise, and sleep are the foundation for

- better stress management;
- spending less time thinking unhelpful thoughts;
- being focused to drive productivity, creativity, and problem-solving;
- building and maintaining robust levels of confidence;
- performing well under pressure; and
- better leadership for improved individual and team performance.

Good DES habits are the foundation for work-life balance.

Now that we have a general understanding about the importance of DES for good brain function—the foundation of health, happiness, and performance—we can explore each area in greater depth.

Diet: What Should I Eat?

A good diet boosts brain function. There are many fantastic books you can read on how your diet impacts your gut and brain performance. Here, I want to share one quick insight that covers a lot of ground and is simple to understand.

BBC broadcaster and phone-in host Stephen Nolan learned how a bad diet with a high proportion of junk food affects our mental health. He discovered it damages the brain, not just the heart and the body.

By his own admission, Nolan has struggled with his diet and body weight. A few years ago, he produced a TV feature in which he traveled to New York to meet Professor Felice Jacka, a leading scientist from the International Society for Nutritional Psychiatry Research.

He learned that a bad diet produces unhelpful changes in the brain and that we must feed our brains well if we want them to function properly.

Nolan was shown that a high consumption of junk food means the hippocampus receives less BDNF. In short, a lack of BDNF can shrink the hippocampus. And brain shrinking is one of the signs of depression.

The broadcaster was told about a recent experiment. A group of healthy males were fed junk food for a week. After that week, the group all showed significant signs of diminished cognitive or brain function.

So when thinking about diet, you should begin with the brain in mind. Your brain needs a combination of energy, building blocks, and antioxidants to work properly.

4 Ways to Improve Your Diet for Brain Function

1. Eat the Right Energy

Although your brain only makes up around 3 percent of your overall body weight, it uses about 20 percent of your oxygen and around 25 percent of your glucose. It is best to eat complex carbohydrates, which release glucose slowly, for example, green vegetables, whole grain or whole wheat bread, whole wheat pasta and brown rice, sweet potatoes, beans, lentils, and peas.

2. Remember Fatty Acids

The brain is a fatty organ, so it needs fatty acids like omega-3 and omega-6 to work properly. Typically, we eat too much omega-6 (poultry, eggs, nuts, cereals, whole grain breads), but not enough omega-3. To boost your omega-3 levels, eat cold-water fish like tuna and salmon, and oily fish like mackerel. Kiwi fruit, soya beans, spinach, flax seeds, chia seeds, and walnuts are also sources of omega-3 fatty acids.

3. Stop Buying Junk Food

There is strong evidence showing that junk food can quickly damage brain function—as detailed in the Stephen Nolan story.

4. Get Plenty of Antioxidants

Having too many "free radicals" can be damaging to brain function. However, a group of molecules known as antioxidants can be used to combat the negative effects of free radicals. Oranges, other citrus fruits, red peppers, almonds, spinach, sweet potatoes, and broccoli all contain antioxidants.

Summary

What you eat can help or hinder your wellbeing, performance, and ability to build new habits. To help your brain function well, consider how you can incorporate the following into a healthy balanced diet:

- Complex carbohydrates
- Omega-3 and omega-6 fatty acids
- Antioxidants

Reflect?

If it is helpful, please use these insights to write down a few notes to help you improve your diet.

Exercise: Why Is It Important?

Exercise boosts brain function. Sometimes we misunderstand the term "exercise" and fail to appreciate that simply walking somewhere is exercise.

We should all recognize that any form of physical activity (especially walking) is beneficial. We would also all probably recognize that it is easy to become inactive and sedentary in our modern lives.

According to molecular neuroscientist Professor John Medina, humans are designed to move around (walk up to 12 miles per day) and solve problems, not to be inactive! But sedentary behavior is on the increase in our society, and this is problematic.

Exercise improves your brain power and boosts BDNF levels. It also makes it easier to HAC (Helpful Attention Control) your brain and

- regulate unhelpful thoughts;
- feel better and more motivated;
- be more productive;
- learn, be creative, and solve problems; and
- improve individual and leadership performance.

It is also important to recognize that different types of exercise impact your brain differently. Here are some examples:

- Lifting weights and strength training are connected to complex thinking, reasoning, and problem-solving.
- Aerobic exercise is thought to boost memory.
- High-intensity interval training helps regulate cravings, addictions, and appetite.
- Yoga is connected to strengthening brain circuits connected to emotional regulation.
- Outdoor daytime exercise (e.g., walking) can improve your mood because natural light helps activate brain chemistry that makes you feel good. Conversely, "seasonal affective disorder" (SAD) is activated by low levels of natural light.

Improving Our Exercise Levels

How much and what type of exercise should you do? A good place to start is by researching the government guidelines in your country. The guidelines I am most familiar with are the UK's—where I live. Here, the government recommends different volumes and types of exercise for people of different age groups. These recommendations include both aerobic and muscle-strengthening details. Please do check out the advice for your age group.

Here are a few quick insights to get you thinking.

Bones and Muscles

The UK government recommends that on three days per week adults do muscle-strengthening exercises. For example:

- Lifting weights
- Working with resistance bands
- Doing exercises that use your own body weight, such as push-ups and sit-ups
- Physical jobs, for example, mowing the lawn

Sweating

It is important that your exercise makes you sweat or perspire. Walking quickly is a good way to do this.

Trackers

There are many apps and physical activity trackers available that can be used as helpful ways of triggering and tracking beneficial levels of exercise. Also, if you are using a tracker beware of the "licensing effect." This means that people sometimes gain weight when they track their calories because they underestimate their calorie intake. For example, some might do a walk that burns 250 calories and then reward themselves with a chocolate muffin. They might not realize the muffin contains 450 calories!

Sitting

Exercise scientists will tell you that doing this for too long every day can kill you! Humans are not designed to sit for long periods in the way modern work often requires. To combat this people are using standing desks and employing tactics like "walking breaks." I have gone one step further and bought a treadmill workstation!

Reflect?

If it is helpful, please use these insights to write down a few notes to help you improve your exercise.

Sleep: The Impact of Poor Sleep

If you want to improve mental health, wellbeing, performance, and leadership in work and life, start by improving your sleep.

Think of your sleep like a bank balance. If you don't put enough in at the end of each day or week, you'll end up bankrupt. A lack of sleep has serious consequences for everyone, especially people focused on performing to their potential and people on whom others depend.

Dr. Matthew Walker, author of *Why We Sleep*, says: "We are socially, organizationally, economically, physically, behaviorally, nutritionally, linguistically, cognitively, and emotionally dependent upon sleep."

Scientists think sleep has two core functions. It removes toxins that build up in the brain during the day and it consolidates memories and learning. Sleep deprivation has some obvious and surprising consequences:

1. **Lack of sleep makes it more difficult to learn and develop.** It makes us more forgetful because it disrupts memory storage. And it has a negative impact on our ability to generate new brain

cells. In the VUCA (volatile, uncertain, complex, and ambiguous) world, where learning fast is a fundamental competitive advantage, doing anything that makes it more difficult to learn and solve problems is not a good use of time.

2. **Poor sleep habits lead to higher stress levels.** Sleep deprivation appears to impair the HAC (Helpful Attention Control) Brain, the part of our brain that helps us regulate our emotions so we can be calm, reasoned, and rational. This makes it more difficult to suppress our primal instincts, so we are more prone to do things we regret and say negative things to ourselves when we are sleep deprived.
3. **Inadequate sleep compromises our judgments and decision-making.** This includes judgments about the importance of sleep itself. A 2015 McKinsey report, *The organizational cost of insufficient sleep*, highlighted that 46 percent of business leaders believed lack of sleep had little impact on their leadership performance. At the same time, 83 percent of these leaders thought their organizations did not spend enough time educating those in high-profile, demanding positions about the importance of sleep. These confused insights suggest these leaders had not been getting enough sleep to make sensible judgments.
4. **Poor sleep habits are thought to increase the onset of prefrontal cortex diseases like Alzheimer's.** A recent edition of *New Scientist* ran a front cover that read: "Why lack of sleep is killing your brain." The research it was referring to shows how poor sleep habits have a long-term negative impact on brain health.

Sleep Quality and Quantity

Both sleep quality and quantity are important to consider. To help you understand more about your sleep quality, I have created the "sleep elevator" metaphor. Your sleep elevator travels over five levels. You move up and down between the five levels as you sleep.

Level 5: You are awake.

Level 4: You move from being awake into rapid eye movement (REM) sleep.

Level 3: You move from REM sleep to "Stage 1 non-REM sleep."

Level 2: You move from Stage 1 non-REM sleep to "Stage 2 non-REM sleep."

Level 1: You move from Stage 2 non-REM sleep to "Stage 3 and Stage 4 non-REM sleep," called "slow-wave sleep."

You start at Level 5 and slowly move down to Level 1, then slowly back up to Level 4, and so on. As you sleep, you move up and down in your sleep elevator. It is natural to arrive back at Level 5 during the night, meaning you wake up.

The most difficult sleep to achieve is probably Level 1. But you should aim to visit Level 1 in your sleep elevator three or four times per night.

Although everybody's need for sleep varies, modern science suggests our average nightly needs are as follows:

- 10–13 hours if you're aged 3–5
- 9–11 hours if you're aged 6–13
- 8–10 hours if you're aged 14–17
- 7–9 hours if you're aged 18–64
- 7–8 hours if you're aged 65+

But you are not average; you are unique.

So, do some personal research to work out how much sleep you need to be at your best every day. Personally, I think about an ideal target for the week (e.g., approximately 55 hours). This means if I have a bad night's sleep,

I can catch up at the weekend and also use power naps to top up my sleep during the week.

18 Ways to Improve Your Sleep

I have tried all these ideas, and many have become part of my sleep routine. As ever, nothing here is prescriptive, but I do encourage you to try things out to see what works best for you.

1. Develop Consistent Sleep Patterns

The time you get up has an impact on the time you can go to sleep. If you oversleep one morning (e.g., Sunday morning), it might be difficult to fall asleep early that night (e.g., Sunday night). Keeping regular sleeping habits is important for good, consistent sleep. As flexible work becomes the norm, this can be more challenging. I know that consistency is not always possible, and sometimes it is helpful to sleep in (to recharge your brain batteries). But aiming to be consistent will give you a better chance of being consistent, and improving your sleep.

2. Exercise

Doing enough exercise during the day can help you sleep better at night.

3. Take Care with Caffeine

Data shows that consuming caffeine six hours before going to bed has a negative impact on sleep, making it more difficult to get down to Level 1.

4. Reduce Your Alcohol Intake

Although alcohol can sometimes make you fall asleep quickly, be aware that it reduces sleep quality. This will potentially lead to poorer brain function, higher stress levels, and lower productivity levels the following day.

5. Drink Sour Cherry Juice

A research study in adults showed that people who drank two glasses of sour cherry juice per day achieved an extra 34 minutes of sleep per night. This study claimed sour cherries contain high levels of melatonin, a hormone responsible for sleepiness.

6. Eat for Sleep

Eating small carbohydrate and protein snacks before bed can help you have a good night's sleep.

7. Take Power Naps

Using short power naps to top-up on sleep can be helpful. Do some personal research to find out what works best for you. I find about 15 to 20 minutes optimal. But do not use power naps to replace a good night's sleep.

8. Avoid Social Media and Emails

Checking social media and emails before bed can make you feel anxious, thereby making it difficult to fall asleep and get good quality rest.

9. Monitor Your Tech Use

The light produced from smartphones, tablets, or laptops can make your brain think it is daytime and stop the release of melatonin, a hormone responsible for sleepiness. So I would recommend that you stop using these devices one hour before you go to bed and not using them in bed.

10. Dim Your Lights

Light is a signal to the brain that it is daytime, so take time to dim your lights one hour before you want to go to bed.

11. Stay Hydrated

Dehydration can make it more difficult to fall asleep and reduces sleep quality. On average, men are recommended to drink two liters of water a day. Women are urged to drink 1.6 liters of water a day. Be aware that caffeinated and sugary drinks (like sour cherry juice) will dehydrate you.

12. Control the Temperature

Sleep is triggered as body temperature reduces. If your bedroom is too hot, it will be difficult to fall asleep. Taking a warm bath or shower before bed is a way to deliberately increase your body temperature and subsequently induce a sense of sleepiness as your body temperature drops afterward.

13. Have a Getting-Back-to-Sleep Routine

Many people wake up in the middle of the night and struggle to get back to sleep. This can become an unhelpful and unwanted habit. To break this habit, you should build a "get back to sleep" routine. Do some research and develop a routine that works well for you.

14. Build the Right Environment

Humans are designed to sleep when it is dark and quiet and you feel calm. Make sure your bedroom and sleeping practices promote all three. For example, some people use eye masks to block out light and help them sleep.

15. Get the Right Bed, Pillow, and Mattress

What you sleep on will impact sleep quality. If you are sharing a bed with your partner, is it big enough? Is the mattress helping you secure a great night's sleep? Take time to invest in the best possible solution.

16. Use Habit Mechanic Stress Management and Confidence-Building Tools

Sometimes sleeping is a problem because we have unhelpful and wanted thoughts in our minds. In later chapters (21, 22, 23), I'll show you some specific Habit Mechanic Tools you can use to de-stress your brain at the end of each day, and improve your chances of sleeping well.

17. Use Sleep Tape

There is an increasing amount of research showing the benefits of mouth taping when you sleep. The main reason for doing this is to force you to breathe through your nose. The reported health and brain function benefits of breathing through your nose (inhaling and exhaling) are very interesting. This is something I am currently looking into.

18. Quit Smoking

Be aware of the negative impact smoking can have on your sleep. It is thought that nicotine's psychoactive properties are particularly disruptive for good quality sleep.

Creating a Getting-to-Sleep Routine

Through personal research, these are the things I've found useful to give myself the best chance of getting a great night's sleep:

- Go for a 25-minute run first thing in the morning—if I don't want to run, I walk.
- Use walking breaks through the day to top-up my exercise and make me feel tired at the end of the day/bedtime.
- Drink two liters of water throughout the day.
- Only have three caffeine drinks per day and stop drinking caffeine at 4 p.m.

- Finish my working day with some reflective writing to help me focus on what went well and what I can improve tomorrow, and to reframe any difficulties I came up against (I will talk about these techniques in more detail later in the book).
- Don't eat too much, or too heavy, close to bedtime.
- Stop using my phone, tablet, and laptop at least one hour before bedtime and don't use these devices in bed.
- Dim the house lights about one hour before bedtime.
- Be in bed reading a fiction book about 20 minutes before I want to go to sleep.

Reflect?

If it is helpful, please use these insights to write down a few notes to help you improve your sleep.

KNOWLEDGE AND SKILLS TO BUILD NEW DES HABITS

Whenever we try to improve our DES (diet, exercise, or sleep), we must remember that steady, tiny changes can lead to the development of powerful new habits and major behavior change. We should not try to change too much too quickly.

When you want to make a successful change (in any area of your life), it is useful to pay attention to two important concepts and big ideas.

Do your best to be your best: We have more control over our own wellbeing and performance than anyone else. For example, if you prepare to have a great night's sleep, you'll have a much better chance of sleeping well than if you did not prepare (but, success is never guaranteed). And while you can't control a family member waking you, you can control your get-back-to-sleep routine.

Similarly, while you can't control a colleague upsetting you, you can control how you react and manage your emotions.

Plan ahead: Our APE (Alive, Perceived, Energy) Brain is so powerful and potentially overwhelming that we must plan to outsmart it. For example, if we know we'll be tempted by unhealthy, high-calorie food in the work cafeteria, we should make a specific plan to help us make a healthier choice (e.g., take a packed lunch).

To make it easier for you to take responsibility for what you can control and plan ahead, I have created a range of Habit Mechanic Tools. Here is another called the "SWAP (Self-Watch, Aim, Plan) Cycle."

To begin building any new habit, including sleep, diet, and exercise, you can follow this simple three-step process.

Step 1—**S**elf-**W**atch
Step 2—**A**im
Step 3—**P**lan

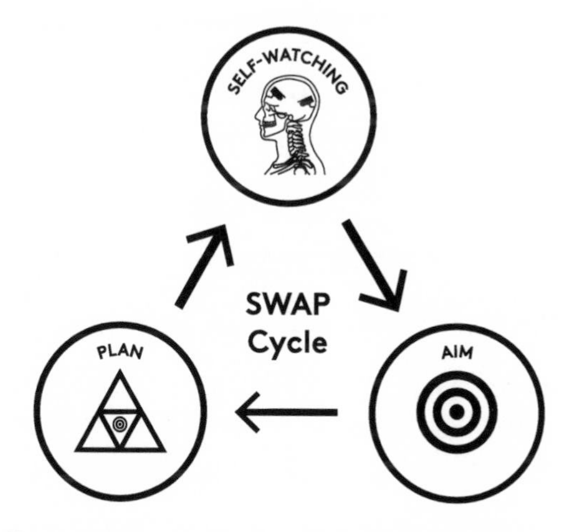

Figure 19.3: You can use this simple three-step process to help you begin making positive tiny changes.

Here's how the process works:

Step 1—Self-Watch

Our HAC (Helpful Attention Control) Brain is the prefrontal cortex. We can switch it on by Self-Watching (remember the Novak Djokovic example from the beginning of this chapter).

Most of our behavior is just a habit, so intelligent Self-Watching is a powerful technique you can use to identify and begin changing your bad habits. We do not need to be as painstaking or as adept at Self-Watching as a high-performance athlete like Novak Djokovic. We just need to get a little bit better at it.

The P2 Scale

To Self-Watch intelligently, we can use what I call the "P2 Scale" (Figure 19.4). P2 is an abbreviation meaning "poor (1) to perfect (10)." It helps us understand that we are neither useless nor faultlessly excellent at anything we do. We are in fact somewhere on a continuum.

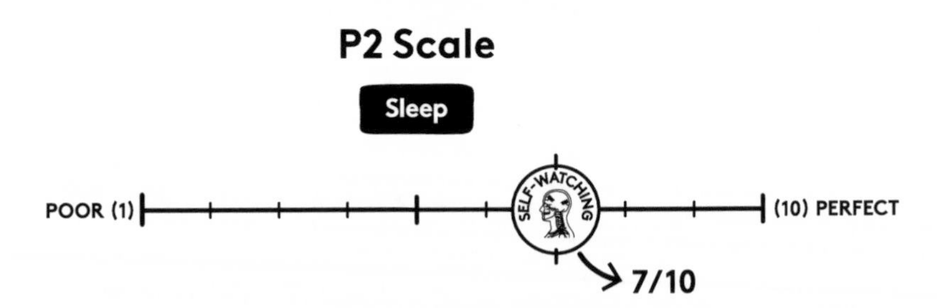

Figure 19.4: You can use the P2 Scale to put any area of your life that you want to improve (e.g., sleep or stress management or leadership or work performance or parenting performance, etc.) into perspective.

To understand how *you* can use the P2 Scale to help you Self-Watch and build new habits, I'll now show you how to create a SWAP Cycle. First, intelligently Self-Watch your DES habits.

- Rate your **sleep** last night on a scale of 1 (poor) to 10 (perfect). *Score:* _____ */10*
- Do the same thing for your **diet** in the last 24 hours. *Score:* _____ */10*
- Finally, rate your **exercise** (walking counts) in the last 24 hours. *Score:* _____ */10*

Step 2—Aim

Next, you need to create an Aim.

Here is my example (Aim): I am going to work on sleep. I scored 7 out of 10. I want to achieve a sleep score of 7.5 tonight. To achieve this, I will get an extra 10 minutes of sleep tonight (compared to last night).

To create your Aim, first highlight the DES area you want to work on in the next 24 hours.

Remember, we can only make one tiny change at a time. Select the area that will be most helpful for you to work on (diet, or exercise, or sleep). This will not necessarily be your lowest score.

Good Aims are carefully written down, are specific (using times and locations), state a positive action ("I will" instead of "I will not"), and can be measured (using quantities). Bad Aims are "get more sleep," "do more exercise," or "eat healthier." These are too vague to be helpful.

Remember, too, to start small (e.g., instead of aiming for one hour of extra sleep, start with one minute and build up). Build some change momentum!

Using the above instructions, why not take a minute to write down your sleep, or diet, or exercise Aim for the next 24 hours:

____

____

Step 3—Plan

The final step is to create a detailed and actionable Plan to help you achieve your Aim.

Like Aims, good Plans should be specific and measurable (e.g., turn my phone off, have a piece of fruit with lunch, get off the bus a stop early to boost my exercise). A bad Plan would be "go to bed earlier." This is too vague to be helpful.

I strongly encourage you to create a Plan that has at least three parts. This is because the APE Brain is very powerful, and without a multifaceted Plan your chances of failure will increase.

My Plan to get an extra 10 minutes of sleep tonight is:

Part 1—Stop drinking caffeine by 4 p.m.
Part 2—Turn off my laptop and phone by 9 p.m.
Part 3—Be in bed reading my book by 10 p.m.

Here are good and bad exercise SWAP examples:

✓ Good Example

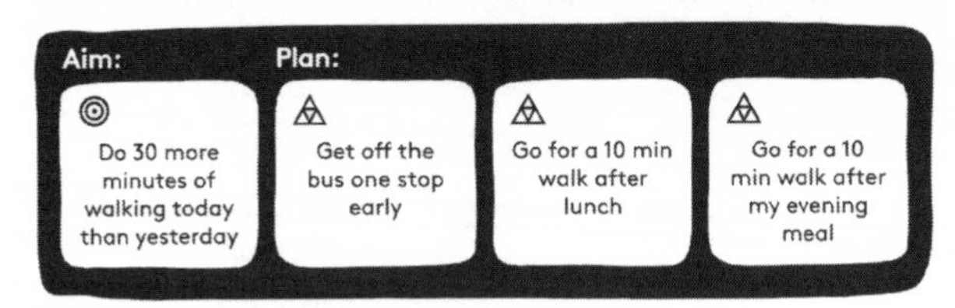

✗ Bad Example

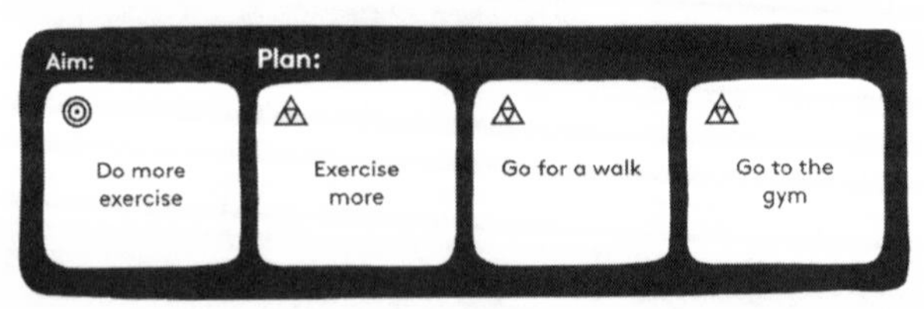

Figure 19.5: Creating great SWAPs is a skill you will get better at with practice.

Look back at the tips I shared for improving DES earlier in this chapter to help you create a powerful plan:

Part 1—

____.

____.

____.

Part 2—

____.

____.

____.

Part 3—

____.

____.

____.

ANOTHER HABIT MECHANIC TOOL TO HELP YOU

Why not use our "Seven-Day Diet, Exercise, and Sleep SWAP" tool to make it easier for you to begin building better habits every day? Go to tougherminds.co.uk/habitmechanic and click on "Resources" to download your copy.

Remember, you can only make one tiny SWAP at a time.

Test?

If it is helpful, write down what SWAP stands for to test your memory!

HABIT MECHANIC LANGUAGE AND TOOLS YOU HAVE LEARNED IN CHAPTER 19...

Core Language

DES—Simple shorthand for diet, exercise, and sleep. ☑

Planning Tools

SWAP (Self-Watch, Aim, Plan)—A simple tool to help you begin building any new habit. ☑

Seven-Day "Diet, Exercise, and Sleep" SWAP tool—A tool to help you build better DES habits daily. ☑

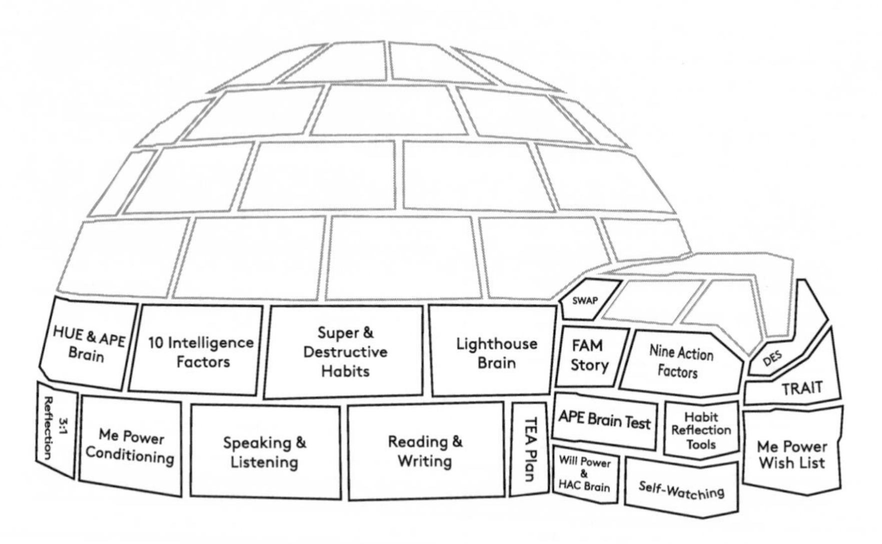

Figure 19.6: Your Habit Mechanic intelligence igloo is building up!

Next, we'll look at how to sustain good DES habits and introduce a simple plan you can use to activate the Nine Action Factors and build sustainable new habits in any area of your life.

20

CREATE YOUR OWN HABIT BUILDING PLAN USING THE SECRETS OF BEHAVIORAL SCIENCE

Olympic gold medal–winning triathlete Jonathan Brownlee converted the conservatory in his home into what he called a "kind of heat chamber." He has explained it gets as hot as 37 degrees Celsius (98.6 degrees Fahrenheit), so he can "sweat away in there on a turbo bike trainer…"

Brownlee's desire to transform part of his house began in Mexico, when he was leading a race where a win would have seen him crowned world champion. With 700 meters to go, he was so exhausted that he started to lose control of his legs. He slowed from a run, to a jog, to a standstill. The finish line was only 200 meters away. It looked like he couldn't take another step, but his older brother—double Olympic gold medalist and world champion Alistair Brownlee—sacrificed his own chance of winning and grabbed his brother by the arm, eventually carrying him over the finish line.

Jonathan Brownlee did not win the race and did not become world champion. When he reflected on his failure to win, he identified that he needed to improve his ability to perform in the heat.

Leaving no stone unturned, he consulted a medical doctor. Then he went to train with the British military to understand how he could best perform in such extreme conditions.

Jonathan Brownlee's inability to perform to his best in the heat of Mexico highlighted that his practice (training) was not as effective as it needed to be. His approach did not address all Nine Action Factors (in particular how the Mexico heat would impact his Brain State), and therefore it did not properly prepare him to perform to his potential.

If you want to give yourself the best chance of developing sustainable new habits that help you fulfill your potential, you need to take into account all Nine Action Factors. If you get behavioral science working for you, instead of against you, making positive changes in life will be much easier.

In this chapter, I'll show you how to put the Nine Action Factors framework into practice so that you can systematically build sustainable habits time and again.

ACTIVATING THE NINE ACTION FACTORS

Creating a SWAP Cycle is a great way to start making a positive change to any behavior, because it brings together steps one and two of the habit building process.

In Step 1, we recognize we need to improve a certain habit.

In Step 2, we consider the knowledge and skills required to make the change.

But to supercharge our chances of building a new habit, we need to consider Step 3—and use the Nine Action Factors to create a "Habit Building Plan." I will show you how.

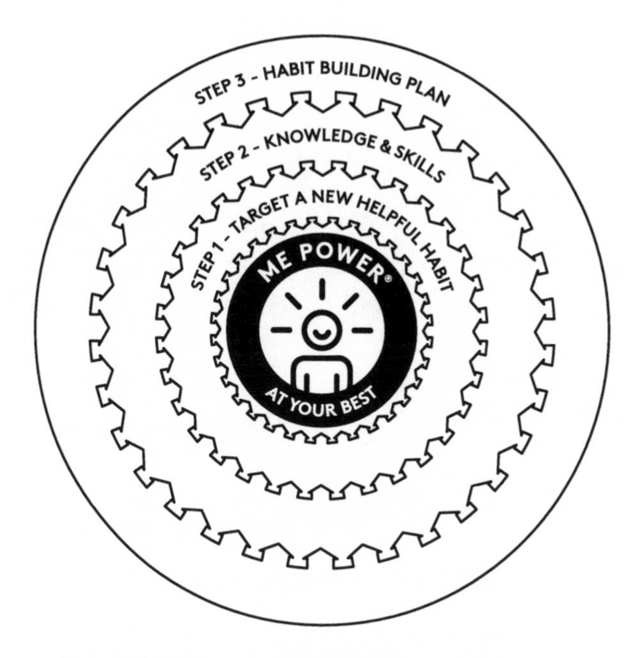

Figure 20.1: Steps 1, 2, and 3 of the habit building process.

I will use "building a better sleep habit" as an example to show you how to create your own Habit Building Plans. To begin, let's recap the Nine Action Factors and how they relate to sleep.

Imagine you want to build a better sleep habit. Here is how the Nine Action Factors can help you:

1. Habit Mechanic Mindset

Hopefully by now you have seen enough evidence to convince you that your brain is not fixed, and you can change (e.g., build better sleep habits).

2. Brain State

Plan to complete your daily diet, exercise, and sleep SWAP Cycle at a time of the day when you have enough Will Power to complete the task (e.g., in the morning).

3. Tiny Change Factor

The Aim you set within your SWAP Cycle should be tiny, clear, and well-defined (e.g., get five more minutes of sleep tonight than last night). This improves your chances of success and therefore helps build some positive change momentum.

4. Personal Motivation

Why do you want to improve your sleep habits? Maybe you're worried about your long-term brain health, or you might want to be more productive at work so you can get a pay raise. You should connect improving your sleep to your long-term goals and your FAM (Future Ambitious Meaningful) Story.

5. Personal Knowledge and Skills

You now know more about why sleep is important and the tactics you can use to improve your sleep. Think of the SWAP Cycle as a tool you can use to apply your new knowledge and skills. The more you practice your SWAPs, the better you will get.

6. Community Knowledge and Skills

If you share your new knowledge and skills about improving sleep with other people, it will help you reinforce your own understanding and help others build new helpful habits.

7. Social Influence

This works both ways. If we model new helpful behavior in our families, in our workplaces, and among friends, we will be helping and influencing them. Equally, if you want to build a new sleep habit, you need to encourage people at home to model this (i.e., work on their own sleep habits) as well because it will make it easier to build your own new habit.

8. Rewards and Penalties

You may want to sleep better tonight for an important day at work tomorrow. You will be rewarded if you sleep well (you will feel refreshed and ready to go), but you will be penalized if you sleep poorly (you will feel lethargic and not very mentally sharp). Your reasons for wanting to change will be connected to your Personal Motivation and FAM Story. Whatever the reasons, identifying the rewards or penalties on offer for a successful or unsuccessful change will be helpful.

9. External Triggers

These are the physical and digital reminders in our immediate environment that trigger our behavior. You may choose to set an alarm that signals it is time to go to bed. Completing a DES SWAP will also be a trigger. Finally, if everyone at home is working on building better sleep habits, that will also be a great trigger.

THE IMPACT OF YOUR HUE ON HABIT BUILDING

Before you create your Habit Building Plan, you need to consider how your HUE (Horribly Unhelpful Emotions) might hinder helpful behavior change. To help you do this, I have created a specific Habit Mechanic reflection tool called "How HUE Hinders Change."

How HUE Hinders Change

This tool will make most sense if you have already selected a habit to work on. If you have not, working through this exercise will still be insightful because it will help you understand all the ways HUE can make it more difficult for you to make positive changes.

The following 15 statements suggest the reasons your HUE might use to stop you from building new helpful habits and make you maintain your current unhelpful habits. If you agree with a statement, put a tick next to it. If you disagree, put a cross next to it.

1. If the new helpful habit does not give me a fast reward, it will be very difficult to build. ☐
2. If the current unhelpful habit feels good in the short-term, but I might regret it later, it is still worth doing. ☐
3. It will feel better in the short-term if I give up on this difficult new helpful habit. ☐
4. It is fine to give up when something gets difficult. ☐
5. It is better to give up than to be bored or frustrated. ☐
6. Feeling good in the short-term is better than being successful in the long-term. ☐
7. Everybody else in my social group is still using the old unhelpful habit, so building a new helpful habit might have a negative impact on their opinion of me. ☐

8. If I am not good at something after a little bit of practice, I will never be good at it. ☐
9. It is not my fault when I behave badly. ☐
10. Everyone is always judging me, so I cannot afford to try something new and fail. ☐
11. The positives of building this new habit far outweigh the negatives, but doing it will make me look odd (e.g., leaving my desk to go for a quick walking break). ☐
12. Admitting I can get better will make me look weak. ☐
13. Giving in to temptation today is fine, because I will start building the new habit tomorrow. ☐
14. If I try to build a new helpful habit and fail, that means I am a failure. ☐
15. Everyone else has the unhelpful habit, so why shouldn't I? ☐

Now reflect on the statements you have ticked. Write down in detail why, or how, you think HUE could stop you from building a new helpful habit. Start with the sentence "*My HUE could stop me because…*"

____

____

____

____

____

YOUR HABIT BUILDING PLAN

Finally, you need to create a Habit Building Plan, which helps you activate the Nine Action Factors (i.e., getting them working for you, instead of against you).

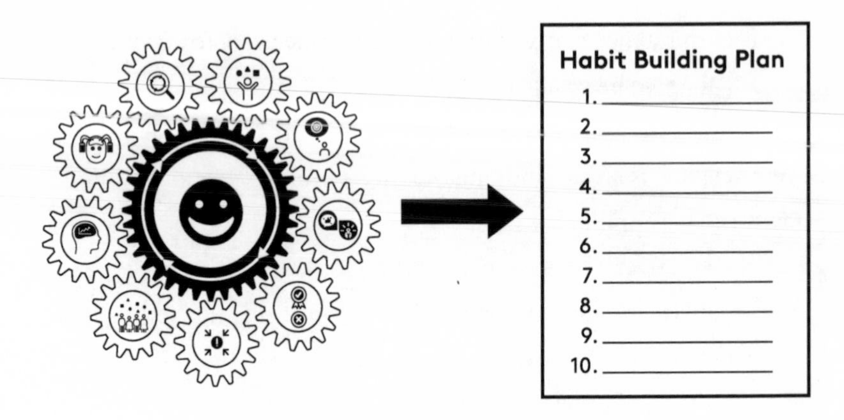

Figure 20.2: The Habit Building Plan is designed to help you activate all Nine Action Factors.

This form will make most sense if you have already selected a habit to work on (e.g., your Aim from the DES [Diet, Exercise, Sleep] SWAP [Self-Watch, Aim, Plan] you created in Chapter 19). If you have not, working through this exercise will still be insightful because it will help you understand what it takes to build a sustainable new habit.

Write down your answers...

1. Describe the SMALL specific new helpful habit you want to build (your Aim):

   ____

   Example answer: Get 10 minutes more sleep tonight than last night (rather than a vague or loose Aim like "get more sleep").

2. Describe what you currently do (your unhelpful habit instead of the new helpful habit you want to build):

   ____

   Example answer: Stay up watching TV instead of going to bed on time.

3. Describe what reminds or triggers this unhelpful habit:

   ____

Example answer: There are unlimited things to watch (on-demand) that are entertaining—sleep is boring.

4. Describe how you will remind yourself (trigger) to practice your NEW habit daily:

___

Example answer: Use my "Daily DES SWAP Plan," which I will stick on the fridge to remind me to complete it every day. Also set an alarm to remind me to go to bed.

5. Describe the new knowledge and skills you will need to help you secure your new habit:

___

Example answer: Do some personal research to gain an improved understanding of the factors that impact my sleep quality and the skills I can use to combat these.

6. If it is helpful, describe where and how you will acquire the new knowledge and skills you need:

___

Example answer: Re-read the "sleep" section of Chapter 19.

7. Describe in detail why you want to build this new habit:

___

Example answer: To give myself a better chance of being my best every day so I can perform well in my job and secure my next promotion.

8. Who can you ask to help you build your new habit? (Ideally they will also be building the same or similar habit at the same time.):

___

Example answer: My family. Also get them to use the "Daily DES SWAP Plan."

9. What will be the reward for building the new habit? Remember, rewards can be internal, external, or social.

___

Example answer: I will feel better, waste less time, and spend more time doing productive work, and I can spend more quality time with loved ones.

10. What will be the cost/penalty for not building the new habit?

    ____

    Example answer: The opposite of all the above.

I have created a PDF template of the "Habit Building Plan." If you want it, go to tougherminds.co.uk/habitmechanic and click on "Resources" to download your copy.

YOU ARE DOING GREAT!

I just want to take a moment to say well done on being prepared to be your best by becoming a Habit Mechanic. It is not easy, and it takes an enormous amount of courage. Many people are simply not prepared to go there. I am not blaming them because we are in a Learning War, and the odds are stacked against them.

But you are different—you are being proactive and putting your best foot forward to be your best. You are taking control of your own future. You are taking responsibility for your health, happiness, and performance. Remember, perfection is not the aim. The goal is simply to feel and do a little bit better every day.

When you analyze your habits, you probably will not like everything you see. But don't worry, you are not alone. Challenging ourselves to do a little bit better is an essential part of being a Habit Mechanic. If you keep persisting and trying and testing things out, I promise you will see results, one tiny habit at a time.

HABIT MECHANIC TOOLS YOU HAVE LEARNED IN CHAPTER 20...

Planning Tool

The Habit Building Plan—A tool to help you activate all Nine Action Factors when you are developing a new habit. ☑

Self-Reflection Tool

How HUE Hinders Change—An exercise to help you reflect on all the ways HUE might make it more difficult for you to build new habits. ☑

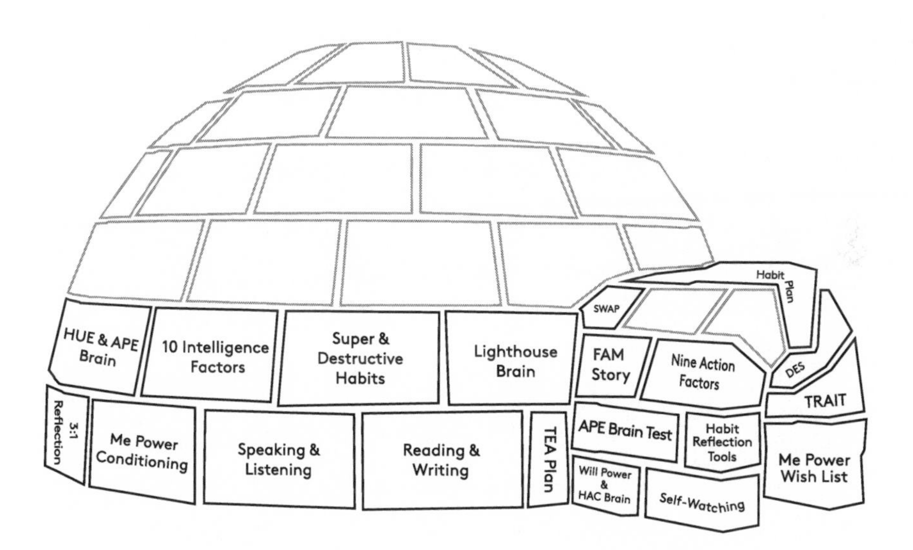

Figure 20.3: Your Habit Mechanic intelligence igloo is building up!

Next, we'll look at Activation management—which is just as important as DES for building new habits.

21

CONTROL YOUR ACTIVATION LEVELS TO FEEL BETTER AND MAKE EVERYTHING YOU DO EASIER

The New Zealand All Blacks are arguably one of the most successful sporting teams in human history. They are the only team with an overall winning record against every other country in the world. Their win rate over 100 years is around 77 percent. In recent history, it is 80 percent. And, in October 2015, they became the first team to win back-to-back Rugby World Cups.

In both the build-up and aftermath of that tournament, much press coverage highlighted how the All Blacks drew on collective and individual mental resilience to help them prevail in the face of on-field setbacks and challenges.

These high levels of resilience were not an accident, but something the All Blacks purposefully developed through a deliberate process of acquiring key mental skills. This was undertaken in the noughties (the decade from

2000 to 2009) as a response to several high-profile defeats that appeared to be the result of choking under pressure.

The All Blacks sought to develop a culture that focused on individual character and outstanding leadership. One of their mantras was "Better People Make Better All Blacks." A central pillar of their on-field performance approach was to "keep a blue head," that is, an optimal performance state, and avoid often unhelpful and panicky "red head" states. I think of this as an All Black intelligent Self-Watching process. You can learn how to use a similar approach to manage what I call "Activation."

In this chapter, I'm going to introduce the concept of Activation, and also show you how to proactively manage your "Activation levels."

THE POWER OF ACTIVATION

Another way to describe the All Blacks' blue and red head states is Activation. Being able to manage your mental and physical Activation is essential if you want to be your best and fulfill your potential.

Activation is a concept I've developed to make it easier for people to better manage their sleep, relaxation/downtime, focus, and stress levels.

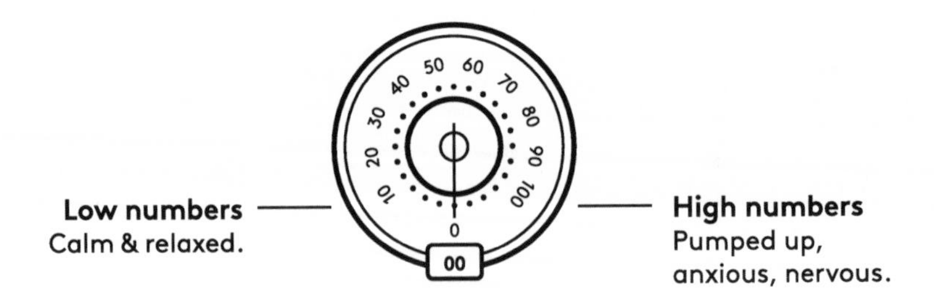

Figure 21.1: A simple overview of the Activation scale, or sometimes I refer to it as the Activation dial.

Optimizing diet, exercise, and sleep (DES) habits will be the foundations for your health, happiness, and success. But building better "Activation management" habits comes a close second. All four are interconnected. Achieving the correct Activation levels can make DES habits easier to build. And building better DES habits can make it easier to achieve optimal Activation levels.

Activation management is essential for building more helpful habits in all the areas I have discussed:

- Improving diet, exercise, and sleep for better brain performance
- Better stress management
- Spending less time thinking unhelpful thoughts
- Being focused to drive productivity, creativity, and problem-solving
- Building and maintaining robust levels of confidence
- Performing well under pressure
- Better leadership for improved individual and team performance

All make it easier to manage work-life balance.

WHAT DO WE MEAN BY "ACTIVATION"?

Imagine a scale that runs from zero all the way to 100.

Only those who are no longer with us are at zero on the Activation scale. Low numbers represent feeling sleepy, calm, and relaxed. High numbers represent being excited, pumped up, or nervous. If your heart is beating as fast as it can, you'd be at 100 on the Activation scale.

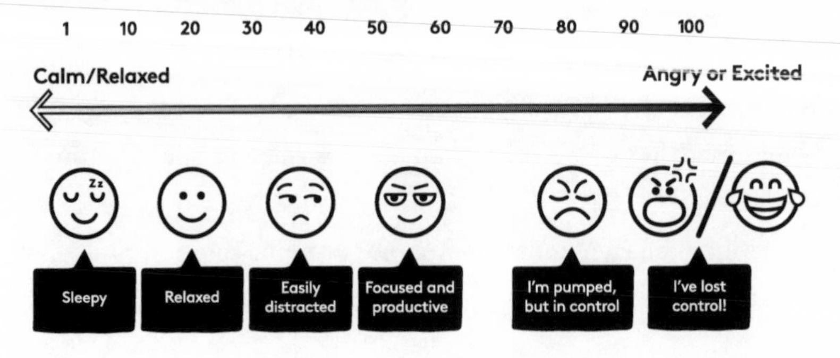

Figure 21.2: A more in-depth insight into different Activation levels. These are my personal examples.

Understanding your ideal Activation level for different tasks and activities, and having the knowledge and skills to control your Activation, is a core ingredient of health, happiness, and performance (imagine trying to sleep if you were at 100!).

By doing some personal research on my Activation levels over the years, I have worked out my ideal levels for different tasks and activities. Here are some examples:

- Sleep—between 1 and 5
- Relaxing/Switching off—between 10 and 20
- I find that when I am between 30 and 50 it is easier for me to get distracted and procrastinate on difficult jobs I need to get done.
- Focused work—between 55 and 60
- Delivering a presentation—65
- Pumped up enough to make a good rugby tackle—between 80 and 85

But your optimal levels will be different than mine, although I am sure there will be a lot of similarities.

THINKING ABOUT YOUR IDEAL ACTIVATION LEVELS

A simple Self-Watching exercise can help you learn more about your daily Activation levels. Remember, Self-Watching is the first stage of a SWAP (Self-Watching, Aim, Plan).

Don't worry if you are not 100 percent certain of your answers. If you are unsure, go with your gut. The more you think about your Activation, the more you will learn which Activation levels work best for you.

First, write down the Activation level (number) you think you are at right now. _____

Next, if you can, stand up. Then, if you can, jump up and down on the spot for 5 or 10 seconds. Now, write your new Activation level. _____

Tip: Getting up and moving around can quickly increase your Activation level.

Next, write down the ideal Activation level you think you need to achieve to fall into a deep sleep tonight (e.g., 1). _____

Next, think about how easy you find it to achieve the correct sleeping Activation level. Rank this from 1 (difficult) to 10 (easy). _____ */10*

To perform well at work, you need to achieve a certain Activation level. On average, people feel they need to be around 50 on the scale to work efficiently and effectively. I call this the "Ideal Work" Activation level.

Write down your Ideal Work Activation level (e.g., 55). _____

How easy is it for you to consistently achieve the correct Ideal Work Activation level? Rank this from 1 (difficult) to 10 (easy). _____ */10*

Reflect?

If it is helpful, write down a few notes on what you have learned about your Activation levels.

LEARNING MORE ABOUT YOUR OPTIMAL ACTIVATION

Different Activation Levels to Boost Your Learning

Activation can positively or negatively impact many other areas of your life. Have you ever been trying to read a complicated report and it feels like the words are bouncing off your eyes, and that nothing will go into your brain?

Part of the problem here is that your Activation level is incorrect. Alertness is the first part of concentration—if you are not alert, it will be harder to learn the information in a complicated report. So, the first step to maximizing your focus, learning, and performance on a given task is understanding which Activation level is ideal for that task.

Write down the ideal Activation level (number) YOU think you need to be at to successfully complete a difficult piece of reading. For me, it is 60. ______

It is highly likely that your Ideal Work Activation level has a range, and different learning tasks, at different times of the day, might require slightly different ideal Activation levels. It is important to be aware of your ideal Activation levels (for different tasks and activities) to give yourself the best chance of achieving that correct level—whether for the first task in the morning, at lunch, or at the end of the day. I will explore this in more detail in Chapter 25, where I will explain Brain States in more detail, and show you how to create a "Will Power Story" to optimize your focus each day.

Different Activation Levels to Boost Your Performance

Activation can also be used as a performance skill. For example, to deliver an excellent presentation you need to achieve a certain Activation level (e.g., 65).

According to reports, New Zealand rugby players consciously managed their Activation during training and matches. Rugby is a physical sport, and certain skills require high Activation to perform them well. For example, making a successful rugby tackle requires high Activation—say an 85. But if your Activation is too high (99), you might give away a penalty.

However, other actions in rugby—such as taking a successful penalty kick—require much lower Activation—maybe a 50.

So different activities have different ideal Activation levels. You might have to switch between these to optimize your performance.

Relaxation Activation Levels

As well as considering ideal Activation levels for learning and performance, we should also think about ideal levels for relaxation (e.g., taking a break and switching off). Sleep is the ultimate way to recharge your brain, but you also need to use relaxation activities for the same purpose. I call these activities "Non-Sleep Recharge."

Research shows many of us do not make optimal use of relaxation and downtime. Our brains are not recharging properly during these periods. After a break, you should feel refreshed and recharged. Yet many of us feel more tired than we did before.

One of the challenges here is HUE (Horribly Unhelpful Emotions). It is on a constant search for threats and problems or new, exciting, fun things that make us feel good. These activities require higher levels of Activation than are helpful when we are trying to recharge our brains (e.g., spending breaks on our smartphones or social media or worrying about things we cannot control is not a good way to recharge our brains).

Think about the ideal Activation level you should be trying to achieve during breaks and downtime to help you quiet your mind and recharge your brain (e.g., at break times I Aim to reduce my Activation level to a 20). Think of this as your Optimal Non-Sleep Recharge Activation level.

Write down your Optimal Non-Sleep Recharge Activation level: _____

HOW CAN I MANAGE MY ACTIVATION LEVELS?

Self-Watching and recognizing which Activation levels YOU need to achieve (your Aim) during different tasks, performances, and times of the day is the first step to successful Activation management. But you also need Plans to make your ideal Activation levels a reality.

To help you make better Plans, we are going to explore the brain science behind Activation management. We will begin by introducing the brain chemistry connected to Activation.

Getting the Basics Right—Activation Science

Brain activity is generated partly by electric impulses and partly by chemical messengers called neurotransmitters. Some of your neurotransmitters can help you manage your Activation.

Glutamate and GABA are two important neurotransmitters in relation to Activation. Glutamate excites the brain, and GABA slows down activity. Many scientists also recognize three other types of neurotransmitters as being particularly important:

Serotonin helps keep brain activity under control and helps you reduce Activation levels.

Noradrenaline or **Norepinephrine** is essential for achieving the type of Activation levels you need for focused work, study, and practice.

Dopamine allows you to sharpen and focus your attention onto the things you need to learn. Best known for making you feel good, it also acts like a save button for the brain, making it essential for learning new information.

Successfully managing DES (diet, exercise, sleep) is key to giving your brain, and therefore your brain chemistry, the best chance of working properly. That's why I ask you to focus on developing good daily DES habits, because it makes managing your Activation levels easier.

Now that we've covered the basics, let's think about some specific techniques and tools you can use in your Activation management Plans.

Breathing Management

Breathing management is the most powerful technique you can use to both increase and decrease Activation.

Increased Activation is strongly connected to what is commonly called the fight or flight (or freeze) response. This is driven by a reaction in our brain's HPA (hypothalamic-pituitary-adrenal) axis when we experience a stress response.

In the 1970s, Professor Herbert Benson from Harvard University wrote *The Relaxation Response* about successfully managing the fight/flight response.

Benson showed that breathing is the fight/flight factor we have the most control over. By reducing our breathing rates, we can also reduce our heart rate, blood pressure, metabolism, muscle tension, and mental arousal. So **Activation can be lowered by reducing breathing rates**.

Equally, when we increase our breathing rate, our heart rate, blood pressure, metabolism, muscle tension, and mental arousal also increase.

So, **Activation can be increased by breathing faster** or by doing activities that cause you to breathe faster.

To master breathing control, you need to understand how thinking works. Imagine that your thoughts have two different but connected parts: self-talk and mental imagery.

Controlling Your Thoughts

To understand this, let's think about how the All Blacks controlled their Activation during a game. Former All Black Brad Thorn is one of the most successful rugby players of all time. He won 20 major titles, including a World Cup, in a 22-year career.

In an article for the *Independent* newspaper, Brian Ashton (former England rugby union coach) reported that Graham Henry (the then head coach of the All Blacks) had disclosed Brad Thorn's very practical trigger for cooling down his emotions. He poured a bottle of water over himself. This helped him move himself from an unhelpful "red head" state (e.g., approximately 90–100 on the Activation dial) during a game to a more helpful "blue head" state (e.g., approximately 50–80 on the Activation dial).

Often in sport, people talk about having fire in your belly and ice in your veins and head—and not letting the fire melt the ice. This was Thorn's way of making sure his fire did not melt his ice.

What Can We Learn from This?

First, it is important to recognize that Thorn made a conscious decision to pour the water over his head and face to help him achieve a more helpful thinking state. So, this is an example of Brad Thorn deliberately HACing (hacking) his brain (or regulating his emotions).

To understand what Thorn might have been thinking, and what we can learn from this, let's dig deeper into "self-talk," or the words we say in our heads.

Self-Talk and Focus Words

To prompt ourselves to do things, we talk to ourselves: "I need to finish this report by tomorrow." "I am so tired; I need to get an early night." "That donut looks so good; it will taste amazing, and I need to have it!" "I am getting angry so I will pour some water over my head and face to help me calm down." ☺

You are talking to yourself right now as you read these words. Previously we used the example of wearing an invisible pair of headphones to illustrate this point.

Gaining control over your self-talk is vital if you want to gain control over Activation. When we deliberately use words to help us think more effectively,

I call them "Focus Words." For example, telling yourself to "Focus" and "Get on with it" can help increase your Activation. Telling yourself to "Focus on my breathing and slow it down" can help you reduce your Activation and relax.

If you don't have control over your self-talk, you might be telling yourself things that have a negative impact on your Activation—for example, "I am nervous," "I am useless," or lying in bed at night telling yourself how terrible tomorrow will be if you don't get a good night sleep. These examples will not help you control your Activation and will trigger a stress response (we will dig deeper into "the stress response" in Chapter 22). The good news is you can learn how to get better at controlling your self-talk with practice, and I will show you how later.

Mental Imagery and Focus Pictures

As well as self-talk, we also think in pictures or mental imagery. Mental imagery is an important part of your thought process. You constantly use it.

For example, picture, in your mind's eye, your home's front door. Without having any visual stimulus, you can see a picture *in* your mind's eye.

Visually, you are constantly switching between what you can see through your eyes (e.g., this book) and what you can see in your mind's eye.

When we deliberately use pictures to help us think more effectively, I call them "Focus Pictures." For example, picturing the Activation dial (in your mind's eye) getting lower and lower as you deliberately slow down your breathing can help you reduce your Activation level. Imagining the Activation dial increasing can help you increase your Activation level. Equally, you could imagine yourself lying on a peaceful beach to help you relax, or imagine a person who has upset you in the past to pump yourself up.

If you don't have control over the pictures in your mind's eye, you might be seeing the worst-case scenario unfolding. This will not help you control your Activation. The good news is you can learn how to get better at controlling your mental imagery with practice, and I will show you how later.

Brad Thorn's Self-Talk and Mental Imagery

When Brad Thorn was pouring water over himself, I do not know exactly what he was thinking. But I do know his thoughts were likely a combination of both self-talk (or Focus Words) and mental imagery (or Focus Pictures). So below I have mapped out a hypothetical example of his thinking process. This is designed to help you understand how you can better use Focus Words and Pictures to manage your Activation.

First Thorn had to do some intelligent **Self-Watching**: he noticed he was not at the correct Activation level. This would have involved him talking to himself: "You need to get out of the red head zone and into the blue head zone."

As he did this, he might have also pictured the Activation dial in his mind's eye and noticed it was too high.

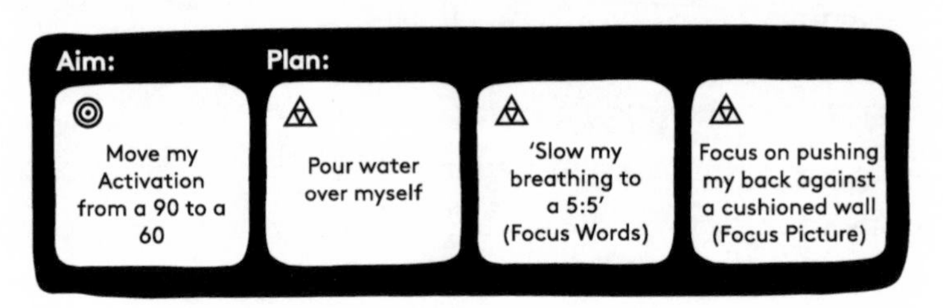

Figure 21.3: Brad Thorn's hypothetical Aim and Plan.

Next, he might have set an **Aim**. He might have said to himself, "I need to move down from a 90 to a 60." So achieving an Activation level of 60 was his Aim.

Finally, to change his Activation he needed a **Plan**. The first part of his Plan was getting a bottle of water and pouring it over himself.

The second part of his Plan—which was triggered by pouring water over his head and face—might have been to control his breathing.

He might have used a relaxation technique called "centering," which is designed to begin and manage the Relaxation Response by reducing breathing rates and body tension. This is achieved by first standing or sitting in a comfortable position with your body weight equally distributed between the left and right sides of your body.

Brad Thorn was standing, and to achieve a centered position he might have imagined (a Focus Picture) that he was pushing his back flat against a soft cushioned wall, making sure that his legs were straight and flat against this wall. Next, he might have used self-talk (Focus Words) to focus on slowing his breathing pattern down to what I call a 5:5—talking himself through the process of breathing out for five seconds and then breathing in for five seconds, and repeating this pattern.

He might have told himself to inhale through his nose and draw the air down into his stomach. He might have used words such as "loose" and "relax" to help release some of the tension in his neck and shoulder muscles. Finally, he might have pictured the Activation dial in his mind's eye, and focused on moving the dial down from a 90 to a 60 as he exhaled.

This might have all happened within a period of 60 seconds. And because Brad Thorn had spent time practicing his Activation management, moving it from knowledge-to-skill-to-habit, it was a reasonably effortless process for him.

I know that pouring a bottle of water over your head is not that practical when sitting at your desk, so don't feel you have to follow this example step by step ☺. I will show you how to apply these ideas in your day-to-day life shortly.

Reflect?

If it is helpful, write down a few notes about what you have learned about using breathing, and Focus Words and Pictures, to manage your Activation.

ACTIVATION MANAGEMENT HABITS

We can think about my description of Brad Thorn's Activation management within the TRAIT Habit Loop.

The **Trigger** is him recognizing his red head state.

His **Routine** used self-talk and mental imagery to slow his breathing, relax his body, and pour cold water over his head and face.

The **APE** (Alive, Perceived, Energy) **Incentive** was that this routine would help him perform better and reap all the associated rewards—like winning the Rugby World Cup.

Finally, the **Training** effect was the more Brad Thorn practiced this routine, the easier it became.

In the context of the Lighthouse Brain, we can imagine Brad Thorn was using this technique to help Will Power get HUE's attention onto what was most helpful. The more Thorn practiced, the more automatic it became for Will Power to help HUE pay attention to helpful thoughts.

The Brad Thorn example demonstrates the importance of breathing management, self-talk, and imagery in successful Activation management.

HOW TO SELF-WATCH YOUR ACTIVATION DURING THE DAY

To help you effectively match your daily tasks and activities to the correct Activation levels, I have created a Habit Mechanic Tool called the "Optimal Activation Review."

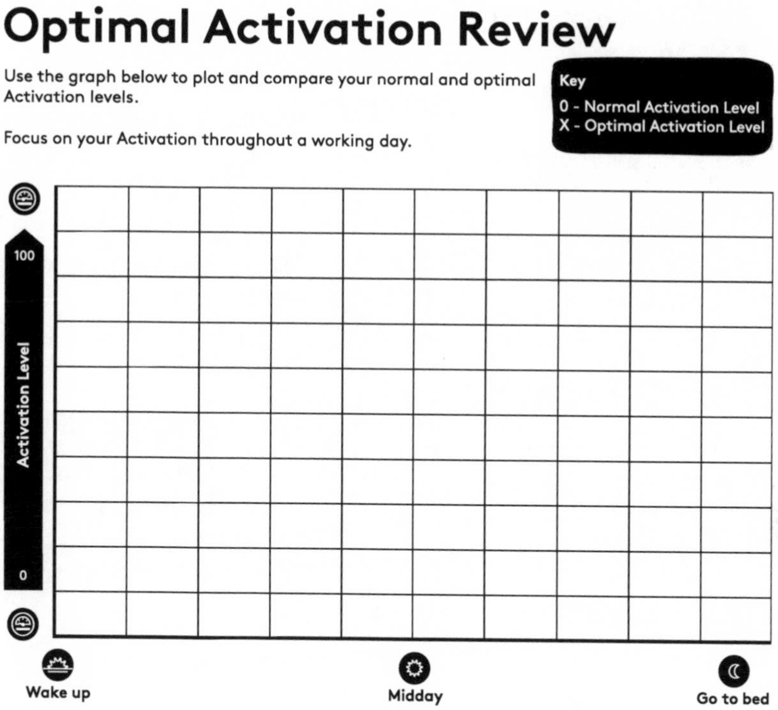

Optimal Activation Review

Use the graph below to plot and compare your normal and optimal Activation levels.

Focus on your Activation throughout a working day.

Key
0 - Normal Activation Level
X - Optimal Activation Level

100
Activation Level
0

Wake up
Midday
Go to bed

Figure 21.4: A blank Optimal Activation Review template.

You can use the Optimal Activation Review to track and compare normal and optimal Activation levels throughout a working day. If you work in the office some days, and from home on other days, you might want to create a separate profile for each situation.

This is a very visual process. To download the Optimal Activation Review PDF, go to tougherminds.co.uk/habitmechanic and click on "Resources" to get your copy.

Once you have downloaded it, take time to complete it.

Completing Your Optimal Activation Review

This tool will help you learn more about your Optimal Activation. The horizontal scale represents one day—from waking in the morning to going to bed in the evening. The vertical scale shows your Activation level from 0 to 100.

I have used a personal example to help you understand how the Optimal Activation Review tool helped me improve my Activation management. First, I plotted "Os" to show my normal Activation profile.

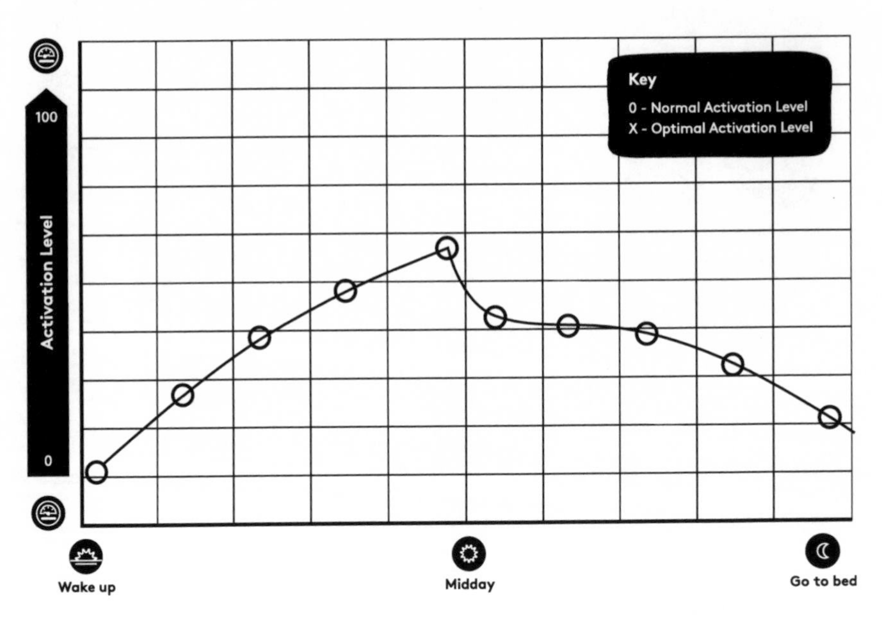

Figure 21.5: Optimal Activation Review showing my normal (now my old) Activation profile.

Before I improved my Activation management, I woke in the morning and my Activation level gradually rose as midday approached. It reached approximately 60 on the scale. But then it fell relatively quickly after lunch, which did not feel ideal.

Once I'd plotted my normal Activation profile, I then used crosses (Xs) to plot my ideal (or optimal) Activation levels throughout the course of a day.

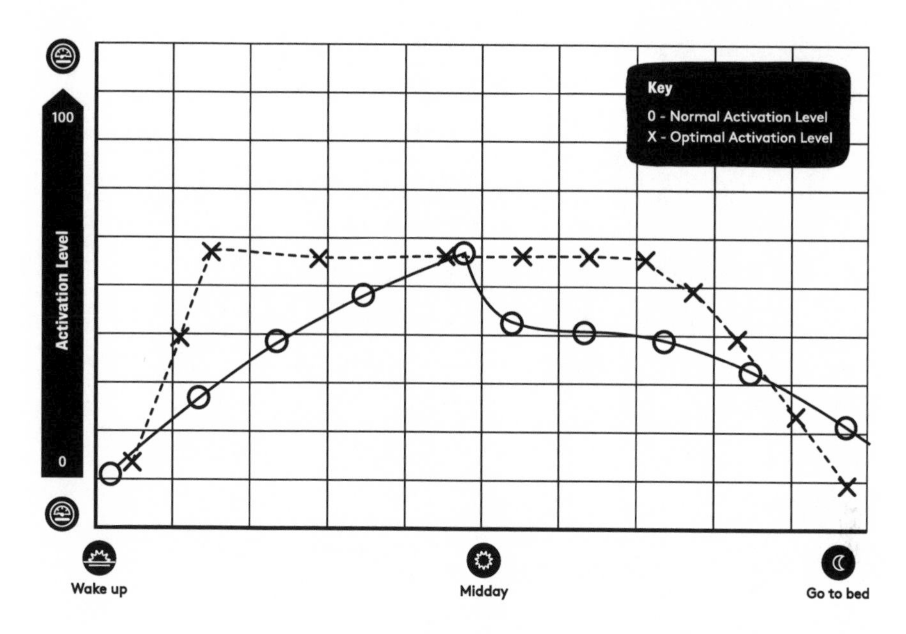

Figure 21.6: Optimal Activation Review showing my normal (but now old) Activation profile (Os) and my ideal (now my current) Activation profile (Xs).

By doing this, I was able to identify my biggest Activation challenges throughout the course of the day (which were in the morning and after lunch) and improve my Activation management. I will explain exactly how I did this in Chapter 25 when I show you how to create a daily "Will Power Story." But now I will share some specific Activation management skills you can begin using immediately.

HOW TO IMPROVE NIGHTTIME ACTIVATION MANAGEMENT

Now that you have identified your biggest daily Activation challenges, let's dig deeper into Activation management improvement skills. We will build on the breathing management and Focus Words and Pictures skills I have already introduced.

Let's start with sleep. When you want to sleep, you need to lower your Activation levels. Think about the sleep elevator metaphor from earlier in this book (Chapter 19), where sleep has five levels and you move between them like an elevator does between five floors in a building.

You start at Level 5 (awake) and slowly move down to Level 1 (slow-wave sleep), then back up to Level 4, and so on. As you sleep, you move up and down in your sleep elevator, and it is natural to arrive back at Level 5 (awake) in the night.

Let's think about how you can reduce your Activation to secure better quality sleep.

STOP Your Technology Unintentionally Increasing Your Activation Levels!

To bring down your Activation levels low enough to fall asleep, you need sufficient levels of a sleeping hormone called melatonin to be present in your brain. Melatonin production is controlled by light. During daylight hours, your melatonin production is low. And using a hand-held screen that produces light, like a smartphone, tablet, or laptop, also reduces melatonin levels.

As well as reducing melatonin levels, the information you see on your devices might be exciting. This increases neurotransmitters like noradrenaline and dopamine. Or it might be stressful and increase hormones associated with the fight/flight response, like cortisol. Either way, it is not helping you achieve your ideal sleeping Activation level.

So the first step to achieving your sleep Activation level is to turn off technology one hour before you go to bed, and don't use it in bed.

Use Warm Water

You can use warm water (e.g., take a bath or shower) to help you reduce Activation levels before bed. We now understand that a reduction in body temperature is a trigger for sleep. Your body cools when you get out of the warm water, helping lower Activation levels and trigger sleep.

Use Focus Words and Pictures

Another technique you can use to decrease Activation levels at bedtime relates to Focus Words and Pictures. One example of using this technique to directly reduce Activation is imagining the Activation dial in your mind's eye—a Focus Picture—and at the same time use Focus Words to help you slow your breathing pattern. You might want to create a 4:7 breathing pattern (or whatever works best for you), telling yourself to breathe in slowly for four seconds—feeling your stomach expanding like a balloon—and breathe out slowly for seven seconds—feeling your shoulders and your neck relax. As you are doing this, you might see the Activation dial in your mind's eye getting lower and lower. You might repeat this until you achieve the desired Activation level. Do some personal research to learn which breathing pattern works best for you.

An example of a less direct way of using Focus Words and Pictures to reduce Activation is focusing on recalling a holiday that provided lasting positive memories. The Focus Words are you talking yourself through what happened on the holiday from start to finish, and the Focus Pictures are you seeing the holiday unfold—like you were watching a movie of it. You could use a similar approach, but instead focus on going on one of your favorite walks.

Other things can help lower your Activation levels:

- Making sure your bedroom is cool, quiet, and dark

- Being mindful of your daily caffeine intake
- Drinking enough water during the day to prevent dehydration
- Learning to relax your muscles with a routine called *progressive muscular relaxation*

Progressive Muscular Relaxation

This is a relaxation technique that can be used directly before you go to sleep, or while you are in bed. The aim is to systematically relax different muscles in the body. For example, you might start with the muscle groups in your feet and work up to your neck and head.

You focus on relaxing one muscle group at a time by learning to deliberately contract and relax muscles until all tension in that muscle group has disappeared. Self-talk (Focus Words) and imagery (Focus Pictures) are very important here. To learn how to do this, you can start with your right hand. Using self-talk, tell yourself to clench and squeeze your hand into a fist. Then tell yourself to open your hand and relax it—imagine it is as light as a feather. Once your hand feels relaxed, you can move onto your right forearm, again telling yourself to tense it as tightly as you can, and then relaxing it, and so on. So progressively, and systematically, you target different muscle groups in your body until all feel relaxed, and you have lowered your Activation level.

Reflect?

If it is helpful, write down a few notes about what you have learned about lowering your Activation levels before you go to bed.

HOW TO IMPROVE DAYTIME ACTIVATION MANAGEMENT

If you are achieving good sleep Activation levels and therefore sleeping well, it will be much easier to control your Activation during the morning. So let's imagine you are struggling to achieve ideal Activation levels after lunch.

You might recognize your post-lunch Activation is typically at 40 when you would ideally like it to be 60. So you set an Aim to improve your score to a 60 more regularly.

Here are some Activation management techniques you could use in a Plan to increase your post-lunch Activation levels:

Food

Consider how the food you eat for lunch can impact your afternoon Activation. One way to categorize food is with the Glycemic Index (GI), which measures the speed at which food that contains carbohydrates increase your blood sugar levels. Foods that score high on the glycemic index are known as high GI. Foods with low GI contain sugars that enter the bloodstream slowly.

High GI food, like white bread, white rice, potatoes, chocolate bars, and sugary drinks, can give you an initial spike in your Activation levels, but then quickly reduce your Activation levels so you feel tired and sluggish.

Low GI food, like whole grain bread, nuts, and some fruits and some vegetables, allow you to maintain a more constant Activation level by releasing sugar into your blood more slowly.

Visit the NHS (or USDA) website for a helpful overview of GI foods.

Exercise

Exercise after lunch will also boost your Activation. Whether you take a short walk or do something more intense like going to the gym, it will help boost essential Activation-increasing brain chemicals like dopamine and BDNF, which will then enhance your focus in the afternoon.

Self-Talk and Mental Imagery

Another technique you can use to increase Activation levels is to use self-talk and mental imagery, just like we discussed in your sleep routine.

Imagine in your mind's eye the Activation dial getting higher (Focus Picture). At the same time, use self-talk (Focus Words) to help you increase your breathing pattern. Using a physical trigger like standing up and clenching your fist might also help. With practice, you will find a strategy that works to help you quickly increase your Activation. This should be a short, sharp—and if you are working in an office with others, quiet—technique ☺.

Music

One extra element that might be useful for Activation level management is background music. Aim not to listen directly to the music, but for it to add a background rhythm and a tempo to your work. For example, I find familiar classical music works best to help me focus on mentally challenging work.

HOW TO IMPROVE PERFORMANCE ACTIVATION MANAGEMENT

Let's think about pumping yourself up for a physical task like making a presentation or playing a sport. Sometimes you might need to increase your

Activation level to help you perform at your best in these types of activities.

To increase your Activation, you can use short, sharp, intense exercise, like jumping up and down on the spot. Using Focus Words (e.g., "Come on, I can do this!") and Focus Pictures (e.g., in your mind's eye seeing your Activation dial increase to the desired level) at the same time can make this even more effective. Playing some upbeat music might also help.

Reflect

If it is helpful, write down a few notes detailing what you have learned about how to better manage your Activation levels.

In this section, we've introduced many insights and techniques you can use to both increase and decrease Activation. Good DES habits will help you manage your Activation, meaning you can focus, learn, perform, and relax much more effectively.

As we move forward, you will see how good Activation habits are central for stress management, confidence, focus, being productive, performing under pressure, outstanding leadership, and ultimately becoming a Habit Mechanic and Chief Habit Mechanic.

HABIT MECHANIC LANGUAGE AND TOOL YOU HAVE LEARNED IN CHAPTER 21...

Core Language

Activation levels—A concept I've developed to make it easier to understand and manage your energy levels, alertness, and anxiety. ☑

Focus Words and Focus Pictures—Skills you can use to help control your thoughts. ☑

Planning Tool

Optimal Activation Review—A tool to help you track, compare, and improve your Activation levels through the day. ☑

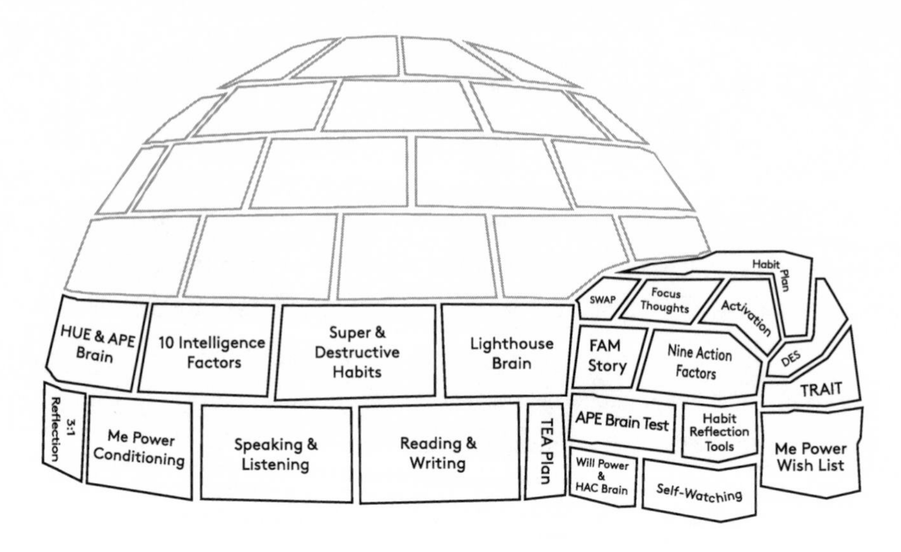

Figure 21.7: Your Habit Mechanic intelligence igloo is building up!

Next, we will look at how to manage stress better and how to spend less time thinking unhelpful thoughts.

22

SIMPLE AND PRACTICAL STRESS MANAGEMENT SKILLS TO STOP NEGATIVE THINKING IN ITS TRACKS

In the build-up to the 2008 Beijing Olympics, a little-known British athlete named Jessica Ennis-Hill suffered three fractures in her right foot in training. The injury was so severe that not only did she miss the Beijing Games, but she was also told she might not be able to compete again as a professional athlete.

She was forced to change her take-off foot for the long jump. For a professional athlete, this was like changing the hand you write with, and then also having to quickly become the best in the world at writing with that "new" hand. Fundamentally, Ennis-Hill was undertaking a brand-new event: the left-footed (or legged) long jump. If she didn't master it quickly, her funding would be cut—and she would not fulfill her dream of becoming the world's best heptathlete. One week she was readying herself to win gold at the 2008

Olympics; the next week she was being told that she might not be able to compete again. It was a confidence-shattering period that resulted in major stress and anxiety about her future.

But she didn't give in. She persisted and found the mental strength to refocus. Jessica worked hard to manage her stress and rebuild her confidence. It wasn't easy, but she dug deep and persevered.

The result? In August 2009, she won heptathlon gold at the World Championships in Berlin. She went on to win two more World Championship golds in 2011 and 2015, and an Olympic gold at London 2012. Jessica Ennis-Hill is now recognized as one of the all-time great athletes in Track and Field.

But how did she do it?

In this chapter, I will show you how Jessica, and other world-leading performers (including Sir Paul McCartney), overcome stress to achieve their goals and fulfill their potential. Then I will show you how to use a range of science-based Habit Mechanic stress management tools. These will allow you to spend more time focusing on what is helpful for you—in life and work.

Let's begin by learning more about the brain science of why we get stressed.

WHAT IS STRESS?
(YOU NEED TO UNDERSTAND THIS.)

It's helpful to remind ourselves what our APE Brain is designed to do:

1. Help us stay **A**live
2. Make us aware of how we are **P**erceived
3. Conserve **E**nergy

These things drive us and our habits. But in the modern world, we are often required to delay gratification, work toward long-term goals, be diligent, and quickly adapt to change. What's expected of us conflicts with how we have evolved to behave as humans. So we can find that HUE (Horribly Unhelpful Emotions) constantly hijacks us.

The result? Stress. And too much stress can make us feel unwell.

Stress is partly a chemical process that occurs in the brain. When stress-related chemicals are released, this can be referred to as the fight or flight (or freeze) response.

Not all stress is bad. Some degree of stress can even be helpful to us for our personal growth and development. However, too much stress is bad for our health, happiness, and performance.

To fully understand our stress response and how to manage it, let's consider the process in greater detail.

Any stress response begins with an experience, or what scientists call an "event."

For example:

- Event: holding the door open for somebody in the office

As the event unfolds, we have a subconscious "expectation" of what should happen.

For example:

- Expectation: for the person to be courteous and say "thank you"

Psychologists describe the expectation of what will happen as our "global meaning." But the reality of the situation—what *really* happens, such as the person ignoring us and not saying "thank you"—is known as the "situational meaning."

When there are differences between what you **expect to happen (global meaning)** and what **actually happens (situational meaning)**, you experience a stress response. This is called a "dislocation of meaning systems."

For example, you hold the door open for someone and expect them to say thank you. But the person ignores you. This creates a stress response.

It's important to point out that dislocations do not have to be real. Imagine you are traveling to a meeting. You pride yourself on being punctual and arriving for all your meetings on time. But your train is delayed and arriving on time is now in doubt. So HUE then starts to run through all the worst-case scenarios—and the possible consequences.

So stress happens because either what's happening is not what you expected to happen, or HUE tells you that what you expect to happen will NOT happen.

Neurologically, the brain reacts to these dislocations with varying degrees of stress response. It is a complex and super-fast reaction. But we can break it down into two simple parts:

1. In the space of milliseconds, our **breathing changes** and our Activation level increases, typically meaning it is too high to be helpful.
2. Our attention drifts onto **unhelpful thoughts**. We focus on them for too long and waste time.

The challenge with stress responses is they add up and can quickly become overwhelming. In the mathematics of stress, one stress response plus one stress response does not necessarily equal two. One plus one can feel more like 26, depending on the nature of the stress!

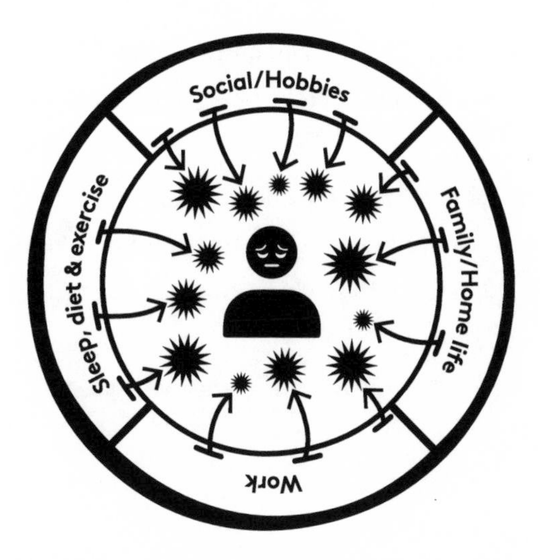

Figure 22.1: Getting overwhelmed is extremely easy in the VUCA world. Small stresses quickly add up.

Stress Reflection

To help you understand your own stress, think about or write down one stressful thing that is bugging you, or that is on your mind at the moment. It could be something small (e.g., the person sitting next to me is playing their music too loud) or something big (e.g., I have upset one of my work colleagues).

____

____

____

Next, try to understand the root causes of this stress. What did you expect to happen versus what is happening? For example, I do not expect the person sitting next to me to play their music so loud that it distracts me. Or, I expect to have good relationships with my work colleagues.

____

____

____

QUICKLY UNDERSTAND AND MANAGE STRESS—USE THE LIGHTHOUSE BRAIN MODEL

Here is a quick recap to help you understand how the Lighthouse Brain model relates to successfully managing stress. Remember, the heart of this process is emotional regulation, which is what Habit Mechanics are really good at.

Let's imagine a scene inside your lighthouse to demonstrate a stress response.

HUE spots something it does not like: the tone your boss has used in an email to you. It feels like you are being unfairly judged. Subconsciously, HUE has identified a social status threat.

You have just experienced a dislocation of meaning systems—what you expected to happen did not happen. You don't expect your boss to speak to you like this, so it triggers a stress response. This entire process unfolds in milliseconds.

Next, two things happen:

1. Your **breathing becomes quicker**, increasing your Activation to unhelpful levels.
2. HUE lets Will Power know there is a problem by flooding your conscious brain with **unhelpful thoughts** (you might start to worry or be too self-critical).

When your brain is functioning properly, Will Power can come to the rescue and help out HUE. I call this the Will Power Mentoring process. We can use this process to help us organize our thinking about how to get better at managing stress. Here's how it works (for a visual see Figure 10.4 in Chapter 10):

Step 1

Stress response. HUE signals Will Power for help.

Step 2

Will Power receives the message.

Step 3

Will Power analyzes the message (problem, worry, threat).

Step 4

Will Power categorizes the problem in one of three ways:

1. It is a real problem that needs to be addressed;
2. It is a false alarm or an uncontrollable problem; or
3. It is a problem, but HUE's reaction is over the top.

Step 5

Will Power coaches HUE. They either create and deploy an action plan, or HUE learns how to interpret similar signals in a more helpful way.

Step 6

Some of the behavior used to solve the problem becomes more automatic, making it easier for HUE to stay calm and resolve similar problems by itself in the future.

"Calmer HUE, better you."

Reflect?

Take a moment to make a few notes, or think about, the relationship between your HUE and Will Power when it comes to stress.

Remember, whatever state the current relationship is in, you can learn how to make it better. Let me show you how.

HOW TO BUILD HELPFUL HABITS TO EFFECTIVELY MANAGE YOUR STRESS

Managing stress effectively can be difficult. The foundational factor for successful emotional regulation is your brain functioning properly.

In a challenging world, this is not a given. If your diet, exercise, or sleep (DES) habits are poor, Will Power will not be in any fit state to help out HUE.

Also, stresses do not typically occur one at a time. Individual stress responses can add up and rapidly create a feeling of being overwhelmed (remember, HUE is actively looking for threats and problems in the past, present, and future).

When we experience prolonged periods of stress, the APE Brain effectively takes over all other areas of our brain—including the HAC (Helpful Attentional Control) Brain, which we lose the ability to use effectively. This means Will Power is not able to help HUE.

And remember, you become good at what you practice. So, practicing becoming stressed strengthens the neural circuitry connected to threat detection and stress responses. This means getting stressed quickly becomes a very unhelpful habit.

The good news is you can retrain your brain to get better at managing and reducing stress.

Here's an overview of a helpful approach to building new stress management habits.

1. Adapt a Habit Mechanic Mindset. In other words, be prepared to do your best to be your best and take responsibility for what you can control. For example, proactively manage the stress, rather than worrying about the uncontrollable factors that caused you to become stressed.
2. Step back and put perspective on thoughts rather than panic. A quick way to do this is creating a SWAP (Self-Watch, Aim, Plan).

Self-Watch

Let's begin the SWAP process with some stress Self-Watching. Start by thinking of stress as a continuum ranging from 1 to 10 (1 is low stress; 10 is high stress).

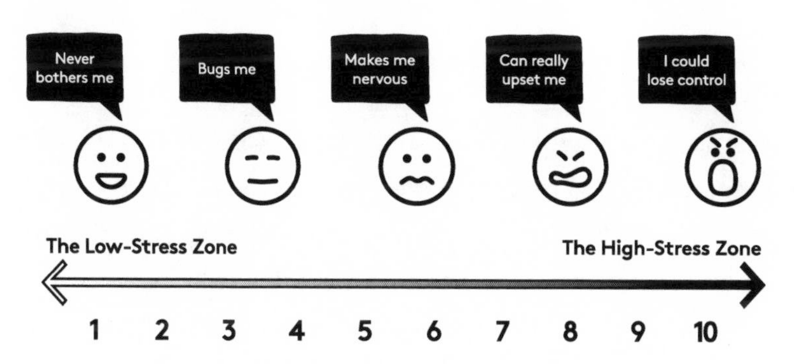

Figure 22.2: Stress is a natural response you experience, but your stress levels can change quickly.

What score best reflects your current stress level? If it's high, write down the problems causing you stress.

____

____

____

By reflecting, you are encouraging a positive interaction between your Will Power and HUE.

Aim

Now let's Aim to reduce your stress level by a small amount (remember the Tiny Change Factor—we can only make one small change at a time).

Current stress level number (e.g., 8):

New target number (Aim) (e.g., 7):

Plan

If you want to reduce your stress levels in the immediate future, you need a Plan.

But what practical things can you Plan to do?

Plan to Control Your Breathing

When we are stressed, one of the clear physical changes is in our breathing. This is the only physical part of the stress response we have direct conscious control of. We can slow down and regulate our breathing. This calms us and reverses the stress response. Slowing our breathing reduces our Activation levels.

Want to try a breathing exercise?

If you can, please stand up. If you cannot, sit upright or lie down.

Place your left hand on your stomach and your right hand on the top of your chest.

Notice your current breathing patterns. How many seconds does it take for you to breathe in? How many to breathe out?

Now I want you to deliberately take control of your breathing and slow it down.

For example, try breathing in through your nose (or your mouth) for five seconds. Then breathe out slowly through your mouth (or your nose) for five seconds. Feel free to adjust these numbers so they work best for you.

Repeat this process until you create a rhythm.

As you breathe out, visualize your shoulders deflating like a balloon and your Activation dial moving from the high numbers down to the low numbers.

It is also possible to reverse this process and raise your Activation levels again (gently jumping up and down for a few moments should do the trick).

Now that you understand more about controlling your breathing to overcome the stress response, you can Plan to do this when needed. Countering the fight/flight response through breathing can become a key part of your stress management Plan.

Take a moment to make a note of your ideal breathing ratio for effective stress management. I use five seconds in and five seconds out, and breathe in through my nose and out through my mouth. More recently, I have also been experimenting breathing out through my nose because of some research I read about the benefits.

Breathe in for _____ seconds through your _______________

Breathe out for _____ seconds through your _______________

Controlling your breathing should not be seen as an emergency response. It is something you should practice regularly. Even 30 seconds of practice will help and can leave you feeling recharged and refreshed. I often do this as I'm walking.

Well done! You just HAC-ed (hacked) your brain. You did it by using Focus Words and Focus Pictures.

Your Focus Words came when you talked yourself through the breathing count. You used words to control your attention and focus on something helpful (i.e., your breathing).

Your Focus Pictures came when you used an image of a balloon deflating, and the Activation dial. These Focus Pictures helped you focus your attention on your breathing, which is much more helpful than focusing on a stress or a problem.

You can now use this technique to help Will Power calm down HUE when it is stressed.

Plan to Manage Your Thoughts

In the second part of the stress response, our attention typically drifts and becomes glued onto unhelpful thoughts. For example, we ruminate, beat ourselves up, and worry. So we need to get better at managing our thoughts.

Using Focus Words and Pictures

The good news is that we can also use Focus Words and Pictures techniques here.

To understand why, let's think about how HUE and Will Power communicate.

When HUE is stressed, it makes Will Power aware through thoughts—essentially, words and pictures. By learning how to get more control over what you say to yourself (Focus Words) and what you see in your mind's eye (Focus Pictures), you can take more control over how you think.

When unhelpful thoughts come into your head, you need to be prepared to challenge them.

In other words... do not believe everything you think!

HUE's job is to warn us about threats. It's designed to make us aware of the worst-case scenario. But the thoughts it puts in our head are often not true and will never become reality.

However, controlling our thoughts is not easy. We know that trying to suppress threatening thoughts does not work and can make them more powerful. So simply trying NOT to think about unhelpful thoughts is not very effective.

Trying to counter HUE's unhelpful thoughts by only thinking positive thoughts, and arguing with HUE in our mind through self-talk, is also not very effective.

To get more control over our thinking, we should first focus on welcoming unhelpful thoughts. By doing this, we disarm HUE—making it less worried or angry, and less powerful. This makes it easier for Will Power to coach HUE and gives us a better chance of managing the unhelpful thoughts. As I am welcoming unhelpful thoughts, I sometimes imagine Will Power giving HUE a relaxing shoulder massage to calm it down (Focus Picture).

Also, when I notice an unhelpful thought from HUE, I say something to myself like, "It is only HUE doing its job" (Focus Words). Typically, I do this with a big smile on my face and sometimes even laugh at myself, because my HUE can say some silly things. By doing this, I am "labeling" the thought. This simple process is quick and can be very powerful.

It's Good to Talk

I have already highlighted the importance of positive social relationships for healthy brain function. One of the reasons this is helpful is that talking to people you trust about your feelings can help you "get things off your chest," make sense of your thoughts, and defuse some of them. So, do speak to people you trust about your feelings, because social emotional support is very powerful—especially if the people you speak to can make you smile and help you think about the challenges you are facing from a different perspective.

However, although talking is a great starting point for managing the unhelpful thoughts that HUE is focusing on, in my experience it is not enough. To truly develop better thinking habits, we need to go further. To do this, I would also recommend using a technique I call "Focused Reflection."

Focused Reflection

Focused Reflection can help us manage our thinking and actually build new thinking habits. Focused Reflection supercharges our ability to focus on helpful thoughts. The central part of this technique is writing things down.

To make the Focused Reflection techniques I am about to show you even more powerful, it is helpful to deliberately activate brain circuits that naturally make you feel more positive. You can quickly do this by creating a pre-writing routine. Here is one example (but do some personal research to find something that works best for you):

1. Go for a five-minute walk (you can focus on your breathing as you do this to help manage your Activation levels) or jump up and down on the spot for 5 to 10 seconds (or more).
2. Then, before you start writing, quickly open and close your right hand several times.
3. At the same time, force yourself to smile ☺.
4. Start writing (using the techniques I will show you shortly).

In simple terms, a pre-writing routine should help activate your accumbens-striatal-prefrontal cortex network. Dr. Kelly Lambert calls this the "effort-driven-reward" circuit. Activating this brain network should make focusing your attention onto helpful thoughts easier.

The reason for using your right hand, and not your left, is that the left prefrontal cortex is associated with positive emotions. The left side of your brain is activated by the right side of your body. So quickly opening and closing your right hand several times should help activate the left side of your prefrontal cortex. Forcing yourself to smile while you write will also have a similar impact! ☺

Have a WABA

One Focused Reflection writing technique (or Habit Mechanic Tool) I teach people is to have a "Written APE Brain Argument" (WABA). Instead of just rehearsing unhelpful thoughts and stories in your mind, write them down. Then write down structured arguments against each one.

If it is helpful, make a list of some of your worries/unhelpful thoughts (e.g., I'm never going to finish writing this book; it is just too difficult):

- ______________________________
- ______________________________
- ______________________________
- ______________________________
- ______________________________

Then you could use some of the following guidance to help you manage and reframe these unhelpful thoughts:

- *Life-threatening score*: Give each unhelpful thought a score out of 10, where 10 is life-threatening and 1 is HUE focusing on an extremely unlikely worst-case scenario. Write down the score.
  This quickly helps put the thought into perspective.
- *More details*: Add more details about each unhelpful thought you are experiencing.

- *Is this true?*: Note whether or not these thoughts are true or correct.
- *More helpful thoughts*: Write down what thoughts might be more helpful to pay attention to instead.

For example (note: the below ideas are helpful for me, but might not be for you):

- *Original thought:* I'm never going to finish writing this book; it is just too difficult.
- *Life-threatening score:* 1
- *More details:* This is HUE wanting to avoid doing work that does not give it an immediate reward.
- *Is this true?:* No! I have achieved far more difficult things in my life than writing this book.
- *More helpful thoughts:* If I don't finish this book, I will be letting people down because helping people become Habit Mechanics is more important than ever. Create a new plan to help me finish, and keep persisting. I will finish this book, even if it takes me longer than planned.

Creating these types of written reflections is a skill you will get better at with practice.

The Power of Writing

When we write something down, we are no longer victims of our short-term memory. The information does not disappear within 30 seconds, or if we write down more than five to seven thoughts.

Learning from a Beatle

Former Beatle Sir Paul McCartney can testify to the power of writing for successful stress management. He has spoken about how he uses writing to process stress, negative experiences, and thoughts. The legendary co-founder of The Beatles was discussing the song *I Don't Know*, from his solo album *Egypt Station.* McCartney spoke about how he finds he can take a memory, sometimes of an argument, and "work it out" in the song-writing process, which "makes [him] feel better." He added that one of the great things about writing songs is the way in which it is "almost like a therapy."

Why? Because writing helps us reframe and address difficult thoughts and ideas.

At Least Three Positives for Every Negative

We can also use Professor Barbara Fredrickson's Grounded Positivity theory to supercharge our stress management writing. Research has shown that people who are thriving and flourishing pay attention to at least three positives for every one negative thought they experience.

Three-to-one is a minimum ratio. This is because HUE is so effective at putting unhelpful thoughts into our heads. Sometimes, we might even need a ratio as high as eleven-to-one.

At the beginning of the book (Chapter 5), I showed you the Daily 3:1 Reflection, a quick technique (or Habit Mechanic Tool) to practice refocusing onto more helpful thoughts at the end of each day.

Here's a quick recap: at the end of each day, write down three positive or helpful things you've done and one thing you can improve on in the next 24 hours.

For example:

- + I went for a jog (not easy, but felt great after).
- + I learned about all the positive changes a team I've been working with has made.
- + I did some writing this morning (I'm currently working on a book).
- – Get to sleep 10 minutes earlier tonight.

Writing down thoughts is a great way to get more control over the words and pictures in your mind. Take a moment to write a three-to-one reflection of your day so far.

- +
- +
- +
- –

Deliberately controlling your breathing, and writing WABA-type reflections, is a great way to calm down HUE.

This makes it easier for your Will Power to function properly and coach HUE through the problem at hand.

FAB Thinking

"FAB Thinking" is another Focused Reflection stress management technique (or Habit Mechanic Tool). It's about proactively shifting our attention onto helpful thoughts through the process of reframing and changing the meaning of an event. **FAB** stands for:

Fortunate—what have I been fortunate to be able to do today?
Adapt—how can I adapt my goals to reduce stress?
Benefits—what benefits can I identify in this current difficult situation?

Studies of people with terminal illnesses, and those who care for them, have revealed that many become highly adept at reframing their experiences, so they have more positive or helpful thoughts.

Let's think about each of these in turn.

Fortunate

What have I been fortunate to be able to do today?

Consider your own situation. Do you live in one of the world's richest countries? Don't take this for granted. For example, I was so lucky to have three meals today (breakfast, lunch, and evening meal). Many people in the world might not have had anything to eat.

Adapt

How can I adapt my goals to reduce stress?

You may have missed a promotion at work, but dwelling will not help. Can you reset your goals and aim for something new? This might include using feedback from last year's appraisal to change the way you work and reapply for promotion next year.

Benefits

What benefits can I identify in this current difficult situation?

When we emerge from challenging circumstances, over time we can often look back and recognize that we have gained valuable experience that improves us or makes us mentally tougher. We can accelerate this process if we purposefully look for the benefits as we experience difficulties. For example, this is a difficult situation, but I am learning a lot about myself and those around me. I will be a better person when I get through this, and will be better equipped to deal with other challenges in my life.

Meaning-Focused Coping

Another way to describe FAB Thinking is "Meaning-Focused Coping." This is a conceptual coping framework created by the distinguished academic Professor Susan Folkman.

I started this chapter with a mention of world champion athlete Jessica Ennis-Hill. Let's return to her career to understand more about Meaning-Focused Coping and FAB Thinking.

Ennis-Hill suffered a major injury setback in 2008. She recovered by using something very similar to a Meaning-Focused Coping approach. A BBC documentary about potential medalists at London 2012 gives us insight into the Sheffield-born superstar. Archives of her national newspaper column also provide additional understanding of her situation and mental state.

I took a particular interest in this story because Jessica trained for javelin at the same leading sports university I was teaching at and completing my PhD.

Jessica's injury created a dislocation of her meaning systems: what she thought should be happening—going to the Olympics—was different than what was actually happening. Remember, these differences trigger the stress response.

Her HUE was no doubt on red alert. It would have been difficult to pay attention to anything that was not a worry or major threat to her future. Her confidence was taking a battering, and she was most probably in a heightened fight/flight state, meaning her brain was not functioning well.

It was clearly unhelpful for her to keep paying attention to worries and threats. If her HUE was left to its own devices, it could potentially have a profoundly negative effect on her. But the difficulty for her was that there were just no obvious positives she could focus on. Nothing was going right.

Thankfully, Ennis-Hill was clearly able to engage her Will Power and start paying attention to helpful thoughts. In doing this, she was using her own version of FAB Thinking.

One example of this is the way she was using Benefit Finding. She said and wrote the following things:

- "There must be a reason (good) for what has happened."
- "I'll be tougher for this experience."
- "Now I can go to watch *Sex in the City* at the cinema…"

The last point is connected to her leisure time normally being restricted when she was in full-time training. A connected Meaning-Focused Coping technique is called Benefit Reminding, which is simply reminding yourself of the benefits you previously identified.

Another Meaning-Focused Coping tactic Ennis-Hill used is called Infusing Ordinary Events with Meaning—or taking pleasure in the everyday things that we take for granted.

For example, after she was told her career might be over, she said:

"I've been so lucky to be able to have the experiences in athletics that I've had."

And by stating that her new priority was "getting over the injury and getting back for winter training," she seemed to be using a technique called Realigning Priorities, which is reordering your priorities to focus on the things that are important right now.

Finally, by stating that she was now going to "focus on London 2012," she seemed to be using Adaptive Goal Processes. When your goals become unattainable due to a change in your circumstances, you have to reset them. Remember, goals are not set in stone.

By becoming skilled at reappraising and reframing difficult events in her life, Jessica Ennis-Hill was able to focus more on helpful thoughts. Ultimately, she got her career back on track and become the world and Olympic champion.

Reflection?

If it is helpful, take a moment to note, or think about, what you've learned about managing your emotions so far.

Expressive Writing

A song by Nina Simone illustrates another way of understanding, reappraising, and reframing our thoughts, feelings, and ultimately our emotions.

The first few verses of *Ain't Got No—I Got Life* reveal a lonely singer living in poverty. Halfway through the lyrics, the focus changes to what the singer does have, including her hair, head, brains, ears, eyes, nose, mouth, and smile.

This is a great example of what scientists call emotional or "Expressive Writing." This Focused Reflection technique (or Habit Mechanic Tool) is an excellent method to combine WABA, 3:1 Reflections, and FAB Thinking into a longer-form stress management skill.

Professor James W. Pennebaker (whom I have studied with) is the most high-profile proponent of this powerful technique. The concept is simple. You write about your deepest thoughts and feelings connected to a prominent trauma or emotional challenge you've experienced. In other words, HUE has become obsessed by this event and cannot stop thinking about it. These are often the types of thoughts that can keep you awake at night.

Experts in Expressive Writing encourage you to write about the same stressful event for 20 minutes a day for four consecutive days. I've personally benefited from this long-form Focused Reflection technique. I find it helpful to have some questions I can ask myself. I generally don't need to provide an answer to every question every time I reflect because they are not all always relevant. Here are the questions I use:

- What event caused you to be stressed and why? (e.g., I expected to get a pay raise.)
- What is the unhelpful thinking habit you want to replace? (e.g., Dwelling on the fact that I did not get a pay raise and beating myself up because of this.)
- What are the social status implications of the event? (e.g., People

might not think I am very good at my job; I feel like work doesn't value me; my family might be disappointed. But deep down I know that my close colleagues, real friends, and family will not think any less of me.)

- What reminds you about the event and why? (e.g., HUE, because it perceives this as a threat—i.e., the P (perceived) in APE. Also, seeing my boss because she gave me the bad news.)
- How can you reframe these reminders? (e.g., This is an opportunity for me to get better and learn how to overcome a setback.)
- How could the event have been worse? (e.g., I could have been given a pay reduction or lost my job. I know many people who would love to have my job.)
- What are the benefits of the event? (e.g., It has given me an opportunity to learn how to manage stress; it has made me reevaluate my long-term goals and FAM Story.)
    - What did you learn? (e.g., I have a clearer understanding of what I need to achieve in the next three months to secure a pay raise.)
    - How did you grow? (e.g., Previously I would have dwelled on this for weeks and months, but now I am learning how to take positive action.)
    - How will you be better able to deal with a similar event next time? (e.g., I will write down a reflection sooner after the event to help me get my attention back onto more helpful thoughts faster.)
- What is a more helpful story to tell yourself about this event? (e.g., This is part of my journey to becoming a Habit Mechanic so that I can be a happier and better version of myself.)

Like any of the techniques/skills/tools I highlight, you will only find out what works best for you by trying out Expressive Writing and creating a list of reflective questions that help you.

DAILY PRACTICE

You now have some knowledge and skills relating to stress management. But this is not enough: you need to practice using these skills every day. When HUE calls for help, you need your Will Power to be trained in these techniques so it can respond efficiently and effectively.

Practicing these skills will help you turn some elements of how you manage stress into helpful habits.

Breathing

We now understand how regulating our breathing can help us manage stress. Why not try practicing 30-second bouts of controlled breathing as you walk around during the day?

Writing (Focused Reflection)

Why not practice writing things down as part of your efforts to reframe difficult situations, using 3:1, WABA, and FAB Thinking? You can also extend this into long-form techniques like Expressive Writing. Finishing each day with a Daily 3:1 Reflection is a great start.

Have a RABA

There is also another technique that we can use. It is called a "**R**unning **A**PE **B**rain **A**rgument" (RABA). This is where we exercise or move around at the same time as thinking through and reframing some stressful thoughts. We can then write down a written reflection when we return from our run or walk.

None of these things are prescriptive. Please try them all and work out which is best for you.

RAW Back

Finally, here's one more reflection process you can use to bring together all the other core stress management tools I have shared: **RAW** Back. This stands for **R**educe **A**ctivation and **W**rite. During a stress response, you purposefully reduce your Activation levels by slowing down your breathing, and writing to refocus your attention onto more helpful thoughts.

HOW TO HELP WILL POWER MENTOR HUE

Here is the Lighthouse Brain model again, but this time including the knowledge and skills you've learned in this section.

Step 1

Stress response. HUE signals Will Power for help.

Coaching point: Regular Self-Watching means you will respond faster.

Step 2

Will Power receives the message.

Coaching point: To reverse the stress response, welcome the unhelpful thoughts. Slow down your breathing and have a WABA.

Step 3

Will Power analyzes the problem.

Coaching point: Building up your Habit Mechanic intelligence will make it easier to analyze problems because you will have greater self-knowledge.

Step 4

Will Power categorizes the problem in one of three ways:

1. It is a real problem that needs to be addressed;
2. It is a false alarm or an uncontrollable problem; or
3. It is a problem, but HUE's reaction is over the top.

Coaching point: Again, building up your Habit Mechanic intelligence will make it easier to solve problems because you will have greater self-knowledge.

Step 5

Will Power coaches HUE. They either create and deploy an action plan, or HUE learns how to interpret similar signals in a more helpful way.

Coaching point: All the stress management Habit Mechanic Tools you've learned could be helpful here, including FAB Thinking and Expressive Writing. Whatever you decide to do will work better if you build it into a Habit Building Plan.

Step 6

Some of the behavior used to solve the problem becomes more automatic, making it easier for HUE to stay calm and resolve similar problems in the future.

Coaching point: Your first Plan, or elements of it, will probably fail. And this is good because we learn how to improve when we fail. So, keep refining your Plan, and use the Habit Building Plan framework to supercharge it until it is working well for you.

YOUR STRESS MANAGEMENT CHECKLIST

As a recap, here are 10 waysto help you manage stress better and spend less time thinking unhelpful thoughts.

1. Develop good DES habits.
2. Reduce Activation by using your ideal breathing ratio.
3. Welcome unhelpful thoughts.
4. Refocus your attention with a WABA.
5. Refocus your attention with a RABA.
6. Close each day with a Daily 3:1 Reflection.
7. Change the meaning of difficult problems with FAB Thinking.
8. Refocus and regulate your emotions with long-form Expressive Writing.
9. "RAW Back" to counter stress responses quickly.
10. Focus on helping your Will Power and HUE work together more effectively.

Several of these ideas might be helpful to you. Why not add these to your Me Power Wish List?

BUILD THE HABIT

Remember, it's only realistic to Aim to build one small new habit at a time. So if it's helpful, **write down one habit you would like to prioritize** to improve your ability to manage stress. Think of this as an Aim, and remember that good Aims are carefully written down, are specific (using times and locations), state a positive action ("I will" instead of "I will not"), and can be measured (using quantities).

Here's my example Aim: "I will complete a Daily 3:1 Reflection at my desk at the end of every day."

If you want to work on a stress management habit, write down your Aim:

___

___

Once you have a clear Aim, you might want to revisit the "How HUE Hinders Change" self-reflection tool (Chapter 20). This will help you think about how HUE might try to stop you from building this new habit.

Finally, create a Habit Building Plan to activate the Nine Action Factors and supercharge the habit building process. Answer the following questions:

1. Describe the SMALL specific new helpful habit that you want to build (your Aim):

   ___

   Example answer: Complete a Daily 3:1 Reflection at my desk at the end of every day (rather than a vague or loose Aim like "get better at managing stress").

2. Describe what you currently do (your unhelpful habit instead of the new helpful habit you want to build):

   ___

   Example answer: Check the BBC (or CNN) website to see the latest news.

3. Describe what reminds or triggers this unhelpful habit:

   ___

   Example answer: It is very easy to access on my smartphone.

4. Describe how you will remind yourself (trigger) to practice your NEW habit daily:

   ___

   Example answer: Set a daily calendar alert to remind me to do this (3:1 Daily Reflection). Create a space in my daily diary to write down the reflections. Encourage one of my team members, or a family member, to do the same so that we will trigger each other.

5. Describe the new knowledge and skills you will need to help you secure your new habit:

Example answer: Do some personal research to gain an improved understanding of the factors that impact my stress levels and the skills I can use to manage my stress.

6. If it is helpful, describe where and how you will acquire the new knowledge and skills you need:

Example answer: Revisit my notes on FAB, WABA, and Expressive Writing and experiment with these ideas.

7. Describe in detail why you want to build this new habit:

Example answer: To save time (spend less time dwelling on unhelpful thoughts) and give myself a better chance of being at my best so I can perform well in my job and spend more quality time with my family.

8. Who can you ask to help you build your new habit? (ideally, they will also be building the same or similar habit at the same time):

Example answer: James, my colleague at work. I also want to get my kids doing this.

9. What will be the reward for building the new habit? Remember, rewards can be internal, external, or social.

Example answer: I will feel better, waste less time, and spend more time doing productive work and can spend more quality time with loved ones.

10. What will be the cost/penalty for not building the new habit?

____

Example answer: The opposite of the rewards I describe above.

Congratulations, you now have a robust plan to build a new helpful stress management habit!

HABIT MECHANIC TOOLS YOU HAVE LEARNED IN CHAPTER 22...

Planning Tools

WABA (Written APE Brain Argument)—A structured approach to managing unhelpful thoughts. ☑

FAB (Fortunate, Adapt, Benefits) Thinking—A structured approach to reframing unhelpful thoughts. ☑

RABA (Running APE Brain Argument)—A structured approach to managing unhelpful thoughts. ☑

RAW (Reduce Activation and Write)—A summary of how to manage your stress. ☑

Expressive Writing—A long-form stress management and confidence-building tool. ☑

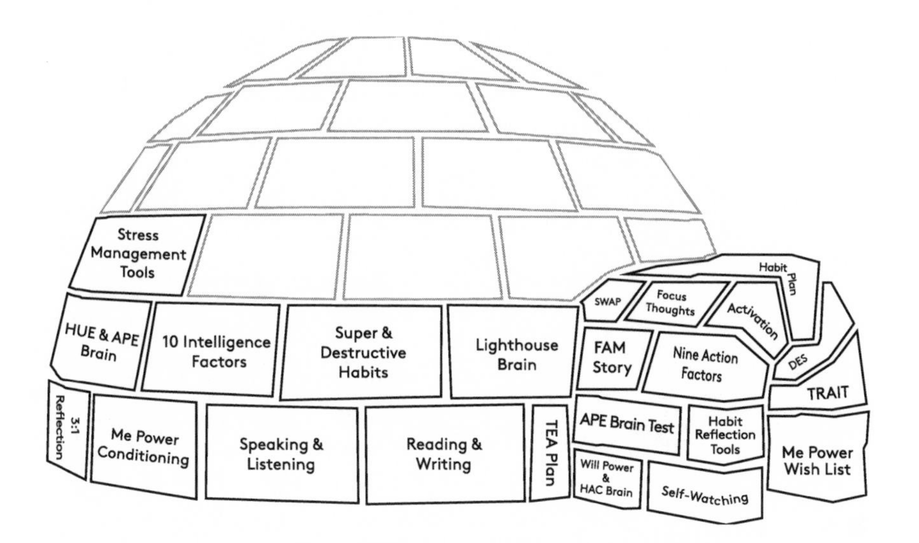

Figure 22.3: Your Habit Mechanic intelligence igloo is building up!

> *If you truly want to master stress, you also need to learn how to develop robust confidence. In the next chapter, I will explain more.*

23

DEVELOP ROCK-SOLID CONFIDENCE WITH OUR SCIENCE-BASED SKILLS

Let's again consider the career of heptathlete Jessica Ennis-Hill. Remember: in 2008 she missed the Olympics after suffering three fractures in her right foot. She was told she might never compete again.

But in 2009, she competed in the heptathlon at the World Athletics Championships in Berlin. Ennis-Hill had been trying to master left-leg long jump for eight months before this competition, and it was her first major competition in two years.

The fly-on-the-wall BBC documentary about her during this event, and the build-up to it, gives us great insight into the stressful, confidence-destroying, and confidence-building processes Ennis-Hill went through.

In Berlin, she led the field after the first day of heptathlon competition. But the first event of the second day was the long jump. A bad outcome could have stopped her from winning a medal. She admitted she was very nervous. She said: "I thought I might fall over."

But she performed superbly and won gold. Jess also ended up being able to jump further off her left leg in the long jump than she ever could off her right leg. The rest is history!

In this chapter, I'll show you simple and practical confidence-building skills that will help you improve your confidence in every area of your life and fulfill your potential, just like Ennis-Hill.

HOW WE GOT CONFIDENCE WRONG

I was sitting in a beautiful room in the UK government's Department of Education building, and I was in shock. I had been invited to contribute to a roundtable discussion about resilience with the then Secretary of State for Education and leading education experts. Every person had five minutes to share their insights about the benefits of developing resilient young people and how it could be achieved.

As one leading thinker began to speak, I was immediately taken aback. The person essentially said that the schools they worked with tried to boost confidence in their young people to help them do better, but it did not work. "We tried confidence, but it failed."

This wasn't the person's fault. They had just been given bad advice about how to develop confidence in others. To me, this underscored a problem first highlighted in Professor Jean Twenge's book *Generation Me: Why Today's Young Americans Are More Confident, Assertive, Entitled—and More Miserable Than Ever Before.*

In short, it tells a story about the well-intended systems that were put in place by education authorities to develop confident young people. They recognized that confidence was essential for life success. Some examples of the tactics used included

- giving everyone, win or lose, a trophy that is the same size; and
- making it easier for people to achieve higher academic grades (e.g., the quality of work that would have previously been graded a C will now be graded a B or even an A).

The result (according to Professor Twenge's research)? A generation of people with very fragile confidence. Why? Because the confidence-boosting approaches had a design flaw. They were not based on good science. The tactics used only boosted self-esteem (the general belief about how good we are at an activity), and not self-efficacy (the evidence as to why we are good, an understanding that also highlights areas that need improvement). This was not the fault of the young people. It was the approach they were exposed to that was faulty.

We can help ourselves and others develop robust confidence, but only if we use a science-based approach. Let me show you how to really develop rock-solid confidence. I will start with the basics.

WHAT IS CONFIDENCE AND HOW CAN WE BUILD IT?

A useful way to explain how confidence can be developed is to imagine it as a house. In simple terms, the house (the "House of Confidence") can be built up one brick at a time.

Figure 23.1: The House of Confidence with a 3:1 ratio of positives to negatives (e.g., instead of only beating yourself up about your weaknesses, also focus on your strengths).

To develop robust confidence, most people need to get better at focusing on positives. This is because research shows that a 3:1 ratio of positive thoughts over negative thoughts promotes "helpful thinking" and is connected to flourishing.

Someone who has low confidence and high stress might not be able to experience any positive thoughts at all. And someone who has high levels of confidence and low stress might rarely experience negative thoughts. But this might lead to overconfidence.

The 3:1 ratio of positive to negative thoughts indicates robust confidence levels and is called "grounded positivity."

The negative thought, or stress, is a useful check for the individual. It provides an incentive to keep persisting and working hard. At the same time, the three positive thoughts create an optimistic outlook. Robust confidence also makes it easier to bounce back when life is difficult, and not sink into a spiral of negative thinking.

The scientific fact that our brains can change and adapt means we can learn how to become more confident, building our House of Confidence up over time.

NO STRESS? NO THANKS

The negative thought in the 3:1 ratio is helpful to us. It is not helpful to have no stress (in other words, areas for improvement) whatsoever.

By having one negative thought (or something we need to address), we have goals to work toward. It gives us a focus. And the three positive thoughts give us confidence and an energy to persist, fueling our efforts. Little successes motivate us to keep trying, and help us make the type of progress (Habit Mechanic development) that is essential for our long-term happiness. If our efforts always result in failure and negative feedback, we very quickly quit.

The optimal mix of positive to negative thoughts that leads to grounded positivity gives us what I call "Robust Confidence." This is a state in which we never become too down in the dumps, but nor do we ever become unrealistically overconfident. The optimal mix is not always 3:1. It differs for different people in different circumstances. For example, someone might need 11 positive thoughts because they are experiencing a particularly traumatic negative thought.

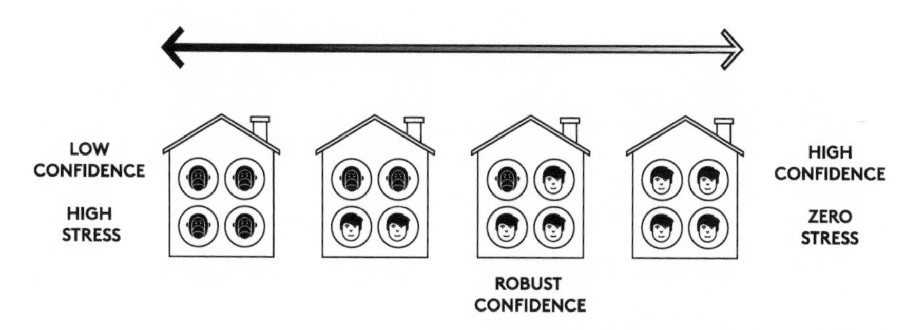

Figure 23.2: High levels of confidence are not necessarily the same as Robust Confidence.

To develop Robust Confidence, we do not want to completely eliminate stress and challenge. So retaining the ability to be constructively self-critical is important if we want to keep improving and developing ourselves.

BUILDING CONFIDENCE WITH THE FAM STORY ICEBERG

The FAM (Future Ambitious Meaningful) Story Iceberg helps us build confidence as we achieve the goals we set. To make it an even more powerful confidence-building tool, let's merge the iceberg concept with our House of Confidence concept.

An iceberg is a large structure. We can imagine it is built from small ice cubes. Let's adjust how we think of our House of Confidence and think of it in ice terms. We can call it an Igloo of Confidence.

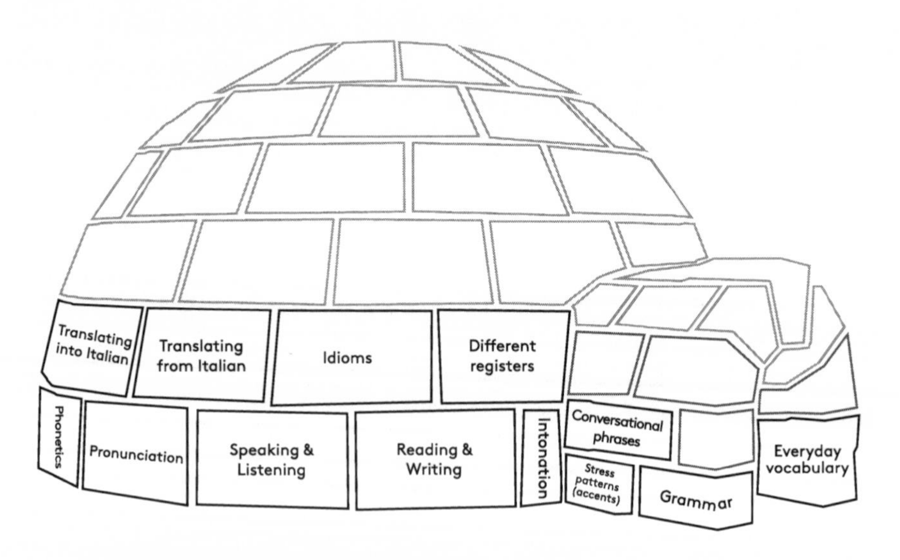

Figure 23.3: Example Igloo of Confidence for becoming an expert in speaking Italian. This igloo is only about 30 percent complete, so there is still room for improvement.

IGLOOS OF CONFIDENCE

Simply working on your "general confidence levels" is too vague to be helpful. So, imagine you have an Igloo of Confidence for every important area of your life—like a housing estate of igloos. Your entire igloo housing estate represents your overarching confidence in yourself and your abilities. So to begin improving your confidence, you must start by doing very specific work on a specific igloo.

Each igloo will be in a different state, depending on your confidence levels in that area. So some igloos will need more work than others.

I will now show you how to build up each igloo.

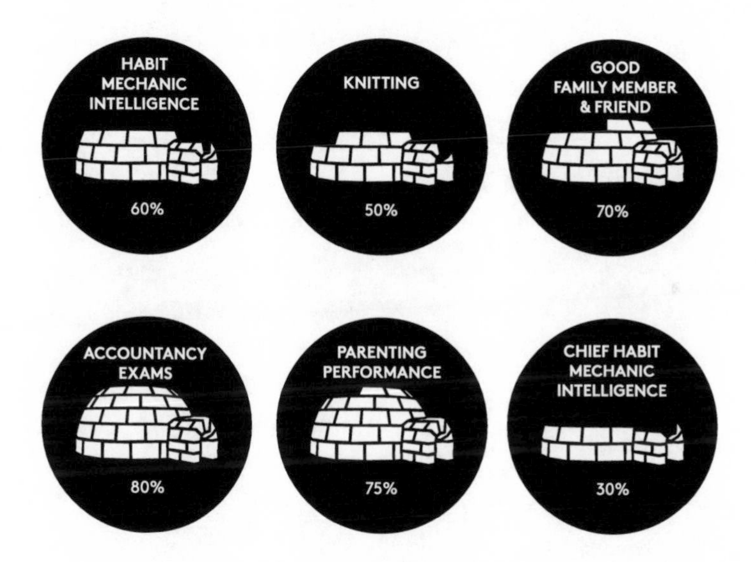

Figure 23.4: Your confidence will be much more robust if you have evidence (ice cubes) to back up your beliefs (igloos).

Ice Cubes (Evidence) and Igloos (Beliefs)

Confidence has two parts: belief (self-esteem) and evidence (self-efficacy).

We have a general belief about how good we are at an activity. Think of the *belief* as the structure of the igloo.

The *evidence* you are good at an activity is represented by the individual ice cubes within the igloo.

To develop Robust Confidence, you need both belief and evidence.

For example, your "Habit Mechanic intelligence" Igloo of Confidence might frequently be challenged and damaged. However, if you understand the different pieces of evidence (ice cubes) that underpin your beliefs about your ability to proactively be your best and build new habits, your confidence will not crumble when it is challenged.

By making sure you always connect your beliefs to evidence, it is less likely you will develop false confidence, which can be very unhelpful for health, happiness, and performance.

Test?

If it is helpful, write down the two components of confidence to test your memory!

Building Up Your Confidence Igloos

Let's begin to think about how we can practically build up our confidence levels.

To begin building confidence in anything, we first need to step back and put perspective on our lives.

If we do not deliberately step back from daily occurrences and activities and reflect, it is much easier for HUE (Horribly Unhelpful Emotions) to focus on unhelpful and negative thoughts.

To achieve perspective, we should do intelligent Self-Watching daily. I have already shown how our 3:1 Daily Reflection tool is very useful for this. But we can go much further.

Make a list of your top five roles and responsibilities (at work and/or in life). Rate your current performance on each role from 1 to 10—remember the poor to perfect (P2) scale (Chapter 19, Figure 19.4).

Here are some examples of areas that are important for me:

1. Developing my Habit Mechanic intelligence—so I can be my best (8)
2. Developing my Chief Habit Mechanic intelligence—so I can help others (8)
3. Writing this book (6)
4. Creating new Habit Mechanic and Chief Habit Mechanic Tools—to help others (8)
5. Being a good family member and friend (8)

Now, please try to do the same for your own life (e.g., relationships, family, social activities) and work:

1. ?
2. ?
3. ?
4. ?
5. ?

Then, after each area, give yourself a score out of 10 for your current performance, where 10 means you are perfect.

Think of each area you have highlighted as an igloo. The score you have given each area indicates how well developed the igloo is.

Now, circle one area (igloo) you want to prioritize improving before the rest (i.e., make a small step forward in the area or activity). For example, I might select "Habit Mechanic intelligence" from my list. Or in other words, my "Habit Mechanic intelligence igloo." I want to improve my confidence in my Habit Mechanic abilities by building up my Habit Mechanic intelligence igloo.

By completing this process, you are Self-Watching and starting to make an Aim. But you need to make your Aim specific. Let me show you how by using the "Confidence Profile" (a Habit Mechanic Tool).

Developing My Habit Mechanic Intelligence Igloo

I am focusing on my "Habit Mechanic intelligence igloo." I have scored myself 8 out of 10, therefore recognizing that I do have Habit Mechanic knowledge, skills, habits, and strengths (my evidence or ice cubes) already in place. But there are also other ice cubes I need to freeze to become an even better Habit Mechanic.

To help me organize my thoughts, I write them out in a confidence planning tool I have created called the Confidence Profile. This is designed to help you highlight

- your current performance (in important areas of your life and work);
- your current knowledge, skills, habits, and strengths (evidence/ice cubes); and
- what you can work on to further develop each igloo (the next ice cube(s) you want to freeze).

Here is my example Habit Mechanic intelligence igloo:

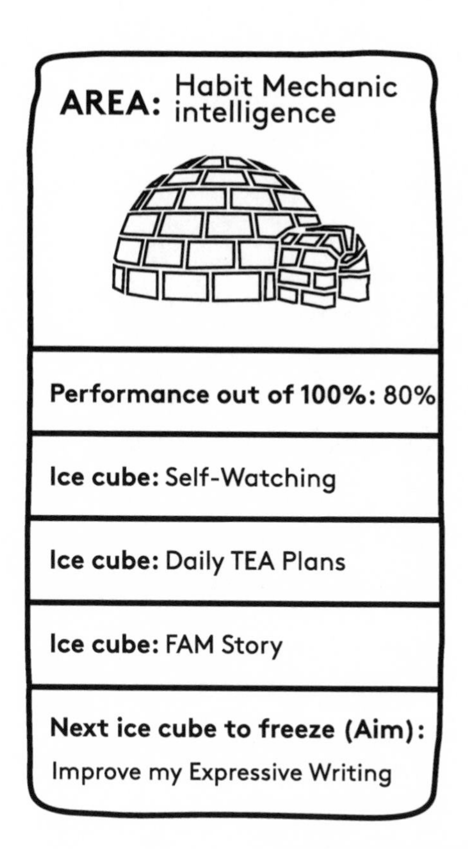

Figure 23.5: Example Habit Mechanic intelligence igloo. Think of the "Next ice cube to freeze" as the improvement Aim, that is, the A in SWAP (Self-Watch, Aim, Plan). Please note that my 8 out of 10 translates into 80 percent, that is, I think this igloo is 80 percent complete.

In this hypothetical example, I have highlighted my top three Habit Mechanic intelligence ice cubes (evidence—i.e., knowledge, skills, habits, and strengths):

1. I am good at intelligently Self-Watching my habits, and know my strengths and areas for improvement.
2. I create a TEA Plan on most days, which makes it easier to be my best.

3. I have created a detailed FAM (Future Ambitious Meaningful) Story, which I periodically update.

Note: I could write down more of my Habit Mechanic intelligence ice cubes. I would do this in my notebook or create a "Confidence Profile" Word document. The Confidence Profile template below (Figure 23.6) only has space for three ice cubes because its purpose is simply to get you started on your confidence-building journey.

To develop my Habit Mechanic intelligence igloo further, I need to get better at managing stress. But to achieve this I need to be more specific, so I have highlighted "Expressive Writing" as the next ice cube I want to freeze (this is my specific improvement Aim). I will explain my Plan for building an Expressive Writing habit in the "Build the Habit" section at the end of this chapter.

Create Your Own Igloos

Confidence Profile:
Health, happiness & performance overview

Name: **Date:**

AREA:

Performance out of 100%:

Ice cube:

Ice cube:

Ice cube:

Next ice cube to freeze:

AREA:

Performance out of 100%:

Ice cube:

Ice cube:

Ice cube:

Next ice cube to freeze:

AREA:

Performance out of 100%:

Ice cube:

Ice cube:

Ice cube:

Next ice cube to freeze:

AREA:

Performance out of 100%:

Ice cube:

Ice cube:

Ice cube:

Next ice cube to freeze:

AREA:

Performance out of 100%:

Ice cube:

Ice cube:

Ice cube:

Next ice cube to freeze:

AREA:

Performance out of 100%:

Ice cube:

Ice cube:

Ice cube:

Next ice cube to freeze:

Figure 23.6: The Confidence Profile is a simple tool to help you reflect on and build confidence in different areas of your life.

First, I want to give you the opportunity to create some of your own igloos (like my Habit Mechanic intelligence example). So, if it is helpful, use Figure 23.6 to have a go at creating some. You could start by using the top five roles and responsibilities (one igloo for each area) you detailed earlier.

Write down a minimum of three ice cubes (evidence—i.e., knowledge, skills, habits, and strengths) for each igloo. You can write more if you wish (e.g., in your notebook or elsewhere).

Then, circle the igloo you want to prioritize improving before the rest.

Finally, in this igloo write down one small improvement you want to make (i.e., this is your Aim; in my example, I targeted improving my Expressive Writing). Remember, we think of these small improvements as building or freezing new ice cubes to make the igloo more robust. Over time, you can freeze more and more ice cubes for each igloo. But for the time being, just focus on improving one small area in the igloo you have deemed to be most important.

A World Champion Confidence-Building Example

Let's return to the story of Jessica Ennis-Hill to learn more about building our own confidence.

Ennis-Hill might have had a Long Jump igloo. After she sustained the injury to her right foot, she may well have rated her long jump performance at just 60 percent.

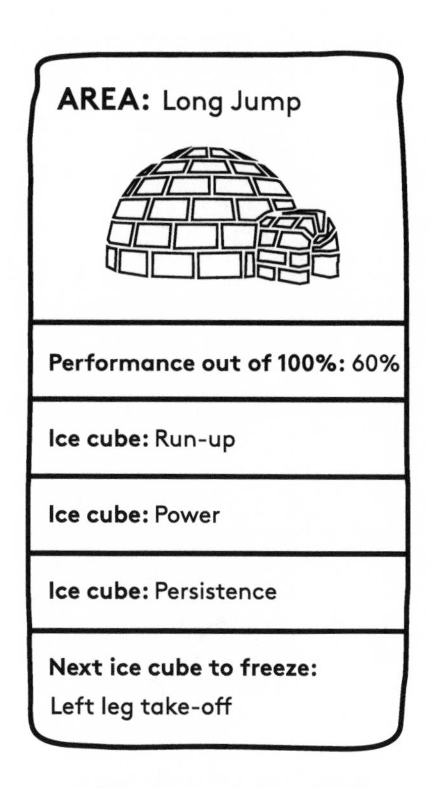

Figure 23.7: An example Long Jump igloo.

Notice the score is not zero. The Confidence Profile would have helped her realize that even though she had injured her take-off foot, she still had long jump knowledge, skills, habits, and strengths, or evidence (ice cubes) about her long jump abilities (a quick run-up, good leg strength, etc.). This evidence prevented her Long Jump igloo from crumbling.

Jessica Ennis-Hill could then have identified one area for improvement to focus on. This might have been improving her left leg take-off performance. In this way, she would have been Self-Watching and making an Aim (improving left leg take-off performance).

Once we've identified the ice cube we want to freeze (our Aim), we need to understand how we will build our confidence in this area.

"KOSY Confidence" is a planning tool (a Habit Mechanic Tool) to help us achieve this. It helps us identify what we need to **do** to improve (i.e., freeze the new ice cube). It also helps us reflect on personal strengths and relationships we already have that can help us with our confidence building.

K stands for **Knowledge**. We can build confidence by acquiring more knowledge.

Knowledge

Figure 23.8: "Knowing" more about how to do Expressive Writing can improve my confidence in my stress management abilities.

O stands for **Others**. Other people (e.g., a family member, a mentor, a senior colleague, a close friend) can help us build confidence by sharing helpful knowledge and skills, listening to us, and giving us emotional support. Further, we can also gain confidence in our ability to successfully complete a task by seeing others doing it. This is called a vicarious experience.

Note: I know that seeking advice from others can be difficult, because you might have been led to believe it makes you look weak. This is simply not true. Asking for help means that you want to grow and improve and shows that you are resilient. If some people don't like this, that is their problem, not yours. This is also one of the reasons I have created the Habit Mechanic app—to provide a place where like-minded people can seek support from each other without being judged.

Others

Figure 23.9: "Other" people can help me improve my stress management abilities by acting as a sounding board, giving me emotional support, and teaching me about their Expressive Writing knowledge and skills.

S stands for **Skill**. Knowing something is different from being able to do it. Skill is the application of knowledge.

Skills

Figure 23.10: Knowing how to do Expressive Writing is one thing; doing it is another. To get better at Expressive Writing, I need to practice doing it (i.e., develop my Expressive Writing skills).

Y stands for **You**. You have transferable skills, for example, self-control, optimism, your ability to learn (reading and writing skills), etc. You can use these to help build confidence in any situation or area of your life.

Figure 23.11: Remember, learning is your superpower. You can use it to build confidence in any important area of your life.

The overall idea with KOSY Confidence is to use it as a helpful framework to freeze new ice cubes and build confidence in any part of our lives. Let me show you an example.

Using KOSY to Build Your Confidence

We can apply the KOSY Confidence framework to Jessica Ennis-Hill when she needed to develop some confidence in using her left leg take-off for the long jump.

Let's recap on the "P2 (Poor to Perfect) Scale" (initially shown in Chapter 19, Figure 19.4). Remember, we are neither useless nor faultlessly excellent at anything we do. At the poor end of the P2 Scale, your igloo doesn't exist. At the perfect end, your igloo is flawless—which from my experience will never be true, because of the challenging nature of the modern world.

In terms of Ennis-Hill's P2 Scale for the long jump, perhaps she was over halfway toward her long jump being good enough to win in top-level competition. In other words, her Igloo of Confidence was 60 percent built. This means she still had some work to do.

Let's imagine she wanted to increase her long jump Igloo of Confidence to being 80 percent built before the World Championships (her first major competition after her foot injury).

To help her achieve this, she may have used a "KOSY Confidence plan" (a Habit Mechanic Tool).

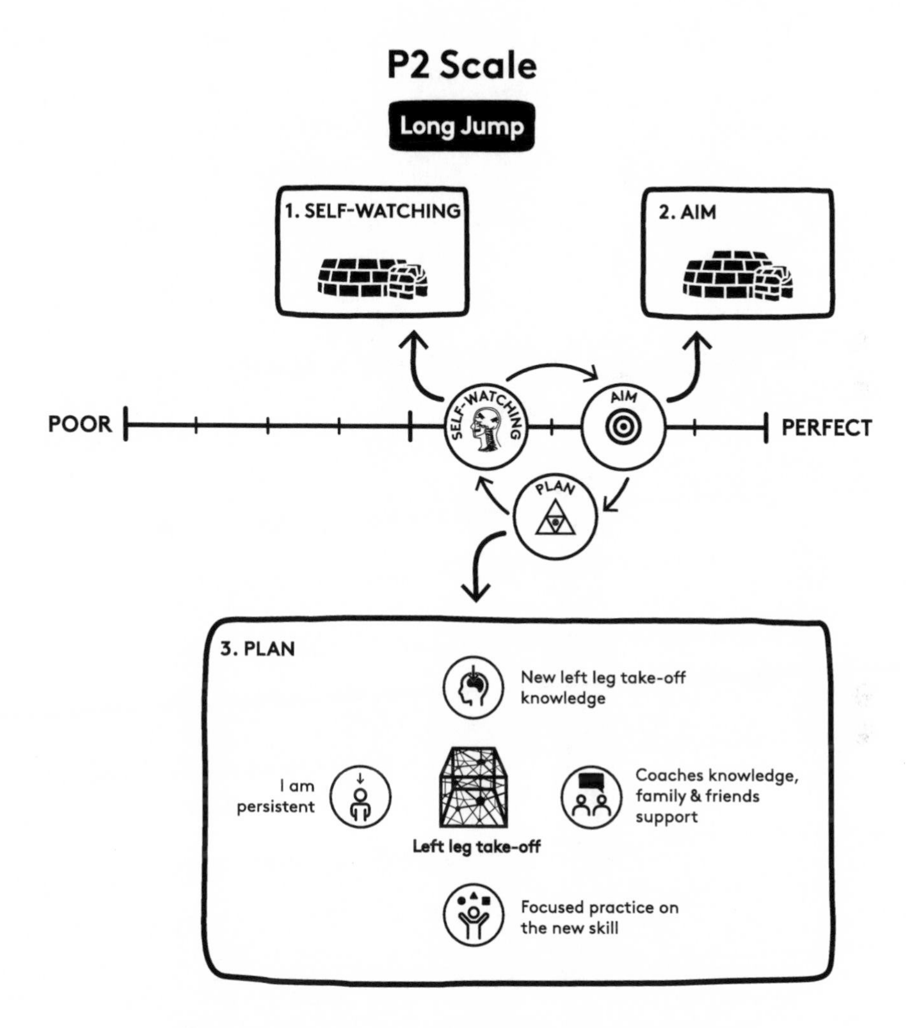

Figure 23.12: An overview of an example KOSY Confidence plan. In real terms, Ennis-Hill's left leg take-off ice cube might have been several different ice cubes. I'm just calling it one to keep this example simple.

Her Aim was to improve left leg take-off. To do this, she could:

- Gain **knowledge** about the best way to approach the long jump using her left leg.
- Ask **others** for technical knowledge (her coach) and emotional support (family and friends).
- Improve her **skill** by putting the knowledge she had gained about left leg take-off technique into focused practice.
- Draw on her persistence (one of her "**You**" qualities) when things got difficult.

Building Confidence in Your Ability to Build Confidence

Here is another KOSY example:

Aim: to be more confident in my ability to build my confidence up. To do this, I could:

- Gain more **knowledge** about building confidence by re-reading this chapter several times.
- Ask **other** Habit Mechanics how they build confidence in themselves and others, and post about my confidence-building journey in the Habit Mechanic app to get emotional support.
- Improve my confidence-building **skills** by completing a Confidence Profile, creating specific KOSY plans for different ice cubes I want to build, and reviewing and updating these monthly.
- Draw on my resilience (one of my "**You**" qualities) to help me keep persisting when HUE is encouraging me to give up.

Try this for yourself. Think about the next ice cube you want to freeze in the igloo you want to develop, and use KOSY to make a confidence-building plan.

STABILIZING OUR CONFIDENCE AFTER A SETBACK

Of course, none of our lives are straightforward. We all experience events that dent and damage our confidence. So, we invariably need to stabilize our confidence as well as build it.

For example, our confidence gets damaged when something we think we are good at gets questioned (e.g., I gave a presentation I thought was very good, but someone told me they did not think it was). In other words, what I expected to happen (get praise for my presentation) didn't happen. So, I experience a dislocation of meaning systems. This is the stress response process I outlined in Chapter 22.

Stabilizing our confidence requires us to directly address the stress response. The good news is we already know how to do this (re-read Chapter 22 for a full recap). You might remember, there are several approaches:

- You can use breathing management techniques.
- You can also use our Focused Reflection (writing) techniques:
  - FAB (Fortunate, Adapt, Benefits) Thinking
  - WABA (Written APE Brain Argument)
  - RABA (Running APE Brain Argument)
  - Expressive Writing
  - RAW (Reduce Activation and Write) Back

Proactively using these techniques will make it much easier for you to regulate your emotions and get your thinking back on track. Remember, we can't avoid feeling bad, but we can work on our emotional response so that these feelings do not last as long as they otherwise would have. For example, instead of it taking five days to start feeling better after a setback, you might be able to do it in three days—**if** you proactively manage your emotions and build back your confidence.

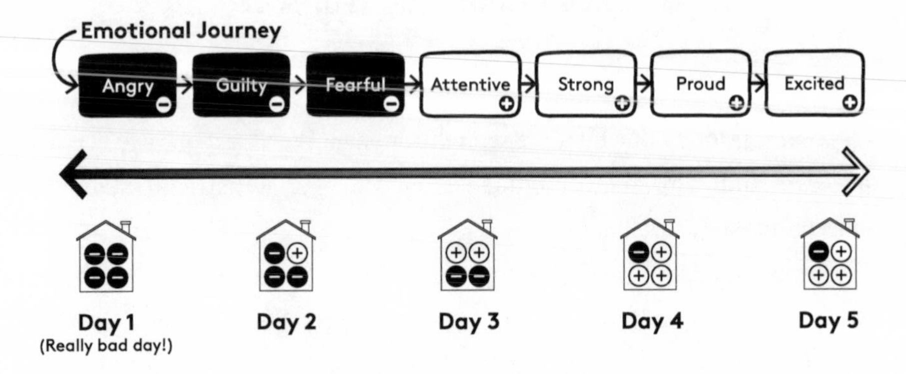

Figure 23.13: You cannot avoid getting stressed and having your confidence knocked, but you can choose to use Habit Mechanic Tools to proactively manage stress, rebuild your confidence, and spend more of your time being at your best.

Once you have stabilized your confidence, and you can think clearly, you will be in a much better place to accurately reflect on the events that dented your confidence. In my example, I could consider whether the feedback I received about my presentation was valid. If it was (or elements of the feedback were valid), I could use my confidence-building skills to help me freeze more ice cubes to make myself an even better presenter.

CONGRATULATIONS ARE IN ORDER!

You now know how to build confidence and how to stabilize it. Well done for persisting with this learning! You are building up your "Habit Mechanic intelligence Igloo of Confidence"!

BUILDING BETTER CONFIDENCE HABITS

In this part, I have considered how you can build and maintain Robust Confidence. I've shared some knowledge to try and make confidence easier to understand, and some practical skills you can use to build and stabilize your confidence in different areas of your life.

If you want to build up your confidence, it is helpful to engage in monthly, weekly, and daily confidence-building activities.

Monthly

- Create and update your Confidence Profile and clearly target the new ice cubes you want to freeze (e.g., improve my Expressive Writing skills).
- Having a well-developed FAM (Future Ambitious Meaningful) Story will make it easier to develop a Confidence Profile.

Weekly

- Reflect on the work you have done to freeze new ice cubes (e.g., "How well have I done my best to improve my Expressive Writing skills?").
- Record your successes (e.g., What new knowledge did you acquire about improving your Expressive Writing skills? Which skills did you try out? What feedback did you get from others about your improved stress management abilities? Did you feel less stressed?).
- By reflecting and recording, you are collecting evidence about your abilities (i.e., this is the process of freezing new ice cubes to build up your igloos).

Daily

- Keep working on your DES (diet, exercise, sleep) habits to ensure your brain is working properly, so you can think clearly.
- Reflect and record. Complete something like a Daily 3:1 Reflection or a short Expressive Writing style reflection. This process will help you reflect on and record evidence about the ice cubes you already have, and the new ones you are freezing.

OVERVIEW

Here is an overview of my key points about building Robust Confidence:

1. Develop good DES (diet, exercise, sleep) habits to make it easier to build and manage your confidence.
2. Use the 3:1 ratio and remember Robust Confidence includes an element of negativity or healthy self-criticism.
3. Confidence has two components: belief (the igloo) and evidence (the ice cubes).
4. The Confidence Profile can help you gain perspective.
5. Focus on freezing one ice cube at a time.
6. Use the KOSY Confidence framework to build up important igloos.
7. Use stress management skills to stabilize confidence when you experience a setback.
8. Plan to build your confidence daily, weekly, and monthly.

There might be several ideas on this list you think would be helpful for you. I suggest you add those ideas into your Me Power Wish List.

BUILD THE HABIT

We can also use the Habit Building Plan to help us freeze new ice cubes.

Let me give you an example. I want to improve my Habit Mechanic intelligence igloo, and the specific ice cube I want to freeze is "improve my Expressive Writing."

To help me achieve this, my Aim is to "Write a short Expressive Writing style reflection at the end of each working day. This will help me to focus on what I have done well, and to reframe and defuse any challenges I have experienced." This Aim will allow me to build up my Habit Mechanic intelligence igloo.

Next (if you want to), **make a written note of one ice cube you would like to prioritize freezing** to help you improve one of your Igloos of Confidence. Think of this as an Aim, and remember that good Aims are carefully written down, are specific (using times and locations), state a positive action ("I will" instead of "I will not"), and can be measured (using quantities).

Your Aim:

Once you have a clear Aim, you might want to revisit the self-reflection tool "How HUE Hinders Change" (Chapter 20) to help you think about how HUE might try to stop you from building this new habit.

Now it is time to create a Habit Building Plan to activate the Nine Action Factors and supercharge the habit building process.

To do this, you need to answer the following questions.

1. Describe the SMALL specific new helpful habit that you want to build (i.e., your Aim to help you freeze a new ice cube):

   Example answer: Write a short Expressive Writing style reflection at the end of each working day.

2. Describe what you currently do (your unhelpful habit instead of the new helpful habit you want to build):

   ___

   Example answer: Dwell on all the things that didn't go well and generally beat myself up.

3. Describe what reminds or triggers this unhelpful habit:

   ___

   Example answer: My HUE is very powerful and is constantly reminding me of the problems in my life.

4. Describe how you will remind yourself (trigger) to practice your NEW habit daily:

   ___

   Example answer: Set a daily calendar alert to remind me. Create a specific Word document on my laptop where I will write down/type out these reflections.

5. Describe the new knowledge and skills you will need to help you secure your new habit:
   Example answer: Learn more about the different Focused Reflection techniques I can build into my Expressive Writing.

6. If it is helpful, describe where and how you will acquire the new knowledge and skills you need:

   ___

   Example answer: Re-read Chapter 22.

7. Describe in detail why you want to build this new habit:

   ___

   Example answer: Give me a better chance of thinking clearly and being my best so I can perform well in my job, and I think it will help with family life as well.

8. Who can you ask to help you build your new habit? (ideally, this person or persons will also be building the same or a similar habit at the same time):

   Example answer: Start getting my kids to do Daily 3:1 Reflections at the end of each day; this will be a helpful trigger for my Expressive Writing.

9. What will be the reward for building the new habit? Remember, rewards can be internal, external, or social.

   Example answer: I will feel better about myself, I will have a better chance of getting the promotion I want, and I will be better able to help colleagues and family members.

10. What will be the cost/penalty for not building the new habit?

    Example answer: The opposite of the rewards I describe above.

Congratulations, you now have a robust plan to develop a new confidence-building habit!

HABIT MECHANIC LANGUAGE AND TOOLS YOU HAVE LEARNED IN CHAPTER 23...

Core Language

The House of Confidence—A concept developed to make confidence easier to understand and build. ☑

The Igloo of Confidence—A concept developed to make it easier to understand and develop the two core components of confidence (belief [self-esteem] and evidence [self-efficacy]). ☑

Planning Tools

The Confidence Profile—A simple tool to help you reflect on and build confidence in different areas of your life. ☑

KOSY (Knowledge, Others, Skills, You) Confidence—A simple confidence-building framework. ☑

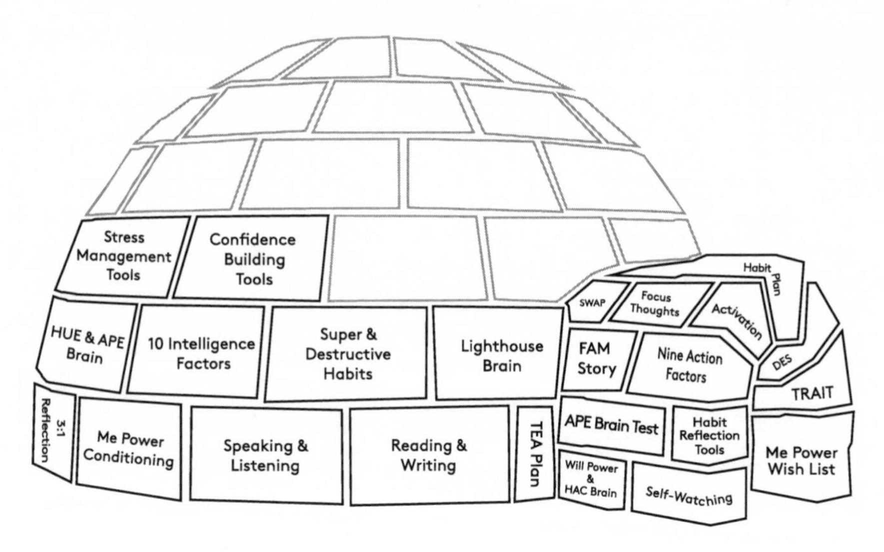

Figure 23.14: Your Habit Mechanic intelligence igloo is building up!

> *Next, we'll build on what we have learned about stress and confidence management by looking at some simple Habit Mechanic Tools we can use to get better at performing under pressure.*

24

PERFORM UNDER PRESSURE USING SECRETS FROM WORLD-CLASS PERFORMERS

American billionaire and philanthropist Warren Buffett is regarded as one of the world's most successful investors and is ranked as one of the wealthiest people on the planet. The so-called "Oracle of Omaha" provides a great example of a highly successful individual, who it is easy to believe is just a natural. But if we look in detail at his career, we can see that, just like all of us, he had to deliberately learn to overcome challenges to fulfill his potential.

He said: "Someone once said that the chains of habit are too light to be felt until they are too heavy to be broken."

When he started his career in the 1950s, by his own admission Buffett was terrified of public speaking. He said: "I couldn't do it. I would throw up!" He knew he had to improve to achieve his life goals. So he enrolled in a popular public speaking training program.

By moving from knowledge-to-skill-to-habit, Buffett described how the course improved his performance under pressure. He has explained that had he not learned to be an accomplished public speaker, his life would have been different and not as successful. Buffett has always been proud to display his course certificate. In fact, he says, it has pride of place over his prestigious academic degrees.

In this chapter, you will learn how to better manage all the elements that impact your performance when the pressure is on. Because you already understand how to manage stress and build your confidence, handling pressure will now be much easier. But in this chapter, I will go further by digging deeper into the science of "learning how to focus when the pressure is on." You will learn how to systematically prepare for specific events and situations where you need to perform under pressure. If you want to pressure-proof your performances, keep reading.

PRACTICING TO PERFORM—LESSONS FROM KING GEORGE VI

To perform under pressure, there are several factors you need to consider when practicing. The following story will explain them to you.

The film *The King's Speech* focuses on the true story of King George VI's stutter and his relationship with his speech therapist, Lionel Logue. The basis of the film was hundreds of diary entries, documents, and letters written about the unusually close relationship between the King and this man.

Lionel Logue was not the first speech therapist asked to help the King. In fact, George VI had seen so many, and had experienced so much failure trying to cure his stutter, that he had given up hope and did not even want to meet Mr. Logue.

Eventually, the King agreed. In the film, at the end of their first consultation, the speech therapist declared: "I can cure you, but it will need a tremendous effort by you. Without that effort, it can't be done." Logue insisted that the King needed to engage in regular focused practice (meaning you focus hard, make mistakes, and use feedback about your mistakes to get better).

One of the central focuses of the film is the King's coronation at Westminster Abbey, where he needed to speak publicly in a high-pressure situation.

According to the film, Logue didn't just ask the King to practice his speech at home or in Logue's Harley Street office. They went to Westminster Abbey, where the coronation would take place. He also made the King sit in the coronation chair and talk through the speech in real time, in the same way he would need to during the hugely important state occasion. Logue also played the part of the Archbishop of Canterbury, so the King could replicate the exchanges between the two.

Logue was exposing the King to **five conditions** that would be present at the real coronation. This wouldn't be the case if the King had simply practiced the speech in his private rooms.

1. First, the therapist was allowing the King to experience what it would be like to perform the speech in Westminster Abbey, so he could become comfortable with the **environment**.
2. Second, by asking him to sit in the coronation chair, Logue was trying to make the King's practice **as similar as possible to the real performance**.
3. Third, by asking the King to practice his responses and speech in Westminster Abbey's coronation chair, Logue was allowing him to experience and practice **managing the Activation levels** he would experience on Coronation Day.
4. By playing the role of the Archbishop of Canterbury, Logue was trying to **make the task (performing the speech) as similar as possible** in rehearsals as it would be in the real ceremony.
5. Finally, and connected to the last point, Logue tried to **make the timing of the task as similar as possible** to the real thing.

> This meant the King had to speak with a rhythm and a pace that would make it more difficult for him to stutter, allowing him to practice at the same speed he would have to perform at on Coronation Day.

Lionel Logue's detailed training plan for the King appears to have paid off. George VI completed his speech at Westminster Abbey without a single stutter. The same practice strategies were used to help the King deliver other powerful and important speeches throughout his reign, including during the difficult days of the Second World War.

FIRING THE SAME NEURAL CIRCUITRY

Our knowledge of these events is drawn largely from a film. But although we do not have a firsthand account, it is safe to assume that Lionel Logue's techniques were very effective at firing the same neural circuitry in the King's brain during practice that would need to fire for him to make successful public speeches. This is perhaps why he succeeded in helping the King where so many had failed.

For your practice to be successful, it needs to trigger the same neural circuits you will need to use when performing under pressure.

Imagine you are rehearsing an important presentation and consider the following points.

Environment

First, think about the environment in which your presentation is taking place. Are you familiar with the room? The more comfortable you feel in that environment, the less likely it will have a negative impact on your performance.

Activation

Next, consider Activation. What is your ideal Activation level when you are giving a great presentation? Replicate that same level when you're practicing your presentation.

It is also worth thinking about how the presentation environment might affect your Activation. If you think you will feel nervous during the presentation—and therefore your Activation will be high in the presentation—you might want to try to replicate this when practicing.

Physical Elements

The third factor focuses on the physical elements connected to giving the presentation. When you give your presentation, will you be sitting at your desk—or will you be standing up? How will you be dressed? Replicate these factors in your practice as closely as possible.

Tasks

The fourth factor to consider is the tasks you perform during the presentation. Will you be reading your presentation from a script? Will you be presenting without notes? Will you be using a clicker to move through your slides? Practice what you will actually be doing in the real presentation.

Timing

The final factor to consider is timing. What time of the day is your presentation? How much time will you have? How much time will you have on each slide? Practice using the same presentation timings.

TE–TAP Learning Framework

To recap, you need to consider the following factors during your practice to prepare you to perform to your potential under pressure:

1. The performance environment
2. Your optimal performance Activation level
3. The physical elements of the performance
4. The tasks you will be completing
5. The performance timings

To make it easier to remember these five factors, I created the acronym "**TE–TAP** Learning": **T**ask, **E**nvironment, **T**imings, **A**ctivation, and **P**hysical. By activating all these factors in your practice, you will be firing the same, or similar, neural circuitry in your brain that you will need to fire during your actual performance.

Test?

If it is helpful, write down what TE-TAP stands for to test your memory!

BUILDING ROUTINES TO HELP US PERFORM UNDER PRESSURE

In the summer of 1998, the England rugby union team set out on a tour to Australia, New Zealand, and South Africa. The team included a young player who had been touted as the future of English rugby. His name was Jonny Wilkinson.

When Wilkinson read that he'd been selected for the squad, he thought it must be a mistake. He was thrilled when he discovered it was true. He had played for England before, but only as a substitute. Now, in Brisbane, he was set to make his full debut, starting the game in the fly-half position against Australia, one of the best teams in the world.

England coach Clive Woodward said: "He had come on as a sub before, but this was his first full start... big difference."

When the game started, England quickly won their first penalty and decided to go for goal. It was Wilkinson's job to take the kicks. The TV commentator said: "For a man of his talent, this is a simple kick." Wilkinson missed. The same commentator began to criticize him.

England won another penalty, giving Wilkinson another opportunity. As he prepared to take the kick, the commentator added: "This is a real test for him after what was an easy miss." Wilkinson missed again.

As the game went on, Wilkinson seemed to make mistake after mistake. At one point, the commentator said: "He must wonder what international rugby is all about."

England lost the game 76–0. During the tour, the team suffered a series of heavy defeats and the media dubbed it "The Tour from Hell."

For many, such a negative experience might have been the end. But not for Jonny Wilkinson. He wanted to learn from this setback and use it as a platform to become an even better player. He would go on to score more World Cup points than any other player in history. But how?

Wilkinson recognized that pressure, which is created by HUE (Horribly Unhelpful Emotions), was having a negative effect on his game—and, in particular, his kicking. So he set out to improve his ability to perform under pressure.

Wilkinson describes kicking successfully under pressure like this: "Dealing with the pressure of kicks comes back to process. You get away from the outcome and you take it back to understanding that if I do this in the zone that I can control around the ball, with the parts of me that I can control... then I will get [a successful kick]."

Wilkinson means there is no point in focusing on the result of the kick. You will only achieve the ideal outcome if you get the process right. Thinking about the possibility of the outcome **not** being positive can make you more nervous and add more pressure. The only thing it is sensible to focus on is the process of making a good kick. Here, Wilkinson is talking about HACing (hacking) his brain and taking responsibility for what he can control (i.e., managing his thoughts and physical actions).

To give himself the best chance of successful goal kicking, Wilkinson focused on making his routine as robust as possible. Although he evolved and developed the routine over time, I will share one version with you to help you understand the process. This version comes from firsthand accounts of what Wilkinson said.

First, I will focus on the physical actions.

1. Wilkinson began by placing the ball down and teeing it up.
2. He then took a specific number of steps backward and tapped the toes of his kicking foot on the floor.
3. Then he cupped his hands together.
4. Next, he looked up and down at the target.
5. Finally, he ran and kicked the ball.

Whether they recognize it or not, all goal kickers have a physical routine like this, although probably not as elaborate. This is because all goal kickers have to tee up the ball, then pace backward, and finally kick the ball. Human nature means the way they do this for each kick will be fairly consistent. Remember, our brain likes to turn things into habits to save energy.

You also have physical routines in your daily life. For example, think about going into the office, sitting at your desk, and beginning work. Typically, it goes something like this:

1. You walk into the room.

2. You sit down at your chair.
3. You turn on your computer.
4. You engage, or try to engage, in the work you have to do.
5. Finally, at the end of a period of work you save your work, turn off your computer, stand up, and leave the room.

CREATING A MENTAL ROUTINE

What makes Jonny Wilkinson's routine stand out is that he not only understood the physical elements, but he also recognized the mental aspects.

The experiences of his first full Test match against Australia taught him that if he let HUE control his thoughts he would not perform to his potential.

When he was putting the ball down, he recognized it was not helpful to be saying to himself: "Don't miss this kick, because you will let everyone down." Nor was it helpful to see himself missing the kick in his mind's eye.

In the same way, when you stand up to give your presentation, you might be saying to yourself: "This is going to be so difficult; I am bound to make a mistake." But thoughts like these are unlikely to help you perform to your potential.

To help you understand how you can think more effectively under pressure, I am going to show how Jonny Wilkinson planned to think during his routine. To do this, we are going to use Focus Words and Pictures, concepts I have covered earlier in this book (Chapters 21 and 22). Using Focus Words and Pictures will help you HAC (Helpful Attention Control) your attention when you are under pressure, so you can perform to your potential.

Jonny Wilkinson added Focus Words and Pictures to each physical step of his routine to allow him to pay attention to helpful information. He developed and evolved these over time, but here is one version based on firsthand accounts.

Step 1

Physical action: placing the ball down and teeing it up

Focus Pictures: seeing the best kick he had made from that position

Focus Words: "Come on, you can do this."

Step 2

Physical action: pacing backward and tapping the toes of his kicking foot on the floor

Focus Pictures: imagining his foot becoming like a block of concrete, so that when he kicked the ball it was solid and powerful

Focus Words: "Concentrate, hard foot."

Step 3

Physical action: cupping his hands

Focus Pictures: imagining a shield popping up around him blocking out all noise and distractions

Focus Words: "Concentrate."

Step 4

Physical action: looking up and down at the target and assessing the kick

Focus Pictures: an elderly lady called Doris. He imagines her sitting behind the posts, reading a copy of the *Sunday Times*.

Focus Words: emphasizing his focus on his kicking target, which was to hit a particular section on the *Sunday Times* front cover

Step 5

Physical action: running and kicking the ball

Focus Pictures: a surge of energy running down his leg so that when he makes contact with the ball it goes a long way

Focus Words: emphasizing the rhythm of the run-up and timing of the kick

Jonny Wilkinson became the best goal kicker in world rugby, and a global sporting icon for his ability to perform under pressure when it mattered the most.

His last-minute drop-goal, kicked off his weakest foot, secured England a World Cup victory in 2003. Since then, professional athletes around the world have tried to copy Wilkinson's routine to give them an edge over their competitors when the pressure is on.

You can do the same. The best way to help HUE in pressure situations, like giving an important presentation, is to pre-plan how you are going to think—just like Jonny Wilkinson.

You could pre-plan a sequence of key Focus Words and Focus Pictures, and practice these as part of your preparation. Planning and practicing these techniques will make it easier for you to perform when the pressure is on.

I call these "in-performance routines" and I will show you how to build one.

But first I want to show you how to create a "pre-performance routine," which will also help you deal with pressure.

Pre-performance Routines

José Mourinho is one of the most successful soccer managers of all time. He has coached teams to league title wins in the English Premier League, Italy's

Serie A, and La Liga in Spain. He was once asked in a television interview if he wanted his players to be nervous before a big game.

The interviewer put their question like this: "Sometimes nerves are thought to be good, because nerves cause adrenaline and adrenaline focuses the mind, and because sometimes if you are a bit laid back before a big match you are not quite on edge."

Mourinho answered:

> *Nerves, no. But relaxation, clearly no. And as I was saying in relation to myself, we need to feel in the moment, in the right state of mind, and that is something very, very personal.*
>
> *I want them to feel comfortable. That is why before the game I leave with them the way they feel comfortable. Some of them like a short and aggressive warm-up. Others, they start warming up one-and-a-half hours before the game. They like to do it very slowly with a completely different profile. Some they like music, some don't. Some like aggressive music, some don't. Some like to speak on the phone with their family, or whoever. Some disconnect the phone three-hours before the game, they want to be completely isolated. It is something very, very personal.*

José Mourinho is saying that every person's ideal preparation to perform to their best under pressure is different. I agree.

He lets each of his players perform their own pre-match routines, empowering each player to optimize their preparation to perform to their potential under pressure.

Find Your Optimal Activation Level

Mourinho's approach is also similar to our own. For example, every person has an optimal Activation level they need to achieve to perform to their potential under pressure. Everyone's optimal Activation level will be slightly different.

To help you achieve the correct Activation level as you are beginning your performance, I encourage you to develop a pre-performance routine.

A pre-performance routine will make it easier to consistently begin your performance at the correct Activation level. Without this type of routine, HUE is more likely to make it difficult for you to succeed.

The first thing you need to work out is what Activation level you want to achieve at the beginning of your performance. The ideal Activation level might differ for different tasks, for example, a presentation to your immediate team (might be 50) versus a presentation to the board of directors (might be 60) versus a presentation to 500 people in a large lecture theatre (might be 65).

Get in Your Performance Zone

Once you've worked out which Activation level you want to achieve, you need to build a pre-performance routine that helps you get to the correct level.

Activation levels will be much easier to control if your diet, exercise, and sleep are optimal. So ask yourself:

- "Will the food I eat in the build-up to a performance help me achieve and sustain my ideal Activation level throughout the performance?" (e.g., high GI versus low GI food—discussed in Chapter 21)
- "How can I use pre-performance exercise to help me achieve the correct Activation level in my performance?" (e.g., going for a pre-performance walk or run)
- "Do my nighttime sleeping habits allow me to sustain the correct Activation level in my performances?" and "Would a power nap before a big performance help?"

You can also use specific skills to both increase and decrease your Activation levels. We covered these skills in detail in Chapter 21. Below I will recap some of the core techniques.

The basic skill for Activation management is breathing control. To increase your Activation, you can exercise and also use a Focus Picture of the Activation dial in your mind's eye, seeing it increase to the correct level, and use Focus Words to pump yourself up.

To reduce your Activation levels, you might go for a slow walk to burn off some nervous energy. You can also use centering and progressive muscular relaxation techniques to calm yourself.

Creating a music playlist to boost or reduce Activation levels can also be a good pre-performance Activation management technique.

Once you have created a pre-performance routine, you need to create an in-performance routine (e.g., similar to Jonny Wilkinson's goal-kicking routine).

In-Performance Routines

I created a specific tool to help people do this called the Pre-Shot Training System, which I described in Chapter 8. The insights I share in this section are drawn from that tool.

To help you build an in-performance routine, I'm going to use an example of a routine I use when giving a presentation to a large group of people. The core components of this example can be used to build in-performance routines in any area where you want to improve your ability to perform under pressure.

Preparing Properly

In-performance routines are only useful if you have thoroughly prepared for your performance.

To help me prepare my presentations properly, I have created the "EXPANDS Plan" tool. It helps me build my confidence in the presentation's quality.

1. **E**motions
2. E**X**cite
3. **P**ictures
4. **A**ctive
5. **N**otes
6. **D**iscussion
7. **S**hort

It is based on insights about how people's brains actually work, and so helps me maximize audience engagement and learning.

Here is a quick overview of EXPANDS and some examples of how I activate each element when I am presenting.

First, I typically start my presentations with an engaging, exciting, or evocative video. This is designed to:

1. Activate positive **E**motions in people in the audience.
2. Create some e**X**citement.

I use the following tactics to activate the other elements:

3. **P**ictures beat words—I pack my presentation slides full of videos and images. I only use words on my slides where it is absolutely necessary. This makes it easier for the audience to process my slides. People cannot read your slides and listen to what you are saying at the same time.
4. **A**ctive engagement beats passive engagement—I design quick tasks for my audience to complete during the presentation, for example, "Rate how well you did your best to be your best and achieve your goals yesterday?" 1 = you failed, 10 = perfect.
5. **N**otes and tests beat listening—taking notes extends short-term memory, which on average only lasts 30-second. So, I ask people

to write down answers to test questions. The more correct answers they get, the more points they receive!

6. **D**iscussion beats listening—I ask people to discuss key questions I set and what they are learning.
7. **S**hort activities beat long presentations—attentions spans are short and concentration seems to reset every 10 minutes. I aim to break all my presentations into 10-minute blocks. I use tests, activities, and discussions to break up the presentation.

You can also use the EXPANDS plan to help you prepare high-quality presentations.

My Presentation In-Performance Routine

We can think of Jonny Wilkinson's kicking routine as a timeline that started when he placed the ball on the kicking tee and finished when he kicked the ball.

You can also think about the task (e.g., giving a presentation; sitting an exam) or skill (e.g., driving your golf ball off the first tee; taking a penalty in soccer; serving in tennis) you want to get better at performing under pressure along a timeline.

I think of my presentation as a timeline. The timeline starts when I enter the presentation room, or when my audience enters the presentation room. It ends when I sit down after I have finished giving my presentation.

If it is helpful, you can draw your timeline on a piece of paper and plot the key physical actions that take place during your in-performance routine. For example, here are the five stages of my presentation timeline:

Step 1—I build rapport with my audience (as I enter the room, or they enter the room).

Step 2—I stand up and move toward the front of the room.

Step 3—I turn the computer or laptop into presentation mode so my slides appear on the presentation screen.

Step 4—I begin talking.

Step 5—At the end of the presentation, I go back to my chair and sit down.

Your timeline might have more or fewer steps than mine.

Now I am going to explain what I focus on during each step.

Step 1—I build rapport with my audience (as I enter the room, or they enter the room).

I want my audience to feel comfortable, and I want to show I am genuinely interested in helping them, which I absolutely am. So, I very deliberately speak to as many people in the audience as I can before I present. I shake their hand, introduce myself, and ask them what they are hoping to get out of the talk.

Why do I do this? There are myriad neurobiological reasons why this simple act sets a positive tone for the presentation. Some of these relate to mirror neurons, Activation, and building trust.

Do you need to do this when you are giving a presentation? No, not necessarily. It is completely up to you. I have tried and tested many other approaches over the 20-plus years I have been teaching people. This is the one I have found to be most helpful in building audience rapport.

If it is helpful, think about or make some notes about what you can do to optimize your performance during Step 1 of your timeline.

____

____

____

____

____

Use Focus Words and Pictures to supercharge Steps 2 through 5

Before we move on to Step 2, I wanted to point out that you can also plan to use Focus Words and Pictures during your routine. You don't necessarily need to use both Focus Words and Pictures for every step. Just try some things out and see what works best for you.

To help you think about developing your own Focus Words and Pictures, I am going to share some that I use during Steps 2 through 5 of my routine.

Step 2—I stand up and move toward the front of the room.

Before standing up, and as I am standing up and moving toward the front of the room, I focus on achieving the correct Activation level. Being optimally activated is the first step to delivering a great presentation.

When I give a presentation, I like to achieve an Activation level of around 60.

If it is helpful, write down the Activation level you would ideally like to achieve during the task or skill you are building a routine for: _____

To help me achieve the correct Activation level for the presentation, I use Focus Words and Pictures as I am walking to the front of the room, or sometimes as I am entering the room. My Focus Picture is of the Activation dial set at the number 60. My Focus Words focus on my breathing: three seconds in and five seconds out.

If it is helpful, on your timeline, write down some Focus Words and Pictures (you might not need both) to help you manage your Activation during your performance.

____

____

____

____

Step 3—I turn the computer or laptop into presentation mode so my slides appear on the presentation screen.

Once I have achieved the correct Activation level, I want to keep HUE nice and calm.

Sometimes I use a Focus Picture of Will Power giving HUE a gentle shoulder massage.

My Focus Words might be a positive self-affirmation like, "I am well prepared." I will repeat this over and over. Or I might talk myself through the first couple of slides.

I might also keep focusing on my breathing: three seconds in and five seconds out.

If it is helpful, on your timeline, write down the Focus Words and Pictures (you might not need both) you can use to get your attention onto helpful thoughts.

____

____

____

____

Step 4—I begin talking.

As I begin and progress through the presentation, I know I will probably get distracted.

This could be an internal distraction. For example, HUE warning Will Power the presentation is not going well. Or it could be an external factor (e.g., an audience reaction) that is making me doubt myself. Distractions will happen. But if you have a plan, you'll be better able to deal with them.

To refocus your attention after a distraction, you need to activate a specific part of your HAC Brain called the orbito-frontal cortex.

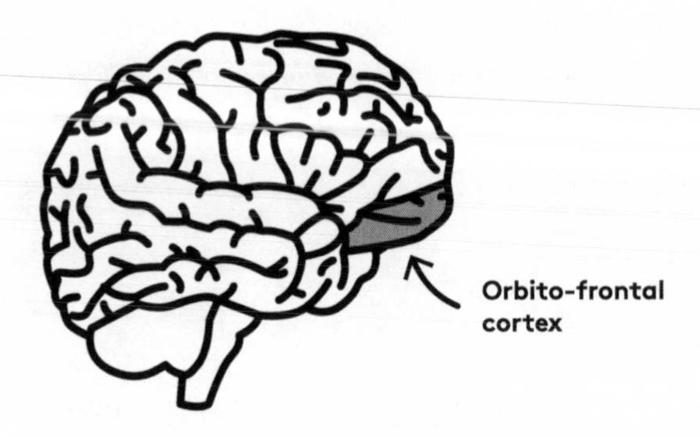

Figure 24.1: A cartoon brain highlighting the orbito-frontal cortex area of the prefrontal cortex region.

You can plan out **Refocus** Words and Pictures to help you do this. For example, here are some I use:

- Refocus Picture: imagining Will Power giving HUE a shoulder massage or seeing my Activation dial at 60
- Refocus Words: "Slow down."

Why do I say "slow down"? Because negative distractions can put a lot of unhelpful thoughts into my mind. So I find telling myself to "slow down" is a good way to calm my thoughts and get my focus back on track.

If it is helpful, on your timeline, write down some Refocus Words and Pictures (you might not need both) you can use during your performance.

____

____

____

Step 5—At the end of the presentation,
I go back to my chair and sit down.

The final part of my in-performance routine is my thoughts after the presentation has finished. At the end of a performance, HUE might dwell on the negatives. This is not very helpful. It is much more helpful to think about at least three things that went well, and one thing you can improve next time.

To trigger a 3:1 reflection, your Focus Words might be "3:1 reflection." I ask myself these types of questions:

1. Out of 100, how well did you do?
2. What was the best part?
3. What was your second-best part?
4. What can you do better next time?

If it is helpful, write down some questions you can ask yourself at the end of your performance to help you reflect consistently.

Recap

Hopefully you now have a better understanding of how to begin creating a robust in-performance routine that can help you manage pressure and perform to your potential. However, this routine will only be helpful if you practice properly using the TE-TAP (Task, Environment, Timings, Activation, Physical) Learning approach.

Efficient and effective practice with proper effort prepares your brain for peak performance. Great pre-performance and in-performance routines make it easier for your brain to perform in the moment. But your routines will only help you perform to your potential if you have prepared properly.

Reflect?

If it is helpful, make a few notes about what you have learned about performing under pressure so far.

PLANNING TO PERFORM TO YOUR POTENTIAL

To help you build and refine your performance-under-pressure habits, I have designed the "Performance HAC Plan." This will help you intelligently Self-Watch your current performance habits and build better pre-performance and in-performance routines.

Although you might want to improve your general ability to perform under pressure, you need to start with one specific area (e.g., giving a presentation to a large group of people). The insights you gain from your approach to that area can then be used to help you in others.

It will be helpful to make written notes as you work through the Performance HAC Plan.

Start with this question:

In which area do you want to improve your performance under pressure? Be specific, for example, a presentation to the board of directors; taking a penalty; short putts (golf); accountancy exams.

____

____

____

____

Score yourself out of 100 for the overall effort you put into preparing for the last performance you gave in this area (if you have not delivered this type of performance before, rate the overall effort you put into preparing for the last performance you gave that was most similar to this one):

_____ */100*

Remember, you can have the best performance routines and techniques possible, but if you have not done suitable practice, you will not fulfill your potential.

Now, consider the following seven questions and write down your answers to help you think about how you usually prepare to perform under pressure. Rate yourself out of 10 for each statement, where 1 means "I didn't do this" and 10 means "I did this as well as I could."

1. During preparation, did you use the TE-TAP Learning framework to optimize your practice?
   Score: _____ /10
2. When preparing for the performance, did you purposefully plan to OPTIMIZE YOUR DIET, EXERCISE, AND SLEEP in the days leading up to the performance?
   Score: _____ /10
3. When preparing for the performance, did you use a pre-performance routine to help you achieve THE CORRECT ACTIVATION LEVEL before and during the performance?
   Score: _____ /10
4. When practicing, DID YOU KNOW YOUR TIMINGS (e.g., the Timings factor in the TE-TAP Learning framework)?
   Score: _____ /10
5. DID YOU DEVELOP A ROBUST IN-PERFORMANCE ROUTINE to help you optimize your performance?
   Score: _____ /10
6. During the performance, did you use FOCUS WORDS AND PICTURES TO HELP YOU RE-FOCUS your attention onto relevant thoughts and information?
   Score: _____ /10
7. Did you REFLECT AFTER THE PERFORMANCE to identify what went well, and what you could improve next time?
   Score: _____ /10

Once you have scored yourself on each question, you will be able to better understand the current strengths and weaknesses of your pre-performance and in-performance routines.

If it is helpful, make some notes about what you have learned:

BUILDING BETTER PERFORMING-UNDER-PRESSURE HABITS

Here is an overview of the main points I have considered in this chapter.

1. To learn how to perform better under pressure, start by selecting one specific task or activity to work on. This will give you a focus and help you refine your performance-under-pressure skills.
2. Use TE-TAP Learning to help you practice to perform under pressure.
3. Understand your physical routine.
4. Create a mental routine, including Focus Words and Pictures, to complement your physical routine.
5. Combine these together into an in-performance routine and practice this routine thoroughly.
6. Good DES (diet, exercise, sleep) habits will make performing under pressure easier.
7. Create a pre-performance routine that helps you manage your Activation levels throughout your performance.

Add the performing-under-pressure habits you would like to develop to your Me Power Wish List. Although there might be several areas you want to work on, remember, it is only realistic to build one tiny new habit at a time.

BUILD THE HABIT

If it is helpful, highlight one habit you would like to prioritize to help you improve your performance under pressure.

As an example, the new performing-under-pressure habit I want to develop is as follows: I want to improve my Activation management. To help me improve, I want to do regular "Activation management training." So my Aim is to "Do at least 10 minutes of pre-work walking (every workday) to deliberately get to my 'Ideal Work Activation level' (I introduced this concept in Chapter 21) before I start work."

This is like doing a "mini pre-performance routine" and is good Activation management training. It is good preparation to help me manage my Activation when I need to perform under pressure. It will also help me be my best at work.

Think of the habit you want to develop as an Aim, and remember that good Aims are carefully written down, are specific (using times and locations), state a positive action ("I will" instead of "I will not"), and can be measured (using quantities).

If you want to work on a performing-under-pressure habit, write down your Aim:

____

____

____

Once you have a clear Aim, you might want to revisit the self-reflection tool "How HUE Hinders Change" (Chapter 20) to help you think about how HUE might try to stop you from building this new habit.

Now it is time to create a Habit Building Plan to activate the Nine Action Factors and supercharge the habit building process.

To do this, you need to answer the following questions:

1. Describe the SMALL specific new helpful habit that you want to build (your Aim):

   ____

   Example answer: "Do at least 10 minutes of pre-work walking (every workday) to deliberately get to my 'Ideal Work Activation level' before I start work."

2. Describe what you currently do (your unhelpful habit) instead of the new helpful habit you want to build:

   ____

   Example answer: If I am working from home, I don't do any pre-work exercise. If I am going to the office, I drive to work and only need to do five minutes of walking.

3. Describe what reminds or triggers this unhelpful habit:

   ____

   Example answer: These are just the habits I have established.

4. Describe how you will remind yourself (trigger) to practice your NEW habit daily:

   ____

   Example answer: Set a daily calendar alert to remind me to do this. Set "10-minutes of pre-work exercise" as a goal on my Me Power Weekly Wall Chart (introduced in Chapter 18).

5. Describe the new knowledge and skills you will need to help you secure your new habit:

   ____

   Example answer: Update my "Optimal Activation Review" (introduced in Chapter 21).

6. If it is helpful, describe where and how you will acquire the new knowledge and skills you need:

   Example answer: Re-read Chapter 21 to learn more about managing my Activation levels.

7. Describe in detail why you want to build this new habit:

   Example answer: So that I am better able to control my Activation when the pressure is on. It will also help me be more productive in the mornings. Both of these factors will give me a better chance of progressing my career and achieving my long-term goals.

8. Who can you ask to help you build your new habit? (ideally, they will also be building the same or similar habit at the same time):

   Example answer: I am going to change our weekly team meeting to a standing meeting and explain the concept of Activation to my team. I will also tell them about my new pre-work exercise habit.

9. What will be the reward for building the new habit? Remember, rewards can be internal, external, or social.

   Example answer: I will feel better, be more focused, improve my ability to perform under pressure, and make my family proud of me.

10. What will be the cost/penalty for not building the new habit?

   Example answer: The opposite of the rewards I describe above.

Congratulations, you now have a robust plan to build a new helpful performing-under-pressure habit!

HABIT MECHANIC TOOLS YOU HAVE LEARNED IN CHAPTER 24...

Planning Tool

TE–TAP (Task, Environment, Timings, Activation, and Physical) Learning—A simple framework to pressure-proof your ability to perform. ☑

Self-Reflection Tool

Performance HAC Plan—An exercise to help you reflect on how well your practice helps you perform under pressure. ☑

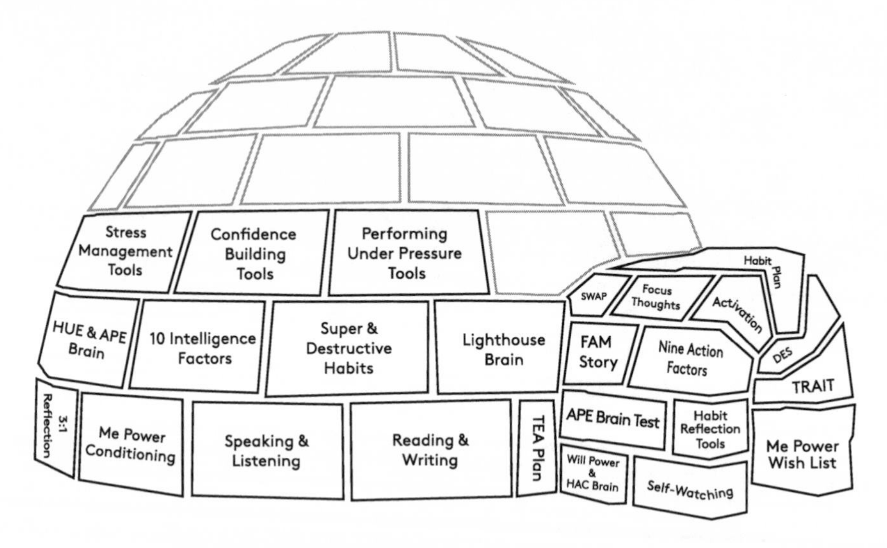

Figure 24.2: Your Habit Mechanic intelligence igloo is building up!

Next, we'll look at focus and productivity-boosting habits that make creativity and problem-solving easier.

25

SUPERCHARGE YOUR PRODUCTIVITY AND FOCUS (IN THE OFFICE OR AT HOME) FOR BETTER WORK-LIFE BALANCE

The Amazon Prime documentary *Chasing Great* follows All Black rugby legend Richie McCaw through his final season as a player. It lifts the lid on McCaw's life as he guides New Zealand to back-to-back Rugby World Cup triumphs. And while McCaw is now retired, he is a sporting legend and remains a hero to a nation.

The film provided a great insight into an athlete whose sporting achievements are well documented. By using the McCaw family video archive, and candid interviews with the former All Black captain, *Chasing Great* provides a revealing psychological profile of a champion's mindset.

Significantly, the film reveals that McCaw has his own Self-Watching process. He is disciplined in the way he does this. He has a journal, and at the beginning of every day, he writes down "Start again." This is one tool

McCaw uses to help himself be at his best, as often as possible. We will return to Richie McCaw later on.

In this chapter, we'll examine insights to boost both focus and productivity, consider how to optimize any 24-hour day, and outline how to get more done in less time. I will also show you how to get your most challenging work done. All of the above will also help boost your creativity and problem-solving abilities.

WHY IS IT CHALLENGING TO BE PRODUCTIVE?

Why do we procrastinate on mentally challenging work? (1) This type of work burns a lot of energy. (2) When we do mentally challenging work, we don't gain an immediate reward. Our HUE (Horribly Unhelpful Emotions) doesn't like that. So instead, it encourages us to quit the mentally challenging work and to do things that require less mental energy, and that do give us immediate rewards (e.g., checking your emails or your phone).

In many ways, humans are designed to procrastinate. We prioritize instant gratification over achieving our long-term goals. In today's world, this once-advantageous trait can undermine human happiness and success.

It encourages humans to build short-term attention habits that restrict our ability to make the type of personal progress (Habit Mechanic development) that is essential if we want to succeed and thrive in the VUCA (volatile, uncertain, complex, and ambiguous) world. Humans have evolved to survive, rather than thrive, in 21st century life.

But we can do better, and we can learn how to delay short-term gratification by developing better focus and productivity habits. To do this, it is useful to revisit the two cornerstone concepts that underpin all habit building success:

Do Your Best to Be Your Best

I have shown that we have a lot more control over what we think and do than we often give ourselves credit for. For example, you might not be able to stop a colleague interrupting you at work—but you can control how quickly you refocus back onto the task at hand.

Plan Ahead

Having a plan helps you manage HUE and be productive. For example, it will be much easier to have a productive day or week if you have planned how to achieve this.

Uncontrollable events happen to us all the time, but these two concepts (doing your best and planning ahead) help you keep HUE in check.

Now I will show you a range of Habit Mechanic Tools you can use to boost your focus and productivity. They will help you spend more of each 24-hour period with your attention on things that are most helpful to your health, happiness, and performance.

WHY DO YOU WANT TO BE PRODUCTIVE TODAY?

In *Chasing Great*, former New Zealand All Black captain and multiple World Cup winner Richie McCaw describes how a McDonald's napkin was the centerpiece for one of the most pivotal moments in his life. In 1998, he was with his uncle in a McDonald's restaurant near his hometown.

After being shown his nephew's training diary, McCaw's uncle asked the youngster if he wanted to be an All Black. "Yes, of course," said McCaw—but he was secretly thinking he would never achieve that dream.

McCaw's uncle then asked him to write down how he would become an All Black. McCaw began to map this out on the back of a napkin. He wrote:

- Make New Zealand U19 in 1999
- Make New Zealand U21 in 2001
- Play for Canterbury Crusaders A team in 2002
- Make the Canterbury Crusaders first team in 2003
- Play for the All Blacks at the 2003 World Cup

After mulling this over, McCaw's uncle told his nephew he should not just aspire to be any All Black. He should aspire to be a great All Black. McCaw felt embarrassed writing that, so just wrote GAB (great All Black) at the bottom of the page. The rest is history.

Like Richie McCaw, if you want to be your best every day, you need to know **why**. So, it is vital to connect your long-term goals to the immediate tasks you need to complete and the habit(s) you want to improve today. So, it will be easier to optimize your productivity today if you have created a FAM (Future Ambitious Meaningful) Story Iceberg (Chapter 16). Remember, this is never set in stone. You need to periodically revisit it and update your goals.

By knowing the "why," you are activating the "Personal Motivation Factor" in the Nine Action Factors framework (Chapter 18).

Reflect?

If it is helpful, make a few notes about what you've learned about improving your productivity so far.

HOW TO USE ICE TO BE MORE PRODUCTIVE AND OPTIMIZE A 24-HOUR PERIOD

Let's use an ice analogy again and apply it to the two main types of jobs we do each day. I liken the easy tasks I need to complete each day to *freezing ice cubes*, and the more mentally complex tasks to *building ice sculptures.*

Freezing Ice Cubes Represents Busy Habit Work

This is the fairly mindless, familiar, easy work we can deal with quickly. It may include answering easy emails or inquiries. It could be a routine task like filing something. This type of work is increasingly becoming fully or semi-automated, sometimes meaning humans are no longer required (e.g., online banking, accounting software, meeting scheduling software).

Figure 25.1: Think of doing your busy work like freezing ice cubes.

Building Ice Sculptures Represents Focused Work

This is creative, innovative, and mentally challenging work. It could involve creating new products or writing long reports. This type of work is typically not completed in one sitting. Humans are increasingly valued for their ability to do this type of work because it is not easily automated.

Figure 25.2: Think of doing your focused, creative, and problem-solving work like building ice sculptures.

Reflect?

If it is helpful, make a list of your daily ice cube tasks, and a separate list of the ice sculpture tasks you are currently working on.

WE CAN CHARGE UP OUR BRAINS TO BE MORE PRODUCTIVE

Imagine your brain is like a battery that has three specific operating states or modes. I call these "Brain States." This concept is connected to the Nine Action Factors' Brain State Factor, which I introduced in Chapter 18.

Brain State 1—Recharging

In any 24-hour period, we need to do some recharging. This includes sleeping, relaxing, eating, and for some people light exercise. Effective recharging activities will be individual to you. To work out what recharges your brain, do some personal research.

Recharging

Figure 25.3: Recharge your brain daily.

Brain State 2—Medium Charge

We use this Brain State to do simple, familiar, and largely undemanding tasks (freezing ice cubes). In other words, anything that is mainly a habit, and therefore requires minimal conscious effort. People sometimes call this busy work.

Medium charge

Figure 25.4: Use your medium-charge brain to complete daily ice cube freezing tasks.

Brain State 3—High Charge

This is the most valuable Brain State. We need this to do clever, focused, creative, and problem-solving work (building ice sculptures). However, high charge is a limited cognitive resource. It rapidly runs out.

High charge

Figure 25.5: Use your precious high-charge Brain State to build ice sculptures.

There is an interdependence between these three Brain States. For example, if we do not spend sufficient time recharging in any 24-hour period, it will be hard for us to properly use our other two Brain States. Also, in the recharge and medium-charge Brain States, you are still subconsciously working on high-charge tasks. For example, that is why a solution to a difficult problem you have been working on sometimes comes to you after a good night's sleep, or in the bath—like Archimedes' Eureka moment! Switching off can create insight.

Of the three Brain States, in any 24-hour period, we should aim to use the recharge Brain State the most. The next most-used state is medium charge. We spend the least amount of time in any 24 hours in a high-charge state.

Your Pyramid of Brain States

Think of the relationship between your Brain States as a pyramid. The foundation is recharge, the middle section is medium charge, and the tip is high charge.

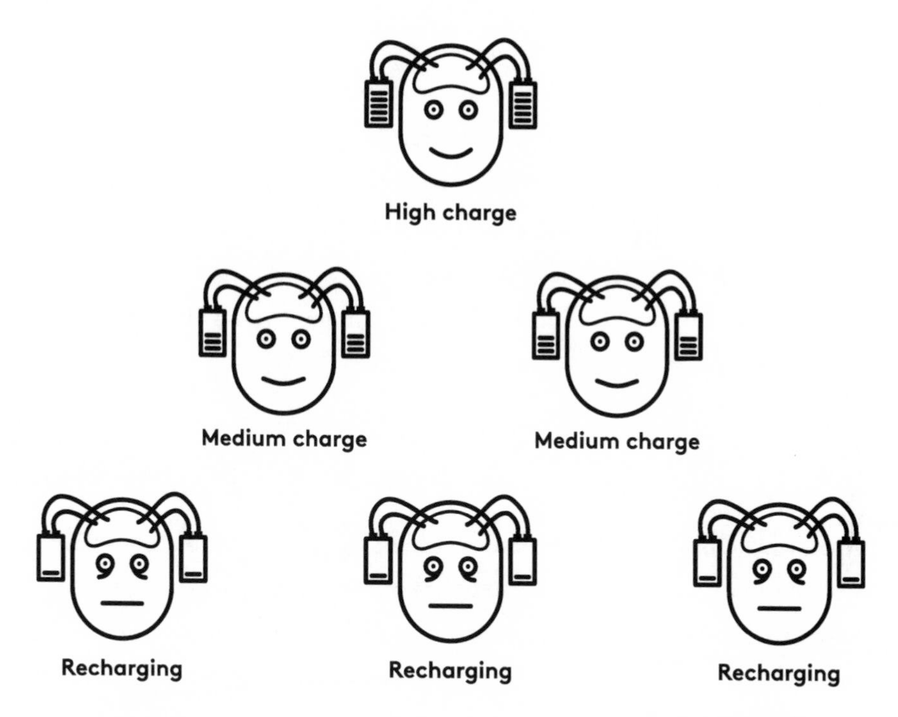

Figure 25.6: To optimize your productivity, creativity, and problem-solving abilities, you need to strike the right balance in your use of all three Brain States.

Here is a personal example for a working day. For me to optimally use a 24-hour period (on a working day), I need to

- spend about 11 to 12 hours in recharge Brain States (including sleeping, relaxing, exercising, eating, etc.);
- spend approximately seven to eight hours in medium-charge states, both personal (home life) and work related (doing fairly mindless, easy tasks); and
- spend the least amount of time (about four to five hours) in high-charge states (doing challenging, demanding, clever, problem-solving work).

Doing this allows me to do valuable sessions of high-charge work five or six days a week. I also aim to have at least one day per week where I do no high-charge work, and really focus on recharging my brain batteries. This is essential if I want to perform to my potential, because focus, creativity, and problem-solving are crucial for me to do my job well.

These timings are personal, but they are also fairly typical for most people I've worked with. But everyone's life is different, and you will need to work out your own timings via some personal research.

Unlike the Lottery, There's No Rollover

If I do not achieve four to five hours of high charge today, I cannot carry it over to tomorrow (i.e., do 8 to 10 hours of high-charge work in one day). Nobody can. That is not how our brains work. That is why it is important for us to achieve the high-charge state every working day, so that, over an extended period, we build-up time during which we're highly effective and productive.

There are many myths about the rest and work habits of famous people. Margaret Thatcher, the UK's first female prime minister, said she only slept for four hours per night. If that's true, we must question how helpful this was for her day-to-day performance and long-term health.

Winston Churchill's sleeping habits are also well reported. It is said the former UK prime minister only slept for five to six hours per night. What is less well conveyed is that he often had several power naps during the day. In the book *Churchill by Himself*, he is reported to have said: "You must sleep sometime between lunch and dinner, and no half-way measures. Take off your clothes and get into bed. That's what I always do."

It is easy for your HUE to get drawn into anecdotal stories that tell us we can get by without much sleep or relaxation time. But if we look at the science, it is very clear: sufficient rest and recovery is vital for our health, happiness, and performance. Without it, your brain does not work properly in the short- or long-term.

Please do some personal research and work out the optimal amount of time you need to spend in high, medium, and recharge Brain States during the course of 24 hours to help you be your best. This will be different for work days and nonwork days.

For example, if I work (a mixture of high- and medium-charge activities) for more than 12 hours each day, it will have a negative knock-on effect for the next day. If this continues throughout the week, doing any sustained, mentally challenging work on Friday (the final day of my working week) will be difficult. I would regard that day as a cognitive write-off.

Multitasking Is Not Effective—Do Not Mix the Brain States

We sometimes fall into the trap of believing we can multitask to accomplish more in less time. But is this true?

In the US health system, statistics show one of the biggest causes of patient death while in hospital is incorrect prescriptions. Reports suggested nurses were often interrupted by their colleagues during their medication rounds.

The nurses were being involuntarily moved from a high-charge state, when concentrating on their prescriptions, to a medium-charge state, when they had to answer routine questions from colleagues. When they returned to their prescribing task, mistakes were being made and patients were dying.

This phenomenon was identified in the American health system and procedures were changed. Now some nurses wear red bibs, indicating they are not to be disturbed on their (high-charge) medication rounds.

I have not seen any scientific data showing that being interrupted while you are doing a high-charge task is helpful. Interruption leads to more mistakes, more pressure, more stress, and less time. One study showed that a single interruption can cost you 23 minutes and 15 seconds of your time. There is also data showing that each time you get distracted, it takes a little bit longer to refocus. In other words, there is a cumulative effect, and wasted time quickly adds up.

A term I really like is "single-tasking." This helps us boost productivity and get more done in less time. We should not mix our Brain States. For example, if you want to relax to recharge, then don't do anything else but relax. The same goes for medium- and high-charge work.

In other words, you only have 100 percent attention. Whichever Brain State you are working in, put 100 percent of your attention into it. This will help you optimize your uptime, downtime, and work-life balance.

Habit Mechanics frequently report that following this advice, and using the tools I am about to show you (in combination with other tools I have already shown you), saves them at least one hour per day. This includes me.

Test?

If it is helpful, write down the three different Brain States to test your memory!

HOW TO TAKE MORE CONTROL OF YOUR BRAIN STATES

We can connect our three Brain States to the concept of Activation (introduced in Chapter 21). Each state will require a different optimal level on the Activation scale.

To illustrate this, I will show you mine.

- For recharge, I need to be around 20 to 10 to do Nonsleep Recharge and between 5 to 1 to sleep.

- For medium charge, I need to be around 30 to 50.
- For high charge, I need to be around 55 or 60.

Make a note of your own ideal Activation level for each Brain State. You can always adjust these later:

Recharge (sleep) level: ______________________

Nonsleep Recharge: ______________________

Medium-charge level: ______________________

High-charge level: ______________________

We should always try to match the tasks, activities, and challenges we face in life and work with the right Activation level.

For example, if I arrive in the office early in the morning and I need to tackle some complex, challenging work, I will be incapable of doing this properly if I'm extremely tired and have low Activation.

Equally, if I'm trying to go to bed early and need a good night's sleep, I won't be able to achieve the correct sleeping Activation level if I have just checked my work emails and have been agitated by a difficult message—making me highly Activated.

Now that you have a better understanding of your Brain States, I would encourage you to review and update your Optimal Activation Review (Chapter 21).

MORE ON THE POWER OF FOCUS WORDS AND PICTURES

Focus Words and Pictures are powerful Brain State management tools. I will show you how to use them to both reduce and increase your Brain State. Before I do, I want to give another example of how a world-class athlete used them to help him break the world record for the distance cycled in one hour.

In an interview with the BBC's Breakfast program, Britain's Olympic cycling hero (winner of five gold medals) and Tour de France winner Sir Bradley Wiggins explained how he used Focus Words and Focus Pictures to help him become a world-record breaker.

Professional cycling is a grueling activity. It takes a physical and mental toll on the athlete. But Wiggins was able to overcome these hurdles by deliberately controlling his thoughts. In other words, the things he said to himself and what he saw in his mind's eye.

He said: "No matter how hard something is or feels, there is always an endpoint. And I always kept thinking of that endpoint. What is it going to feel like when you've done it and smashed the record?"

So, his Focus Words were something like, "Keep thinking about the endpoint," and his Focus Picture was something like seeing himself get over the finish line and smash the record.

By managing his thoughts, Wiggins helped his Will Power talk HUE through these challenging moments, making it much more difficult for HUE to dwell on difficulties and potential pitfalls.

Many successful individuals use these mental skills to overcome adversity and personal challenges and to be successful. We can all benefit from the same skills, and they are essential for becoming a Habit Mechanic.

HOW TO OPTIMIZE YOUR RECHARGE BRAIN STATE

We have already outlined a great deal of information about diet, exercise, and sleep (DES). This has been done very purposefully to help you to optimize your recharge state.

Unfortunately, there are no DES shortcuts. If we do not do these things correctly, our brains will not work properly.

As well as sleep, let's also think about "Nonsleep Recharge" activities. To understand this, we need to consider where we need to be on the Activation scale to achieve Nonsleep Recharge. This is your target Nonsleep Recharge Activation level you wrote down earlier. Mine was 20 to 10.

Securing high-quality recharge feels more challenging than ever, because in the context of the Learning War, the temptation is to always be on. Smartphones, for example, are constant barriers to securing good quality Nonsleep Recharge. The attention economy in which we live means our brains are constantly being hijacked and interrupted, so we need to consider if our downtime really is helping us recharge our brains.

Deliberately Reduce Your Activation to Boost Recharge

To get better at controlling your recharge, you need to get better at controlling your Activation. One of the ways you can do this is by using Focus Words and Pictures.

This is how I do it. In my mind's eye, I picture (Focus Picture) the Activation dial at my current Activation level. For example, it might be at a 40. Then I use Focus Words to help me slow down my breathing. As I'm breathing out, I imagine the Activation dial needle moving toward 20, which is the correct level for my Nonsleep Recharge. I typically do this for between 30 seconds and five minutes. I do this periodically throughout the day and call it a "micro-recharge."

Some years ago, when I created the first Optimal Activation Review, I noticed that I experienced a dip as the afternoon progressed.

So I created and deliberately began using these "micro-recharge techniques" at lunchtime to reduce my Activation level and achieve my recharge

Brain State. I combined this with some lunchtime diet modifications and light exercise. Now, when I return to my desk after lunch, I'm in a better state to do my work efficiently and effectively because my brain has been refreshed and recharged.

Help Will Power Calm HUE

Let's consider how this looks inside your Lighthouse Brain. Because downtime can be boring, HUE can get distracted by worries and threats or by looking for something more interesting to do. This means that our recharge time can get sabotaged.

Simply being aware of this means we can proactively respond. To make it more difficult for HUE to disrupt my downtime, I help Will Power create a plan. So, when HUE calls my Will Power for help (e.g., to make it aware of a worry, or to help HUE get my smartphone out to relieve boredom), it is ready. My Will Power knows I have designated this period for Nonsleep Recharge. So when HUE signals Will Power, it coaches HUE to focus on reducing Activation by using the pre-planned "Focus Words and Pictures micro-recharge technique." I also turn my phone off to make it harder for HUE to get its own way.

When I don't have such a detailed plan for recharge, I can quickly find myself moving into high or medium Brain States, meaning I am not able to secure the high-quality recharge time I need to function at my best.

Reflect?

If it is helpful, plan your own Nonsleep Recharge Focus Words and Focus Pictures.

HOW TO OPTIMIZE YOUR HIGH-CHARGE BRAIN STATE

The high-charge Brain State is the most precious resource we have in the VUCA world. High charge helps us do clever, focused work so we can solve problems, be creative, and innovate. Using this resource efficiently and effectively is vital in helping us be our best so we can achieve the meaningful goals that make us feel good about ourselves. In our terms, high charge is about creating ice sculptures.

Many of us will have "To Do" lists. We can extend and expand these to make them even more powerful for us:

- Label the different tasks on your list as being either ice sculptures or ice cubes.
- Set yourself a specific amount of time to work on each task on the list.
- Add Habit Mechanic activities to your list (e.g., walking breaks, Nonsleep Recharge activities, Daily 3:1 Reflection, Daily TEA Plan).

This enhanced list is one quick way to help us take responsibility for what we can control and plan ahead, but we can go much further.

A Lesson on How to Focus from Elite Sport

Another way to gain the most from high-charge states relates to our physical environments.

In our work, we are often surrounded by distractions. Many office spaces are open plan, so colleagues can attract our attention easily. But whether working in the office or at home, we can also be distracted by our smartphones, emails, and thoughts. Sometimes, we think there is little we can do to control these distractions, and we are unable to improve our productivity in these contexts. In reality, we can do more to plan ahead and take responsibility for being our best.

To understand how, let's return to the story of Richie McCaw. We can learn a great deal about controlling our attention from the processes he followed before a game. At another point in the *Chasing Great* documentary, McCaw explained part of his pre-match routine.

He wrote down both the physical actions and the types of beneficial behavior he needed to achieve during the chaos and confrontation of Test match rugby. He did this in the morning, well ahead of kickoff.

He wrote things relating to how he wanted to play, such as "get involved early," "work rate," and "get up and go." He also wrote words related to his conduct and demeanor as the captain and leader of an iconic team, such as "calm, clear, and decisive" and "presence." He regularly wrote down the same words, because writing them meant he was far more likely to do them.

This example further reinforces the power of planning, which helped McCaw regulate his emotions. He made it easier for Will Power to help HUE pay attention to helpful things on the rugby field. McCaw knew if he didn't do this, HUE would have been more likely to get distracted by mistakes and unfair decisions, making it harder for him to perform to his potential.

By planning ahead, you, too, can get much greater control over how HUE responds to your environment. Planning ahead gives you more control over how quickly you refocus by making it easier for Will Power to get HUE's attention back onto what is most helpful.

The Will Power Story

To help you plan ahead and take more control in your daily life, I have created the Will Power Story. This Habit Mechanic Tool helps you plan to control your attention so you can better control the controllables.

By creating daily Will Power Stories, it will be easier to keep your HUE calm and get more done every day.

Today

Plan Your Day - create a Will Power Story

i) Use the timeline to plan out the commitments you have tomorrow or today. Then circle the activity or commitment that will be most challenging.

Plan when you will use Will Power Boosters and Strengths to help your day run smoothly:

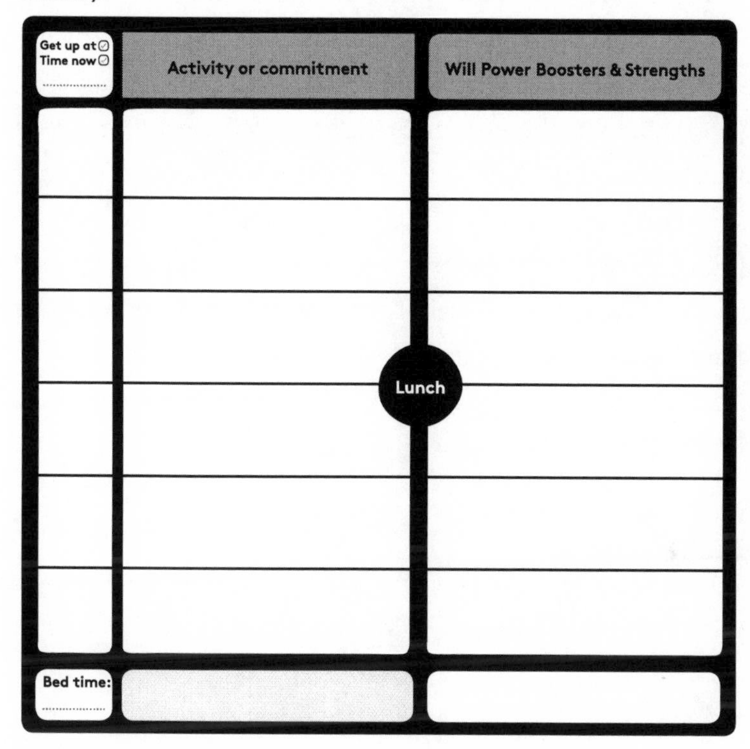

ii) Why not create a small specific SWAP to help you manage the most challenging part of your day, which you have circled, more effectively?

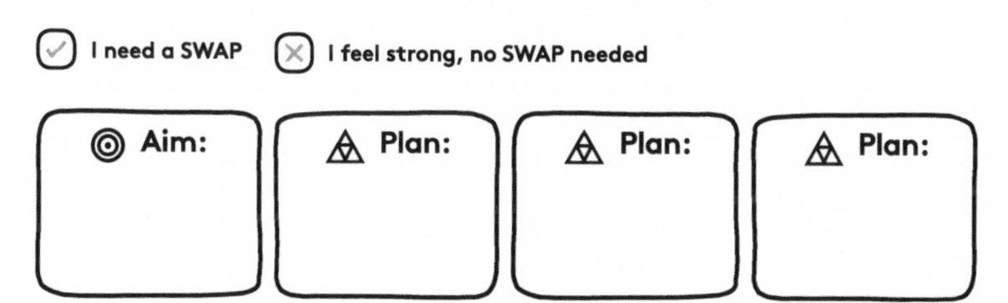

Figure 25.7: A blank Will Power Story template.

At the end of each day, I complete my Will Power Story for the following day.

I begin by deciding when I will get up. Then I plan what time I will go to bed. This sets a timeframe for the following day, so I know how much time I have to get things done.

Within that timeframe, I can plan the various tasks and activities I have to do—work, family, social, relaxation, using different Habit Mechanic Tools. I can categorize tasks as *freezing ice cubes* or *creating ice sculptures*. This helps me think about the different Brain States I will need. I can also use my Optimal Activation Review to consider my Activation levels throughout the course of the day and when it might be best to do different tasks and activities.

Here's an example Will Power Story. I will explain the "Will Power Boosters and Strengths" element shortly. By the end of the chapter, you will understand how to create your own.

EXAMPLE

Plan Your Day - create a Will Power Story

i) Use the timeline to plan out the commitments you have tomorrow or today. Then circle the activity or commitment that will be most challenging.

Plan when you will use Will Power Boosters and Strengths to help your day run smoothly:

Get up at / Time now: 6am	Activity or commitment	Will Power Boosters & Strengths
6.15am 7.15am 8am	- 25 minute run - increase Activation - DES SWAP - Travel to work.	- Self-controlled
8.30am - 10am	- Write a proposal for a new client - Graze (have a piece of fruit)	- Internet Management
10.30am - 1pm	- Run lunchtime webinar for investment bank client - 12 noon start	
1.30pm - 2.30pm	- Lunch [If I eat too much I will procrastinate in the afternoon!] - 15 minute walk	- Self-controlled
3pm - 5pm	- Reply to emails - Call Andrew - Plan tomorrow - Will Power Story - End of day written reflection	- Phone management - Workspace plan - Concentration control
5.30pm - 9pm	- Travel home - Food shopping, eat with family, relax with family	
Bed time: 10pm	- Get ready for bed - Reading in bed by 9:30pm	- Phone management

Lunch

ii) Why not create a small specific SWAP to help you manage the most challenging part of your day, which you have circled, more effectively?

☑ I need a SWAP ☒ I feel strong, no SWAP needed

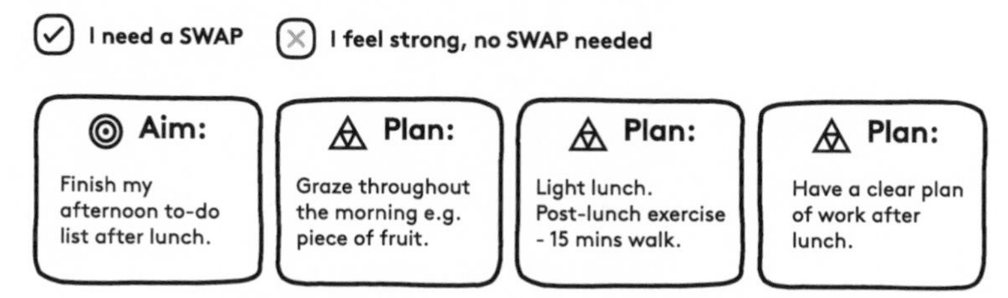

Figure 25.8: An example Will Power Story.

I have put an ice sculpture task at the start of the day (writing a proposal for a new client) because I know I will be mentally fresh. I have prioritized getting a good night's sleep so that I can wake up feeling refreshed. And I've exercised before I begin my work. This means I will be at the correct Activation level to build my ice sculptures.

You will see I haven't just planned the tasks I want to complete. I've also included what I call "Will Power Boosters and Strengths."

Strengths

Self-controlled
You stay focused on your priorities and avoid distractions.

Persistent
You motivate yourself to keep going even when things are tough.

Perspective
You step-back from the here-and-now to reflect and plan.

Efficient
You are organized & do things with little wasted effort.

Leading
You help others to get the best out of themselves.

Empathic
You understand how your colleagues, family, and friends are feeling when they are having a tough time.

Optimistic
You stay hopeful and positive even when things are not going to plan.

Will Power Boosters

Confidence booster
Do not beat yourself up if you make a mistake, keep trying.

Phone management
Turn off your phone to minimize distractions & get more done.

Mindset
Approach tasks & activities on time & in the right frame of mind.

Internet management
Disconnect the internet to reduce the temptation of quickly checking your emails, or favorite website.

Concentration booster
At the start of a challenging task or job, write down a concentration plan to help you focus.

Activation booster
Exercise at lunch or break to boost Activation e.g., a 10-minute walking break.

Workspace plan
Create a workspace with minimal distractions.

Concentration control
Use Focus Words and Pictures to control concentration.

Figure 25.9: Use Strengths and Will Power Boosters to improve your focus and productivity.

In my example, I have ensured that writing a new client proposal goes alongside what I call "Internet management." In practical terms, I don't need the internet for this particular task. If it is available to me, it might be distracting. So I've planned to turn off the Wi-Fi connection on my laptop. This will help Will Power manage HUE and give me a better chance of being efficient and effective while I'm writing the proposal. This helps me do the work faster.

You can use Will Power Boosters and Strengths to help you

1. plan how you will behave;
2. control your environment; and
3. ultimately make it easier to control your attention.

They can help you keep persisting so that you can build better habits. Will Power Boosters can relate to things like your personal workspace or your use of electronic devices. You can also use them to help you with mental skills like concentration and mindset.

When I first created it, the Will Power Story tools acted like stabilizers to help me develop excellent productivity habits. This means that over time I have been able to add less and less detail into my daily timeline/plans and still get really powerful results. However, when I feel like my productivity has gone off track, I do revert back to using the full Will Power Story process. This helps me build back my best productivity habits.

Reflect?

If it is helpful, use all the productivity insights I have shared so far to begin completing your first Will Power Story. I will explain the SWAP section of the Will Power Story later in this chapter.

The more detail you add, the more powerful it will be in helping you develop the productivity habits that allow you to be your best.

Over time, as you develop better and better productivity habits you will be able to add less and less detail into your daily timeline/plans and still get great results. This is because you will have developed some excellent productivity habits. However, if your productivity ever worsens, you can always revert back to using the full Will Power Story process to help you reestablish your best productivity habits.

Use Your Torch of Concentration to Supercharge Your High-Charge Work

When we are doing high-charge work, every time we unintentionally break concentration we are likely wasting a small amount of this precious resource. Remember, we only get a small amount of high-charge brain power each day. But we can reduce time wastage and "single-task" more effectively by learning more about how concentration works, and how we can refocus faster.

Think of human concentration as a torch. We only have a limited amount of battery charge. Also, think of your concentration on a continuum, where one end is very narrow (focused like a spotlight) and the other end is very broad (like when we use our peripheral vision). We can all learn how to focus our concentration in different ways, moving from very broad to very narrow and vice versa.

To understand more about concentration, we can learn from a BBC documentary on tennis superstar Serena Williams. Williams has won every major Grand Slam tournament multiple times. One section of the documentary showed her facing an opponent getting the better of her in a key match. The footage showed Williams engaged in a dispute on the court after she had just lost a point. The sequence then went on to show her responding and subsequently dominating the opponent and winning the match.

In the voiceover, Williams explains how the dispute impacted her concentration levels. We can use these insights to help us understand more about concentration.

Neurobiologically,
Concentration Has Three Parts

Part 1: Switch on your brain in the same way you switch on a torch. This is about reaching the right Activation level, so you have the most helpful neurotransmitters (like noradrenaline and dopamine) in your brains for focusing and learning.

Serena Williams can aid our understanding here. She says she plays better and hits good shots when an opponent makes her angry. We can reasonably assume the stimulus from her opponent takes her to her optimal Activation level for high-performance tennis.

Part 2: Focus your attention on what you want to achieve, which requires you to activate your HAC brain (specifically the dorsolateral part of the prefrontal cortex).

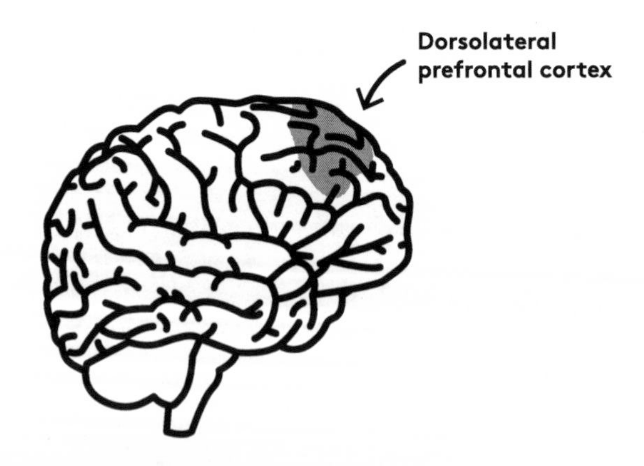

Figure 25.10: A cartoon brain highlighting the dorsolateral region of your prefrontal cortex.

To do this, Williams talks about following up on her feelings of anger by specifically "talking herself through" and "focusing on the actions" she is going to take. In Williams' example, she is talking herself through the process of moving off the baseline and attacking the ball.

To focus your attention in a work context, you could write down your goals. For example, in the next hour I will:

1. First, turn my phone off to help me focus.
2. Finish the report I am working on.
3. Write a draft email about this report to my client (do it in Word so I don't have to open my emails).

This is an effective way of aligning your attention with what you want to achieve. It is why I strongly encourage you to create a Will Power Story (i.e., clear goals for your day).

Part 3: Sustain and refocus your attention. To do this, you need to activate a specific part of your HAC Brain called the orbito-frontal cortex (see Chapter 24, Figure 24.1).

Having a "refocus plan" will help you do this, making distractions less problematic and less time consuming. (To help me refocus, I plan to use specific Focus Words and Pictures, which I will explain shortly.)

But again, you can learn from Williams here. For example, to sustain her focus, she suggested she used Focus Words like "move up" and "attack the ball."

Using Focus Words and Focus Pictures to Refocus

When I feel I need to refocus my concentration, in my mind's eye I picture (Focus Picture) a spotlight focusing back onto the task at hand. The words (Focus Words) I say in my head are: "Come on, get on with it." This means whenever I become distracted, I'm only in this state for 30 seconds or so, rather than minutes. By refocusing faster, I am saving time and increasing my productivity levels. By the end of the day, this technique can save me 15 to 20 minutes. By the end of the week, I could be hours better off. Small changes add up.

People I've worked with tell me they've found the following Focus Pictures effective for refocusing:

- A torch
- A magnifying glass
- A microscope
- A telescope
- Their eyes emitting laser beams onto their work

Refocus Word examples:

- Refocus
- Keep going
- HUE, stop it! ☺

Reflect?

If it is helpful, write down some Focus Words and Focus Pictures you can use to help you refocus.

The Focused Practice Framework

Another tool you use to supercharge your high-charge work is the "The Focused Practice framework." I will show you how to use this in Chapter 26.

HOW TO OPTIMIZE YOUR MEDIUM-CHARGE BRAIN STATE

Arguably, for most people, medium-charge Brain States are the easiest state to achieve in the VUCA world. But this means we can spend more time in them than is helpful. Because of this, we need to be mindful of using our daily medium-charge Brain State capacities efficiently and effectively to complete our daily ice cube tasks (at work and in our home lives).

In my Will Power Story example, I deal with my ice cube jobs (e.g., replying to emails, simple phone calls, etc.) in the afternoon because my natural afternoon Brain State is more suitable for work of this type. And because I have planned and committed to doing these tasks, I have a much better chance of completing them efficiently and effectively.

You can plan when you will complete your ice cube jobs on your daily Will Power Story.

LOOK FOR THE BIGGEST CHALLENGE IN YOUR DAY

The most challenging part of your day (i.e., when it is most difficult to do what you need to do) might not always be the same. But many people find there is some level of consistency in what they find challenging. The Optimal Activation Review (Chapter 21) is a powerful tool to help you identify this.

For example, your biggest challenge might be one of the following:

- Achieving the correct Activation level to work efficiently in the morning
- Achieving the correct Activation level to work efficiently after lunch
- Achieving the correct Activation level to get a good night's sleep

In my own case, the Optimal Activation Review showed the biggest challenge during my day came immediately after lunch (in Chapter 21, Figure 21.6, notice the big mismatch between the Xs and Os at this time of day). I felt drowsy after eating. This was not ideal if I needed to work efficiently on my medium-charge tasks in the afternoon, so I needed to address the situation.

The foods I ate for lunch were not helping me be productive in the afternoon. So, I changed my diet slightly.

I also sometimes had to attend work lunches with colleagues or clients. I felt it polite and proper to stay for the duration of the meal. If and when these lunches happened, I was often unproductive in the afternoon and sometimes had to catch up on work on weekends.

So, I created a plan to help me successfully manage the situation. I used the SWAP Cycle for this. Remember, this entails Self-Watching and making an Aim and Plan (there is a space at the bottom of the Will Power Story template to do this). Here is my specific Plan:

My Aim was to complete my afternoon to-do list after lunch.

The first part of my plan was to ensure I did not arrive at the restaurant too hungry. So, I grazed on snacks throughout the morning.

Then I looked online at the restaurant menu and planned to order a light dish.

I also planned to walk to the restaurant, giving me the chance to do some micro-recharge breathing work. I also planned to walk back to my office from the restaurant (instead of taking a taxi).

Finally, I planned to write a clear list of work for the afternoon before I left the office for lunch so I'd know exactly what I needed to accomplish on my return.

Reflect?

If it's helpful, write down your own workday SWAP to help you overcome the biggest challenge of your day. You can use your Will Power Story to do this.

BUILDING BETTER FOCUS AND PRODUCTIVITY HABITS

I want you to think of one small thing you can change to be more productive, so you get better at optimizing every 24-hour period. These reminders might be helpful:

1. Understand why you want to be productive today by connecting the work you need to get done with your big long-term goals (FAM Story).
2. Use Will Power Stories to optimize your Brain States.
3. Build better DES habits.
4. Use downtime to deliberately recharge.
5. Plan to create ice sculptures.
6. Use Will Power Boosters and Strengths to help you accomplish complex, clever work and to help you switch off.
7. Use Focus Words and Pictures.
8. Use the SWAP Cycle to manage and overcome your greatest daily challenge.

Add any areas of improvement you have identified and new habits you'd like to build to your Me Power Wish List.

BUILD THE HABIT

Next, if it is helpful, identify one habit you'd like to prioritize developing to improve your focus and productivity. This will be your Aim.

My example Aim is: "Every lunchtime, focus on my breathing for five minutes as I am walking to get my lunch. This will help me secure more micro-recharges."

If you want to work on a productivity-boosting habit, write down your Aim:

____

____

Once you have a clear Aim, it might be helpful to revisit the "How HUE Hinders Change" self-reflection (Chapter 20) tool to help you think about how HUE might try to stop you from building this new habit.

To create a Habit Building Plan that activates the Nine Action Factors and supercharges the habit building process, answer these questions:

1. Describe the SMALL specific new helpful habit that you want to build (your Aim):

   ____

   Example answer: Every lunchtime, focus on my breathing for five minutes as I am walking to get my lunch to help me secure more micro-recharges.

2. Describe what you currently do (your unhelpful habit) instead of the new helpful habit you want to build:

   ____

   Example answer: Typically HUE would be focusing on threats (e.g., work problems) and looking for interesting things to do (e.g., checking my phone).

3. Describe what reminds or triggers this unhelpful habit:

   ____

   Example answer: HUE and my phone.

4. Describe how you will remind yourself (trigger) to practice your NEW habit daily:

____

Example answer: Plan it into my Will Power Story (e.g., five minutes of focused breathing every lunchtime). Keep my phone on airplane mode as I am doing focused breathing. Time the five minutes on my watch.

5. Describe the new knowledge and skills you will need to help you secure your new habit:

____

Example answer: N/A (I already know what to do).

6. If it is helpful, describe where and how you will acquire the new knowledge and skills you need:

____

Example answer: N/A (I already know what to do).

7. Describe in detail why you want to build this new habit:

____

Example answer: Help me to be efficient and effective in the afternoons. Give me a better chance of being my best so I can perform well in my job, help colleagues, and free up time to spend with my family.

8. Who can you ask to help you build your new habit? (ideally, they will also be building the same or similar habit at the same time):

____

Example answer: Tell my team about this and invite others to give it a try.

9. What will be the reward for building the new habit? Remember, rewards can be internal, external, or social:

____

Example answer: I will feel better about myself, I will have a better chance of getting the promotion I want, I will be better able to help colleagues, and I will get to spend more quality time with my family.

10. What will be the cost/penalty for not building the new habit?:

____

Example answer: The opposite of the rewards I describe above.

Congratulations, you now have a robust plan to build a new productivity-boosting habit!

HABIT MECHANIC LANGUAGE AND TOOLS YOU HAVE LEARNED IN CHAPTER 25...

Core Language

Brain States—A concept created to help a person think about their brain as being like a battery that has three specific operating states: recharge, medium charge, and high charge. ☑

Ice Cubes and Ice Sculptures—Terms created to help a person separate their daily tasks into two distinct categories: easy work (ice cubes) and mentally challenging work (ice sculptures). ☑

Planning Tools

Will Power Story—A tool to help you be more focused and productive every day so you can better balance work and life. ☑

Will Power Boosters and Strengths—Tactics you can use to supercharge your Will Power Stories. ☑

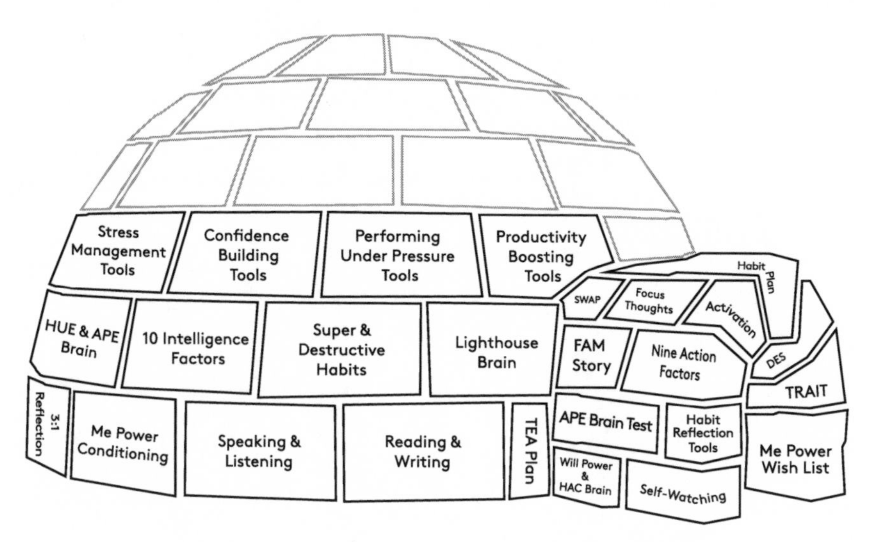

Figure 25.11: Your Habit Mechanic intelligence igloo is building up!

Next, we'll look at how you can supercharge your learning to sharpen your intelligence and make building new habits in any area of your life easier.

26

PRACTICE SMARTER, BOOST YOUR INTELLIGENCE, AND BUILD ANY HABIT FASTER BY USING OUR LEARNING STRENGTHS PLAN

You now know about a range of Habit Mechanic Tools you can use to build new habits to be your best. These tools are designed to make it easier for you to practice turning your new knowledge into new habits. But building new habits takes time and persistence, and not all forms of practice are equal. Some help you learn faster than others.

Also, your intelligence is not a gift or fixed. It is earned and developed through focused practice. By learning how to practice smarter, you will develop your intelligence faster—including your Habit Mechanic intelligence.

In this chapter, I will show you how to supercharge your practice so that you can harness your learning superpower (introduced in Chapter 5), develop your Habit Mechanic intelligence, and build new habits faster.

WHAT CAN WE LEARN ABOUT LEARNING FROM THOMAS EDISON AND MARIE CURIE?

To understand more about high-quality practice, let's consider how two of the greatest scientific minds of all time made the most of their learning superpowers to discover insights that changed our world.

Thomas Edison was one of America's greatest inventors. He held over 1,000 patents for his creations. His most famous invention is probably the first commercial light bulb.

The concept of a light bulb was not new, but Edison made the first one that was reliable enough to be sold to the public. He said: "Of the 200 light bulbs that didn't work, every failure told me something that I was able to incorporate into the next attempt."

He also said: "I have not failed. I've just found 10,000 ways that won't work."

Thomas Edison's willingness to work hard and acquire new insights from his mistakes seems to have been very important to his success.

It turns out that this formula of "focused or deliberate practice" (where you focus hard, make mistakes, and use feedback about your mistakes to get better) did not only work for Edison. Strong research evidence shows time and again that this special type of practice is essential if you want to improve and develop in any area of life.

Another famous scientist that can help our understanding of the power of focused practice is Marie Curie. She was the first woman to be awarded a Nobel Prize, and the only person to be awarded a Nobel Prize in two different sciences (physics and chemistry).

Curie's love of learning, and her passion for science, was sparked from a young age by her father. At just four years old, she was already a confident reader—an essential skill for focused practice at school and beyond. This allowed her to fully engage in her studies and become a dedicated pupil who received a gold medal when she completed secondary school.

However, as a woman, she was not allowed to attend university in her home country of Poland. For a short period after school, she abandoned her studies. But she soon made a pact with her sister that would allow her to attend the Sorbonne University in Paris.

At the age of 18 or 19, while waiting to move to Paris, she joined a secret Polish laboratory and started to learn chemical analysis. This was the "Flying University"—an underground academic collective that constantly moved location to evade Russian officials, who controlled Poland at the time.

When Marie Curie described her early work in physics, she explained how "from time to time, a little unhopeful success would encourage me... and at other times I sank into despair. But on the whole I discovered my taste for experiments during these trials."

Here she is describing pushing herself out of her comfort zone and making mistakes. This is an example of the focused practice that would help her become an expert and uniquely successful scientist.

When she got the chance to study in Paris, her hard work and dedication resulted in her graduating first in her class.

After marrying her scientific partner, Pierre Curie, she became pregnant with their first child. She worked in the lab throughout her pregnancy and returned there a couple of days after the birth of her daughter Irene. A few weeks later, her first paper was published to worldwide acclaim.

The work she endured to win her two Nobel Prizes has been described as "repetitive, tedious, and drudgery"—but, despite that, she persisted.

One of the hallmarks of Marie Curie's professional life was the way she documented everything in journals and notebooks. This will have supercharged her learning. Remember, short-term memory only lasts about 30 seconds.

Within these documents, she detailed insights about the radioactive qualities of radium and polonium. These insights helped fuel a creative spark that would save many lives in the First World War. Through her research,

Curie knew about the power of X-ray technology in helping see injuries deep inside the human body that were invisible to the naked eye. She created the concept of mobile X-ray units that could be used on the battlefield to more accurately diagnose soldiers' injuries. These life-saving mobile units became known as "Little Curies."

Many would say that people like Marie Curie and Thomas Edison were just talented, and naturally intelligent,[5] and that is why they were successful.

However, Marie Curie didn't agree. She said of her success: "I was taught that the way of progress was neither swift nor easy."

And Thomas Edison famously said: "Genius is one percent inspiration and ninety-nine percent perspiration."

As we learn more about what allows people to fulfill their potential in life, we increasingly understand that having a genetic advantage seems to be less and less important. Focused practice and your ability to learn are just as important. This is because they allow you to develop the knowledge, skills, and habits to be healthier, happier, and at your best more often.

But focused practice and successful learning can be difficult to do because HUE (Horribly Unhelpful Emotions) will often get in the way. So, I am going to show you how you learn, and how to supercharge the learning process. You'll learn how to get your HUE out of the way of your learning so you can fulfill your potential.

HOW DOES LEARNING HAPPEN?

Learning is not magic. It is a biological process.

When you pay attention to (concentrate on) information, by training,

---

[5] For clarity, I am defining intelligence as the ability to acquire and apply knowledge and skills. This means learning and intelligence are interconnected. By learning to be a Habit Mechanic, you are boosting your Habit Mechanic intelligence.

practicing, studying, revising, observing, or listening, your brain builds new neurological connections to help you remember and learn that information.

The first step to learning new information is concentrating on what you want to learn. So, let's recap on the concentration ideas we introduced when we covered high-charge work (building ice sculptures) in Chapter 25.

The way that we think about human concentration is that it is like a torch. And in the same way a torch has limited battery life, our ability to concentrate is limited.

Neurobiologically, we can think of concentration having three parts (revisit Chapter 25 for an in-depth recap):

Part 1—**Switching on your brain** (like switching on a torch)

Part 2—**Focusing your attention** (like focusing the torchlight onto what you want to learn)

Part 3—**Sustaining and refocusing your attention** (when the torchlight drifts off the target, refocus it back onto the target)

Like concentration, learning can also be broken down into some simple steps. First, you pay attention to some new information. This information goes into your short-term memory. But if you don't repeat the information within about 30 seconds, your short-term memory will dump it. It will disappear without a trace.

However, if you repeat the information quickly—for example, by saying it to yourself again or writing it down—this information will start to be turned into a memory. Your brain will begin to form neurological connections that represent the new information you have learned. It is like turning fragile cobweb-like connections into thin cable-like connections. The more you repeat the information, the thicker the connections become. I call this process "cobwebs to cables" (I have already told you about this [Chapter 5], but by repeating it here I am trying to strengthen your learning ☺).

For example, you are moving from cobwebs to cables when you do these two things:

1. Use your knowledge about creating a Daily TEA Plan to actually create one (i.e., moving from knowing to doing [skill]).
2. Repeat this process regularly until it becomes a habit (i.e., moving from doing [skill] to habit).

However, if you stop using the information (e.g., completing Daily TEA Plans), the cables will reduce to cobwebs and eventually disappear. So it seems that the most important part of learning is repetition. Here are some examples of how you can do this:

- Write down new information
- Test yourself
- Talk to someone else about it
- Talk to yourself about it
- Physically practice the skill

To make this important repetition process easy to remember, I use the term R2R (repeat to remember and remember to repeat).

HOW TO LEARN FASTER

To help you supercharge your learning so you develop your Habit Mechanic intelligence and build new habits faster, I am going to show you four interconnected frameworks and tools:

1. The E3 Learning framework
2. The 10 Intelligence Factors (I will go into more detail than in Chapter 5)

3. The Focused Practice framework
4. The Learning Strengths Plan

THE E3 LEARNING FRAMEWORK

The science is clear: you can learn how to get better with practice, because practice changes your brain. You can learn how to improve (one tiny step at a time) any area including sleep, stress management, confidence, productivity, performing under pressure, and leadership.

But insights from cutting-edge science show us that the most impactful types of practice include three core factors: Effort, Efficiency, and Effectiveness. I call optimal learning "E3 Learning."

Here is a quick overview to help you do more E3 Learning.

Effort

To learn anything new, effort and focused practice are essential. To apply focused effort, you need to be Activated, have clear aims about exactly what you are going to practice, and have concentration strategies to maintain focus on what you want, or need, to learn.

Efficiency

As well as effort, you also need to organize your time efficiently. This means planning exactly what you need to practice, planning when and where you will practice, and reflecting on how your practice is progressing. Two efficiency ideas I recommend exploring are "variable practice" and "spaced learning."

Effectiveness

As well as effort and efficiency, you also need to make sure that your practice is effective. Effective practice means what you're learning helps you build the habits you will need in order to perform in real-world situations. For example:

- Practicing hitting balls on a golf range is very different from playing a round of golf.
- Practicing giving a presentation alone sitting down when you are calm and relaxed is very different from giving a presentation where you are standing up in a room full of people and you feel under pressure.
- Reading about how to be a great leader is very different from building better leadership habits so you can put great leadership into action.
- Making revision notes to help you do well on an exam (which is memory storage work) is very different from what you need to do on an exam to secure a good grade (memory recall).

To optimize the time you spend learning, you must work on all E3 areas.

For example, let's think back to Roger Bannister's story (Chapter 4). His research allowed him to do higher quality E3 Learning than his competitors. All three athletes were undoubtedly putting a lot of effort into their training, but Bannister was able to make his more efficient and effective. This was because he uniquely understood that a core aim of his training was to help him get better at conserving oxygen as he ran. So he adjusted his training to allow him to do this.

THE 10 INTELLIGENCE FACTORS

You can use the 10 Intelligence Factors (first introduced in Chapter 5) to help you supercharge your E3 Learning. Below I have explained each factor in greater detail so you can understand more about how each can supercharge or block your learning.

Just to recap, the 10 Intelligence Factors are:

1. Your motivation to learn (including your belief that you can learn)
2. Your diet, exercise, and sleep habits
3. Your emotional state while learning
4. Your Activation levels while learning
5. Your attentional style
6. Your working memory and memory recollection capacities
7. The brain friendliness and quality of the learning material (or how you encode information)
8. The skill of your teacher(s)
9. The volume and quality of your prior learning (i.e., what you have already learned)
10. The volume and quality of your current learning (i.e., are you doing lots of focused practice?)

All of these factors interact, so get as many working for you as you can.

Remember, learning is your superpower. But it does not happen by osmosis. If you are struggling to learn something, it doesn't mean you can't learn it. It means one or more of the following factors are stopping you.

Now let's dig deeper into each area.

1. Your Motivation to Learn (Including Your Belief That You Can Learn)

The first factor that can block or enhance learning is your motivation. Remember, in Chapter 16, we defined motivation as "direction and intensity of effort." If you are not motivated to learn, it will be difficult to do so. Incorporating the things you need to learn into your FAM (Future Ambitious Meaningful) Story will boost your motivation to learn them.

What about your beliefs in your learning abilities? People with a "Habit Mechanic Mindset" (the first Action Factor in Chapter 18) believe they can improve anything with practice and take responsibility for being their best. I hope reading and engaging in the exercises in this book have helped you develop your Habit Mechanic Mindset.

2. Diet, Exercise, and Sleep (DES)

The second factor that can block or enhance learning is DES. If you optimize these three areas, it will be much easier to concentrate and for new neurological connections to grow in your brain.

3. Emotional State

The third factor is your emotional state. Emotions drive attention; attention drives learning. For example, if you are feeling fearful, angry, or guilty, it is very difficult to pay attention to anything but these emotions—making it equally difficult to focus on the things you want to learn.

4. Activation Level

The fourth factor is your Activation level. Achieving the correct Activation level means that your brain is alert enough, and has the right type of chemical messengers, to allow you to learn new information. You will have different optimal Activation levels for learning different things (as discussed in Chapter 21).

5. Attentional Style

The fifth factor is attentional style. Different types of learning require different attentional styles. Here are some examples:

Academic Focus

In education and at work (office based), many of the things you need to learn are written down, whether in a book or on a screen. This means that you need to focus the spotlight from your torch of concentration quite tightly onto these written words in order to read them and to secure learning. This requires a "narrow spotlight," or what is called a "narrow attentional style."

Playing Sport Focus

Learning that requires a different attentional style might be found in some types of sports training. For example, imagine that you are practicing soccer or hockey, and you are learning about attack, and where to pass the ball among teammates, to break through the opposition's defense.

This requires you to switch between a narrow focus of concentration—understanding where the ball is in relation to your foot or stick—and a broad focus of concentration—understanding where your teammates are and where the spaces are in the opposition's defense. It is important to point out that the narrow focus in this situation is still much broader than the type of narrow focus that you need to read the words in a book—as the words are much smaller than a football or a hockey puck.

The point of explaining these two different learning examples is to emphasize how different attentional styles are advantageous for different situations.

What Is Your Natural Attentional Style?

Now here is the challenge: everybody seems to have a different natural attentional style. Some people have a very broad style, some have a very narrow style, and others have styles somewhere in between. Most formal learning (in education and at work) is done using a very narrow style, so those who naturally have a narrow attentional style will probably find it easier to concentrate and learn in these settings. Those who have a broader attentional style might find it easier to learn things like playing sports.

However, the good news is that it does not matter what your natural style is because you can learn how to focus your attention more narrowly, or widely. For example, by creating a Will Power Story and planning Refocus Words and Pictures, you are learning to focus your attention more narrowly.

6. Working Memory and Memory Recollection

The sixth factor is your working memory and memory recollection. To help you understand working memory, I want you to read out the following numbers once, close the book, and see if you can write them down.

2-0-3-5-3-7-1-8-4-7-8-9-3-0-8-2-9-5-8-3-7-2-9-3-5

How did you do?

It is highly likely I have just overloaded your working memory. Your working memory is where you temporarily hold information while you are thinking, learning, making decisions, and solving problems. Sometimes it is called the mind's workspace.

People can typically hold five to seven chunks of information in their working memory. In this exercise, I asked you to remember 25 pieces of information. So, after you read the first five to seven numbers, your brain probably started dumping the early ones so it could focus on the new numbers. Your working memory is similar to a leaky bucket, and some people seem to have more holes in their bucket than others.

Memory Recollection

As well as working memory, memory recollection also influences learning. Memory recollection is the ability to recall things you have previously paid attention to or experienced. For example, if you are reading a book, you often need to recall what you have previously understood from earlier in the book to make sense of what you are currently reading. Or, when you are in a meeting, you have to recall insights from previous meetings and events to answer questions you are asked.

Working memory and memory recollection are often used together. To understand this, I want you to complete the following task:

Without writing anything down or using a calculator, divide 160 by 20.

To find the answer, you needed to hold both the number 160 and 20 in your working memory. Then you might have recalled other information you have previously learned. For example, there are five 20s in 100, and three 20s in 60. Then you might have recalled your ability to do addition, adding five and three together. This would have given you the correct answer: 8.

A combination of both working memory and memory recollection allowed you to solve this mental arithmetic.

For some people, the process would have been very subconscious—meaning that they barely noticed how they solved the problem—because solving these types of math problems is a well learned habit. For others, it would have been a much more conscious process, because they might usually use a calculator to solve these types of problems.

It appears that different people have different working memory capacities. Some have larger capacities than others. Also, different people have different abilities to recall memories. Some people are better at recall than others.

The good news is that **working memory and memory recall are learnable skills**. The areas of your brain that are responsible for these crucial learning capacities can be changed and strengthened with focused practice. So, you can improve your working memory and memory recall.

Is Technology Impacting Your Memory?

One major 21st-century challenge that we face when training our memory is that instead of using our memory to store and recall information, we use technology like smartphones and search engines. So we are not training it like we might have done in the past.

One way you can practice improving your working memory and memory recall is reflecting at the end of each day by writing a summary of the day's key events. When doing this, it is helpful to focus on what you should be thankful for, what went well, and what you could do even better tomorrow—just like the reflective writing processes (Focused Reflection) I introduced in Chapter 22.

7. Encoding Information (The Brain Friendliness and Quality of the Learning Material)

The seventh factor is how the information we need to learn is presented. Some information (e.g., the plot of your favorite film) seems to be more memorable, or memory friendly, than other information (e.g., the details of a technical presentation, or the periodic table).

The first step to moving information from outside your brain to inside is called encoding. Brain scientists have identified different types of encoding, but the one that appears to be the most effortless (for most people) is called automatic processing (i.e., this is happening when you learn new information very easily).

So whenever possible, we should try to find information in a format we can learn with relatively little effort (meaning you process that information automatically). For example, I often find it easier to learn from a TED Talk presentation than an academic textbook. So I can spend 10 minutes watching a TED Talk and learn a lot very easily. But if I spend 10 minutes reading an academic textbook on the same subject, I will typically not learn as much as easily, because I find the information harder to process.

Another example: to optimize my learning from a nonfiction book, I will buy both the audiobook and the physical book. I will listen to the audiobook as I am walking and then return to my office to make notes in the physical book. This helps optimize the way I encode the information.

Please note, these are my personal examples. But the way you optimally encode information might be different. So please do some personal research to work out the format in which information is easiest for you to learn.

8. The Skill of Your Teacher(s)

The eighth factor is the skill of your teacher(s). For example, imagine you want to learn how to drive. You can be taught by either someone who has only just passed their test or an experienced driving instructor. Selecting the former will probably hinder your learning, and selecting the latter will probably supercharge your learning.

9. Volume and Quality of Your Prior Learning (i.e., What You Have Already Learned)

The ninth factor is the volume and quality of your prior learning. Your ability to learn new knowledge, skills, and habits is limited by your current knowledge, skills, and habits. For example, if you do not know your alphabet, it is difficult to spell. If you do not know how to structure a sentence, it is difficult to structure a paragraph. And if you cannot add and subtract, it is difficult to do long division.

If you are struggling to learn something new, it might be because you have not learned other important information. So you need to identify and fill the gaps in your current knowledge and skills before you can learn the new information.

Everything you can do has many interconnected layers of learning. I've used the igloo concept throughout the book to highlight this. The igloo concept helps show how learning is built up over a long period of time. What I did not show is that if you miss one learning step, like your alphabet, you can be stopped from learning something else, like spelling. Another example: if you do not know how to manage your Activation, it is much more difficult to manage your stress.

If you think back to when you were at school, you might have missed key learning steps for many reasons, such as

- you didn't find one area of a subject at school particularly interesting so you didn't do the work necessary to learn it; or
- perhaps you were ill while the rest of your class was learning a key part of a subject.

Some knowledge and skills within certain areas are essential for learning other knowledge and skills.

So, when you are struggling to learn something new, it might be because you have not learned other important information. Therefore, you need to identify and fill the gaps in your current knowledge and skills before you can learn the new information.

10. Volume and Quality of Your Current Learning (i.e., Are You Doing Lots of Focused Practice?)

The tenth and final factor that can block or enhance learning is the volume and quality of your current learning. Just because you are sitting at your desk with your accountancy exam books open does not mean you are learning what is written in the textbook in front of you. For example, you might be thinking about the family holiday you are going on next week, and therefore not learning anything useful for your accountancy exams. To supercharge your learning, you need to do focused practice.

THE FOCUSED PRACTICE FRAMEWORK

You can use the "Focused Practice framework" to improve the quality of your current learning. It helps you break down the learning process into four distinct parts, making it easier to do high-charge ice sculpture building working.

It doesn't matter what you are learning (e.g., golf putting, stress management, leadership skills, arithmetic), this overarching four-part process is always the same. It will help you optimize any "learning session"—for example, a training or practice or study or revision session.

Here is an example of the four-part process in action:

Part 1—Task Selection

First, you take some time to understand what you want to learn in this specific learning session. For example, you need to **watch a 30-minute video** to learn about VAT[6] (value added tax) laws, VAT processes, and VAT returns. Then you need to answer some exam-style questions on these areas. You have one hour to do this.

Part 2—Planning

Next, you plan how to do the work to the best of your ability. First, you make sure that your Activation level is correct for learning. Then you split one page

[6] Not sure what VAT is? It is a basic tax added to most things you buy.

in your notebook into three sections: (1) "VAT laws"; (2) "VAT processes"; and, (3) "VAT returns." This helps you organize your notes so that you can study them coherently before you take the post-video test. Finally, in the top right-hand corner of the page, you write down one or two concentration tactics to help you focus. Here are some examples:

Pause - Pause the video to help me make notes.

Rewind - When it is helpful rewind the video to help me make notes.

Phone Management - Turn off your phone to minimize distractions.

Workspace Plan - Create a workspace with minimal distractions.

Mindset - Approach this task in the right frame of mind.

Figure 26.1: Taking a few moments to plan how you will concentrate will save you time and improve your quality of learning. This is very similar to the Will Power Boosters and Strengths we discussed in Chapter 25.

Part 3—Focus

Here, you do the work. You might call it training, or practice, or study, or revision. For example, you watch the video, making notes about each of the three areas, and then review your notes. Then you close your notebook and answer the test questions. You use your concentration strategies to help you sustain focus.

Part 4—Feedback

Finally, you evaluate what you have learned by taking the test and marking your answers. **The feedback phase is the most important phase of this four-part process.** It is where valuable insights about what you have learned from the video, and what you have not learned, can be evaluated. You can use these insights to improve how you approach Parts 1, 2, and 3 of the learning process in your next learning session. This helps you refine your learning approach and optimize future learning sessions.

Not all practice will result in the same quality of learning. For example, one hour of focused practice using the four-part approach outlined above could result in you learning a lot. But one hour of unfocused practice could result in you learning very little.

To learn more about the "learning science" behind the four-part process I have shown, I recommend checking out Professor Mark Guadagnoli's Challenge Point Framework. Professor Guadagnoli has published over 100 articles and abstracts about how to optimize the learning process and is a professor of neuroscience and neurology. I have learned a lot from his work over the years.

Summary

This is only a quick overview of the core factors that influence your learning, because it is beyond the scope of this book to go into more detail. But think carefully about your current practice strategies to help you optimize your learning. Ensuring your practice quality is as good as possible will give you the best chance of building new habits faster and fulfilling your potential.

Learning how to harness your learning superpower is central for Habit Mechanic success. I will continue to show you how to do this for the remainder of this chapter.

Test?

If it is helpful, write down the 10 Intelligence factors that can block or enhance your learning.

THE LEARNING STRENGTHS PLAN

Cricket legend Sir Alastair Cook was only the second opening batsman to reach 10,000 runs in Test cricket. The record-breaking former England captain said: "All the greats have hard work in common. I haven't been given a talent that makes me better than everyone else. I have made that difference by working hard."

The best learning happens through focused or deliberate practice or study. Practicing in a focused or deliberate way means that you practice to improve. This means you will probably make mistakes. But your mistakes contain the vital information that helps you get better. Without making mistakes, you cannot improve.

To help you do more focused practice or study, I have designed the "Learning Strengths Plan." This will help you intelligently Self-Watch your current learning habits and build better ones.

First, I want you to select an area where you want to improve.

For example: "I want to build better stress management habits."

Once you have selected a specific area, I want you to consider a series of statements to help you think about how well you practice that area. Rate yourself from 1 to 10 for each statement (1 means you never do this, and 10 means you always do it).

Statement 1

I HAVE A CLEAR PLAN of how I am going to approach my learning in this area or subject (i.e., do you map out what you are going to do before you start learning?). *Score: ______ /10*

Statement 2

I always ACHIEVE THE CORRECT ACTIVATION LEVEL before I begin my learning in this area (if you are not at the correct Activation level, it will be very difficult to optimize your learning). *Score: ______ /10*

Statement 3

I SET GOALS to help me concentrate when I am learning (setting goals is closely connected to setting out a clear plan—for example, I will answer questions 1–5, mark my answers, and retest myself on answers I got wrong; I will turn my phone off to help me focus). *Score: ______ /10*

Statement 4

When I don't understand something I want to learn, I GO BACK OVER IT. *Score: ______ /10*

Statement 5

I MAKE A NOTE of things I don't understand so I can follow these up later (e.g., finding a resource that explains it in a different way, or asking someone else who knows more about this area). *Score: ______ /10*

Statement 6

I PRACTICE THINGS OVER AND OVER until I know them or become skilled at them (e.g., I use R2R [repeat to remember, remember to repeat]). *Score: ______ /10*

Statement 7

When I finish my learning in this area, I LOOK BACK TO SEE HOW WELL I DID (e.g., I read back over my work). *Score:* _____ */10*

Statement 8

I TEST MYSELF at the end of the learning session in the same way I will be tested in the exam or in real life (tests are a great way for improving your working memory and memory recall skills, which are important learning and performance capacities). *Score:* _____ */10*

Statement 9

If I am studying for an exam, I MARK MY OWN TEST QUESTIONS using the exam board marking criteria (if relevant and available), and then test myself again until I have achieved full marks in all the test questions.

OR

I TEST MY NEW SKILLS in the same way I will need to use them in real life and (if relevant) get feedback from others (this point is closely connected to TE-TAP Learning introduced in Chapter 24). *Score:* _____ */10*

Statement 10

I USE FOCUS WORDS AND PICTURES to help me concentrate when I am learning, and to refocus when I become distracted. *Score:* _____ */10*

Once you have scored yourself on each statement, you will better understand your learning strengths and weaknesses. You can then target one small area to improve and make yourself a better learner.

You can learn, but it is not always easy. If you put the learning insights I have shared into practice, they will improve your ability to learn and make it easier for you to build more helpful habits so that you can fulfill your potential.

HABIT MECHANIC TOOLS YOU HAVE LEARNED IN CHAPTER 26...

Planning Tools

E3 Learning—A framework to highlight that the most impactful types of practice include three core factors: Effort, Efficiency, and Effectiveness. ☑

Focused Practice framework—Designed to help you improve the quality of your current learning. It helps you break down the learning process into four distinct parts, making it easier to do high-charge ice sculpture building work. ☑

Self-Reflection Tools

The Learning Strengths Plan—An exercise to help you reflect on your current learning habits and build better ones. ☑

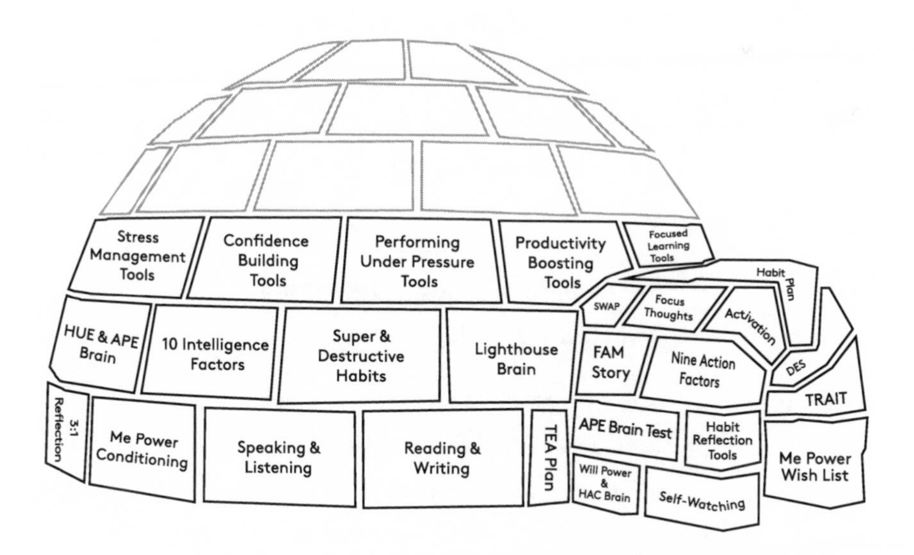

Figure 26.2: Your Habit Mechanic intelligence igloo is building up!

CONGRATULATIONS—YOU HAVE COMPLETED THE HABIT MECHANIC SKILLS SECTION!

But this does not necessarily mean you are a Habit Mechanic. To become one, or to continue to be one, keep working on yourself. Focus on striking that helpful balance between pleasure and Habit Mechanic development (so you can achieve meaningful goals and experience personal growth). For example:

1. Keep updating your FAM (Future Ambitious Meaningful) Story.
2. Regularly analyze your habits.
3. Keep using the Habit Mechanic Tools to help you develop better habits.

Life is a series of ups and downs. Habit Mechanics manage this roller coaster of life by maximizing the ups and minimizing the downs. They do it one tiny habit at a time.

WHAT NEXT?

In the next section, I'll introduce "Team Power Leadership" and show you how you can start to become a "Chief Habit Mechanic."

Who Can Benefit from Becoming a Chief Habit Mechanic?

Anybody who wants to help others do better, from senior leaders and managers to team members. Also, coaches (sports and personal), teachers (you have a team of colleagues and a team of students or pupils), and parents (think of your family as a team).

Why Can All Members of My Team Benefit from Learning How to Be Better Leaders?

As I will discuss in much more detail in the next section, leadership is not a position or a title. It is about the actions you take and the examples you set within your group.

Therefore, every team member has a leadership responsibility. This is because everything anybody in a team does or says has an impact on everybody else's behavior and habits. Every team member has an important part to play in their team's happiness and success.

Is Helping Other People Be Their Best Not a High Priority for You Right Now?

If your answer is no, please skip ahead to the "Bringing It All Together" section, which starts directly after Chapter 35.

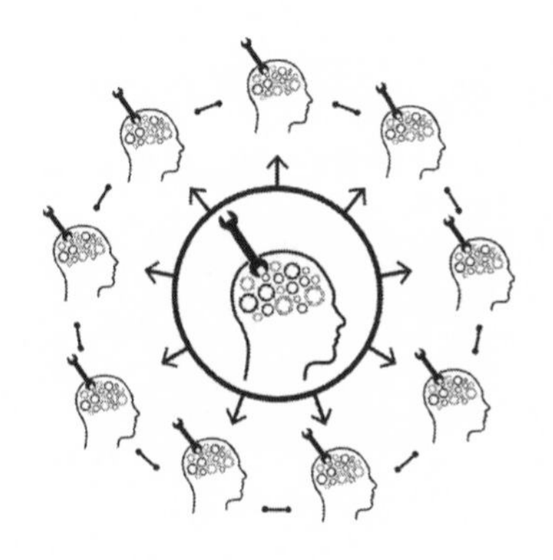

Step 4

CHIEF HABIT MECHANIC SKILLS

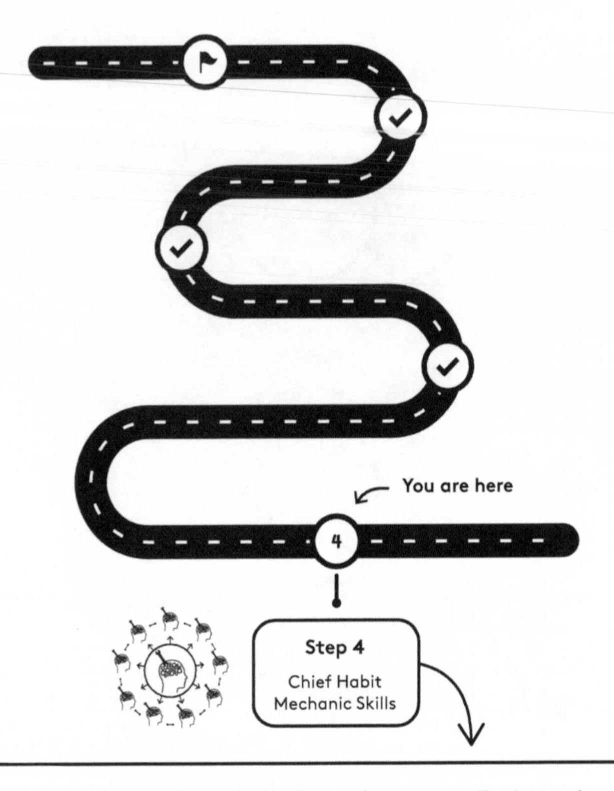

Figure S4.1: An overview of your journey through Step 4.

27

CHIEF HABIT MECHANIC LANGUAGE, TOOLS, AND OVERVIEW

As you read through Step 4, you will learn how to use a set of tools I've created to help you lead. These will help you develop your "Chief Habit Mechanic intelligence" (i.e., your ability to acquire and apply Chief Habit Mechanic knowledge and skills to help others develop new helpful habits) and benefit anybody who wants to help others do better.

I have listed them here so that you can refer back at any point. I will also recap them throughout Step 4 and in the index section at the back of the book.

Five-Stage Team Power model—A model showing the five stages high-performing teams successfully utilize to achieve their collective goals and fulfill their potential. (Chapter 28)

The Team Power Builder—A tool to help teams reflect on their strengths and areas of improvement across the Five-Stage Team Power model. (Chapter 28)

Team Power Leadership—The Chief Habit Mechanic leadership framework, which has four core components: Role Model; SWAP Coach; Cultural Architect; Action Communicator. (Chapter 29)

Role Model self-assessment—A tool to help you analyze your current Role Model strengths and weaknesses and develop better Role Model habits. (Chapter 30)

SWAP Coach self-assessment—A tool to help you analyze your current SWAP Coach strengths and weaknesses and develop better SWAP Coach habits. (Chapter 31)

Cultural Architect self-assessment—A tool to help you analyze your current Cultural Architect strengths and weaknesses and develop better Cultural Architect habits. (Chapter 32)

Action Communicator self-assessment—A tool to help you analyze your current Action Communicator strengths and weaknesses and develop better Action Communicator habits. (Chapter 33)

Team Power Leadership Builder—A tool to help you create a quick summary overview of your Team Power Leadership strengths and weaknesses. You can also use it to "map" every team member's Team Power Leadership skills and areas for improvement. (Chapter 34)

Culture Development Reflection Tool—A tool to help you consider how effectively you are using the Nine Action Factors to make it easier for your people to develop the behaviors/habits needed for team success. (Chapter 35)

BECOMING A CHIEF HABIT MECHANIC

You are now ready to begin developing your Team Power Leadership skills and take the first steps to becoming a Chief Habit Mechanic.

Figure 27.1: Me Power Conditioning + Team Power Leadership = Chief Habit Mechanic.

WHAT IS THE SECRET BEHIND ONE OF THE MOST SUCCESSFUL TEAMS IN HUMAN HISTORY?

Steve Hansen is the former head coach of the New Zealand All Blacks rugby team. He was a central figure in their back-to-back World Cup wins and in achieving a win ratio of over 85 percent. He revealed the secret of his success when he told *The Guardian*, "If you think you've arrived, you probably have—and it'll be the end of the destination. If you keep striving to be better, then you're going to search for ways to do that."

In the same interview he also said, "One of the greatest things you can do in life and in sport is be a faster learner than someone else... reflect and learn."

But Amazon Prime's fly-on-the-wall documentary *All or Nothing: New Zealand All Blacks* showed that knowing what you want your team to do is one thing but getting them to do it is another.

The documentary focuses on the All Blacks team that had won back-to-back Rugby World Cups, but had also seen a number of senior leaders retire. In episode four, the All Blacks are accused of complacency after a poor performance against Australia.

Before their next game against Argentina, Steve Hansen asked players to stand up in a team meeting if they had completed some individual video analysis work required of them. Only 3 out of 25 could say they had viewed the clips of opponents, which were vital for optimal preparation.

Hansen responded by asking his squad to consider and improve their weekly habits.

He said: "What I need you to do if you want to be a great All Black is to have a look at your habits from Sunday to Friday... Saturday [match day] is just the fun part... Every time you look in the mirror you ask that man, am I doing what I need to be doing?... It is not about the talk, boys. It is about what you do."

For me, this insight reinforces two important things I have learned while helping teams fulfill their potential:

1. Habits are the heartbeat of all cultures.
2. Even for very experienced leaders, creating and sustaining cultures where people are happy and high-performing can be very difficult because human behavior is complex.

WHY PURPOSEFULLY DEVELOPMENTAL ORGANIZATIONS WIN IN THE VUCA WORLD

Organizations with a culture of continual improvement are what I call "purposefully developmental organizations."[7] This is the same type of culture Steve Hansen focused on creating.

Harvard University academics, led by Professor Robert Kegan, scientifically analyzed leading companies, including Bridgewater Associates

---

[7] I use "purposeful development culture" and "purposefully developmental culture" interchangability throughout this book.

(arguably the world's most successful hedge fund), that adapted this purposefully developmental approach. Professor Kegan's team found the approach was the perfect antidote to the challenges of our volatile, uncertain, complex, and ambiguous world (VUCA).

The VUCA world demands innovation and change. The purposefully developmental organization approach creates workplaces where resilience, critical thinking (needed to solve problems and innovate), and adaptability (needed to change) become part of the culture. In these organizations, people are empowered to grow and do meaningful work. This makes them feel happier and perform better because they are better able to strike the balance between hedonism (pleasure) and eudemonia (Habit Mechanic development) that I explained earlier in the book (Chapter 14). Happy, focused employees deliver the continuous improvements required for organizations to stay ahead of the competition and win.

These types of organizations have five broad priorities.

1. Creating a culture where people trust each other and feel respected and valued.
2. Creating a mission that people in the organization are excited about and emotionally invested in. Think of this as a Future Ambitious Meaningful (FAM) Story (Chapter 16) for the organization.
3. Creating a culture where everyone is empowered and upskilled to become Habit Mechanics, or in other words, grow and improve every day by deliberately working on small, new helpful habits.
4. Creating a culture where everyone feels empowered and upskilled to become a better Team Power Leader so they can positively influence other people's behavior.
5. Creating a culture where a select group are supported to become expert Team Power Leaders and Chief Habit Mechanics.

This five-pronged approach helps people feel and perform better. It also helps the organization achieve its mission.

CREATING A PURPOSEFULLY DEVELOPMENTAL CULTURE IS DIFFICULT

However, knowing what purposefully developmental organizations do is one thing. Achieving it in your team or organization is another. This is because our brains are not wired to instinctively make the above outcomes easy.

Also, the Harvard scientists found that the purposefully developmental businesses they researched all used a different method to develop their cultures. They evolved this through trial and error over decades. As Bridgewater Associates founder Ray Dalio has intimated, their approach will probably not work for other businesses because it has not been designed to.

But what if there was a scientific, tried-and-tested, and flexible approach you could use to create a purposefully developmental culture in your team and/or organization?

This is what I have been refining over the past 16 years via my research and applied work in contexts of elite sport, business, and education. In this section of this book, I am going to show you the roadmap for becoming a Chief Habit Mechanic and creating a purposefully developmental culture that consistently helps your people feel and perform better, and your team and/or organization thrive.

Whether you're a senior leader, new leader, or aspiring leader, or just want to help others do better, and whether you have face-to-face contact with your team/people or manage them remotely, these insights will help you improve your leadership habits and supercharge your team's and/or organization's performance. The great thing is that this approach is flexible. It can be practically applied in a way that will work for your team and/or organization.

In this section, you will learn how to

- spot outdated and ineffective leadership methods;
- use Leadership Science to create truly world-class teams with our five-step Team Power Builder;
- use Leadership Science to start building world-class leadership habits in four simple steps; and
- use Leadership Science to start developing other world-class leaders in your team and/or organization.

Now, let's think more about the challenges of leading in the VUCA world.

28

USING LEADERSHIP SCIENCE TO CREATE TRULY WORLD-CLASS TEAMS WITH OUR FIVE-STEP TEAM POWER BUILDER

We know that leading is very challenging. In fact, I would argue that it's more challenging than ever before.

WHY LEADERS ARE BEING LET DOWN

The world has a leadership crisis. That was the shocking conclusion of a survey by the World Economic Forum. The data showed that 86 percent of respondents shared this belief. Lee Howell, the Forum's managing director, has argued a root cause of this situation is that our world rewards narcissism much more than the selflessness needed to be a great leader.

I do not think the above conclusions are the fault of leaders. I think leaders and future leaders are being seriously let down. This is because the vast majority of leadership training suffers from exactly the same problems I highlighted about personal development. It is still based on outdated "black-box" theories and presumes that giving people more knowledge will make them better leaders. This approach fails to recognize the centrality of habits in human behavior, and therefore has minimal impact on helping leaders actually do better.

How Do I Know This?

Let me recap one of the stories I told you earlier. In 2006, I was working in the backroom staff of an English professional soccer team. That team won the league against the odds. We spent about 50 percent less on player wages than our direct competitors. It was a phenomenal and record-breaking achievement. We won promotion to the Championship, which I would argue is the most challenging league in world soccer.

The Championship was far more competitive, and I became fascinated by the performance and leadership transitions the team was going through. I pursued a PhD to learn more about the theory behind some of the successes and setbacks I was observing. I began a journey to understand how outstanding leaders could be developed.

On this journey, I have worked with some of the biggest businesses in the world, and with world-class leaders in both sport and business. I will share some specific insights I have gleaned. These include lessons from my work with the head coach of one of the UK's most high-profile rugby clubs, who also coached the England team in a World Cup, and from a former captain of a Great Britain sporting team who faced great adversity in his quest to help his hometown team win the cup final at the national stadium.

Note: I hope that you will appreciate the nature of my work and respect that I cannot always publicly disclose the identities of those people and organizations I work with.

Let me begin by explaining how I learned to spot outdated and ineffective leadership methods.

TRADITIONAL LEADERSHIP DEVELOPMENT

Often, traditional approaches to helping leaders do better are very good at telling them the type of things they need to get good at, for example, the well-intended list shown below.

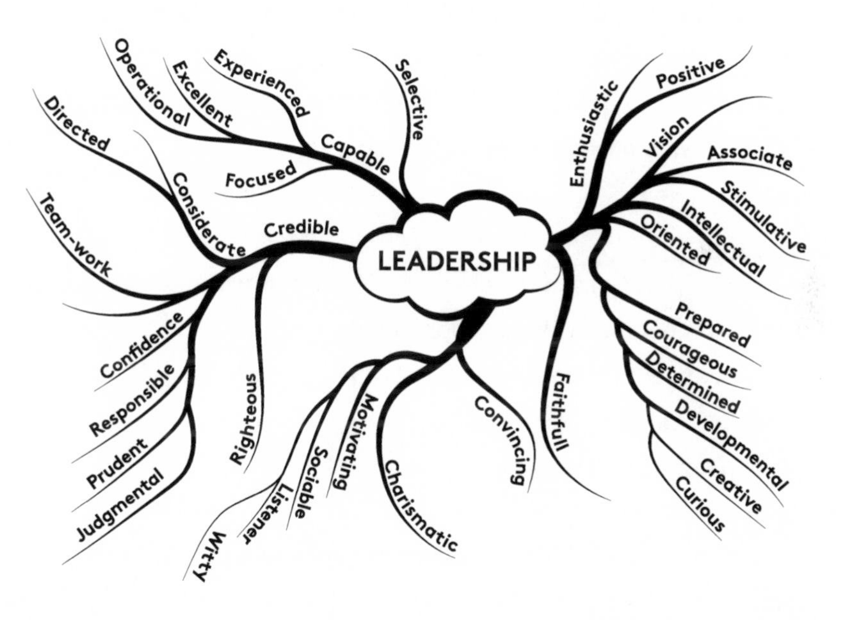

Figure 28.1: Knowing what great leaders do is very different from being able to do these things.

But I've found this approach to be arbitrary, confusing, and not very helpful in supporting leaders to actually do better.

There are also lots of psychometric, leadership, and personality tests available. I have tried and tested this approach, but again, I found that they weren't all that helpful. They are very deterministic about people's abilities. In other words, they can negatively reinforce the idea that you are born a leader or you're not. Also, according to leading neuroscientist Professor Lisa Feldman Barrett (in her 2021 book, *Seven and a Half Lessons about the Brain*), these types of tests have no more scientific validity than horoscopes.

There is clearly a major problem with these leadership development approaches and tests.

Because of advances in neuroscience and behavioral science, I presumed these leadership development approaches must consider what is going on inside people's brains. But when you look closely, they don't. They are largely based on black-box theories. They do not capitalize on what cutting-edge science tells us about what leaders need to do to be at their best. In fact, some of the research is over 100 years old. Most of the leadership training out there doesn't consider (1) how brains actually work (e.g., neuroplasticity, brain maturation, habits) or (2) how to actually help leaders change their behavior (i.e., build new habits).

Also, in the very few instances where some of these insights are considered, I am not aware of any approaches (other than our own) that are also based on cutting-edge behavioral science (the science of why we do what we do). The latter is essential if leaders truly want to understand how to develop high-performing cultures and world-class teams (i.e., help others build new habits).

Lists of good leadership behaviors and leadership tests can be a good starting point, but that is all they are. If this is all we give leaders to help them develop, it will likely do more damage than good, because these traditional approaches will actually stop leaders from improving and fulfilling their potential. This means using traditional approaches alone is a waste of time and money.

A NEW APPROACH TO LEADERSHIP DEVELOPMENT

These leadership development problems made me determined to take insights from cutting-edge neuroscience and behavioral science to create training that would consistently help leaders become outstanding, or what I call "Chief Habit Mechanics."

I don't know of any other leadership training program that does this and considers leadership habits in this way. This approach has proven to be extremely powerful in quickly helping leaders and their teams do better. I am confident it will help you and those people you want to help.

Before we go further, let's take a few moments to think about the role of teams in the VUCA world.

WINNING TEAMS IN THE VUCA WORLD

All my clients have to deal with the VUCA world. There's only one constant in the VUCA world—and that is change. This presents new challenges, but also new opportunities. What's more, the rate of change is getting faster and faster. This means it's not the companies and organizations that are currently financially strongest that will be the most successful in the medium- to long-term. Nor is it the companies and organizations that currently have the most intelligent people.

So who will win? The companies and organizations that best adapt to the new challenges and capitalize on the emerging new opportunities. Challenges and opportunities are just problems that need to be solved.

To be crystal clear what I mean by problems, here are some examples across different contexts:

Business problem-solving examples:

- How do we get better at online marketing?
- How do we create products that delight our customers?
- How do we use new AI technologies to make our business more effective?
- How do we become a world-class hybrid working organization?
- How can we help everyone make the most of our new CRM system?
- How can we get more of our people doing Me Power Conditioning and becoming Habit Mechanics?
- How do we make it easier for our people to become outstanding leaders?

Individual problem-solving examples:

- How can I get better at managing stress?
- How can I study for my exams to maximize my grades?
- How can I become a better leader (Chief Habit Mechanic)?
- How can I become a better Habit Mechanic?

Sporting problem-solving examples:

- How do we break down the opposition's defense?
- How do we disrupt the opposition's attack?
- How do I hit my golf ball straighter and farther?

Education problem-solving examples:

- How do we help our students get more engaged in their learning?
- How can we help more of our students become Habit Mechanics to improve their wellbeing and performance?
- How can we help our students get better exam grades?

Humans are much better at solving problems when they work in effective teams.

A Brief History of Teamwork and Problem-Solving

Humans are designed to survive. To help us stay alive, humans became very good at solving problems and innovating. For example, we learned how to

- avoid and outwit predators;
- create fire;
- build shelter;
- create tools to make daily tasks easier;
- grow crops;
- sanitize water; and
- cure disease.

To help us innovate, we had to become good at learning from mistakes. But more importantly, we also had to become good at understanding each other's emotions and motivations[8] so that we could cooperate and work together. For example, our sophisticated use of language is not an accident. It evolved to help us communicate so we could collaborate.

Why Do We Need to Work Together?

Humans are not the biggest, strongest, or fastest animal on the planet. The main reason we have prospered more than any other is our unique ability to intelligently work together and outsmart competitor species.

The "collective intelligence" of a group can be greater than the sum of its parts, making it easier to innovate, learn from mistakes, succeed, and thrive.

---

[8] This ability is called "Theory of Mind" and humans are much better at it than any other animal.

Being part of a team is central to being human. Communication and collaboration not only help us be healthier and happier, but collective effort—by teams, and not individuals—is the source of all great advancements in our society.

But great teams need great leaders.

To help you understand how to become an outstanding leader and develop others, let's consider what leadership means.

WHAT IS LEADERSHIP?

In very simple terms, leadership is about influence. Outstanding leaders must first get good at influencing their own behavior so that they can be at their best more often. This means getting good at Me Power Conditioning (deliberately working toward being your best) and becoming a Habit Mechanic. Next, you can focus on becoming excellent at "positively influencing" other people's behavior.

I deliberately make the point about "positive influence" because leaders can influence people's behavior in a positive way (think Nelson Mandela) or in a negative way (think Darth Vader—the evil Dark Lord from Star Wars movies ☺).

One of the greatest myths about leadership is that it's just the people with formal titles who are leaders. That is not correct. We all influence each other, all the time. Within any group or any team, influence is shared among everybody.

Figure 28.2: This understanding is essential for team success.

Some people who have many helpful habits might have a major, positive influence. Some people who have many unhelpful habits might have a really negative influence. But everybody has some degree of influence, because everything that everybody says and does (their behavior, which is driven by their habits) influences everyone else's behavior and habits.

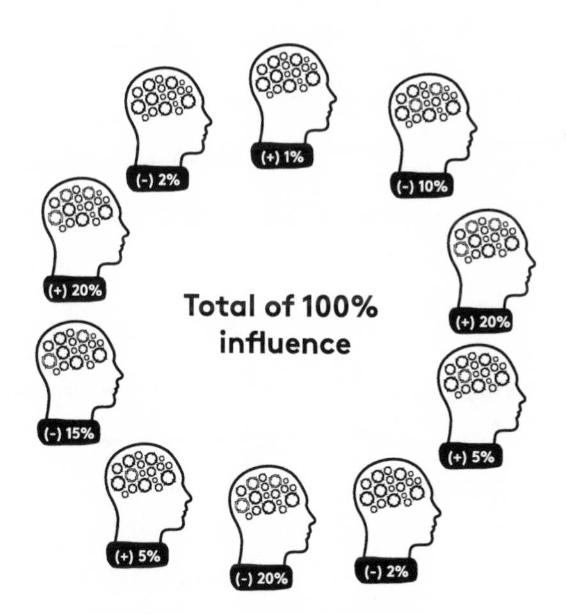

Figure 28.3: Which people have a positive influence (+) on your team, and which have a negative influence (-)?

To truly become an outstanding leader, you must learn how to deliberately and positively influence other people's behavior. The good news is that we can all learn how to do this better.

LEADERSHIP SCIENCE

Leadership is a science, not an art. So to help people become better leaders, I have created what I call "Leadership Science."

Leadership Science is a combination of neuroscience, behavioral science, and psychology. It has the potential to supercharge individual and team performance in the same way that sports science transformed player fitness levels in professional sport. Leadership Science offers a platform to help all teams and organizations reach new levels of performance that will supercharge their success in the VUCA world.

Neuroscience

The first part of Leadership Science is neuroscience. This relates to how brains work—something I have already covered in great detail.

Behavioral Science

The second part is behavioral science. This is about the things that influence what happens in our brains, and the resulting behavior—or, in other words, habits. Although this might sound complex, hopefully using the Nine Action Factors framework (Chapter 18) and the Habit Building Plans you have created shows you this science can be used in a simple and practical way to make behavior change easier. The good news is you can use the same approach to help your team and/or organization do better, and I will show you how.

Applied Psychology

The third part of Leadership Science is applied psychology. This is actually putting the neuroscience and behavioral science into practice to help ourselves and, ultimately, others do better.

I teach Habit Mechanics how to be "Team Power Leaders" so that they can put Leadership Science into practice. Team Power Leaders use Leadership Science to positively influence their team's habits so the team can achieve its mission. In doing this, they also develop Habit Mechanics and other Team Power Leaders in their team. When you pack your team full of Habit Mechanics and Team Power Leaders, team success becomes super easy.

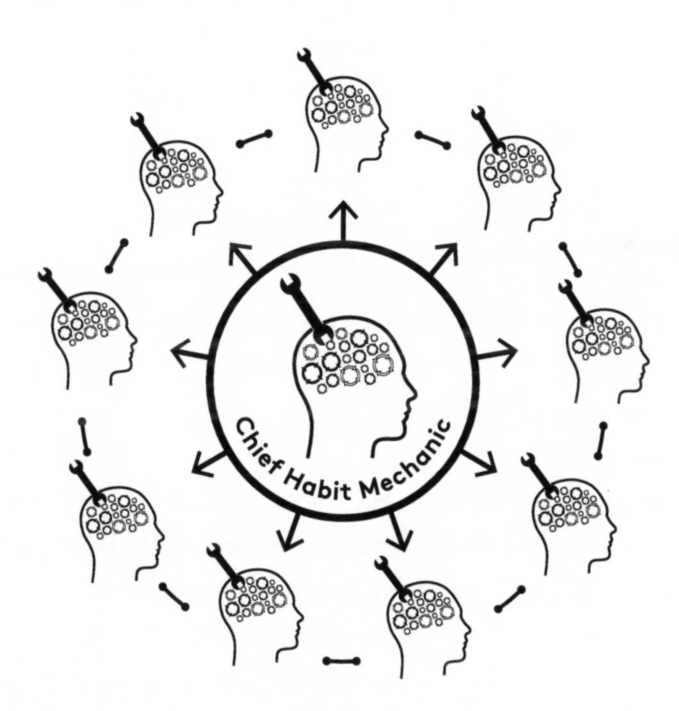

Figure 28.4: Chief Habit Mechanics deliberately use insights from Leadership Science to influence other people's behavior and help them become better Habit Mechanics.

Quick recap: Becoming a Chief Habit Mechanic is a two-step process. First, you have to become adept at Me Power Conditioning so you can become a Habit Mechanic. Then you have to learn how to become an expert Team Power Leader.

Let's dig a little deeper into what Chief Habit Mechanics do.

HOW ARE SNOWMOBILES AND LEADERSHIP CONNECTED?

"Driving the bus" is a very well-established metaphor for leadership. It's often said that the leader is driving the bus and they have to get the right people on that bus. It's also often assumed that because they drive a metaphorical bus, a leader has total authority, the most knowledge, and a crystal clear roadmap of exactly what the team needs to do to achieve success. But the unrelenting changes and challenges presented by the VUCA world have changed that. This metaphor isn't valid anymore.

The metaphor I think is most powerful now is this: imagine everyone on your team is driving their own snowmobile, and a fleet of snowmobiles is moving up a mountain, aiming to reach the summit.

The conditions on the mountain are changing all the time. By reaching the top of the mountain, the team will achieve its mission. It's the leader's job to make it easier for every individual to excel at driving their snowmobile in these challenging and changing conditions. Connected to that, leaders have to take responsibility for helping their team communicate and collaborate. Remember, these two factors are at the heart of problem-solving.

THE CHALLENGES OF LEADING AND MANAGING TEAMS REMOTELY

Communication is not just verbal. It is also visual. Parts of our brain called "mirror neurons" allow us to read other people's emotions and feel what they are feeling. These powerful centers are designed to work in person and are far harder to notice and discern over a video conference call. This makes communication, collaboration, and, ultimately, problem-solving more challenging when working remotely.

Connected to this, the evidence shows us that remote/hybrid working is causing three main challenges:

1. It is more challenging for teams to perform, because communication and collaboration are more difficult.
2. It is more difficult to lead, because traditionally one of the main reasons people have been promoted to these positions is that they are good at getting into a room with people and bringing energy and positive influence—and remote/hybrid working means there are fewer opportunities to do this.
3. We are more reliant on people self-managing (in other words being Habit Mechanics), because it is harder for teams and organizations to positively influence an individual's behavior when they are working remotely.

Chief Habit Mechanics know how to overcome these challenges and make it easier for their people to individually and collectively progress up the mountain on their metaphorical snowmobiles. They do this by creating high-performing cultures.

But what is a culture and how can you build one?

CREATING A PURPOSEFUL DEVELOPMENT CULTURE

In Latin, "culture" relates to agriculture and means to cultivate or grow plants and crops. The word can also refer to nurturing and developing people.

Like a farmer is concerned with creating the right conditions (e.g., the soil, the weather) for their crop to flourish, Chief Habit Mechanics focus on creating the right conditions for their people to thrive. Specifically, a Chief Habit Mechanic's number one priority is to help their people's brains—and, in particular, the prefrontal cortex—work really well so that Will Power or emotional regulation works properly.

If your people's brains are not working properly, they will not be at their best, nor will they be able to effectively communicate, collaborate, and solve problems. Remember: teams that are best at solving problems will most likely win in the VUCA world.

The most basic component of every culture is habits.

So two core factors shape every culture:

1. People's habits—what people in the team or organization say and do (human behavior)
2. The factors that shape and trigger people's habits—the Nine Action Factors

Some of the habits your people have will be helpful for team performance and some will be unhelpful. Remember the barcode metaphor from Chapter 9 (Figure 9.5)? It works exactly the same at the group level as it does at the individual level.

Figure 9.5: Your team's unhelpful habits are represented by the black lines, and their helpful habits are represented by the white lines. The more successful your culture, the more white lines there will be.

So to develop better cultures, we need to do five things:

1. Understand which types of habits we want our people to develop.
2. Analyze people's current habits to see if they match up with the above.
3. Empower people to regulate their emotions so they can build more helpful habits (i.e., train people to do Me Power Conditioning and become Habit Mechanics).
4. Empower people to become better Team Power Leaders so they can positively influence other people's behavior.
5. Support and develop a select group to become expert Team Power Leaders and Chief Habit Mechanics.

To help Chief Habit Mechanics develop high-performing cultures, I have created three interconnected models and tools to guide culture building:

1. Five-Stage Team Power model and self-assessment tool
2. Team Power Leadership framework, self-assessment, and planning tools
3. Culture Development Reflection Tool

These models and tools will help you create a purposeful development culture where the following things are true:

1. People feel respected, feel valued, and trust each other.
2. People are excited about and emotionally invested in the team's/organization's mission.
3. People feel empowered and upskilled to become Habit Mechanics or, in other words, grow and improve every day by deliberately working on tiny, new helpful habits.
4. People feel empowered and upskilled to become better Team Power Leaders so they can positively influence other people's behavior.
5. A select group are supported to become expert Team Power Leaders and Chief Habit Mechanics.

First, I want to show you how to use the Five-Stage Team Power model. It will help you understand some of the basic things great teams do, and get you thinking about the type of habits your people will need to develop to enable your team and/or organization to fulfill its potential.

THE FIVE STAGES OF TEAM POWER

High-performing teams can achieve results beyond what was thought possible. Many of us witnessed this firsthand when we saw teams of scientists create a new, effective COVID-19 vaccine in months. This normally takes 10 years! When a team's mission is epic and the culture is high-performing, the sky is the limit.

But How Do You Create a High-Performing Team?

About a decade ago, I was asked to work as a consultant with one of the UK's biggest professional rugby clubs. This team was notorious for underperforming, despite being as well-resourced as their rivals. The team didn't perform to its potential.

The club brought in a very high-profile, world-class coach. I had been working with that coach when he coached the national team. In the first instance, he wanted me to spend some time around the team and write a report to tell him what I was seeing "through a scientific lens."

One day I arranged to meet the coach early, so I went to the training ground at about seven o'clock in the morning. I saw the coach and he wasn't happy. The team had played a match the day before and had won. But the coach explained to me that two players had been arrested outside a nightclub for fighting during their postmatch celebrations.

So the morning training session began with a team meeting including all the players. It was very firmly focused on the team's culture. Fundamentally, this culture was problematic. It was stopping them from fulfilling their potential.

The coach effectively gave a master class on how to deconstruct a team culture, in a way that was both transformational and empowering for the team members.

This was one of the most powerful experiences I'd had. I was thinking, "How can I make it really easy for more coaches and leaders to get as good as this at culture building?"

I tried different approaches. Some had success; others failed. Eventually, I created a system that was science-based, but simple and practical for leaders to use. I call it the Five-Stage Team Power model.

Five-Stage Team Power Model

Ascending a mountain is a great metaphor to help us understand how to create a powerful, effective culture that produces a high-performing team. Remember, everyone on your team has a snowmobile to help them move up the mountain. And because you're a team, you want to make the ascent in unison.

Based on my research and consultancy work, I believe there are five stages that high-performing teams successfully utilize to reach the top of their mountain and achieve their mission. These stages act as the backbone of your team's culture.

First, I will explain each stage, and then I will show you how to activate them.

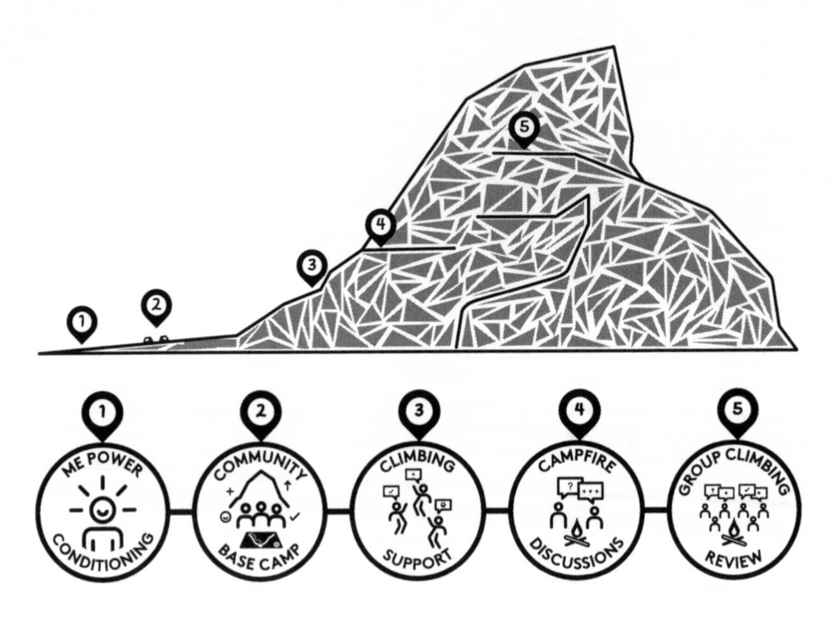

Figure 28.5: Five-Stage Team Power model.

Stage 1—Me Power Conditioning: everyone deliberately chooses to work toward being at their best. This is like everyone committing not only to learning how to use their snowmobiles, but also to keep improving their snowmobile skills so they can continue to be the best version of themselves, and successfully navigate new VUCA world challenges as they emerge.

Figure 28.6: High-performing teams are packed full of high-performing people.

Stage 2—Community Base Camp: the team establishes its mission (e.g., purpose, values, big goals), plans a strategy, decides its priorities, and agrees on individual team members' roles and responsibilities. Before you begin your journey to the top of the mountain, you need to collectively agree on these things.

Figure 28.7: Establish the team's mission and short-term priorities before you start climbing.

Stage 3—Group Climbing Support: everyone on the team deliberately supports and brings the best out in each other. The conditions on the mountain are more challenging than ever before, so it can be harder than ever to do this well. I use the word "climbing" here, but I'm also thinking of this in terms of moving up the mountain on snowmobiles.

Figure 28.8: Respect and look after each other.

Stage 4—Campfire Discussion: one-to-one support to help individuals grow, improve, and deliver results. The VUCA world means that we all need to continually work on ourselves and keep developing our abilities.

Figure 28.9: Build time in for one-to-one coaching and development.

Stage 5—Group Climbing Review: the team collectively steps back, reflects, and adjusts priorities to help it achieve its mission. Because conditions on the mountain are changing all the time, we need to be agile.

Figure 28.10: Build time in to stop and reflect together.

Let's Dig a Little Deeper into Each Stage

As we do this, you might be thinking, "This sounds like a good idea, but I am not sure how to do it." Don't worry, because in the Team Power Leadership section (Chapters 29–34) I will show you a range of simple and practical things you can do to help your team and/or organization thrive by leading better in all five stages. In those chapters, I will clearly highlight how each Team Power Leadership element connects with each of the five stages described below. Right now, all you need to do is focus on learning more about what is involved at each stage.

Stage 1—Me Power Conditioning

Me Power Conditioning relates to each of us purposefully choosing to look after our wellbeing and work toward being at our best. We want to pack our teams full of people who are already Habit Mechanics or, at the very least, have Habit Mechanic Mindsets (e.g., they believe they can improve anything with practice and take responsibility for being their best). This obviously has implications for how you recruit and hire people.

Remember, getting good at emotional regulation is central to becoming a Habit Mechanic. To help your people do this better, you can

- train them how to do Me Power Conditioning; and
- be empathetic that everyone in your team has a HUE (Horribly Unhelpful Emotions) living inside their heads.

The latter point means you need to go the extra mile to show your people that you

- care about them;
- trust them;
- are carefully listening to their feedback and ideas; and
- are a Habit Mechanic and are continually working on yourself—because even you, with all your experience, know it is important to keep improving.

Respecting, valuing, and trusting each other will

- calm people's HUEs;
- get people's brains working properly; and
- make it easier for everyone to do Me Power Conditioning.

The central idea of Me Power Conditioning is preparing to

- bring your best self to work; and
- bring the best out in others at work.

Me Power Conditioning does not stop at Stage 1; it is the backbone of all five stages.

Stage 2—Community Base Camp

Once we are all deliberately trying to be the best we possibly can, and supporting others to do the same, we can consider the journey we are going on together.

First, create a mission that people in the team and/or organization can get excited about and emotionally invested in. What do you want to achieve and why?

Second, work out the strategy you will use to help you achieve your mission. Then set out the immediate priorities, the first steps in your collective journey to achieving the mission.

Finally, empower your people to connect their individual roles and responsibilities to the team's short-term priorities and over-arching mission.

With a few small adjustments, the FAM (Future Ambitious Meaningful) Story Iceberg tool (Chapter 16) can be used to help you in Stage 2.

Stage 3—Group Climbing Support

Once you have agreed on your mission and strategy, and clearly communicated it, you need to implement the plan. Think about your day-to-day work as climbing your metaphorical mountain. You will be able to do this much more efficiently and effectively if you support each other as you climb.

Stage 4—Campfire Discussion

This stage can be compared to personal coaching. It is about having regular senior-to-peer, peer-to-peer, and sometimes expert coaching sessions that help individuals build new helpful habits that contribute to individual and collective success.

These one-to-one coaching interactions are an excellent opportunity to develop empathy (a central component of trust) with every member of your team.

This stage helps people develop personal capabilities, grow, and keep getting better.

As you endeavor to make progress toward your team achieving its mission (the top of the mountain), you will enter a cycle of Group Climbing Support (Stage 3) and Campfire Discussions (Stage 4).

Stage 5—Group Climbing Review

These will take place at different times for different teams, but many groups find it very helpful to have these types of reviews approximately every month or six weeks. A Group Climbing Review helps you reconnect with each other, and with the strategy you created at Community Base Camp (Stage 2).

In Stage 5, you might ask yourself questions like, "Do our priorities still align with our major goals?" in order to help you refine your strategy.

Group Climbing Reviews need to be open and honest, so people say (constructively) what they really think. The alternative is people talking behind each other's backs!

In the VUCA world, regular reviews of our major goals are critical. This is because change is happening so quickly that we need to systematically question whether our goals are still relevant, or whether we need to pivot and change them.

Reflect?

If it is helpful, take a moment to write some notes about the five different stages.

THE TEAM POWER BUILDER

Our "Team Power Builder" tool helps you and your team reflect on your strengths and areas of improvement across the five stages. You can do it in under five minutes.

Team Version (You Do This with Your Team and Ask Everyone to Provide a Score for Each Question)

To get a PDF version that you can share with your team, go to tougherminds.co.uk/habitmechanic and click on "Resources" to download your copy.

Score each statement from 1 to 10, where 1 equals *never* and 10 equals *always*.

Statement 1:

Everyone in our team deliberately chooses to bring their best self to work every day, so they can be their best and help the team fulfill its potential. *Team Members' Average Score:* ______

Based on the team's reflections, write down one simple and practical thing your team can do to improve its "Me Power Conditioning" performance:

____

____

Statement 2:

The team has a clear strategy (a plan of action designed to achieve its mission) that makes everyone feel empowered and helps the team perform well and achieve its mission. *Team Members' Average Score:* ______

Based on the team's reflections, write down one simple and practical thing your team can do to improve its "Community Base Camp" performance:

Statement 3:

Everyone in our team deliberately chooses to support and bring the best out in each other to help the team achieve its mission. *Team Members' Average Score:* _____

Based on the team's reflections, write down one simple and practical thing your team can do to improve its "Group Climbing Support" performance:

Statement 4:

We coach and support each other (i.e., to develop better habits) so that every team member can make a more positive contribution to our success. *Team Members' Average Score:* _____

Based on the team's reflections, write down one simple and practical thing your team can do to improve its "Campfire Discussions" performance:

Statement 5:

Collectively, we periodically review our individual and team performance and create a plan of action to help our team improve. *Team Members' Average Score:* _____

Based on the team's reflections, write down one simple and practical thing your team can do to improve its "Group Climbing Review" performance:

Now, combine the above scores and rank your team's current performance out of 50: ______ */50*

Based on your (the team's) reflection, you can create a "Team Power Wish List" and add in the changes you (the team) want to focus on. You might want to expand this list as you work through the rest of the Chief Habit Mechanic section.

____

____

____

____

Leader's Version (Do This by Yourself)

To get a PDF version, go to toughen minds.co.uk/habitmechanic and click on "Resources" to download your copy.

Next, you could consider the same statements, but through the lens of the team's main (titled) leader.

Score each statement from 1 to 10, where 1 equals *never* and 10 equals *always.*

Statement 1:

I (the senior or titled leader) can easily create a team culture where everyone deliberately chooses to bring their best self to work every day (whether working in the office or remotely), so they can be their best and help the team fulfill its potential. *Score:* ______

Based on your reflections, write down one simple and practical thing you can do to help your team improve its "Me Power Conditioning" performance:

____

____

Statement 2:

I (the senior leader) can easily create a strategy (a plan of action designed to achieve a long-term objective) that makes everyone feel part of the team and helps the team perform well and achieve its mission. *Score:* _____

Based on your reflections, write down one simple and practical thing you can do to help your team improve its "Community Base Camp" performance:

____

____

Statement 3:

I (the senior leader) can easily create a team culture where everyone deliberately chooses to be supportive and bring the best out of each other, to help the team achieve its mission. *Score:* _____

Based on your reflections, write down one simple and practical thing you can do to help your team improve its "Group Climbing Support" performance:

____

____

Statement 4:

I (the senior leader) can easily help individual team members change their behavior (i.e., their habits) so they can make a more positive contribution to the team's success. *Score:* _____

Based on your reflections, write down one simple and practical thing you can do to improve your "Campfire Discussions" performance:

____

____

Statement 5:

I (the senior leader) can easily refine the team's strategy in a way that makes everyone feel part of the team and helps the team be successful and achieve its mission. *Score:* _____

Based on your reflections, write down one simple and practical thing you can do to help your team improve its "Group Climbing Review" performance:

____

____

Now, combine the above scores and rank your current performance out of 50: ______ */50*

Based on your reflection, add any changes you want to focus on to your Me Power Wish List.

____

____

____

____

> *Understanding the Five-Stage Team Power model is a great start to developing a high-performing culture. Next, you need to focus on helping yourself and your people develop the habits that will make your team's and/or organization's mission success a reality.*

CHIEF HABIT MECHANIC MODEL AND TOOL YOU HAVE LEARNED IN CHAPTER 28...

Five-Stage Team Power model—A model showing the five stages high-performing teams successfully utilize to achieve their collective goals and fulfill their potential. ☑

The Team Power Builder—A tool to help teams reflect on their strengths and areas of improvement across the Five-Stage Team Power model. ☑

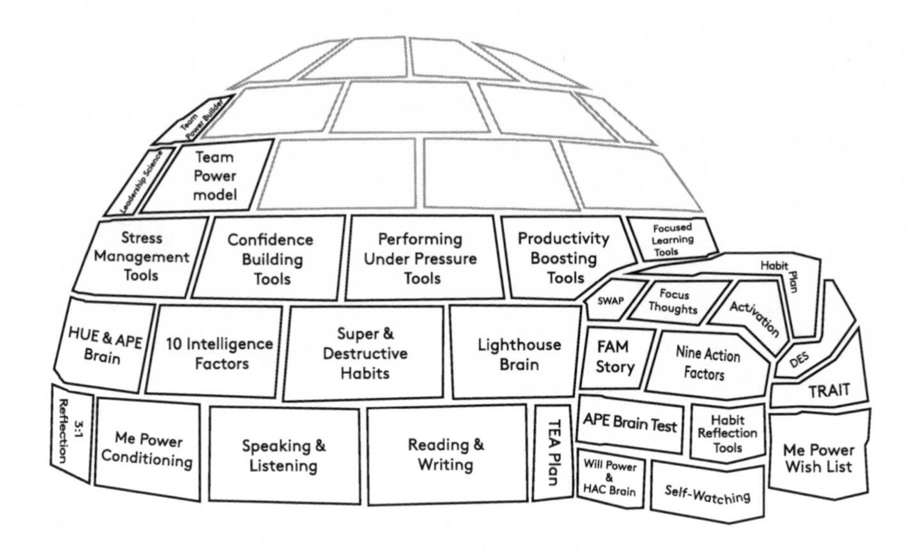

Figure 28.11: Your Chief Habit Mechanic intelligence igloo is building up!

29

LEARN THE FOUR CORE SKILLS THAT WILL MAKE YOU A WORLD-CLASS LEADER

HELPING LEADERS ACTUALLY CHANGE THEIR BEHAVIOR AND IMPROVE THEIR PERFORMANCE

I want to tell you another story. It is also from my work in elite sport.

I was in contact with the head coach of a high-profile international team. He asked me to help him use a psychometric test as part of the preparations for a major tournament in Australia.

Australia was also this team's greatest rival, and this coach and his players were under pressure to make the tournament a success. He wanted to use every advantage he could. So I did some personality leadership-type testing with the senior leaders. The test was supposed to show leaders some of their strengths but also some of their weaknesses.

As I was doing this work, I was also doing other pieces of work in elite sport, using the same model. But I was becoming less and less compelled by personality test approaches.

It was interesting to the leaders, and they liked it because it helped them understand themselves a little bit better. But it didn't help them move from knowing what they needed to do, to actually doing it and building better habits. So I knew there had to be a better way.

I didn't go on that tour with the team. But it didn't go particularly well, which for me reinforced the need to take a different approach to helping leaders do better.

So I carried out in-depth research to understand how I could better serve the leaders I was working with. It became clear to me that using personality and leadership profiling didn't actually help people build better habits. At best, it's the start of a journey for self-improvement, but it literally is just the starting point.

This flawed approach made me redouble my efforts to take what I'd learned from neuroscience and behavioral science to actually help leaders do better. So I used these insights to construct my own leadership model and training approach. I call it "Team Power Leadership."

This model isn't only about knowing what to do. It trains leaders how to deliberately build better habits for themselves and their teams.

Post-tournament, I had kept in contact with some of the international team's senior leaders, including the team's captain. He was one of the sport's highest-profile athletes in the world. About 12 months after that tournament, he sustained a serious injury. We met to discuss this. The injury was particularly problematic because he was going to miss a major showpiece Cup final for his club.

This Cup final has massive importance, prestige, and international profile in this sport. The captain had previously won it playing for another team but never with his hometown club—whom he currently played for. He was heartbroken that he would miss the final. To compound matters, he also felt it was probably his last opportunity to win this famous trophy.

But he knew that he had to turn up and be present for the squad to help the players who were going to play. For me, this was an opportunity to help and test out my new leadership development approach with a very senior and established leader.

I knew he had a good idea of what he needed to do, but I had to help him turn this knowledge into habits.

To help him do this, I created a bespoke *leadership planner* using insights from my new Team Power Leadership framework. This was a tool to help him develop the new leadership habits he wanted to build.

As it happened, the team lost the Cup final. But he was able to extend his career for another three years. And in his final two years, he managed to win the Cup twice. It was a fitting climax to his career, and his laser focus on being his best.

But this piece of work taught me a valuable lesson. Using leadership psychometrics is not very effective or powerful for developing outstanding leaders. Instead, we need to help leaders build better habits.

I use my Team Power Leadership framework to teach Habit Mechanics very simple and practical ways to build tiny new leadership habits—one at a time—so they can start to become Chief Habit Mechanics. I have used this model again and again. It is tried and tested across different contexts (including business, sport, education, and parenting) and gets results very quickly.

TEAM POWER LEADERSHIP HABITS UNDERPIN THE FIVE STAGES OF TEAM POWER

Team Power Leadership habits are at the heart of every powerful team. These habits will make it easier for your team to excel at every stage of the Five-Stage Team Power model ([1] Me Power Conditioning; [2] Community Base Camp; [3] Group Climbing Support; [4] Campfire Discussion; [5] Group Climbing Review).

Team Power Leadership has four core components, which are interconnected. I have listed them below:

1. The Role Model—doing what you expect others to do (connects to all five stages of the Team Power model).

Figure 29.1: Lead by example.

2. The SWAP Coach—coaching others to develop better habits (mainly connects to Stage 1: Me Power Conditioning and Stage 4: Campfire Discussions).

Figure 29.2: Help others become better Habit Mechanics.

3. The Cultural Architect—leading the team's strategy and culture (mainly connected to Stage 2: Community Base Camp and Stage 5: Group Climbing Review).

Cultural Architect

Figure 29.3: Use Leadership Science to help your team fulfill their potential and complete their mission.

4. The Action Communicator—communicating in a way that gets people to take positive action (connects to all five stages of the Team Power model).

Action Communicator

Figure 29.4: Build trust and initiate positive action by the way you communicate.

DEVELOPING TEAM POWER LEADERS THROUGHOUT YOUR TEAM

Leadership is about influencing other people's behavior. And because everyone in your team has influence, they all need a "Team Power Leadership Development Plan." This will help everyone deliberately and progressively become a better leader.

If you are the senior leader in your team, you will no doubt want to improve yourself across all four Team Power Leadership components (Role Model, SWAP Coach, Cultural Architect, and Action Communicator).

But let's imagine a new university graduate has joined your team. Because they are a young person, you might not expect them to have many SWAP Coach and Cultural Architect responsibilities. But you do expect them to become an even better Role Model and Action Communicator. So their Team Power Leadership Development Plan should focus on these areas.

USE SELF-WATCHING TO IMPROVE TEAM POWER LEADERSHIP KNOWLEDGE, SKILLS, AND HABITS

"Only by knowing yourself can you become an effective leader." That's a quote from iconic American football coach Vince Lombardi.

In the following chapters, I want you to engage in some specific Self-Watching to begin improving your Team Power Leadership habits. Many people who are regarded as great leaders readily admit they are not perfect in all four components of Team Power Leadership. You may well already have many strengths as a Team Power Leader, but I believe you will also identify areas you can improve. The best Team Power Leaders never stop learning and refining their practice.

First, we'll look specifically at how to build better Role Model habits.

CHIEF HABIT MECHANIC MODEL YOU HAVE LEARNED IN CHAPTER 29...

Team Power Leadership—The Chief Habit Mechanic leadership framework, which has four core components: Role Model, SWAP Coach, Cultural Architect, and Action Communicator. ☑

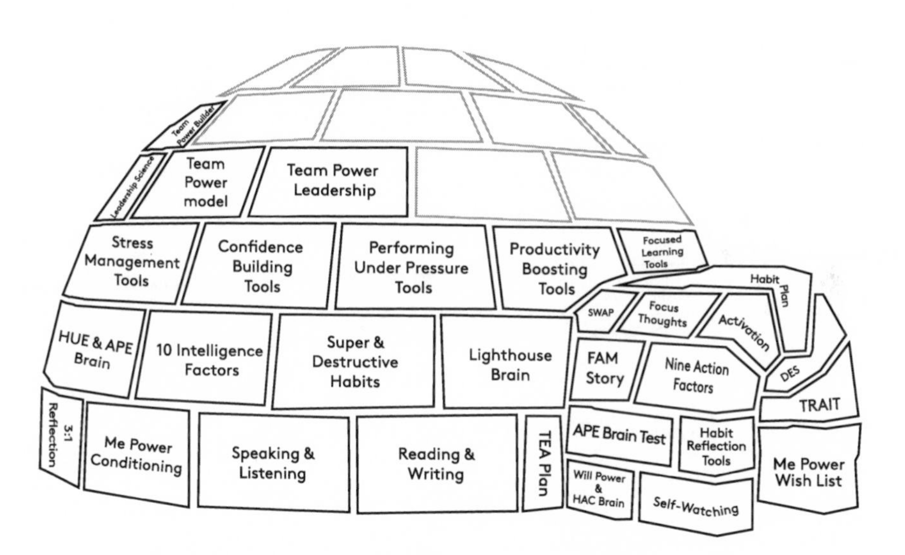

Figure 29.5: Your Chief Habit Mechanic intelligence igloo is building up!

30

THE ROLE MODEL—LEAD BY EXAMPLE

The film *Hidden Figures* tells the story of how the US beat the Soviet Union in the 1950s space race, and how three African American women played a pivotal role in this. Mary Jackson is the main protagonist.

She was a black woman who worked for NASA as a so-called human computer, performing countless mathematical calculations to support scientific research and development. Mary Jackson showed great potential, and this was spotted (in the film) by Karl Zielinski, one of NASA's senior male engineers.[9] He'd arrived in the US after the Second World War as a Polish refugee.

One scene shows Zielinski asking Jackson to give her input into a complex engineering problem relating to the design of an Apollo space capsule. This was despite her still being in her human computer role and being forced to work in a segregated area due to US race laws. After Jackson gives a pertinent

[9] Zielinski is a fictional character but is based in some ways on Jackson's real-life mentor, Kazimierz "Kaz" Czarnecki.

and potentially groundbreaking insight, Zielinski asks her encouragingly if she has ever considered applying to be a NASA engineer.

She said: "I am a negro woman. I'm not going to entertain the impossible."

Zielinski replied: "And I'm a Polish Jew whose parents died in a Nazi prison camp. Now I'm standing beneath a spaceship that will carry astronauts to the stars. I think we can say we *are* doing the impossible. If you were a white man, would you wish to be an engineer?"

Jackson replied: "I wouldn't have to. I'd already be one."

Mary Jackson subsequently fought and won a legal challenge so she could study to become an engineer. In 1958, she became NASA's and America's first female African American aeronautical engineer. She had an exceptional career and went on to achieve the most senior position within her NASA engineering department. She also managed a program that promoted the advancement of women within the organization.

Mary Jackson is a fantastic example of what I mean when I use the term Role Model. The Role Model component of the Team Power Leadership model emphasizes **doing** what you expect others to do. This is about what other people see you doing.

These are the key components of being an excellent Role Model:

- Engaging in Me Power Conditioning (deliberately choosing to work toward being your best), so your brain is working well and you can be at the top of your game.
- Setting good examples for others.
- Being a good person by bringing the best version of yourself into work and being mentally prepared to support others to be the best version of themselves.

The Role Model component of Team Power Leadership is strongly connected to Stage 1 (Me Power Conditioning) and Stage 3 (Group Climbing Support) of the Team Power model.

ANOTHER ROLE MODEL EXAMPLE

Billionaire inventor and tech entrepreneur James Dyson is another good Role Model to learn from.

In a brand film, Dyson explained the company's rigorous design processes. He outlined how he had to use over 5,000 prototypes before arriving at the successful design for the cyclone structure, which is a key component of his powerful, bagless vacuums. He said: "We actually get quite excited when something fails, because that's how we learn."

In this way, Dyson is a Role Model by embodying one of his team's key priorities. He is modeling failure. He is showing his team it is important (and even desirable) to fail as a means of learning, developing, and growing.

Reflect?

If it is helpful, take a moment to write the names of one or two people you think are great Role Models—these could be people you know or people you know of, for example, a famous athlete.

THE ROLE MODEL SELF-ASSESSMENT

To help you analyze your current Role Model strengths and weaknesses, use our Role Model self-assessment tool.

This is an intelligent Self-Watching tool. It helps you understand much more about being a good Role Model. I use this tool, and the other Team Power Leadership self-assessment tools I will show you, as a starting point for the coaching work I do with leaders.

To begin, look through the statements and respond to them.

There is some cross-over in this tool with the Helpful Habits Reflection self-assessment tool (Chapter 17). But now that you have read the "Habit Mechanic skills" section of this book, your answers should be even better informed. You might have also developed some better habits since you read that section of the book.

It is highly unlikely you will be a perfect Role Model. The important thing is that you are thinking about your Role Model habits and identifying your strengths and areas for improvement. If you revisit this process every four to six weeks, you will gradually improve your Role Model habits.

Answer each statement by selecting one of the following options:

a. Not a priority
b. Something I already do well
c. Something that I need to do better

1. It would be helpful if I improve my sleep.

   ☐ a ☐ b ☐ c

   Note: ____________________

2. It would be helpful if I improve my exercise.

   ☐ a ☐ b ☐ c

   Note: ____________________

3. It would be helpful if I improve my diet.

   ☐ a ☐ b ☐ c

   Note: ____________________

4. It would be helpful for me to reflect and highlight what went well, at the end of the day, and what I can improve tomorrow.

   ☐ a ☐ b ☐ c

   Note: ____________________

5. At the end of every week, it would be helpful for me to think about what went well, and to plan how I can improve next week.

☐ a ☐ b ☐ c

Note: ______________________________

6. From time to time, it would be helpful for me to think about my future, and set long-term, medium-term, and short-term goals to focus my efforts and achieve my future goals.

   ☐ a ☐ b ☐ c

   Note: ______________________________

7. It would be helpful for me to regularly update my yearly and monthly calendar to add in important work and life activities.

   ☐ a ☐ b ☐ c

   Note: ______________________________

8. It would be helpful for me to recognize when I am stressed and successfully plan to reduce my stress.

   ☐ a ☐ b ☐ c

   Note: ______________________________

9. It would be helpful for me to monitor my confidence levels and successfully build up confidence in areas where it is low.

   ☐ a ☐ b ☐ c

   Note: ______________________________

10. It would be helpful for me to recognize when my emotions are unhelpful and successfully keep them under control.

    ☐ a ☐ b ☐ c

    Note: ______________________________

11. It would be helpful for me to successfully plan to improve my productivity levels.

    ☐ a ☐ b ☐ c

    Note: ______________________________

12. It would be helpful for me to successfully plan to improve my learning and performance for areas of life and work I want to improve.

☐ a ☐ b ☐ c

Note: ____________________

13. It would be helpful for me to successfully plan to improve my performance under pressure.

    ☐ a ☐ b ☐ c

    Note: ____________________

14. It would be helpful for me to plan out my day to improve my productivity.

    ☐ a ☐ b ☐ c

    Note: ____________________

15. It would be helpful for me to do the daily things I expect from others, for example, complete a Daily TEA Plan.

    ☐ a ☐ b ☐ c

    Note: ____________________

16. It would be helpful for me to embody the organization's, and the team's, priorities, for example, improving my DES (diet, exercise, and sleep) so it is easier for me to be my best every day.

    ☐ a ☐ b ☐ c

    Note: ____________________

17. It would be helpful for me to learn how to become an even better leader.

    ☐ a ☐ b ☐ c

    Note: ____________________

Now that you've considered your current strengths and weaknesses as a Role Model, write down some reflections about your insights. It might be helpful to give each area you think needs work (i.e., your "c" areas, "Something that I need to do better") a priority score (1 = most urgent; 10 = least important).

If it is helpful, consider which small new helpful habits you can build to help you become an even better Role Model and Team Power Leader. Add these to your Me Power Wish List.

Let's now think about how you can become an even better SWAP Coach.

CHIEF HABIT MECHANIC TOOL YOU HAVE LEARNED IN CHAPTER 30...

Role Model self-assessment—A tool to help you analyze your current Role Model strengths and weaknesses and develop better Role Model habits. ☑

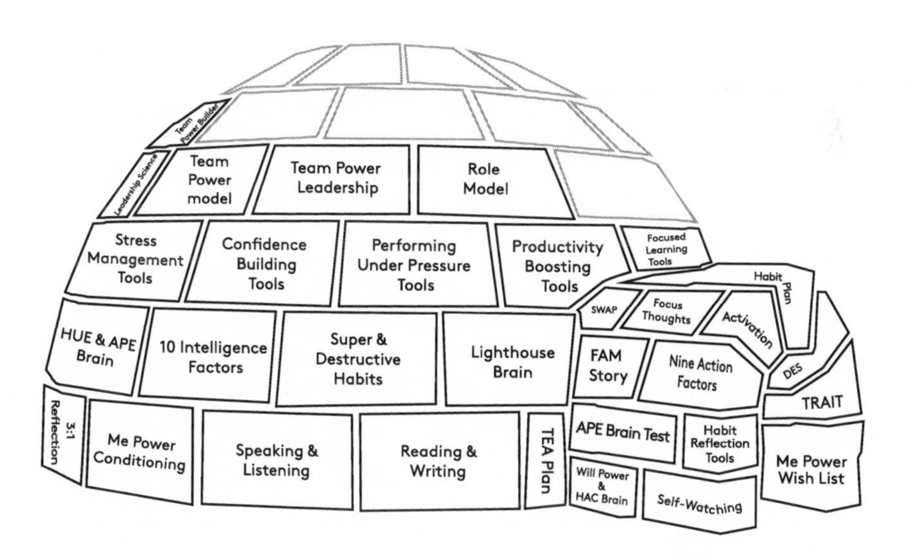

Figure 30.1: Your Chief Habit Mechanic intelligence igloo is building up!

31

THE SWAP COACH—HELP OTHERS BUILD NEW HELPFUL HABITS

In this chapter, I'll examine the "SWAP (Self-Watch, Aim, Plan) Coach" element of my Team Power Leadership model. I'll explain what great SWAP Coaches do and show you how to analyze your own SWAP Coach capabilities and habits.

My first example of a highly effective SWAP Coach is Sir Alex Ferguson.

Ferguson is one of soccer's most highly regarded and successful managers. As Manchester United manager, his side dominated domestic and European soccer and won multiple trophies.

He also oversaw the development of the so-called *Class of 92*. They were a group of players who included club legends David Beckham, Paul Scholes, Nicky Butt, Gary and Phil Neville, and Ryan Giggs.

In an interview with Sequoia Capital chairman Sir Michael Moritz on the Stanford Graduate School of Business YouTube channel, Ferguson explained how, before every game, he conducted a series of one-to-one meetings with players that had not been selected. He gave them his reasons for making that decision.

He said the important part of doing this was to make these players feel like they were contributing to the team's success, even though they were not playing in that particular game. Interestingly, Ferguson said he based this practice on his own experiences of being dropped without reason shortly before kick-off in a Scottish Cup final, when he played for Glasgow Rangers in the 1960s. At the time, he was the team's top goal-scorer.

Successful SWAP Coaches are excellent at helping individual members of a team work toward being at their best. They do this by helping individuals develop their personal capabilities (i.e., knowledge, skills, and habits). To achieve this, they create positive relationships (built on trust), so people feel able to share their unhelpful habits. The SWAP Coach then supports them in building new helpful ones.

There are three core components of being an excellent SWAP Coach:

1. Focusing on individuals and showing you care (building trust)
2. Having great listening and rapport-building skills
3. Coaching and supporting individuals to improve by helping them build sustainable new helpful habits

Campfire Discussions (Stage 4 of the Five-Stage Team Power model) are where SWAP Coaching takes place.

FIRST LEARN HOW TO COACH YOURSELF

To become a great SWAP Coach, you must first learn how to coach yourself, that is, become a Habit Mechanic. Then you can use your Habit Mechanic Tool Kit to help others build new habits.

For example, consider this scenario: you and a member of your team (your coachee) have agreed that you are both going to work together to improve their leadership skills and abilities. To help your coachee build sustainable new habits, you will need to use Habit Mechanic Tools and insights like SWAP, the Nine Action Factors framework, and the Habit Building Plan.

OTHER HIGHLY EFFECTIVE SWAP COACHES

Judy Murray is the mother of tennis star Andy Murray, an Olympic champion, Davis Cup winner, and the first British man to win multiple Wimbledon singles titles since Fred Perry in 1936. She is also the mother of Jamie Murray, who in his own right is a highly successful tennis professional. Judy Murray played a pivotal role in both her sons' careers. She coached both of them when they were young children and aspiring juniors. She has continued to be a huge influence in their development.

In the early part of Andy Murray's career, he was constantly written off. First, it was said he was not strong or fit enough. So he got fitter. Then it was said he was not sufficiently mentally resilient. So he developed his mental game. Andy Murray kept on developing himself until he eventually won his first Grand Slam title. From his comments and other reports, it is safe to assume Judy Murray had a significant input in helping him develop the physical and mental capabilities he needed to become a world champion.

My final example is from Will Carling, the former England rugby captain. He was made captain at the early age of 22 and went on to be one of England's most successful players.

Carling talks about the power of peer-to-peer coaching, where teammates actively help each other get better. He discusses the importance of being able to have difficult conversations. Getting good at having difficult conversations is an important skill for a SWAP Coach.

Reflect?

If it is helpful, take a moment to write down examples of people you think are great SWAP Coaches—these could be people you know or people you know of, for example, a famous business leader.

THE SWAP COACH SELF-ASSESSMENT

Our SWAP Coach self-assessment tool is designed to help you analyze your current SWAP Coach abilities.

This is an intelligent Self-Watching tool. It helps you understand much more about being a good SWAP Coach.

It is highly unlikely you will be a perfect SWAP Coach. The important thing is that you are thinking about your SWAP Coach habits and identifying your strengths and areas for improvement. If you revisit this process every four to six weeks, you will gradually improve your SWAP Coach habits.

Answer each statement by selecting one of the following options:

a. Not a priority
b. Something I already do well
c. Something that I need to do better

1. It would be helpful for me to have a set of questions I can use to help build a rapport with people for both face-to-face and remote interactions.

   ☐ a ☐ b ☐ c

   Note: ______________________________

2. It would be helpful for me to have a set of questions I can use to help me show people I am listening in both face-to-face and remote interactions.

   ☐ a ☐ b ☐ c

   Note: ______________________________

3. It would be helpful if I showed vulnerability first. For example, sharing with your coachees (e.g., team members/colleagues) that you are still working on improving yourself.

   ☐ a ☐ b ☐ c

   Note: ______________________________

4. It would be helpful for me to overemphasize that I am listening and understanding what the other person is saying (this might be especially important in remote interactions).

   ☐ a ☐ b ☐ c

   Note: ______________________________

5. It would be helpful if I learned to improve my listening skills.

   ☐ a ☐ b ☐ c

   Note: ______________________________

6. It would be helpful if I gave advice less often.

   ☐ a ☐ b ☐ c

   Note: ______________________________

7. It would be helpful if I asked my coachees (e.g., team members/colleagues) to explain **why** something was stressful or challenging.

   ☐ a ☐ b ☐ c

   Note: ______________________________

8. It would be helpful if I encouraged my coachees (e.g., team members/colleagues) to think about their long-term goals.

   ☐ a ☐ b ☐ c

   Note: ______________________________

9. It would be helpful if I encouraged my coachees (e.g., team members/colleagues) to think about what they need to achieve in the short-term to achieve their long-term goals (e.g., create a FAM Story).

   ☐ a ☐ b ☐ c

   Note: ______________________________

10. It would be helpful if I had a list of questions (e.g., the Role Model questions) to help my coachees (e.g., team members/colleagues) reflect on how they can be at their best more often, so they have the best chance of achieving their short-term and bigger goals.

    ☐ a ☐ b ☐ c

    Note: ______________________________

11. It would be helpful if I helped my coachees (e.g., team members/colleagues) consider their current performance in areas they want to improve on a scale from 1 (poor) to 10 (perfect).

    ☐ a ☐ b ☐ c

    Note: ______________________________

12. It would be helpful if I explained neuroplasticity to my coachees (e.g., team members/colleagues), so they understand they can change and grow.

    ☐ a ☐ b ☐ c

    Note: ______________________________

13. It would be helpful if I asked my coachees (e.g., team members/colleagues) to write down a SWAP (Self-Watch, Aim, Plan) that will help them move one step closer to 10 on the scale described in statement 11.

    ☐ a ☐ b ☐ c

    Note: ______________________________

14. It would be helpful if my coachees wrote a Habit Building Plan to consider all the factors that would help or hinder them in achieving their new habit.

    ☐ a ☐ b ☐ c

    Note: ______________________________

Now that you have reflected on your current strengths and weaknesses as a SWAP Coach, write down some reflections about your insights. It might be helpful to give each area you think needs work a priority score (1 = most urgent; 10 = least important).

____

____

____

____

____

If it is helpful, consider which small new helpful habits you can build to help you become an even better SWAP Coach and Team Power Leader. Add these to your Me Power Wish List.

> *Let's now think about how you can become an even better Cultural Architect.*

CHIEF HABIT MECHANIC TOOL YOU HAVE LEARNED IN CHAPTER 31...

SWAP Coach self-assessment—A tool to help you analyze your current SWAP Coach strengths and weaknesses and develop better SWAP Coach habits. ☑

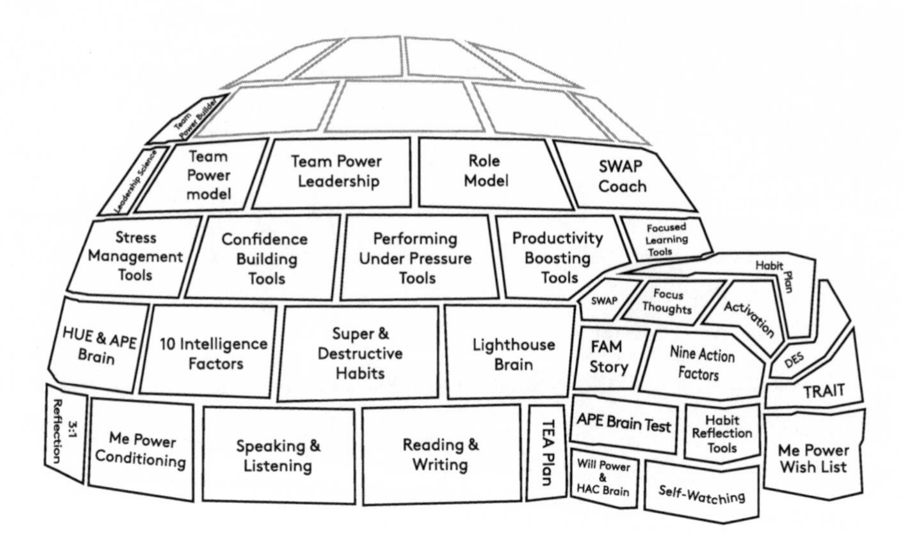

Figure 31.1: Your Chief Habit Mechanic intelligence igloo is building up!

32

THE CULTURAL ARCHITECT—BUILD A CULTURE FOR TRUST, EMPOWERMENT, HAPPINESS, AND SUCCESS

The role of the Cultural Architect is to create an environment that helps all team members cultivate the helpful habits needed for team and organizational mission success. I call this a purposeful development culture[10] where the following things are true:

- People feel respected, valued, and trust each other.
- People are excited about and emotionally invested in the team's/organization's mission.
- People feel empowered and upskilled to become Habit Mechanics or, in other words, grow and improve every day by deliberately working on tiny, new helpful habits.

---

[10] As mentioned previously, I use "purposeful development culture" and "purposefully developmental culture" interchangability throughout this book.

- People feel empowered and upskilled to become better Team Power Leaders so they can positively influence other people's behavior.
- A select group are supported to become expert Team Power Leaders and Chief Habit Mechanics.

SIR CLIVE WOODWARD

My first example is former England rugby coach Sir Clive Woodward. In 2003, he took the team to its first Rugby World Cup triumph—beating their rival Australia in an epic final. Later, he became involved with the British Olympic team and played a role in the highly successful 2012 London Olympics, which generated a record medal haul for Great Britain.

During his time coaching England, Woodward played a pivotal role in the career of record-breaking player Jonny Wilkinson, who came to epitomize composure under pressure. The story of Woodward and Wilkinson provides some useful insights if you want to learn how to become an even better Cultural Architect.

As you have read earlier (Chapter 24), Wilkinson made his debut for England against Australia in 1998's so-called "Tour from Hell." He missed his first two kicks at goal and his debut was not well received. Fast forward 12 months, and the team was knocked out of the 1999 Rugby World Cup. As the figurehead, Woodward came under pressure from external sources. However, many players within the England squad spoke out publicly on Woodward's behalf. They stressed that they felt the overall direction of the team was good. The recent results may have been poor, but the coach was not to blame and should remain with them.

Woodward said this inspired him to redouble his efforts and reset the team's strategy. The mission was for England to become the world's best team. Woodward and his staff identified the assets (people capabilities [i.e., knowledge, skills, and habits] and material resources [e.g., money, equipment, technology]) needed to develop a team that could play winning rugby. He enlisted the support of specialist coaches to strengthen key areas. Finally, he then completely overhauled and remodeled the coaching environment, with the sole purpose of developing players who could perform to their potential under pressure and win.

He distilled the team's new strategy into simple, high-impact messages and ideas. The team created posters with these messages and placed them in their training and performance environments. Woodward said he regarded this form of communication as empowering the players to take ownership of these ideas and actions.

The following year (2000), England's fortunes changed. Victory in Paris against a tough French team was followed by a win against the ultracompetitive South African Springboks. In the autumn, world champions Australia were defeated at Twickenham.

Clive Woodward published *Winning: The Story of England's Rise to Rugby World Cup Glory* and, more recently, *How to Win: Rugby and Leadership from Twickenham to Tokyo.* These are extremely useful insights. Woodward has essentially created a record of what he did to become a highly successful Cultural Architect.

Here are the key components of being a Cultural Architect:

- Creating a culture where people feel respected and valued, and trust each other
- Having a well-defined, overarching strategy that helps the team and/or organization achieve its mission
- Creating a culture where everyone is empowered and upskilled to become Habit Mechanics, or in other words grow and improve every day by deliberately working on tiny, new helpful habits

- Creating a culture where everyone is empowered and upskilled to become better Team Power Leaders
- Creating a culture where a select group are empowered and upskilled to become expert Team Power Leaders and Chief Habit Mechanics
- Creating a culture where everyone is empowered to actively commit to their roles and responsibilities, and help the team and/or organization achieve its mission
- Recruiting people with a Habit Mechanic Mindset, and/or people who already are Habit Mechanics, Team Power Leaders, and Chief Habit Mechanics
- Using behavioral science insights to design performance management systems and performance and leadership development systems that help people be their best and continually improve individually and collectively

The Cultural Architect closely connects to the Community Base Camp (Stage 2) and Group Climbing Review (Stage 5) parts of the Five-Stage Team Power model.

Reflect?

If it is helpful, make a few notes about what you have learned about Cultural Architects so far.

BUILDING TRUST

The cornerstone of a purposeful development culture is trust. Harvard Business School professor Frances Frei calls trust the foundation of leadership. Her work shows that trust has three core components. If people think you are authentic, empathetic, and believable, they are much more likely to trust you.

Great Cultural Architects know how to build and rebuild trust by showing their people they

- care about them;
- will carefully listen to their feedback and ideas;
- continually work on themselves—because even they, with all their experience, know it is important to keep getting better;
- believe in them by allowing them to get on with their work without micromanaging; and
- have a sound logic behind their ideas and methods.

Why is trust so important? When people trust you it is easier for them to calm their HUE, and get their brain working properly. This is the foundation of people being their best.

DEVELOPING A STRATEGY

Once you have trust, you need to co-develop a strategy with your team. I really like the strategy model used in *Playing to Win*, written by A.G. Lafley (former CEO of Procter & Gamble) and Professor Roger Martin. It focuses on the following five core questions, which I have tweaked:

1. What is winning? (What is your objective/mission)
2. Where to play? (Who do you want your products or services to delight?)
3. How to win? (What are the basics of your success? e.g., create a purposeful development culture)
4. What assets (material resources [e.g., money, equipment, technology] and people capabilities [i.e., knowledge, skills, and habits])

must be in place to win? (e.g., we need everyone to be a Habit Mechanic, everyone to be working on themselves as Team Power Leaders, and to have several experienced Chief Habit Mechanics)

Follow-up questions to help you dig deeper into Question 4 are:

a. Which assets do we already have?
b. Which must we develop or acquire?
c. Which must we prioritize developing or acquiring?

5. What performance management systems, and performance and leadership development systems, are required to help people build and sustain the habits that will make all the above a reality? (e.g., Habit Mechanic and Chief Habit Mechanic training programs)

Developing a robust strategy takes time. But without one, your chances of mission success will be seriously diminished.

WHAT ARE PERFORMANCE MANAGEMENT SYSTEMS, AND PERFORMANCE AND LEADERSHIP DEVELOPMENT SYSTEMS?

The foundations of any strategy are people's habits. For example, if you need people to be more positive, or more innovative, or more productive, or better leaders, these outcomes can only be achieved by people changing their habits. Of course, you can recruit people into your team and/or organization who have the correct habits. But you will still have to put systems in place to help them sustain their current good habits, or to help current team members develop new helpful habits.

So, performance management systems, and performance and leadership development systems, help you guide and shape your people's and team's behaviors and habits.

To help you create powerful systems that capitalize on cutting-edge behavioral science and Leadership Science, I have designed the following three interconnected models and tools:

1. Five-Stage Team Power model and self-assessment tool
2. Team Power Leadership framework, self-assessment, and planning tools
3. Culture Development Reflection Tool (based on the Nine Action Factors framework)

You are now familiar with the first two, so I will say more about the third. The "Culture Development Reflection Tool" is designed to make it easier for Cultural Architects to assess the impact the Nine Action Factors are having on their culture—for better or worse. Cultural Architects can then use the Nine Action Factors to shape their culture accordingly.

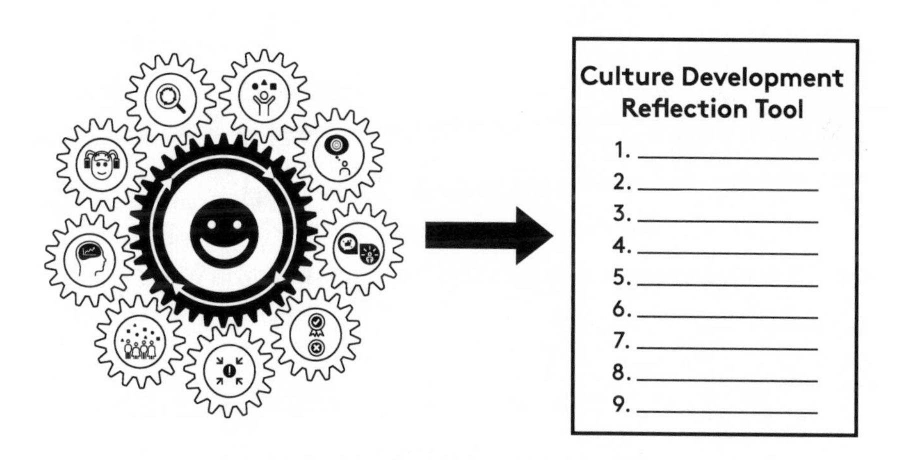

Figure 32.1: I will show you how to use the Culture Development Reflection Tool in Chapter 35.

USING INSIGHTS FROM SELF-DETERMINATION THEORY TO EMPOWER PEOPLE TO SUCCEED

Professors Edward Deci and Richard Ryan's self-determination theory focuses on people's motivation to take action and keep persisting. In simple terms, the theory says that if people feel empowered to choose their own methods of growing and developing, they will be more likely to stick to them and get results.

To be self-determined is to be able to do what you choose to do and be free to make the choices you want to make. But it is helpful to think of self-determination on a continuum. One end is 100 percent self-determined behavior, doing things you have chosen to do. The other end is 100 percent coercion. This is doing things because you have been forced to do them.

When people make self-determined decisions, they are more likely to put in their best efforts, persist, and enjoy the task. When people feel coerced, it has the opposite effect. Self-determination is seen as the most robust type of motivation.

However, it is impossible to create an environment where every decision everyone in a team makes is 100 percent self-determined. But this does not mean that every decision has to be 100 percent coercive.

With the correct knowledge and skills, you can learn how to make the team's mission, strategy, priorities, and individual roles and responsibilities feel more self-determined.

HOW TO CREATE A SELF-DETERMINING ENVIRONMENT

Here are seven practical suggestions (drawing on the excellent of work of Professor of Psychology Robert J. Vallerand and his colleagues) for creating a purposefully developmental environment that makes people feel more self-determined. This means it will be easier for people to be their best. You will notice some overlap between the seven areas as they all focus on increasing autonomy, improving people's confidence, and showing people that you care about them and respect their opinion.

1. Show That You're Listening to Opinions and Suggestions

For example, ask your team to complete the Team Power Builder exercise in Chapter 28. Then set some team goals based on the results.

2. Allow Your Team an Opinion and Show You Value Its Input

Like Clive Woodward did with his rugby players, ask your team to map out the standards it should be expected to achieve (e.g., having your camera on during an online meeting). This will aid better Group Climbing Support (Stage 3 of the Five-Stage Team Power model).

3. Give the Team Choices

For example, ask the team to prioritize the three most important goals to focus on (i.e., the goals that emerged from the Team Power Builder exercise). By letting the team choose which areas to work on, it will be more self-determined to make a positive change in the selected areas.

4. Rationalize Your Decisions

If you have to make a tough choice, explain this in a reasonable and detailed manner. This approach is far less coercive and much more motivational. It is exactly what Sir Alex Ferguson reported he did in his one-to-one meetings with nonplaying members of his squad.

5. Build People's Confidence

When people accomplish something, or do something well, take time to recognize it. This helps build people's confidence. Remember the 3:1 ratio of positive to negative feedback I introduced in the discussion of confidence (Chapter 23)? I will talk more about how you can build people's confidence by what you say to them in the Action Communicator chapter (Chapter 33).

6. Negotiate and Discuss

Don't simply tell someone what to do. This is extremely coercive and counterproductive.

7. Focus on the Task or Process, Not the Ego

When giving feedback, focus on the improvements and progress people are making—and not on how their performance compares to others.

CREATING TEAM COHESION

Another role for the Cultural Architect is to create team cohesion. Theoretically, team cohesion describes a dynamic process that is reflected in the tendency to stick together and remain united in the pursuit of goals and objectives.

The relationship between performance and cohesion has attracted much attention. Research suggests that the effect of performance on cohesiveness is stronger than the effect of cohesiveness on performance. That is to say, the fastest way to improve team cohesion is for the team to achieve a meaningful result.

My most powerful experience of this was when I took part in the UK's National Three Peaks Challenge within the same 24-hour period (i.e., climbing Scotland's Ben Nevis, then England's Scafell Pike, and finally Wales' Snowdon—starting at 12 p.m. on a Monday and finishing by 12 p.m. on Tuesday). I was part of a newly formed seven-member team. Team cohesion was not obvious at the start of the challenge, but good team performances on Ben Nevis, Scafell Pike. and, ultimately, Snowdon built a reciprocal relationship where positive performances bonded the team members. We are all still good friends.

The good news is you don't have to do the National Three Peaks Challenge within 24 hours to improve cohesion in your team! The key is to create situations where the team achieves something meaningful and challenging together. When the team succeeds, recognize this and reward it.

THINK ABOUT BUILDING CULTURAL ASSETS

Cultural assets (resources [e.g., money, equipment, technology] and people capabilities [i.e., knowledge, skills, and habits]) should help team members develop the new *personal capabilities* they need to help the team succeed. For example, Clive Woodward realized that if his team was going to become the best in the world, it needed to get better at performing under pressure. So he created cultural assets (e.g., hired specialist coaches) that helped his players get better at performing under pressure (i.e., developing the player's personal capabilities).

By bringing in specialist outside help, he activated the "Community Knowledge and Skills" Action Factor (first introduced in Chapter 18).

Just to recap, Community Knowledge and Skills are what those around you have that might be helpful for you. For example, Jonny Wilkinson needed more knowledge and skills to help him build better performance-under-pressure habits. In other words, the coaches used their personal capabilities to enhance Wilkinson's capabilities. So bringing in specialist coaches with these knowledge and skills was essential in Jonny Wilkinson's progress from failing under pressure to becoming one of the best under-pressure performers in professional sport.

Recruitment

Woodward has spoken at length about his recruitment and selection policies. He said he preferred to recruit "sponges" (i.e., highly teachable players) instead of "rocks" (i.e., unteachable know-it-alls). Woodward was looking for players who wanted to get better (i.e., develop their personal capabilities). He did not just recruit players on the basis of their current capabilities (i.e., knowledge, skills, and habits). He sought out players who wanted to join the England squad to learn and improve themselves, through practice.

I would describe Woodward's "sponges" as players who had "Habit Mechanic Mindsets."

TWO MORE CULTURAL ARCHITECT EXAMPLES

Sharmadean Reid

Reid is the founder and chief executive of beauty treatment booking app *Beautystack*. Reid has developed her own rule: "Look after your people and they will look after your business."

She allowed members of her team to bring their children into work and interact with them in the office—especially during school holidays. Reid also secured the services of a registered nanny and purchased toys and cushions for a play area in the middle of the working environment.

This might seem extreme and even counterproductive to some. But Reid was using some of the Nine Action Factors to promote helpful change. She had created "External Triggers," and also used the "Community Knowledge and Skills" and "Social Influence" Action Factors to make her team feel more comfortable at work, so they were able to give more of their energies to their roles.

Ray Dalio

As the founder of Bridgewater Associates, Dalio has been incredibly successful in building an organization that seems to be packed with Habit Mechanics. The central focus of the business is continuous improvement. So the culture is designed to empower everyone to get a little bit better every day, and reward people more for their performance than their experience (i.e., a meritocracy). Dalio explains his approach in detail in his books.

Reflect?

If it is helpful, write one or two examples of people you think are great Cultural Architects—these could be people you know or know of, for example, a famous sports coach.

THE CULTURAL ARCHITECT SELF-ASSESSMENT

To help you analyze your current Cultural Architect strengths and areas for improvement, use our Cultural Architect self-assessment tool.

This is an intelligent Self-Watching tool. It helps you understand much more about being a good Cultural Architect.

It is highly unlikely you will be a perfect Cultural Architect. The important thing is that you are thinking about your Cultural Architect habits and identifying your strengths and areas for improvement. If you revisit this process every four to six weeks, you will gradually improve your Cultural Architect habits.

Answer each statement by selecting one of the following options:

a. Not a priority.
b. I already do this well.
c. I need to do this better.

I have broken this self-assessment into two parts.

To understand which parts you need to answer, consider the following: is your organization either going through change or preparing to make changes? If your answer is YES, please answer all questions in Part 1 and Part 2. If your answer is no, ONLY answer questions in Part 2 from 7–28.

Note: If any of the questions in this self-assessment don't make sense to you, just skip to the next question.

Part 1

(Questions 1 to 6 were influenced by Professor John Kotter's "8-Step Process for Leading Change" model.)

1. To transform our team's and/or organization's strategy, or elements of it, it would be helpful if we created a greater sense of urgency around the do-or-die nature of these changes to encourage people to take action.

☐ a ☐ b ☐ c

Note: ______________________________

2. It would be helpful if we got more Social Influencers (as defined in the Nine Action Factors framework in Chapter 18) to believe in the changes we need to make and to proactively help to deliver the changes.

   ☐ a ☐ b ☐ c

   Note: ______________________________

3. It would be helpful to clearly show people how changing our team's and/or organization's strategy, or elements of it, will make things better for them.

   ☐ a ☐ b ☐ c

   Note: ______________________________

4. It would be helpful to use behavioral science insights (e.g., Nine Action Factors framework) to make it easier for people to become part of the change movement.

   ☐ a ☐ b ☐ c

   Note: ______________________________

5. It would be helpful to systematically analyze the barriers that will prevent change and create a plan to remove them.

   ☐ a ☐ b ☐ c

   Note: ______________________________

6. It would be helpful to create a strategic plan that sets out both our short- and long-term goals so that we can focus on securing short-term wins and celebrate them.

   ☐ a ☐ b ☐ c

   Note: ______________________________

Part 2

7. It would be helpful if we spent some time revisiting our team's and/or organization's strategy.

   ☐ a ☐ b ☐ c

   Note: ______________________________

8. It would be helpful if we spent some time revisiting what people need to do regularly (habits) to be at their best and help our team and/or organization achieve its short-term priorities and long-term objectives (mission).

   ☐ a ☐ b ☐ c

   Note: ______________________________

9. It would be helpful if everyone could name our team's and/or organization's priorities and rank them in order of priority.

   ☐ a ☐ b ☐ c

   Note: ______________________________

10. It would be helpful if we internally communicated our priorities with a significant piece of marketing activity that gets people's attention and has lasting impact.

    ☐ a ☐ b ☐ c

    Note: ______________________________

11. It would be helpful if we internally communicated our mission in such a way that it made a genuine, lasting impact with people.

    ☐ a ☐ b ☐ c

    Note: ______________________________

12. It would be helpful if everyone understood how their individual roles and responsibilities helped the team and/or organization achieve its short-term priorities and long-term objectives (mission).

    ☐ a ☐ b ☐ c

    Note: ______________________________

13. It would be helpful if people were empowered to actively commit to their roles and responsibilities.

    ☐ a ☐ b ☐ c

    Note: ____________________

14. It would be helpful if we were better at measuring individual and team performance against our strategic priorities.

    ☐ a ☐ b ☐ c

    Note: ____________________

15. It would be helpful if we were better at celebrating small individual and team performance successes.

    ☐ a ☐ b ☐ c

    Note: ____________________

16. It would be helpful if we were better at holding individuals and teams accountable when they do not perform.

    ☐ a ☐ b ☐ c

    Note: ____________________

17. It would be helpful if everyone in the organization felt like they had a voice.

    ☐ a ☐ b ☐ c

    Note: ____________________

18. It would be helpful to embrace negative feedback to make people feel safe enough to tell the truth.

    ☐ a ☐ b ☐ c

    Note: ____________________

19. It would be helpful if we created more dedicated space where people could collaborate face-to-face and remotely.

    ☐ a ☐ b ☐ c

    Note: ____________________

20. It would be helpful if our onboarding inductions made people feel safer, more valued, and more central to the team's and/or organization's mission.

    ☐ a ☐ b ☐ c

    Note: ____________________________________

21. It would be helpful if we undertook more fun activities to boost team cohesion and morale.

    ☐ a ☐ b ☐ c

    Note: ____________________________________

22. It would be helpful if we focused more on learning together, instead of focusing on winning the argument.

    ☐ a ☐ b ☐ c

    Note: ____________________________________

23. It would be helpful if we had individual and team "best doing" and performance reviews more regularly.

    ☐ a ☐ b ☐ c

    Note: ____________________________________

24. It would be helpful if we separated performance reviews/appraisals and staff development (e.g., training, coaching).

    ☐ a ☐ b ☐ c

    Note: ____________________________________

25. It would be helpful if I stepped back occasionally and let others take more responsibility.

    ☐ a ☐ b ☐ c

    Note: ____________________________________

26. It would be helpful if the team and/or organization was better at managing people who had a negative influence on their colleagues and our clients.

    ☐ a ☐ b ☐ c

    Note: ____________________________________

27. It would be helpful if recruitment had a bigger focus on the candidate's Habit Mechanic and/or Chief Habit Mechanic skills and mindset.

   ☐ a ☐ b ☐ c

   Note: ____________________

28. It would be helpful if colleagues shadowed each other for a few hours and provided constructive feedback.

   ☐ a ☐ b ☐ c

   Note: ____________________

Now that you have considered your current strengths and weaknesses as a Cultural Architect, write down some reflections about your insights. It might be helpful to give each area you think needs work a priority score (1 = most urgent; 10 = least important).

If it is helpful, consider which small new helpful habits you can build to help you become an even better Cultural Architect and Team Power Leader. Add these to your Me Power Wish List.

> *Let's now think about how you can become an even better Action Communicator.*

CHIEF HABIT MECHANIC TOOL YOU HAVE LEARNED IN CHAPTER 32...

Cultural Architect self-assessment—A tool to help you analyze your current Cultural Architect strengths and weaknesses and develop better Cultural Architect habits. ☑

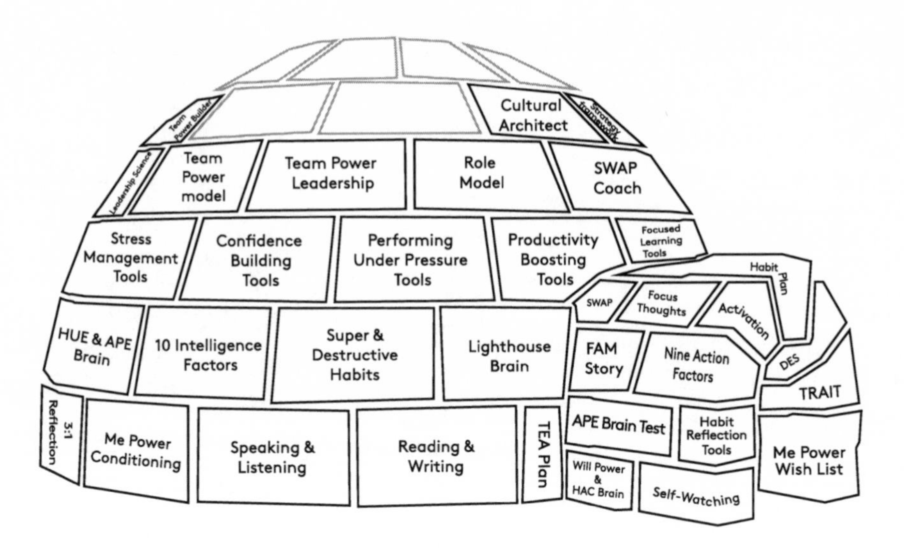

Figure 32.2: Your Chief Habit Mechanic intelligence igloo is building up!

33

THE ACTION COMMUNICATOR—EMPATHIZE, EMPOWER, SUPPORT, AND ENCOURAGE

The fourth and final component of Team Power Leadership is the Action Communicator.

This element of Team Power Leadership focuses on communicating with people in a way that encourages them to be their best and fulfill their roles and responsibilities within the team. Action Communicators help others take positive and helpful action because of how they communicate with them.

An example of a highly effective Action Communicator is former UK Prime Minister Sir Winston Churchill.

The American radio reporter Edward R. Murrow reported from London during the Second World War.

He said that Winston Churchill mobilized the English language and sent it into battle. Of course, Churchill was the Prime Minister who led the UK successfully through the war and led the defeat of Nazi Germany.

The 2017 film *Darkest Hour*, starring Gary Oldman, provided people with a vivid reminder of Churchill's contribution to history. It was a compelling piece of cinema that won Oscars, BAFTAs, and Screen Actors Guild awards. And, of course, it highlighted what is known about Churchill's personal approach to communicating in highly challenging and chaotic circumstances.

Churchill's ability to use evocative and emotionally stirring language is a very useful attribute for an Action Communicator. His example is worthy of note.

But an Action Communicator also has other attributes, such as charisma. I think former England soccer manager Sir Bobby Robson clearly demonstrated this in the way that he communicated with players, staff, and fans of the numerous iconic teams he led to victory throughout Europe. He embodied the idea of a charismatic Action Communicator.

In the documentary *More Than A Manager*, Robson is praised by legendary players like Gary Lineker, Paul Gascoigne, and the Brazilian Ronaldo. He is lauded by senior figures within iconic soccer clubs, including Barcelona, and modern-day managers like Pep Guardiola. Gary Lineker even calls Robson the best English manager of all time.

So what are the key capabilities of an Action Communicator?

- They consider both their verbal and nonverbal communication with people.
- They build trust with people via their verbal and nonverbal interactions.
- People take positive action because of how they communicate.
- They verbally reinforce the group's short-term priorities and long-term objectives (mission).

The Action Communicator is connected to all five stages of the Team Power model (Me Power Conditioning, Community Base Camp, Group Climbing Support, Campfire Discussion, Group Climbing Review).

PROMOTE CONFIDENCE

An effective Action Communicator will make their team feel confident they can achieve their mission. They will make deliberate attempts to gain a thorough understanding of how individual team members are feeling and create different ways of effectively communicating with different people.

The former England cricket captain and psychoanalyst Mike Brearley expressed the need to communicate with different people in different ways when he said, "Trouble the comforted and comfort the troubled."

To help us be even more specific in how we communicate with others, we should remember the ratio of three positive pieces of feedback to one negative. In some cases, people will require many more positive pieces of feedback to sustain Robust Confidence levels.

Good Action Communicators regularly discuss their team's mission, and also connect this to the team's immediate daily priorities.

Successful Action Communicators also make people feel safe and tell them that they care about them and believe in them. In turn, this makes it easier for people's brains to work properly. Remember, when HUE (Horribly Unhelpful Emotions) does not feel safe, it makes clear thinking much more difficult.

Here are some examples of what great Action Communicators say to their teams.

- What do you need from me to make this a success?
- Sorry, my fault!
- I value your contribution.
- You've done a great job!
- How could we do this better?

LESSONS FROM OTHER GREAT ACTION COMMUNICATORS

Eddie Jones

In 2015, Eddie Jones took up the head coach position of the England rugby team. Shortly afterward, he formally changed the name of players who were selected on the bench from substitutes to "Finishers." He explained that he viewed players on the bench as being pivotal to a successful result in any game.

By doing this, Jones had elevated the perceived importance of these players, both within the context of the whole squad and in the eyes of the public. This is a great example of building confidence by changing the way messages are communicated. If a player is not selected to start the match, their morale and confidence may drop. But, by categorizing these players as the group who will successfully conclude (and hopefully win) the match for the whole team, their importance is significantly enhanced.

Sara Blakely

Sara Blakely is a self-made billionaire, the founder of the undergarment brand Spanx, and an excellent Action Communicator. She regularly stages meetings during which team members are encouraged to highlight their own mistakes. These events are known as "oops meetings" and Blakely leads from the front by regularly highlighting her own mistakes and failings.

These meetings have several benefits. First, they create an "External Trigger" (one of the Nine Action Factors, see Chapter 18) that reminds everyone it is okay to make mistakes, but we need to learn from them. Second, they create trust in the group by showing that everyone (even the boss) wants to get better. Trust makes it easier for people's brains to work properly. Blakely realizes the immense value trust and learning from mistakes can bring for her leadership, and the performance of her business.

Sir Alex Ferguson

Sir Alex Ferguson was also a great Action Communicator. Ferguson says the most important phrase in soccer is "well done." He recognized the importance and necessity of constantly building his players' confidence, and their sense that they were valued and valuable.

Ferguson balanced this approach with a strong focus on regularly communicating major goals, to prevent complacency from creeping into team environments. Ferguson's biographies show that he was highly skilled at successfully balancing the reinforcement of competence and challenging his team to improve. This is closely connected to what I have previously described as grounded positivity.

Reflect?

If it is helpful, write one or two examples of people you think are great Action Communicators–these could be people you know or know of, for example, a political leader.

THE ACTION COMMUNICATOR SELF-ASSESSMENT

To help you analyze your current Action Communicator strengths and areas for improvement, use our Action Communicator self-assessment tool.

This is an intelligent Self-Watching tool. It helps you understand much more about being a good Action Communicator.

It is highly unlikely you will be a perfect Action Communicator. The important thing is that you are thinking about your Action Communicator habits and identifying your strengths and areas for improvement. If you revisit this process every four to six weeks, you will gradually improve your Action Communicator habits.

Answer each statement by selecting one of the following options:

a. Not a priority
b. Something I already do well
c. Something that I need to do better

1. It would be helpful to be more aware and purposeful with my body language when communicating different messages to people in different contexts, for example, face-to-face, via videoconferencing.

   ☐ a ☐ b ☐ c

   Note: ____________________

2. It would be helpful to communicate my own weaknesses to others more regularly.

   ☐ a ☐ b ☐ c

   Note: ____________________

3. It would be helpful to help the team understand what it is capable of achieving in the future, both individually and collectively.

   ☐ a ☐ b ☐ c

   Note: ____________________

4. It would be helpful to say "thank you" and "well done" to people more often.

   ☐ a ☐ b ☐ c

   Note: ____________________

5. It would be helpful to know the name of every person who directly and indirectly helps me do my job.

☐ a ☐ b ☐ c

Note: ______________________________

6. It would be helpful to accentuate the positives and give people feedback at a minimum ratio of 3:1.

   ☐ a ☐ b ☐ c

   Note: ______________________________

7. It would be helpful if I approached the communication of important expectations with a significant piece of marketing activity that gets people's attention and has lasting impact.

   ☐ a ☐ b ☐ c

   Note: ______________________________

8. It would be helpful if I delivered negative news face-to-face (either in person or via videoconferencing).

   ☐ a ☐ b ☐ c

   Note: ______________________________

9. It would be helpful if my feedback was less brutally honest (personal and judgmental) and more focused on working well together to get the job done.

   ☐ a ☐ b ☐ c

   Note: ______________________________

10. It would be helpful if I used shared language (e.g., "Keep your HUE calm") to trigger helpful behaviors and habits in my colleagues.

    ☐ a ☐ b ☐ c

    Note: ______________________________

11. It would be helpful if I used phrases or slogans to remind people of essential behaviors and habits that underpin the team's and/or organization's success, for example, "Let's do our best to be our best"; "Calmer HUE, better you."

    ☐ a ☐ b ☐ c

Note: ____

12. It would be helpful if I helped people feel like they were up to the task before asking them to do something difficult.

    ☐ a ☐ b ☐ c

    Note: ____

13. It would be helpful if I asked people to actively agree to my requests, for example, "Will you let me know if this piece of work is going to be late?" instead of "Please let me know if this piece of work is going to be late."

    ☐ a ☐ b ☐ c

    Note: ____

14. It would be helpful if I reminded people about our organization's short-term priorities and long-term objectives (mission) more often.

    ☐ a ☐ b ☐ c

    Note: ____

15. It would be helpful if I had a list of helpful and positive things I could communicate (spoken or written, e.g., messages, emails) to people daily.

    ☐ a ☐ b ☐ c

    Note: ____

16. It would be helpful if I stopped telling people what to do without first asking for their opinion or rationalizing my decision.

    ☐ a ☐ b ☐ c

    Note: ____

17. It would be helpful to be less predictable in how and when I praise people's efforts.

    ☐ a ☐ b ☐ c

    Note: ____

18. It would be helpful to place a verbal warning shot "across the bow," or give a "slap on the wrists" before properly punishing people (e.g., "If ________ happens again, ________ will be the consequence").

    ☐ a ☐ b ☐ c

    Note: ______________________________

19. From time to time it would be helpful if I publicly praised those who were doing a great job.

    ☐ a ☐ b ☐ c

    Note: ______________________________

20. It would be helpful to be more mindful that written communications (e.g., messages, emails) can have a more negative tone than if the message was delivered face-to-face (either in person or via videoconferencing).

    ☐ a ☐ b ☐ c

    Note: ______________________________

Now that you have reflected on your current strengths and weaknesses as an Action Communicator, write down some reflections about your insights. It might be helpful to give each area you think needs work a priority score (1 = most urgent; 10 = least important).

____

____

____

____

____

____

If it is helpful, consider which small new helpful habits you can build to help you become an even better Action Communicator and Team Power Leader. Add these to your Me Power Wish List.

> *Let's now think about how to create more Team Power Leaders on your team, and how to create a Habit Building Plan to help develop the most important small new Team Power Leadership habit on your Me Power Wish List.*

CHIEF HABIT MECHANIC TOOL YOU HAVE LEARNED IN CHAPTER 33...

Action Communicator self-assessment—A tool to help you analyze your current Action Communicator strengths and weaknesses and develop better Action Communicator habits. ☑

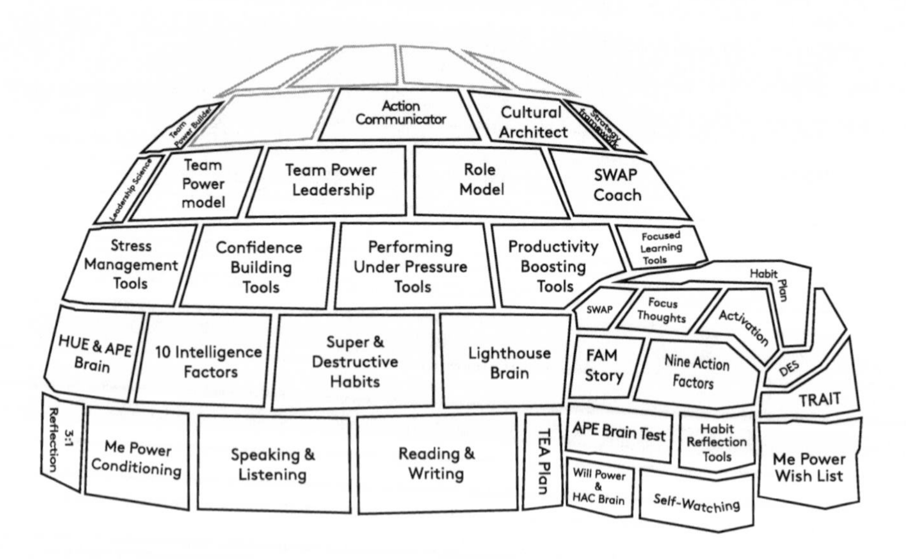

Figure 33.1: Your Chief Habit Mechanic intelligence igloo is building up!

34

BUILDING NEW TEAM POWER LEADERSHIP HABITS

To complete my explanation of Team Power Leadership, I will return to the idea that everyone in your team has influence.

Remember, leadership is not a position or a title. It is about the actions you take and the examples you set within your group.

Everyone in your team has a leadership responsibility. This is because everything anybody in a team does or says has an impact on everybody else's behavior.

So we should aspire to make everybody in the team a better Team Power Leader. But we need a plan to make this a reality.

If you are the designated leader in a team or organization, your first priority is to develop your own Team Power Leadership capabilities.

Part of this work should be making all members of the team aware of the Team Power Leadership framework and encouraging them to work toward becoming better Team Power Leaders.

Successfully executing your team's strategy will be much easier if all team members are continually refining some elements of their Team Power Leadership skills. For example, there is no reason why every team member should not become an even better Role Model and Action Communicator.

To help you quickly assess your own and your individual team members' current Team Power Leadership abilities, I have created the "Team Power Leadership Builder."

INTRODUCING THE TEAM POWER LEADERSHIP BUILDER

The Team Power Leadership Builder tool acts as a summary overview for the specific self-assessments I introduced in the chapters covering the four core Team Power Leadership components.

With a few small adjustments, you can also use it to "map" every team member's Team Power Leadership skills.

Start by completing it with your own Team Power Leadership skills in mind.

Question 1:

a. Rank your current performance as a Role Model out of 100:
 ______*/100* (100 = the best you can be)
b. Based on your reflections, including insights you gained from the Role Model self-assessment, write down one simple and practical thing you can do to improve your performance as a Role Model:

 ____

 ____

Question 2:

a. Rank your current performance as a SWAP Coach out of 100: _____*/100*

b. Based on your reflections, including insights you gained from the SWAP Coach self-assessment, write down one simple and practical thing you can do to improve your performance as a SWAP Coach:

____

____

Question 3:

a. Rank your current performance as a Cultural Architect out of 100: _____*/100*

b. Based on your reflections, including insights you gained from the Cultural Architect self-assessment, write down one simple and practical thing you can do to improve your performance as a Cultural Architect:

____

____

Question 4:

a. Rank your current performance as an Action Communicator out of 100: _____*/100*

b. Based on your reflections, including insights you gained from the Action Communicator self-assessment, write down one simple and practical thing you can do to improve your performance as an Action Communicator:

____

____

Your Total Score:

Combine the above scores and rank your current performance as a Team Power Leader out of 400: _____ */400*

Finally, if it is helpful, add any new Team Power Leadership habits you have highlighted as beneficial into your Me Power Wish List.

Reflect?

If it is helpful, write down one habit you would like to prioritize building to help you improve your Team Power Leadership capabilities.

Think of this as an Aim, and remember that good Aims are carefully written down, are specific (using times and locations), state a positive action ("I will" instead of "I will not"), and can be measured (using quantities). For example, "Start every day with a TEA Plan that focuses on my Team Power Leadership performance." If you want to do this, just adapt the Daily TEA Plan questions from Chapter 1 (e.g., "How well did I do my best to be a Team Power Leader and achieve my goals yesterday?").

____

____

WANT TO BUILD A NEW LEADERSHIP HABIT?

Select the Habit

My example habit is:

"Improve my communication skills to help me become a better Action Communicator."

But to actually help me improve this area I need to focus on something more specific. So my Aim is to:

"Write a reflection at the end of each working day to focus on what I have done well, including the work I have done on improving my communication skills."

Remember that good Aims are carefully written down, are specific (using times and locations), state a positive action ("I will" instead of "I will not"), and can be measured (using quantities).

If you want to build a new Team Power Leadership habit, write down your Aim:

____

____

Once you have a clear Aim, you might want to revisit the self-reflection tool "How HUE (Horribly Unhelpful Emotions) Hinders Change" (Chapter 20) to help you think about how HUE might try to stop you from building this new habit.

Now we'll examine how we can transform what you've just identified into a new helpful habit. To do this, we'll use the Habit Building Plan.

Build the Habit

Now it is time to create a Habit Building Plan to activate the Nine Action Factors and supercharge the habit building process for the new Team Power Leadership habit you want to prioritize building.

To do this, you need to answer the following questions.

1. Describe the SMALL specific new helpful habit that you want to build (i.e., your Aim):

   ____

Example answer: Write a reflection at the end of each working day to focus on what I have done well, including the work I have done on improving my communication skills.

2. Describe what you currently do (your unhelpful habit instead of the new helpful habit you want to build):

   Example answer: Dwell on all the things that didn't go well and generally beat myself up.

3. Describe what reminds or triggers this unhelpful habit:

   Example answer: My HUE is very powerful and is constantly reminding me of the problems in my life.

4. Describe how you will remind yourself (trigger) to practice your NEW habit daily:

   Example answer: Set a daily calendar alert to remind me. Create a specific notes folder on my phone where I will write down these reflections.

5. Describe the new knowledge and skills you will need to help you secure your new habit:

   Example answer: Learn what great communicators do to get others to take positive action.

6. If it is helpful, describe where and how you will acquire the new knowledge and skills you need:

   Example answer: Take the "Action Communicator self-assessment" (in Chapter 33) every four to six weeks to help me build up more and more helpful communication skills and habits.

7. Describe in detail why you want to build this new habit:

   ____

   Example answer: Give me a better chance of being my best so I can perform well in my job and help my team grow and improve, and I think it will help with family life as well.

8. Who can you ask to help you build your new habit? (ideally, this person or persons will also be building the same or a similar habit at the same time):

   ____

   Example answer: Ask one of my direct reports to take the "Action Communicator self-assessment" and discuss it with them. This might give me a few other ideas about what I can improve.

9. What will be the reward for building the new habit? Remember, rewards can be internal, external, or social.

   ____

   Example answer: I will feel better about myself, I will have a better chance of getting the promotion I want, and I will be better able to help colleagues and family members.

10. What will be the cost/penalty for not building the new habit?

    ____

    Example answer: The opposite of the rewards I describe above.

Congratulations, you now have a robust plan to build a new Team Power Leadership habit!

CHIEF HABIT MECHANIC TOOL YOU HAVE LEARNED IN CHAPTER 34...

Team Power Leadership Builder—A tool to help you create a quick summary overview of your Team Power Leadership strengths and weaknesses. You can also use it to "map" every team member's Team Power Leadership skills and areas for improvement. ☑

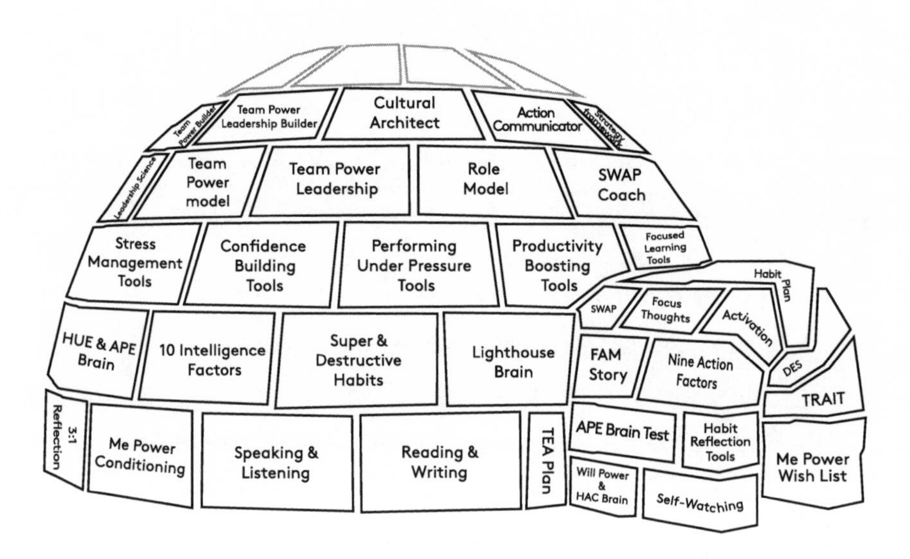

Figure 34.1: Your Chief Habit Mechanic intelligence igloo is building up!

35

YOUR "CULTURE DEVELOPMENT REFLECTION TOOL"

To help you bring everything together, I wanted to quickly recap the Nine Action Factors (for a full overview re-read Chapter 18). These are the levers you can use to make it easier for your people to develop the behaviors and habits needed to drive your team's and/or organization's culture.

Remember, you and your people are in a Learning War. If we don't purposefully use these factors to help us manage our own habits and our team's, others (e.g., people, organizations, etc.) will hijack our attention and control our behavior (e.g., checking our phone too often, staying up too late, eating the wrong type of food, beating ourselves up too much).

Below each Factor, I have posed questions to help you reflect on your team's and/or organization's culture. These are the "Culture Development Reflection Tool" questions. These types of questions are often the starting point for my work with clients. They help me begin helping clients develop more Habit Mechanics, Team Power Leaders, Chief Habit Mechanics, and ultimately a high-performing culture where every individual is deliberately striving to be their best to achieve team success.

NINE ACTION FACTORS RECAP AND CULTURE DEVELOPMENT REFLECTION QUESTIONS

1. Brain State Optimization

In simple terms, this relates to how ready your brain is to learn. For example, if you are sleep-deprived, learning will be more difficult. Equally, if you are stressed or in a bad mood, it will also be more difficult to build new habits that help you be your best. Remember: emotion drives attention; attention drives learning.

Are your people looking after themselves (e.g., doing Me Power Conditioning)?

Does your culture make people's HUE feel safe?

Does your culture make it easy for your people to do Me Power Conditioning?

2. Habit Mechanic Mindset

People with a Habit Mechanic Mindset believe they can improve anything with practice. They also take responsibility for being their best. People with an APE Brain Mindset believe they are only good at certain things, believe they cannot change, and become victims of "VUCA world conditioning" (see Chapter 9).

Do your people have Habit Mechanic Mindsets?

Do you help your people develop Habit Mechanic Mindsets?

Do the people you recruit have Habit Mechanic Mindsets? (Our clients use our tools to help identify this.)

3. Tiny Change Factor

This factor relates to the size or scale of the change we are able to make. In simple terms, we can make changes to behavior, but we can only make one tiny change at a time.

Does your organization understand this (e.g., evolution vs. revolution)?

Do your people understand this?

4. Personal Motivation

It's easier to make a change or build a new habit if you can connect it to a bigger meaningful goal in your life. This is one of the reasons why I asked you to create a FAM (Future Ambitious Meaningful) Story Iceberg (Chapter 16).

Do your people have FAM Story Icebergs?

Are their goals connected to the team's goals, and vice versa?

Do your people understand and believe in the team's and/or organization's mission?

5. Personal Knowledge and Skills

We do not need to acquire new knowledge and skills to eat a donut, but new knowledge and skills are often essential for complex behavior change—like improving our leadership or enhancing our sleep or productivity habits for the new hybrid workplace.

Do your people have the knowledge and the skills needed to do Me Power Conditioning so they can become Habit Mechanics?

Do your people have the knowledge and the skills needed to become Team Power Leaders?

Do your titled leaders (and future senior leaders) have the knowledge and the skills needed to become Chief Habit Mechanics?

6. Community Knowledge and Skills

Do team members have the knowledge and the skills needed to effectively support each other in helping the team achieve its mission?

7. Social Influence

Your APE Brain is strongly influenced by the behavior of those people you look up to and respect. We worry about how we are perceived by these people. We want to be liked by these people.

Do people in your team and/or organization Role Model the right behaviors and habits?

Does working remotely make it more difficult to positively influence each other's behavior?

8. Rewards and Penalties

Our APE Brain is strongly influenced by rewards and penalties. These can be social, intrinsic, or extrinsic.

Do your performance management systems, and performance and leadership development systems, reinforce the habits that are essential for a high-performing culture and mission success?

If your culture is NOT where you want it to be, performance management systems, and performance and leadership development systems, are definitely not helping develop and reinforce essential habits.

9. External Triggers

External Triggers in our modern world can be physical and digital. The smartphone is one of the most powerful External Triggers ever designed.

Do the triggers that surround your people help or hinder them from developing and sustaining the habits that are essential for a high-performing culture and mission success?

If your culture is NOT where you want it to be, these triggers are definitely not helping develop and reinforce essential habits.

Next, let's bring everything together.

CHIEF HABIT MECHANIC TOOL YOU HAVE LEARNED IN CHAPTER 35...

Culture Development Reflection Tool—A tool to help you consider how effectively you are using the Nine Action Factors to make it easier for your people to develop the behaviors/habits needed to drive the team's culture. ☑

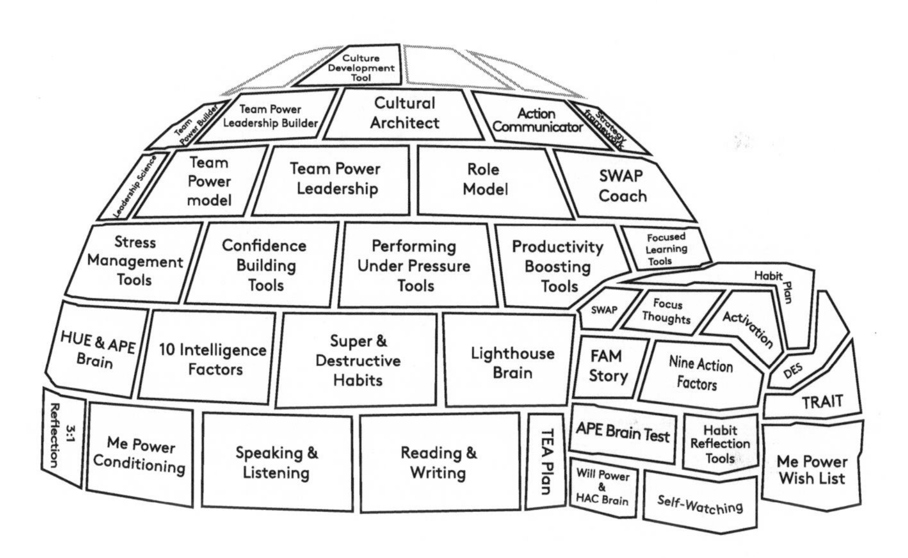

Figure 35.1: Your Chief Habit Mechanic intelligence igloo is building up!

BRINGING IT ALL TOGETHER

"If you want something, you need to go after it. Never give up!"

—SIR LEWIS HAMILTON, record-breaking and World Champion Formula One racing driver

"I was brought up to believe that I could achieve anything I wanted to as long as I studied hard and worked at things."

—BARONESS TANNI GREY-THOMPSON, 11-time Paralympic gold medalist, six-time winner of the London Marathon, UK's foremost campaigner for disability rights

36

DAILY, WEEKLY, AND MONTHLY HABIT MECHANIC TOOLS

We have covered a lot of ground and introduced many Habit Mechanic and Chief Habit Mechanic Tools throughout the course of this book. We could go further, but that would be beyond the scope of what I wanted to achieve in this book. So, to conclude, I want to show you how to bring all the tools together so that you can maximize their collective benefits.

The message in this book is very simple. We live in a challenging world and the number one thing we can do to help us feel and do better individually and collectively is to become Habit Mechanics. You now have the knowledge and tools to do this for yourself, and to help others do this (if you want to become a Chief Habit Mechanic). Your new Habit Mechanic intelligence will make building and sustaining new helpful habits easier.

SUPER HABITS

As you develop more and more helpful habits, your Super Habits (Chapters 8 and 17) will emerge. Remember, these are like hubs that help activate other helpful habits. Here is a recap of my current Super Habits:

Monthly/Bimonthly

1. **Review and update my FAM (Future Ambitious Meaningful) Story:** improves my motivation, productivity, and confidence; helps activate my daily and weekly Super Habits.
2. **Complete the Team Power Leadership self-assessments:** improves my Chief Habit Mechanic intelligence; helps the team and business thrive; helps activate my daily and weekly Super Habits.

Weekly

1. **Weekly reflection and planning for week ahead:** improves my motivation, productivity, and confidence; helps activate my daily Super Habits.

Daily

1. **Morning run:** activates my brain to the correct Activation level, meaning it is easier to focus and be productive; triggers healthy eating habits; contributes to my overall daily exercise, which makes sleeping easier at night; helps me manage my weight.
2. **Completing a Daily TEA Plan:** makes it easier for me to get the most out of my day; triggers a lot of the productivity habits

I have developed (connected to Brain States, Will Power Stories, building ice sculptures, etc.); having a productive day makes me feel better about myself at the end of the day, and helps me better manage work-life balance.

3. **Five-minute lunchtime walk where I deliberately focus on my breathing:** helps me manage stress; be productive in the afternoon; finish work on time; better manage work-life balance; sleep better.
4. **End-of-day planning for the next day, combined with a written reflection on the current day:** helps me manage stress; see progress; build confidence; finish work on time; activates my evening routine/habits; helps me sleep better.

IDEAS TO HELP YOU DEVELOP YOUR HABIT MECHANIC AND CHIEF HABIT MECHANIC SKILLS

What I suggest below are only ideas. You will only learn what works best for you by trying things out.

Monthly/Bimonthly

- Once you have created your FAM Story Iceberg, keep refining it.
- Retake the habit analysis tests that are most helpful for you (e.g., APE Brain Test [Chapter 12], In-Depth Habits Reflection and Helpful Habits Reflection [Chapter 17]).
- If you are working toward becoming a Chief Habit Mechanic, update your Team Power Leadership self-assessments (e.g., Role Model [Chapter 30], SWAP Coach [Chapter 31], Cultural Architect [Chapter 32], Action Communicator [Chapter 33]) and update the Team Power Builder scores [Chapter 28]).

Other Monthly/Bimonthly tools you could use include:

Planning Tools

- *The Habit Building Plan*—A tool to help you activate all Nine Action Factors when you are developing a new habit (Chapter 20)
- *How HUE Hinders Change*—An exercise to help you reflect on all the ways your HUE might make it more difficult for you to build new habits (Chapter 20)
- *Optimal Activation Review*—A tool to help you track, compare, and improve your Activation levels throughout the day (Chapter 21)
- *The Confidence Profile*—A simple tool to help you reflect on and build confidence in different areas of your life (Chapter 23)
- *KOSY (Knowledge, Others, Skills, You) Confidence*—A simple confidence-building framework (Chapter 23)

Self-Reflection Tools

- *Performance HAC Plan*—An exercise to help you reflect on how well your practice helps you perform under pressure (Chapter 24)
- *The Learning Strengths Plan*—An exercise to help you reflect on your current learning habits and build better ones (Chapter 26)

Start of Each Week

Me Power Weekly Wall Chart

If it is helpful, you could answer the following questions, which are part of the "Me Power Weekly Wall Chart" (Chapter 18). They help me achieve a better work-life balance.

1. What Are Your Goals for This Week?

Make a list of your goals for this week (e.g., do 30 push-ups every day; nail my presentation to clients; finish the report; reflect at the end of each day; make progress on the new product; finish work on time every day). If it is helpful, state how long each task will take to complete, and whether the task is easy (ice cubes) or difficult (ice sculptures).

2. Why Do You Want to Achieve These Goals?

Consider how achieving these goals will help you be healthier and happier, and fulfill your potential in the short- and long-term.

3. What Will Help You Achieve These Goals?

Consider how developing better habits will make it easier to achieve your goals (e.g., prioritize sleeping well each night; create a Daily TEA Plan each day).

Other weekly tools you could use include:

Planning Tools

- *Seven-Day "**D**iet, **E**xercise, and **S**leep" SWAP tool*—A tool to help you build better DES habits daily (Chapter 19)
- *The Habit Building Plan*—A tool to help you activate all Nine Action Factors when you are developing a new habit (Chapter 20)
- *Optimal Activation Review*—A tool to help you track, compare, and improve your Activation levels throughout the day (Chapter 21)
- *The Confidence Profile*—A simple tool to help you reflect on and build confidence in different areas of your life (Chapter 23)
- *KOSY (**K**nowledge, **O**thers, **S**kills, **Y**ou) Confidence*—A simple confidence-building framework (Chapter 23)

Self-Reflection Tools

- *APE Brain Test*—A quick Self-Watching exercise to help you reflect on your helpful and unhelpful habits (Chapter 12)

Daily

- Create a Daily TEA (Tiny Empowering Action) Plan at the beginning of each day (Chapter 1).
- End each day with a Daily 3:1 Reflection (Chapter 5).

Other daily tools you could use include:

Planning Tools

- *SWAP (**S**elf-**W**atch, **A**im, **P**lan)*—A simple tool to help you begin building any new habit (Chapter 19)
- *WABA (**W**ritten **APE** **B**rain **A**rgument)*—A structured approach to managing unhelpful thoughts (Chapter 22)
- *FAB (**F**ortunate, **A**dapt, **B**enefits) Thinking*—A structured approach to reframing unhelpful thoughts (Chapter 22)
- *RABA (**R**unning **APE** **B**rain **A**rgument)*—A structured approach to managing unhelpful thoughts (Chapter 22)
- *RAW (**R**educe **A**ctivation and **W**rite)*—A summary of the fundamental stress management framework (Chapter 22)
- *Expressive Writing*—A long-form stress management and confidence-building tool (Chapter 22)
- *Will Power Story*—A tool to help you be more productive every day (Chapter 25)

For a full list of daily, weekly, and monthly Habit Mechanic and Chief Habit Mechanic Tools, please see the index at the back of this book.

HABIT MECHANIC PLANNERS—
GET YOUR FREE RESILIENCE PLANNER

To package these tools together, we create planners for our clients. To download a PDF sample, go to tougherminds.co.uk/habitmechanic and click on "Resources" to download your copy of the "Me Power Resilience Planner."

37

NEED MORE HELP?

This book is a great introduction to becoming a Habit Mechanic and Chief Habit Mechanic, but I know you might want to go much further in developing your own skills—and possibly help other people become Habit Mechanics and Chief Habit Mechanics.

So, what can you do?

PODCAST AND APP

The Habit Mechanic Podcast

Check out the Habit Mechanic podcast. It is packed full of powerful Habit Mechanic insights and will act as a great trigger for your habit building endeavors.

To learn more, go to tougherminds.co.uk/podcast.

Habit Mechanic App

The Habit Mechanic app is designed to make all the ideas covered in the book super easy to put into practice and supercharge your ability to build new habits. You can use it as an individual, as a team, or across an entire business or organization.

To learn more, go to tougherminds.co.uk/habitmechanic and click on "Habit Mechanic app."

COACHING, TRAINING, AND KEYNOTES

Do you want one-to-one Habit Mechanic coaching?

Work with one of our experts and they will help you overcome the unique challenges that are stopping you from being your best and fulfilling your potential.

Do you want to train your people to become Habit Mechanics and Team Power Leaders?

We will work with you to create bespoke webinars, workshops, and in-depth programs to train your people in the science of building new habits.

We also train people to become Chief Habit Mechanics via our Chief Habit Mechanics Leadership Certificate.

Are you a coach? Do you want to train and coach your clients to become Habit Mechanics and Team Power Leaders?

We can help you do this. We are constantly evolving our "training the trainer" program.

Are you an educator? Do you want to train pupils and students to become Habit Mechanics and Team Power Leaders?

We have created a specific program for education that trains young people, teachers, and parents to become Habit Mechanics.

If you want us to help you with any of the above, or you have any other training requests, please contact us at:

contact@tougherminds.co.uk

Or visit our website:

tougherminds.co.uk

38

FINAL THOUGHTS

First and foremost, thank you for taking the time to read this book. Your time and attention are your most precious resources and I deeply appreciate that you have chosen to use some of them on me. I truly hope what you have learned will help you use your time and attention in an increasingly helpful way, to be your best and fulfill your potential.

As I've previously said, nothing I say in this book is prescriptive. You are unique and will only understand what works for you by trying things out (this is what I call "doing personal research").

Learning how to become a Habit Mechanic or Chief Habit Mechanic is a bit like a jigsaw puzzle. But now you have all the pieces, and a good understanding of how to begin putting them together.

But remember, you only get good at what you practice. So, if you want to become a skilled Habit Mechanic or Chief Habit Mechanic, keep this book close by so that you pick it up regularly and revisit the sections that are most helpful for you.

Think of your life as a journey where you travel through peaks and troughs. When you notice yourself going into a trough, deliberately build new habits (or reestablish helpful old habits) to help yourself get out of it faster than you otherwise would. When you feel like you are on a peak, assess whether you really are and if you need to push yourself further or take your foot off the pedal and recharge.

Habits are amazing, and you now have the knowledge and skills to start making them work for you, instead of against you. Now you can win the Learning War!

But you can only change one tiny habit at a time. So be patient. Take baby steps. But understand that tiny changes can lead to huge results. The tiny habit you are currently working on could be the one that unlocks your potential and changes your life.

So keep persisting. You are only ever one habit away!

—Dr. Jon Finn

ACKNOWLEDGMENTS

It would not have been possible to create the body of work that underpins Tougher Minds, the "Habit Mechanic" approach (language and tools), and this book without the support of many other people. Here I would like to thank them for their time, energy, and belief in me. First, thank you to my Habit Mechanic colleagues Andrew Foster, Catherine Grant, Professor Jim McKenna, Andrew Whitelam, and Dr. Laura Lucia Rossi—your support and input are invaluable. Thank you to all the people, teams, and organizations (my clients) for letting me into your lives and trusting me (and my team) to help you fulfill your potential. Thank you to all the researchers and world-class performers that I have referenced within this book. My work and this book would not have been possible without their efforts and dedication to their respective fields. Thank you to all the people who helped create the physical book, including Anna, Katie (and her team), Neil, Nook, Jo, and all of those people that kindly gave feedback on the early drafts. Finally, thanks to my family, friends, former teachers, and coaches who fueled my initial and ongoing interest in striving to be the best I can be and my passion for helping others be their best.

BIBLIOGRAPHY

I am fortunate to be able to stand on the shoulders of many groundbreaking scientists who dedicated their lives to developing some of the insights that underpin the "Habit Mechanic" approach. I have mentioned some of them throughout the course of this book, but also provide an overview of some specific research papers and books that have influenced my thinking over the years in the online bibliography. To access it, go to toughserminds.co.uk/habitmechanic and click on "Bibliography."

QUICK RECAP INDEX

PLANNING AND SELF-ASSESSMENT TOOLS INDEX (A–Z)

HABIT MECHANIC

Planning Tools (A–Z)

Chapter 23

The Confidence Profile—A simple tool to help you reflect on and build confidence in different areas of your life.

Chapters 5 and 23

Daily 3:1 Reflection—A daily positive reflection tool.

Chapter 1

Daily TEA (Tiny Empowering Action) Plan—A two-minute daily exercise to make your life easier.

Chapter 26

E3 Learning—A framework to highlight that the most impactful types of practice include three core factors: Effort, Efficiency, and Effectiveness.

Chapter 22

Expressive Writing—A long-form stress management and confidence-building tool.

Chapter 22

FAB (Fortunate, Adapt, Benefits) Thinking—A structured approach to reframing unhelpful thoughts.

Chapter 16

FAM (Future Ambitious Meaningful) Story—A tool to help you create, connect, and periodically review and update your long-, medium-, and short-term goals.

Chapter 26

Focused Practice framework—Designed to help you improve the quality of your current learning. It helps you break down the learning process into four distinct parts, making it easier to do high-charge ice sculpture building work.

Chapter 20

The Habit Building Plan—A tool to help you activate all Nine Action Factors when you are developing a new habit.

Chapter 23

KOSY (Knowledge, Others, Skills, You) Confidence—A simple confidence-building framework.

Chapter 18

Me Power Weekly Wall Chart—A tool to help you set meaningful goals for the week, and achieve them.

Chapter 21

Optimal Activation Review—A tool to help you track, compare, and improve your Activation levels throughout the day.

Chapter 22

RABA (Running APE Brain Argument)—A structured approach to managing unhelpful thoughts.

Chapter 22

RAW (Reduce Activation and Write)—A summary of how to manage your stress.

Chapter 19

Seven-Day "Diet, Exercise, and Sleep" SWAP tool—A tool to help you build better DES habits daily.

Chapter 19

SWAP (Self-Watch, Aim, Plan)—A simple tool to help you begin building any new habit.

Chapter 24

TE–TAP (Task, Environment, Timings, Activation, and Physical) Learning—A simple framework to pressure-proof your ability to perform.

Chapter 22

WABA (Written APE Brain Argument)—A structured approach to managing unhelpful thoughts.

Chapter 25

Will Power Boosters and Strengths—Tactics you can use to supercharge your Will Power Stories.

Will Power Story—A tool to help you be more focused and productive every day and improve work-life balance.

Self-Reflection Tools (A–Z)

Chapter 12

APE Brain Test—A quick Self-Watching exercise to help you reflect on your helpful and unhelpful habits.

Chapter 17

Helpful Habits Reflection—An exercise to help you reflect on which new habits it would be most helpful to build.

Chapter 20

How HUE Hinders Change—An exercise to help you reflect on all the ways HUE might make it more difficult for you to build new habits.

Chapter 17

In-Depth Habits Reflection—An in-depth exercise to help you begin identifying your most unhelpful habits.

Chapter 26

The Learning Strengths Plan—An exercise to help you reflect on your current learning habits and build better ones.

Chapter 24

Performance HAC Plan—An exercise to help you reflect on how well your practice helps you perform under pressure.

CHIEF HABIT MECHANIC

Tools and Models (A–Z)

Chapter 33

Action Communicator self-assessment—A tool to help you analyze your current Action Communicator strengths and weaknesses and develop better Action Communicator habits.

Chapter 32

Cultural Architect self-assessment—A tool to help you analyze your current Cultural Architect strengths and weaknesses and develop better Cultural Architect habits.

Chapter 35

Culture Development Reflection Tool—A tool to help you consider how effectively you are using the Nine Action Factors to make it easier for your people to develop the behaviors/habits needed for team success.

Chapter 28

Five-Stage Team Power model—A model showing the five stages high-performing teams successfully utilize to achieve their collective goals and fulfill their potential.

Chapter 30

Role Model self-assessment—A tool to help you analyze your current Role Model strengths and weaknesses and develop better Role Model habits.

Chapter 31

SWAP Coach self-assessment—A tool to help you analyze your current SWAP Coach strengths and weaknesses and develop better SWAP Coach habits.

Chapter 28

The Team Power Builder—A tool to help teams reflect on their strengths and areas of improvement across the Five-Stage Team Power model.

Chapter 29

Team Power Leadership—The Chief Habit Mechanic leadership framework, which has four core components: Role Model; SWAP Coach; Cultural Architect; Action Communicator.

Chapter 34

Team Power Leadership Builder—A tool to help you create a quick summary overview of your "Team Power Leadership" strengths and weaknesses. You can also use it to "map" every team member's Team Power Leadership skills and areas for improvement.

CORE LANGUAGE INDEX (A–Z)

Chapters 5 and 26

10 Intelligence Factors—Once we have the opportunity to learn something, I have concluded that 10 factors (some genetic and some environmental, but all changeable) can supercharge or block our learning.

Chapter 21

Activation level—A concept created to make it easier to understand and manage your energy levels, alertness, and anxiety.

Chapter 11

APE (Alive Perceived Energy) Brain—An easy acronym to help you understand your survival brain/limbic regions of the brain.

Chapter 25

Brain States—A concept to help a person think about their brain as being like a battery that has three specific operating states: recharge, medium charge, and high charge.

Chapter 27

Chief Habit Mechanic intelligence—Your ability to acquire and apply Chief Habit Mechanic knowledge and skills to help others develop new helpful habits.

Chapter 19

DES—Simple shorthand for diet, exercise, and sleep.

Chapter 8

Destructive Habits—Habits that trigger lots of other unhelpful behaviors /habits.

Chapter 14

Eudemonia (Habit Mechanic development)—This focuses on delaying short-term gratification and sometimes enduring pain, boredom, and stress in order to develop yourself, grow, and achieve big meaningful goals.

Chapter 21

Focus Words and Focus Pictures—Skills you can use to help control your thoughts.

Chapters 5 and 26

Focused or deliberate practice—Where you focus hard, make mistakes, and use feedback about your mistakes to get better.

Chapter 5

Habit Mechanic intelligence—Your ability to acquire and apply Habit Mechanic knowledge and skills to develop new helpful habits.

Chapter 11

HAC (Helpful Attention Control) Brain—An easy acronym to help you understand your prefrontal cortex.

Chapter 14

Hedonism (pleasure)—This focuses on seeking short-term gratification and immediate rewards.

Chapter 23

The House of Confidence—A concept created to make confidence easier to understand and build.

Chapter 10

HUE (Horribly Unhelpful Emotions)—An imaginary character who lives in your brain who can make you worry and make it difficult for you to be your best.

Chapter 25

Ice Cubes and Ice Sculptures—Terms created to help a person separate their daily tasks into two distinct categories: easy work (ice cubes) and mentally challenging work (ice sculptures).

Chapter 23

The Igloo of Confidence—A concept created to make it easier to understand and develop the two core components of confidence (belief [self-esteem] and evidence [self-efficacy]).

Chapter 10

Lighthouse Brain—A simple model to help you understand the gist of how your brain works so you can begin to improve your thinking.

Chapters 2 and 9

Me Power Conditioning—This means deliberately working toward being your best.

Chapter 12

Me Power Wish List—A list of all the small new helpful habits you would like to build.

Chapter 18

Nine Action Factors framework—Created to make it easy for you to use the latest insights from behavioral science to build sustainable new habits.

Chapter 12

Self-Watching—Reflecting and thinking about yourself in a focused and systematic way.

Chapter 8

Super Habits—Habits that trigger other positive behaviors/habits.

Chapter 17

TRAIT (Trigger, Routine, APE Incentive, Training) Habit Loop—A unique habit model to help people understand how their habits work.

Chapter 10

Willomenia Power or Will Power—An imaginary character who lives in your brain who can help you manage HUE.

TRADEMARKS

Habit Mechanic®
Chief Habit Mechanic®
Lighthouse Brain®
APE®
HUE®
HAC®
Will Power™
SWAP®
TRAIT®
Nine Action Factors™
Personal Change Management™
Focus Pictures™
Focus Words™
TE-TAP®
Will Power Story™
E3™
Me Power®
KOSY®
FAB®
DES®
FAM®
House of Confidence®
Activation®
WABA®
RAW®
Igloo of Confidence®
TEA®
Team Power®
Pre-Shot®

Made in the USA
Middletown, DE
26 August 2024